The Secret Conferences
of Dr. Goebbels

The Secret Conferences of Dr. Goebbels

The Nazi Propaganda War 1939 – 43

Selected and edited by Willi A. Boelcke

Translated from the German by Ewald Osers

E. P. DUTTON & CO., INC.

New York

1970

First published in the U.S.A. 1970 by E. P. Dutton & Co., Inc.

Copyright © 1966, 1967 by Deutsche Verlags-Anstalt Gmbh, Stuttgart
English translation Copyright © 1970 by E. P. Dutton & Co., Inc.,
and Weidenfeld and Nicolson Ltd.
All rights reserved.

First Edition

Printed in Great Britain

This book is a slightly abridged translation of "*Wollt Ihr den total en Krieg?*"
Die geheimen Goebbels-Konferenzen 1939–1943, first published by Deutsche
Verlags-Anstalt, Stuttgart in 1967. Some passages from the complete
edition of the minutes of Goebbels's conferences from October 26, 1939
to May 31, 1941, *Kriegspropaganda 1939–1941: Geheime Ministerkonferenzen
im Reichspropagandaministerium,* first published by Deutsche Verlags-Anstalt,
Stuttgart, in 1966, are incorporated in this translation.
Library of Congress Catalog Card Number: 79-95469
SBN 0-525-19893-8

Contents

Contents

Editor's Introduction

JOSEPH GOEBBELS was born in 1897, at Rheydt on the left bank of the Rhine, the son of a shop assistant and clerk. There were five children in all. The family, devout Catholics, lived in straitened circumstances. In 1917 Joseph Goebbels completed his grammar school education with grades ranging from good to very good. Between 1917 and 1921 he studied at the universities of Bonn, Freiburg and Heidelberg, being enabled to do so by a loan from the Catholic Albertus Magnus Association, which he repaid up to 1930. At Heidelberg he gained his doctor's degree in 1922 with a thesis entitled 'Wilhelm von Schütz as a dramatist. A contribution to the history of the drama of the Romantic school.' His doctoral supervisor was Professor Friedrich Gundolf, the outstanding literary critic – and, incidentally, of Jewish extraction.

Unable to pursue a teaching career – he had not taken the required examinations – Goebbels first tried to make a living as a professional journalist. Constant failure, however, soon turned him towards political militancy. He joined the National Socialist Party in 1922. In 1925 he became its Regional Secretary for the Ruhr, in 1926 Gauleiter of Berlin, and in 1928 was elected to the German Reichstag as a National Socialist Deputy. His marriage in 1931 to Magda Quant, the divorced wife of a wealthy industrialist, marked a turning-point not only in Goebbels's life but also in his political career. The financially independent society woman opened to him, the man from the lower middle class, the doors into high society. Goebbels's elegant home in the West End of Berlin became one of Hitler's 'headquarters' before the Nazis' seizure of power. When in 1933 he was appointed Reich Minister of Propaganda Goebbels had every right to regard his new post as the consummation of his political career. Politics gave him the power he longed for and the comfortable, patrician life he had coveted for more than a decade.

From the very beginning of the war to its very end, from the first few days of September 1939 to April 21, 1945, Goebbels almost every day, at a fixed hour of the morning, summoned his closest collaborators to a secret 'ministerial conference' at the Reich Ministry for Propaganda. During 1940–1 there were about twenty regular participants at the conference. After the beginning of the Russian campaign the number of participants gradually increased to about fifty. These included the departmental heads of his Ministry, the officials responsible for radio, film, the press, representatives of the Berlin Gau Directorate,* of the Reich Directorate for Propaganda in Munich and of the foreign branch of the Nationalsozialistische Deutsche Arbeiterpartei (National Socialist German Workers' Party), as well as liaison officers from the Wehrmacht (Armed Forces) High Command and from other ministries.

With this ministerial conference – though not a 'conference' in the proper meaning of the word – Goebbels created his own secret command post. It was here that, day after day, he would issue his verbal instructions for all spheres of propaganda and, up to a point, supervise their implementation. The conference thus became a kind of 'control tower' of the German propaganda war. Here Goebbels issued his orders, announced propaganda slogans and laid down linguistic usages. The style of the conference was entirely suited to his personality. It was he who shaped it and dominated it. He alone laid down decrees, asked questions, dispensed praise and rebuke, produced scintillating ideas, indulged in critical monologues, outlined arguments and virtually dismissed all counter-arguments. He alone determined what was topical and 'close to the people'. There was never anything like frank discussion, let alone consultation as among colleagues. If other opinions were ever voiced they were, at best, objections raised, during the early years of the war, by Professor Karl Bömer (1900–42), the Head of the Foreign Press Department, by Hans Fritzsche (1900–53), the often brilliant but notorious radio commentator who was indicted but acquitted at Nuremberg after the war, or by some of the Wehrmacht liaison officers. The majority of the participants thought it more prudent not to ask questions or voice misgivings.

When, after the start of the Russian campaign, the conference had been enlarged to more than twice its original size, Korvettenkapitän (Lieutenant-Commander) Hahn, the liaison officer of the Navy and of the Propaganda Department at the Oberkommando der Wehrmacht (High Command of the German Armed Forces), once referred to his conference colleagues as the 'Reich yes-men' – a witticism said to have been acknowledged by Goebbels with a burst of laughter. But he then explained to the OKW representative that he needed this larger audience of people sensible of the particular honour of being allowed to attend – that he needed it in order to 'avoid awkward discussions and preserve the one-sidedness so indispensable for his job.' Goebbels's customary concluding query whether anybody had any questions soon became a fossilized, empty formula.

* The Reich was regionally subdivided into *Gaue* (Regions) with the Nazi Party organization in each *Gau* headed by a Gauleiter. *Tr.*

Goebbels himself regarded the ministerial conference as a highlight, frequently *the* highlight, of his day. Here he was in his element, here he could sparkle and be admired. What was equally admired was the skill he displayed in bluffing and deceiving. Even when he was absent from Berlin and thus unable to conduct the conference in person, Goebbels in a sense still remained present. He would give his instructions to his personal assistant accompanying him; the official would telephone them through to Berlin, where they would be taken down by a shorthand writer in order to be read out verbatim at the conference. In consequence, the participants at the conference were reduced to the role of extras, of bit actors on a stage whose strings Goebbels held in his own hands. For the prompt implementation of his directives the 'Reich yes-men', of course, were indispensable.

The fact that Goebbels's essential observations, his fundamental directives at the conference, were recorded at the time was first revealed by the testimony of witnesses at the Nuremberg war crime trials. The search for these conference minutes, however, was unsuccessful at the time. The minutes – or rather reduced-size copies made at the Ministry for Propaganda – had fallen into the hands of the Soviet occupying forces. That part of them covering the period from June 1941 to the end of the war, i.e. the period of victories and defeats in Germany's campaign in Russia, was, according to trustworthy reports, translated into Russian but has not appeared anywhere since. Copies of the minutes covering the period from October 26, 1939 to May 31, 1941, on the other hand, together with other documents of the Ministry for Propaganda, found their way into the Deutsches Zentralarchiv Potsdam as early as 1952, where they have since been waiting in vain for a comprehensive, scholarly evaluation.

Inspection and use of the extant documents of the Third Reich, including in particular the Goebbels minutes at the Deutsches Zentralarchiv Potsdam, has always been extremely difficult. When an attempt was made by a publisher to get the Goebbels minutes in Potsdam published – needless to say giving a critical interpretation – in East Berlin, by the firm of Ruetten & Loening, the mere suggestion was flatly rejected. Since the evidence produced in the minutes might not fit into the picture of history which is obligatory in Iron Curtain countries on the subject of the Third Reich, the minutes were in the nature of a hot potato which had better be left untouched if one did not wish to incur disfavour with the supreme guardians of the state monopoly in history.

More important, perhaps, is that there is a great deal in the minutes which would throw too clear a light on the rules of the game played by totalitarian states in eliminating the free expression of opinion and in determining and manipulating, by means of linguistic rulings, what may be thought, said and printed. The communists of East Berlin are evidently afraid that readers might draw the obvious parallel between Goebbels's practices and their own techniques of mass-incitement and propaganda. At the same time there is no denying that certain passages of the minutes covering the initial years of the war revealed not so much the diabolical Goebbels as a not entirely unlikable figure. That, of course, is part of an objective portrait of Goebbels which does not therefore necessarily need touching up. A demagogue must from time to time appear 'likable' to his victims, since otherwise his work of seduction cannot succeed in the long run. The parallel with the Mephisto-Faust relationship is obvious.

Without at first requiring any special authority, and independent of the trends of historiography in the German Democratic Republic, the present editor, who was on the staff of the Deutsches Zentralarchiv Potsdam from 1957 to 1959 and there concerned with press and propaganda in the Third Reich, made edited copies of the minutes for himself with a view to subsequent study and publication – although, of course, the date of the latter could not even be guessed at under the conditions then prevailing. Thanks to support from the German Federal Research Council and the Historical Commission of the ARD, the body associating all broadcasting organizations in the German Federal Republic, it was eventually possible, in 1966, to publish, under the imprint of the Deutsche Verlags-Anstalt Stuttgart, a volume of nearly eight hundred pages comprising the minutes together with a critical introduction and explanatory notes.

Of the approximately twelve hundred ministerial conferences held at the Ministry for Propaganda during World War Two, a little more than four hundred took place during the period from October 26, 1939, to the beginning of June 1941; of these, with the exception of about a dozen, the minutes have survived. The number of these, produced at the Ministry for Propaganda, usually by the personal assistants and aides of the Minister, is relatively small compared with the still missing minutes of roughly eight hundred conferences held between June 1941 and April 1945. The assurance of the Director General of the Soviet State Archives that there are no such German documents left in his archives naturally diminished the hopes that it might be possible to fill that substantial gap in the records. This hope shrank further when no trace of the minutes was found among the large bulk of documents seized by the Western Allies and now for the most part restored to the archives of the German Federal Republic.

On October 22, 1941 a long-overdue 'Agreement between the Ministry of Foreign Affairs and the Ministry for Popular Enlightenment and Propaganda' came into effect in Germany, designed to regulate the often conflicting work of the two ministries going back to August 1939. The agreement envisaged that in future a 'chief liaison officer' would attend Goebbels's daily morning conferences. At the end of October 1941 the 'Krümmer Section' was specifically charged with the task of 'liaison' with the Ministry for Propaganda. The head of the section, Ewald Ludwig Krümmer (b. 1896), who had held the senior rank of Vortragender Legationsrat since 1940 and that of a minister in the diplomatic service (Gesandter) since November 1941, was entrusted with all the duties of chief liaison officer between the two ministries. In November 1941 he presented himself to Goebbels and thereafter attended his morning conferences. After January 1942 his colleague, Dr Gerhard Todenhöfer (b. 1913), who held the rank of Legat, was appointed his deputy. He had been brought back from the Finnish front where he had been a lieutenant and 'representative of the Ministry of Foreign Affairs', so that, together with Krümmer, he should tackle the difficult task of watching the interests of his Ministry in the face of those of the Ministry for Propaganda both at and outside the conferences. Punctually at 10.50 a.m. Krümmer or Todenhöfer would make a brief report to Goebbels and subsequently attend the conference which as a rule lasted from 11 a.m. to about 12 noon.

A totally surprising turn of affairs in the search for the Goebbels minutes occurred when Dr Philippi of the Political Archives of the Foreign Ministry handed the present editor three unassuming and dust-covered folders which had been found to contain carbon copies and drafts of notes made by Krümmer and Todenhöfer on the Goebbels conferences covering the period from December 1, 1941, until and including March 14, 1943. The credit for making this genuinely historical find goes to Dr Philippi – a find which many contemporary historians had hardly believed possible and which several Goebbels biographers had either finally written off after an unsuccessful search, or had not thought worth pursuing. These documents proved of considerable value. The most essential directives of Goebbels, issued at roughly three hundred conferences during the first few years of the German campaign in Russia up to his proclamation of total war, were now available at first hand, from an authentic source. This period, moreover, is one which is rather inadequately attested in Goebbels's published and unpublished war diaries. In Lochner's edition of the Goebbels diaries there are entries covering the period from January 21 to May 23, 1942. The diaries for the six months or so from May 24 until December 6, 1942, are missing. We then again have diary entries from December 7 to 20, 1942. Then comes another 'blank' of two months, until March 1, 1943. The diaries thus let us down completely as far as information and reflection on the progress of the battle of Stalingrad goes, and about the origins and the first results of Goebbels's sinister speech at the Sports-palast on February 18, 1943. This vital period of World War Two, when the turning point in the war first became clearly discernible, is thus at last documented, almost without gaps, by the records of the ministerial conferences.

The minutes of these conferences from October 1939 to May 1941, supplemented by records from the Ministry for Propaganda covering the period from June until November 1941, together with the records of the Ministry of Foreign Affairs' liaison officers from December 1941 until March 1943, are here published for the first time. They provide the interested general reader as well as the researcher with an unparalleled insight into the propaganda pattern of World War Two as seen through Goebbels's eyes. The German top-level decisions for the propaganda war, collected together in this volume, represent primary sources of unusual interest. Compressed into one volume and focused on the essential features of the propaganda conducted by Goebbels, and in part by Hitler himself, during the various phases of the war, we can follow the development of the propaganda scene over a period of just under four years – its fascinating documentary authenticity and originality, and its dramatic course culminating in Goebbels's proclamation of total war in early 1943. The minutes of the conferences, here published in chronological order, have been divided up according to the separate phases of the war, into thirteen chapters, each of them bearing as its heading a quotation by Goebbels of the same period – one of those propaganda slogans which he coined and which to us today highlight not only the central issues of the day but frequently also the striking discrepancy between propaganda and reality.

This volume, however, offers only a careful selection from the extant records of the ministerial conferences. There were a number of reasons in favour of such a selective publication in a single, handy volume. Extensive collections of documents, which inevitably and indiscriminately comprise both fundamental and trivial information, frequently lack the clarity and, above all, the readability of edited versions. The present volume, therefore, represents a selection from the confusing mass of subjects touched upon at the conferences, so designed as to illustrate more clearly the guiding principles of Goebbels's propaganda during the various stages of the war. Its aim is to provide information about the underlying principles of the propaganda war and to illustrate both the repetitive and the changing methods of propaganda. If, as a result, it has gained in clarity and also – in spite of the limited vocabulary and the simple officialese of the minutes – in readability, then it will have fully accomplished its task.

An important consideration, needless to say, in devising a volume which would provide 'popular enlightenment about what used to be called Popular Enlightenment' is that it must not cost as much as a large and comprehensive collection of documents would. The discipline involved in compressing and streamlining eleven volumes of official documents into a handy, readable book was, however, by no means a disadvantage. It provided the challenge of finding a way which would meet both the yardsticks of strict scholarly editing and the public demand for factual and concise information in an age when most people's capacity for reading is saturated anyway. For the sake of better understanding, therefore, information relating to the matter in hand, supplementary notes and explanations, and frequently also the results of years of research into sources have been inserted into the text and distinguished from it by smaller type. The aim throughout has been to produce a book which would not only become an indispensable volume in any specialized library but could also claim a place on the private shelves of any reader, and more especially the reader who wants to learn about the entire 'propaganda phenomenon' associated with Goebbels's name.

The directives issued by Goebbels at his morning conferences became the basis for the propaganda campaign throughout the various phases of the war. In matters of detail they were concerned, above all, with information policy and with press and radio comment on the incoming news material. The formulation of polemics came first. But there were also directives for the editorial policies of political and entertainment programmes of domestic and foreign broadcasting. During the first few years of the war Goebbels exercised direct personal control over the content of the broadcasts put out by certain clandestine 'secret transmitters' for foreign listeners. The campaign in France, in particular, proved what an insidious weapon the secret war in the ether could be. Goebbels set his stamp on the German radio and, to a considerable extent, controlled the presentation, tone and contents of the German press. He directed the spreading of rumours at home and abroad. A masterpiece of diabolical insidiousness was, without any doubt, his launching of faked Allied post-war plans in the press of the Western Allies which, quite unsuspectingly, reprinted the stories which he had fabricated in order to goad the German people into hatred and bitterness against their enemies. Thus, in 1942, the German papers quoted the foreign press reports of a plan envisaging that, after Germany's defeat, all German males would be sterilized and all children separated from their mothers and deported abroad.

At his conferences Goebbels concerned himself with leaflet propaganda, the policy to be followed by publishing houses, political and propaganda pamphlets, etc. Even the production of several feature films was due solely to his request. Moreover, he ordered the announcement of new feature films and film newsreels, and prescribed their propaganda interpretation in the press. He even concerned himself, though marginally, with German theatrical, musical and cultural life; he banned certain stage productions and musical performances, and he demanded that other plays should remain in the repertory or be put in it. He was concerned with questions of forces' welfare and, last but not least, with the programmes and the execution of the Sunday Request Concerts. It was from the ministerial conference that various mass demonstrations, parades, and Führer rallies were invisibly stage-managed, and it was from there that the most varied collection campaigns for the Winter Relief Scheme, the Red Cross, etc., were launched. Numerous measures which would appear to have little to do with propaganda were nevertheless inspired or demanded by Goebbels at these conferences, with a view to checking a decline in public morale. Simultaneously he set in motion police action and criminal proceedings, he prevailed on the judiciary to pass sentences of deterrence and saw to it that all courtroom reporting was done with an eye to its propaganda effect.

Nevertheless, there were a few areas in which the Nazi leadership throughout the war failed to impose its will completely. Goebbels found it impossible to prevent the massive listening to foreign broadcasts, in particular British and Swiss transmissions, both at the front and at home – even though 'black listeners' were sentenced to many years of penal servitude or sent to concentration camps, and even though these sentences were regularly and prominently published in the press as deterrents. Similarly, the German press, especially after 1942, continuously reported transgressions or criminal offences against rationing regulations, A large number of death sentences were passed, very largely at Goebbels's suggestion, yet it proved impossible to put an effective stop to black-market dealings or to the illegal slaughter of animals; indeed, the black market grew throughout the war. Almost every day from the beginning of the war onwards, the German press had, furthermore, complained about the 'improper' or 'sentimental' attitude shown by many Germans towards prisoners of war or foreign workers. In rural areas these were frequently treated no worse and no better than any other agricultural worker. Among the popular masses the Nazi doctrine of the German master race did not fall on very fertile ground. Indeed, there was silent rejection, both at the front and at home, of the 'sub-humanity propaganda' staged against the nations of the Soviet Union – a manifestation of imperialist colonialism of the kind found elsewhere in the nineteenth century.

The conferences frequently discussed the discriminatory measures introduced against the Jews, as well as their expulsion; the campaign against the Christian Churches, which were to be destroyed after Hitler's victory, similarly started there. Nevertheless, the attitude of many Germans towards their Jewish fellow citizens and towards the Church was not in line with Goebbels's hopes and ideas. The press, therefore, avoided attacks on the Church and throughout the war was under strict instructions to treat the question of the German Jews as taboo. The 'just punishment of the Jewish bacillus' was to be practised unobtrusively, utilizing the possibilities of secrecy provided by the war. By March 1942, at the latest, Goebbels knew that the 'final solution' of the Jewish question was being put into effect in the gas chambers and cremation furnaces of the concentration camps. He noted in his diary that at Lublin 'a rather barbaric method, not to be described in detail', was being practised, and that 'nothing much is left now of the Jews'. Not a word of this was allowed to reach the German public, since he knew that even those anti-Jewish measures of which the German people were aware frequently met with distaste and opposition. Even though Goebbels had repeatedly urged the German people: 'Don't be too fair,' there is no doubt that the initial indifference towards the Jews living in Germany was increasingly turning into sympathy for them.

Although the effective range of the Ministry for Propaganda extended to very nearly all aspects and spheres of the war, or at any rate was related to them, the actual progress of the war was not significantly affected by Goebbels's decisions. Of course, the conferences were not always concerned with highly political matters. All too frequently they seemed to deal with trivial affairs – but these too form part of the overall picture of Goebbels's conferences and of the broad spectrum of subjects discussed there. In the first winter of the war, the winter of 1939–40, when public morale sagged in an alarming way, Goebbels clearly began to realize that the propaganda machine which directed and controlled all public opinion could not confine itself to the trotting out or repetition of certain basic political arguments or to the drumming in of formulations and slogans concerning the political events of the day, but also had to get down to the 'small troubles and hardships' of everyday wartime life and, if possible, provide remedies for them. Goebbels, as he himself put it, adopted the 'strategy of makeshift repairs'. Thus the propaganda machinery, which had already grown to an almost unwieldy size, began organizing aid programmes covering the allocation of fruit, vegetables and potatoes, babies' layettes and free theatre tickets, coal and tobacco supplies, and even matters concerning old-age pensioners and war victims. This system of 'makeshift repairs' developed into a regular scheme when, following the heavy British air raid on Lübeck in March 1942, Goebbels received from Hitler full powers to undertake instant relief measures in bomb-damaged cities. Goebbels's most effective weapon against the hail of bombs which descended on Germany's dying and groaning cities remained his promise of a 'day of vengeance' and a package of special rations.

For a totalitarian state, where the mood and the views of extensive sections of the population were not in harmony with the intentions and ideas of the dictator or his Minister for Propaganda, the war resulted in considerable stresses and trials: the way in which these were faced necessarily depended in part on the efficiency of the propaganda machine and on the credibility of the propaganda. The impression of monolithic unity between leadership and people had to be preserved at all costs, and it had to be forged anew whenever it threatened to fall apart. The artificial harmony or 'concerted action' of all means of communication, of all mass media, was no more than the prerequisite for a uniform, totalitarian state propaganda. Effective concentration of all means of propaganda, their focusing on one objective, the monopoly of public-opinion shaping, the omnipresence of propaganda, the use of a refined technique of applied psychology in political mass-persuasion backed up by force and coercion – all these characterize the nature of German propaganda during World War Two. Propaganda had to be ubiquitous and the propagandist could not ever 'lose his voice'. Yet propaganda proved most effective where it remained invisible. Thus the political and propaganda war was hidden under a thousand veils and disguises, and the radio waves were employed to re-echo lies with ice-cold deliberation.

The war, therefore, cannot be seen merely as a military fact: from its very start it grew, both at home and abroad, into a propaganda war of previously unknown dimensions, a war in which all means of psychological warfare became important operational weapons. Technical progress favoured the range and efficacy of propaganda. It was its task to undermine the enemy's spirit of resistance, to win over or at least isolate the neutral nations, and last but not least to buttress the German people with a confident belief in victory or the conviction of invincibility.

Goebbels, of course, realized, as early as the Polish campaign, that in the long run victories could not be won merely with propaganda, let alone with lies. Propaganda could not remain entirely untouched by reality. True, for the most part it preferred to remain silent in the face of uncomfortable facts and in its news policy it gave precedence, as a matter of principle, to tendentiously coloured half-truths. By his relatively frank admission of half-truths and by his occasional sworn 'hour of truth' Goebbels not only invested his propaganda with an air of credibility but also made sure that the whole truth, which was frequently available from the lips of the enemy, scarcely gained ground among the people.

If one tried to list Goebbels's propaganda technique in detail one would find it reduced to a few basic principles to which he personally adhered from the beginning to the abrupt end of his career. At his ministerial conferences he treated his collaborators to an *haute école* of propaganda, lecturing them on the principles of the subject. Propaganda, as defined by him, meant:

1. The art of simplification, the art of finding the most primitive arguments in popular terms because only such arguments would carry the necessary force and ensure the support of the masses;

2. The art of continuous repetition, of the unceasing driving home of theses, slogans and captions, not necessarily in the same words but certainly long enough until even the stupidest had grasped them;

3. The art of appealing solely to the instincts, the emotions, the feelings and the passions of the people, while never attempting what was hopeless from the outset – i.e. trying to convince intellectuals by the use of rational arguments;

4. The art of reproducing facts with an air of objectivity but tendentiously coloured by their selection and manner of reproduction;

5. The art of keeping silent about uncomfortable facts unless, of course, the truth had reached the public in other ways;

6. The art of lying credibly, remembering that the continuous repetition of a lie, which need be limited only by its credibility, frequently worked wonders.

Propaganda and all forms of political persuasion – a kind of salesmanship applied to politics – was to Goebbels an art which he not infrequently likened to Wagnerian music. Propaganda, he emphasized, had 'nothing at all to do with truth.' It was not its task, he argued on another occasion, 'no more than it is the task of art, to be objectively true.' The sole aim of propaganda was success. By proclaiming the principle that 'in propaganda as in love' all things were fair that led to success, and by declaring simultaneously that the value of a propaganda campaign was determined solely by its success, Goebbels proclaimed for propaganda what Machiavelli had set out as the supreme principle of statesmanship nearly five hundred years before. Ranged alongside a Machiavellian policy was now a Machiavellian propaganda which, like an autocratic ruler, was not subject to any higher responsibility, to any moral law, and even less to the judgement of the people.

While it would be criminally foolhardy to underestimate the effect of modern political mass propaganda, so, on the other hand, it would be a mistake to overrate Goebbels or his propaganda. Goebbels was by no means, as is sometimes claimed, the virtuoso able at will to manipulate the morale of a whole nation throughout the war, who could suddenly change a 'psychological low' into a 'psychological high' or who could transform what the leadership regarded as the people's negative attitude to the war into sudden enthusiasm for it,

There was never, either in 1939 or during the subsequent years of Hitler's 'blitz victories', any question of enthusiasm for the war, let alone the kind of war hysteria which had seized and inspired the masses in Berlin and Paris in August 1914. The unexpected outbreak of the war in September 1939, which came as a complete surprise to the majority of Germans, following as it did Hitler's political successes and the conclusion of the Hitler-Stalin Pact of August 23, 1939, produced, to begin with, a dejected mood among large sections of the German people. The outbreak of the war was not welcomed with enthusiasm or flag-waving; during the early days of September there was an oppressed silence among the people. The campaign in the West in May 1940 similarly took the German people by surprise; its first few days were marked by profound gravity and dejection. Although in the spring of 1941 the German people still generally believed that the Balkan campaign would end with a rapid German military victory, the campaign against Yugoslavia and more particularly the war against the courageous, small Greek nation were decidedly unpopular. Even before the beginning of the campaign in Russia a slogan from World War One was suddenly resuscitated throughout the country: 'We shall kill ourselves with our victories!' The opening of the German campaign in Russia on June 22, 1941, shocked the public into a state of paralysis. But as in all previous campaigns the first victory fanfares of the special announcements produced a noticeable swing in morale. Yet each military victory, no matter whether it was won in the west, in the east, in the north or in the south, gave rise – in spite of full acclaim of German military achievements and all pride in soldierly heroism – not so much to a desire to conquer further countries and subjugate ever new nations as to a longing for peace. It was this hope of peace which determined the mood in the country throughout the war and which was deceived year after year.

Goebbels had to deal ceaselessly with 'peace rumours' at home and abroad. In the early years of the war he prohibited genuine peace initiatives from being reported by the press or radio. Frequently foreign reports about armistice negotiations had to be denied and others had to be countered by whispered propaganda. 'Tough action' was to be taken, if necessary, against 'rumour-mongers'. From time to time, moreover, Goebbels was compelled to deal with the much discussed subject of 'the end of the war' in an editorial article, though as a rule he would appease his readers with commonplaces. The war would end as suddenly as it had begun, Goebbels repeated from one editorial to another. He wanted to, and indeed had to, avoid the idea of a rapid end to the war gaining ground among the people. As for his own reflections about peace, since early 1942 Goebbels appears to have tried to brush these aside: 'Just as a wanderer in the desert should not continually think of water, so a man waging war should never think of peace.'

By September 1941, the beginning of the third year of the war, the German people had largely abandoned hope of an early peace. Everywhere the anxious question was being asked: 'How much longer is this war going on?' At the beginning of the fourth year of the war, in September 1942, the German people asked themselves: 'Is an end to the war still in sight?' Gradually the illusion of an inevitable German victory also began to fade. It was during the German winter crisis on the outskirts of Moscow in 1941–2 that the German people first experienced the anxiety that peace might possibly be available only at the price of defeat, a defeat which, admittedly, might well entail even greater suffering than the war itself. The incipient German summer offensive of 1942 was followed by large sections of the people in a mood of reserved scepticism. The public already seemed to have retreated behind an armour of lethargic indifference. Reports of victories were acknowledged without comment, whereas any cut in food rationing or any other difficulties in supplies produced violent reactions.

Public morale reached its lowest ebb with reports of the incipient disaster of Stalingrad. When Goebbels, on February 18, 1943, asked the question at the Berlin Sportspalast: 'Do you want total war? Do you want it, if necessary, even more total and radical than we can even imagine today?' it was very well realized, both inside and outside the Berlin Sportspalast, that the war had reached, or possibly even passed its climax. A mood of nervous depressive tension seized not only those who had once been confident of victory.

Weeks before his Sportspalast speech Goebbels had developed a positively hectic activity, setting himself far-reaching targets, initiating fundamental Führer-level decisions, all in order to lend even greater momentum to what he himself had set in action. He triumphed as a master of public-opinion shaping. About mid-December 1942 Hitler had received a Goebbels memorandum about the totalization of the war effort. On December 28, 1942, Bormann, the head of the Party Chancellery and Hitler's confidant, a dangerous intriguer in the corridors of power, visited Goebbels in Berlin to discuss with him his memorandum and the measures to be taken in the future. Goebbels was given the go-ahead. He was entrusted with the drafting of laws for 'the totalization of the war' on the basis of an appropriate 'Führer Draft', and in the shortest possible time. On January 13, 1943, Hitler signed the 'Führer Decree on the comprehensive employment of all men and women capable of work for the task of the defence of the Reich,' which had been drafted by Goebbels and his closest collaborators. The decree envisaged the freeing of manpower by way of extensive closing down of commercial, trade and small-craft enterprises and their redeployment in the war economy; in this way, men fit for active military service would be released on a major scale by the civilian war economy. The details of the implementation of these measures were to be supervised by a committee.

The amateurish nature of Goebbels's proposals for the totalization of the war are revealed by the 'Führer Draft' attached to the decree. It showed that Goebbels was still unreservedly sharing Hitler's optimistic belief in victory, that he evidently accepted as genuine the assessment of the situation given him by Hitler and on this basis had made statistical calculations which from the very outset were totally inadequate, even in Hitler's judgement. In order to march as far as Stalingrad on the Volga and to start a retreat from there, Hitler had virtually sacrificed an army of over two million men, including killed, missing and wounded. Yet Goebbels believed that a mere additional half a million troops, something like thirty to forty divisions, would be enough to pin victory finally to the German colours in the spring or early summer of 1943! The military gave notice that they needed a further two million – but this demand, of course, was unrealizable. It is not therefore surprising that Goebbels was not included in the committee for the co-ordination of the totalization measures, although he had firmly counted on membership. Towards the end of January 1943 Hitler intimated to him that he would have to content himself with the part of 'herald of total war' while leaving the practical realization of the idea to the experts.

The plan of demonstrating to Hitler the German people's unreserved readiness for total war by way of a mass rally was first conceived by Goebbels in late January 1943. The unquestionably sensational success of the rally eventually staged on February 18, 1943, was almost certainly due in equal measure to the public's attitude in a situation of incipient desperation and to a speech which pulled out all the stops of suggestion and persuasion. To a lesser extent, no doubt, it was due to the obligatory stage-management and to the applause provided during the rally by a *claque* which this time consisted of canned ovations on gramophone records which were unobtrusively faded into the loud-speaker system in the hall. Nevertheless, no amount of technical refinement and sophisticated stage-management could have achieved the persistence of the applause, for minutes on end, or the spontaneous shouts of approval, or finally the excesses of hysteria which were in fact observed. All these must be attributed to the skill of the speaker and to his ability to electrify an audience tense with latent charge, an audience representing a broad spectrum ranging from the Party fanatic to every shade of fellow-traveller. Goebbels's speech was, broadly speaking, composed of two roughly equal main parts. About half of it was concerned with the dangers of bolshevism, proceeding from the situation on the Eastern Front and culminating in two axiomatic assertions: (1) Europe was exposed to the bolshevik world danger, synonymous with the 'world revolution of the Jews,' the 'bolshevik-capitalist tyranny,' synonymous with 'terror,' 'anarchy,' 'hunger,' 'misery' and 'slave-labour,' (2) only the German Wehrmacht and the German people, together with their allies, were strong enough to achieve Europe's salvation from this menace. Not the Anglo-Saxon powers but Germany alone was able to oppose successfully those 'motorized robot divisions' of the East. But to accomplish this – and here he moved on to the second part of his speech – appropriate counter-measures must be taken 'unless we wish to give up the game as lost.' 'Total war, therefore, is the command of the hour.' And now Goebbels, supported by the spontaneous applause of his audience, explained the new style of life and, by a skilful exploitation of popular criticism of existing social contrasts, prepared his audience for the radical nature of the measures envisaged. He proclaimed as the 'decisive task' the creation of 'a strategic reserve' for the Führer; he announced the drive for the scrapping of 'hundreds of thousands of reserved occupations in the home country'; he appealed to the women to volunteer for work; he hinted at 'large-scale amalgamations' in the economy, and in general, by pointing to the coming summer offensive, aroused those hopes of victory for which his audience was only too ready. The final climax of his speech was provided by ten psychologically well-prepared questions. By applauding or chanting in unison the crowd was to demonstrate and confirm its faith in victory, its readiness to do battle, its resolution to work harder, its will to total war, its absolute faith in Hitler, etc. With satisfaction and approval Goebbels concluded the rally with the promise of an imminent victory, with a reminder of the demands of the moment, and with a new slogan in the form of the well-known line from the poet Körner: 'Now, people, arise; now, storm, break loose!'

There is no doubt that with his Sportspalast speech Goebbels succeeded in overcoming, at least for a few weeks, the crisis of morale among large sections of the German people. But his speech was by no means accepted uncritically. In the territories occupied by Germany it encountered icy rejection; in the neutral countries of Europe and even among Germany's allies it frequently encountered sceptical reserve. There, a victory of German arms was no longer expected, and hopes and confidence were placed in the superiority of the Anglo-Saxon military potential. Sporadically in Germany, universally among the neutral nations, and partially also in the countries allied with Germany, the view was expressed that it would be a good thing if the British and Americans intervened in Europe as soon as possible.

Thus, while the momentum generated by Goebbels for total war was by no means petering out, it nevertheless proved impossible to raise and equip an army of two million men within a matter of months. Goebbels had fanned hopes·and energies; these did not however, as he believed, serve 'the shortest possible war' but merely the continuation of one that they had already lost. True, he himself continued, in January–February 1943, to live with the dangerously naïve conviction, based on a total misjudgement of the military ratio of strength, that the war could still be won. This was no longer so in mid-1944 when Hitler appointed the indefatigable Goebbels to be his 'Reich Plenipotentiary for the Total War Effort' in what was then generally seen to be a hopeless situation. But Goebbels nevertheless proclaimed a programme for 'final victory', a programme willingly believed by quite a few, but which for him personally included the 'battle of Berlin'. The prolongation of his own life at no matter what cost was more important to him than the lives of millions of other human beings in Germany and throughout the world. At the Berlin Sportspalast on February 18, 1943, he had provoked a kind of plebiscite *Yes* to self-destruction; on May 1, 1945, his personal self-destruction, suicide at the last minute, seemed to him the only solution to his own insoluble problem.

Translator's Note

A glance at the German text of the minutes of Goebbels's secret propaganda conferences reveals that these are genuine notes jotted down while the conference was in progress, with – obviously – no thought of publication or even of circulation outside the small, privileged circle of participants. They are, in consequence, recorded snatches of Goebbels's remarks rather than polished departmental minutes. They are slipshod, in the kind of linguistic shorthand used by people who meet every day and know what they are talking about; they abound in awkward and clumsy passages resulting from off-the-cuff speech, and they are often repetitive.

It would have been easy to smooth out this linguistic and stylistic roughness in the translation. It was felt, however, that this would deprive the minutes of much of their spontaneity and impair the reader's sense of eavesdropping on the conferences.

E.O.

Publisher's Note

To facilitate distinction between the text of the minutes and the editor's commentary, the latter is printed one type size smaller than the text of the minutes.

'Victory will be ours'

October–December 1939

October 26, 1939
Herr Fritzsche* reads out a letter from a Jew in England, which was seized from a Prague lawyer. The letter contains highly revealing material, especially about the Jewish backers of the pro-war party in Britain, and is to be exploited after accurate translation.

This letter, allegedly confiscated in Prague, was published by the Deutsches Nachrichtenbüro (German News Agency) on October 31, 1939, with the approval of Reichsprotektor† von Neurath; dated October 18, it had been sent by a Jewish refugee to Dr Zdenek Thon, a lawyer in Prague. The letter speaks of the collaboration of Jewish refugees in England with the Czech Jews, alludes to contacts with Hore-Belisha, the British Secretary for War, and contains recommendations for anti-German actions aiming at a 'revolution'.
By its contents alone, which gravely incriminated its recipient and thus ran counter to all the rules of any underground movement, the letter would appear to be a rather clumsy propaganda fake, even though its origin has not so far been established beyond doubt.

October 27, 1939
Oberregierungsrat‡ Neumann reports that coal supplies, as well as potato supplies in Berlin, Hamburg and other big cities, appear at present to be seriously threatened. As a result of the ten-day transport stop supplies have largely been sold out, and potatoes, in particular, will be in danger if they cannot be brought under cover before the onset of frost. Parteigenosse§ Jetter, on the other hand, points out that the shortages in potato supplies have now largely been eliminated since some 6,000 to 7,000 tons of potatoes are at present reaching Berlin each

---

* For identifications of participants see the list of participants, p. 343.
  † After their invasion of Czechoslovakia in March 1939 the Germans partitioned the country by setting up a Slovak puppet state under Mgr Tiso and turning the Czech Lands (which had already lost considerable areas to the German Reich under the Munich Agreement of 1938) into the 'Protectorate of Bohemia-Moravia'. This was placed under a 'Reichsprotektor' (Reich Protector). *Tr.*
  ‡ See the list of ranks in the German Civil Service, p. 347.
  § Party Comrade – the official form of address in the NSDAP, the Nazi Party. *Tr.*

1

day as against a normal quota of 3,000 tons. Coal supplies are similarly assured, provided the promised increase in transport facilities can be maintained until December 10.

At the conference on October 28, 1939, Gutterer reported that the necessary measures had been taken to ensure regular supplies of coal in future. But there was in fact no question of that. Coal supplies, especially in Berlin, were heading towards near disaster in the winter of 1939–40. (*Cf.* January 9, 1940.)

October 30, 1939

On October 28, 1939, the Czechoslovak national day, there were demonstrations in Prague, with massive support from the Czech public and with distribution of leaflets. At first the Germans attempted to hush this up, or at least to play it down. At the press conference on October 29, 1939, an extensive DNB report about the disturbances in Prague was withdrawn. It was merely announced that there had been demonstrations by Czech juveniles, mainly students, and that arrests had been made and persons wounded. Stricter counter-measures, it was said, had become necessary. One of these turned out to be the closure of all Czech colleges and universities on November 7, 1939, which resulted in student demonstrations on November 15. The German reply to these was mass arrests among the Czech students. Moreover, nine students were executed in Prague on November 17.

To avoid a repetition of the incidents in Prague on 28.10. the following suggestions are to be submitted to Freiherr von Gregory for passing on.

As a matter of principle, anything that is permitted should be safeguarded, while anything that is forbidden must be brutally suppressed by force of arms. Appropriate measures should be taken in advance, and not when it is too late. Punitive and preventive measures should hit everybody – not just the thin layer of intelligentsia who have to be regarded as the authors of the demonstrations. Examples:

If the Czechs boycott the cinemas even for a single day, then all cinemas are to be closed for three months.

If they boycott the trams even for a few hours, no trams are to be run for several weeks.

If they proclaim a short-term tobacco strike, they are to be told that for a number of months all tobacco supplies earmarked for the Czechs will be sent to the German front.

If they pull down street names, then the plates are to be expensively replaced at the cost of the Czech state.

If foreign broadcasts are found to be responsible for demonstrations, then all receivers should be confiscated – in a small-sized town to begin with – and sent to the German front.

In future, foreign rumours about the intentions of the German military command are not to be refuted, so that nervousness and suspense, and even the growth of rumours, are intensified as much as possible.

At the press conference of the same date (October 29, 1939) the following was said in this context: 'The more silent we are the greater will be the nervousness on the other side.' Moreover, at the conference of November 18, 1939, Goebbels demanded that speculations in the foreign press about German military plans should be answered 'by a campaign of figures and statistics about German successes.'

Herr Berndt is to consult with the Ministry of Foreign Affairs and the OKW, and set in motion the necessary preliminary work, with a view to setting up a French communist secret transmitter and an Irish secret transmitter for England.

Two secret transmitters directed against France and one directed against Britain began operations in January–February 1940.

On November 5, 1939 Goebbels made a speech to inaugurate the Hitler-Jugend and Bund Deutscher Mädel* film festival. This speech deserves some attention since it contains remarks which are diametrically opposed to the directives issued at the ministerial conference. Thus Goebbels said: 'Because we know what is at stake we are totally immune to foreign, and in particular British, attempts to deceive us. The stupid and foolish leaflets dropped by British aircraft over German cities and villages cannot affect our morale. In Germany no one listens to the voices which are carried to us from enemy countries; we now listen only to the voice of the Führer.'

November 6, 1939

Dr Hippler is instructed to withdraw American feature films from public showing. Dr Hippler reports that favourable contracts have been concluded with American newsreel companies.

Because of the objections voiced by Hippler, Goebbels's instruction was not implemented. Although, acting under pressure from the Reichssicherheits-hauptamt† (Reich Security Directorate), Goebbels again demanded the immediate withdrawal of American films from German cinemas at the conference of January 12, and again on February 14, 1940, these directives were again not put into effect. (*Cf.* February 16, 1940.)

---

* The Hitler-Jugend (Hitler Youth) and Bund Deutscher Mädel (German Girls' League) were the Nazi Party's youth organizations for boys and girls respectively. *Tr.*

† The Sichesheitsdienst (Security Service) was principally concerned with the political attitude and morale of the German population. *Tr.*

November 8, 1939

Herr Gutterer reports that clothes rationing will be introduced on November 15, 1939, and that each person will receive a card with 100 points. The purchase of overcoats will not be covered by the clothing card. The Minister directs that appropriate measures should be taken to prevent available stocks being sold out within a few days of the issue of the clothing card.

The introduction of the first clothing card was made under the Decree on the Control of Textiles of November 14, 1939. Even before its introduction the public harboured the gravest misgivings about it. In particular, it was feared that the workers would run short under the envisaged points system. Moreover, there was dissatisfaction about the inadequate allocation, or total suspension, of the vouchers which continued to be necessary for the purchase of overcoats and footwear. True enough, Goebbels successfully opposed the view put forward in October by the Ministry of Economics, namely that the public would just have to make do with the available footwear for the duration of the war – but this did not improve supplies of footwear. There was even a shortage of footwear for working, so that, as the war went on, wooden clogs were increasingly used.

Press publicity about the introduction of the clothing card increased the public's irritation. From a letter by the Minister of the Interior, Frick, to the Ministry for Public Enlightenment and Propaganda, dated December 22, 1939, it appears that the news of the issue of the clothing card was carried by the press at a time when local authorities knew nothing about it, so that 'intolerable scenes' were said to have taken place at the rationing offices.

Herr Gutterer is to be responsible for the compilation of material about the Jewish infiltration of the British press, banking and government circles. The press should start at once to criticize the 'Jewish warmongers' in Britain and to concern itself less with organizational shortcomings. In this connexion, remarks by famous Englishmen about the Jewish question are to be collected and used.

Directives along these lines were issued to the press that same day. When, on January 9, 1940, the *Völkischer Beobachter* carried a lengthy story about the alleged Jewish origin of British and French statesmen it clearly overshot its mark. Thus the paper alleged that Duff Cooper's wife was a Jewess. In actual fact, as was pointed out at the Berlin press conference of January 9, 1940, she was 'the most Aryan among the Scottish nobility.'

November 11, 1939

The Minister issues directives for the further treatment of the attempted assassination in the Bürgerbräukeller. The moral responsibility of the western democracies, in particular Britain, proved by her continuous murder propaganda, is to be pilloried and exposed. A comprehensive compilation of material is to be carried out to this end.

The first directives in connexion with the Munich attempt on Hitler's life were issued by Goebbels in the afternoon of November 9, 1939, after he had returned to Berlin with Hitler by express train from Munich. At the midday press conference of November 9, which was quite short, remarks about the attempt in the Bürgerbräukeller were clearly still rather cautious. As far as can be established, more definite instructions were not issued to the press until the publication of the *Vertraulichen Informationen* (*Confidential Information Bulletin*). This states that, in discussing responsibility for the attempt, this should not be attributed to groups inside Germany (Jewish, clerical or monarchist) since this might lead to excesses against the putative culprits. Instead, accusations against those foreign powers which were also responsible for the war were to be hinted at. However, until the results of the investigation were disclosed, the volume and extent of the reporting was not to abate.

Further directives on the press coverage of the attempt were given by Goebbels at the conference of November 10, 1939. According to the minutes of the press conference, the event was to dominate the make-up of the papers. Moreover, the sacrifice of the simple, old Party comrades was to be recorded and the German people were to sympathize with their families in their grief. Finally, the Ministry for Propaganda expressly asked that for the time being no notice should be taken of the incidents on the German-Dutch frontier which had led to the arrest of the heads of the British intelligence service in Europe, Best and Stevens.

November 13, 1939

The Minister points out that there is no reason whatever to ban Shakespeare and Shaw in Germany, as some *Gaue* have already done. Schmidt of the office of the Führer's Deputy is to make the necessary arrangements with the Party bodies concerned.

As a result of repeated directives from Goebbels, G. B. Shaw's works continued to be performed in Germany throughout the war, although with certain restrictions. One of the arguments advanced was that Shaw, as an Irishman, could not be regarded as directly involved in the war. It should also be mentioned that Shaw's *Atrocities of Denshawai, and Other British Atrocities* (Berlin, 1940) fitted into the pattern of German propaganda and was therefore published in the series *England Unmasked*.

November 16, 1939

As for a possible ban on Shakespeare and Shaw, the Führer himself shall decide.

5

November 18, 1939

The press is to publish a cartoon of Chamberlain in slippers.

At the conference of December 16, 1939, Goebbels amended his directive to say that Chamberlain 'must no longer be portrayed in the press as an incompetent, helpless figure with an umbrella, but as a vicious old man.'

November 22, 1939

Publications about prophecies are to be banned. Nostradamus, on the other hand, can perhaps be used in a French leaflet. Gutterer is to submit proposals.

On November 25, 1939, Gutterer was instructed by Goebbels 'to have the Nostradamus leaflet prepared as quickly as possible.' On December 5, 1939, a 'Nostradamus brochure', whose final version was to be submitted to Goebbels within a few days, was mentioned at the conference. Goebbels declared that the brochure should 'have not a scientific but a propaganda character'.

The French astrologer and physician Nostradamus, Michel de Notre-Dame (1503–66) wrote his *Centuries,* his controversial predictions until AD 3000, while living at the court of Henry II of France, who had seized Calais and Boulogne from the English. Particularly useful for the German campaign in France in 1940 was the thirty-third *Century,* which reads:

'Brabant, Flanders, Ghent, Bruges and Boulogne/are temporarily united with the great Germany./But when the passage of arms is finished/the great Prince of Armenia will declare war./Now begins an era of humanity of divine origin,/the age of peace is founded by unity,/war, now captive, sits on half the world,/and peace will be preserved for a long time.'

According to Sommerfeldt, Goebbels, speaking on the subject of Nostradamus, said at the conference: 'This is a thing we can exploit for a long time. I forbid all printing of these forecasts by Monsieur Nostradamus. They must be disseminated only by handbills, hand-written, or at most typed, secretly, and in the manner of snowball letters. The thing must have an air of being forbidden. The following points are to be added by word of mouth: The magic agreement between the thirty-third *Century* with the year 33, our Seizure of Power. Interpretation: Introduction of the new order in Europe by Greater Germany, occupation of France only temporary, Greater Germany ushers in the thousand years' Reich and a thousand years' peace. Naturally, all this silly rubbish must also go out to France over the transmitters. As for the great Prince of Armenia, we'll put him on ice until Herr Stalin from Georgia declares war on us – or we on him. Any other questions or remarks on the subject? Thank you.'

November 27, 1939

It is reported that students in small university towns are behaving badly.

Gutterer is instructed to investigate these reports and to see that appropriate measures are taken by way of the regions.

On December 11, 1939, Gutterer was further instructed to examine complaints about the behaviour of students in Göttingen and to report back. To this end he was to telephone the Mayor of Göttingen on December 12, to find out details. Moreover, Goebbels demanded that the blanket exemption of medical students from military service should be abolished.

Details are contained in an SD report of January 5, 1940. This states that the staff of Göttingen university are for the most part perplexed at the bad behaviour of the students. Never in their academic practice had they come across such things as small paper balls being thrown at the blackboard, or students coming to lectures armed with crackers, or the explanation of sexual matters in medical colleges triggering off sniggers and silly remarks.

Similar phenomena were observed at nearly all German universities. In Leipzig, too, students who had done a period of labour service or military service were exhibiting 'character immaturity' which manifested itself in poor performance. Reports from Venna spoke of political apathy among the students and considered it alarming that they did not give *Heil Hitler* salutes.

December 2, 1939
Dr Bömer is to make arrangements for Kipling's poem *Big Steamers* to be broadcast in the English-language service.

December 11, 1939
The Minister forbids all publicity for British kite-flying of a peaceful settlement of the war. He directs that emphasis should be given in the press to successes in the war at sea.

At the same time, Goebbels demanded that the press should concern itself 'in the strongest possible way with British war aims'; on the other hand he warned against 'belittling the British as to their military value.' Nothing was allowed to seep into the German press of the attempts at peace negotiations made by way of the neutral countries during the winter of 1939–40. The word 'peace' had to disappear from German public opinion because it was feared that it might be interpreted by the enemy as a sign of German weakness, that it might sap the German people's willingness to fight the war, and that it might interfere with German military plans.

Herr Gutterer is instructed to devote the most careful attention to British leaflets, which have become very much more skilful. Discussion of these leaflets in the press is forbidden.

In the past a limited polemic accompanied by the contents of British leaflets had been permitted in the press. The best known and most widely read British leaflet of that time was the *Wolkiger Beobachter,* which appeared in several issues and was at that time mainly concerned with the *NS-Heimkrieger.**

December 12, 1939

The Minister instructs Herr Fritzsche to see to it that greater emphasis is put by the press on

(a) the fact that the war ahead of us will not be child's play, and (b) the other side is determined to annihilate Germany for good.

In future all enemy remarks of this kind are to be recorded; there must be no word in the German press about any lame peace.

In line with this point of view any sentimental note in connexion with Christmas must be avoided in the press and on the radio. The only Christmas Day is December 24 – otherwise politics must always predominate in the newspapers.

In order to testify to the unity of front and homeland, the radio's Christmas programme had the theme 'Soldiers' Christmas – People's Christmas'.

December 14, 1939

Major Cohrs is instructed to obtain information about the treatment of Polish officers in German POW camps, in particular also about possible contact with the population, and to report to the Minister as soon as possible.

At the conference on December 4, 1939, Goebbels had directed that the attention of the public should 'continually be drawn to the indignity of contact with prisoners of war'. In spite of propagandist and police counter-measures the problem continued to be topical for the next few years. Appropriate decrees were issued first by Hess and later by Himmler. Deterrent sentences were passed by courts. The official gazette of the NSDAP announced that on January 8, 1940, a married woman was sentenced to ten years' penitentiary for sexual intercourse with a Polish prisoner of war; the prisoner was sentenced to death. By December 1942, however, the German leadership seemed agreed that in the 'treatment of certain moral phenomena among the female population' allowance should be made for wartime conditions. 'On no account, however,' Goebbels wrote, 'does the Führer desire a slackening of legislation concerning relations of German women with prisoners of war. And this is quite right – one has got to draw the line somewhere.'

* Literally: 'Observer from the Clouds', a pun on the official National-Socialist *Völkischer Beobachter. NS-Heimkrieger* is also a pun, meaning both 'National-Socialist Warriors at Home' and someone 'trying to get back home from the front.' *Tr.*

December 15, 1939

The Minister discusses with Herr Fritzsche, Dr Börner, Lieutenant-Colonel Wentscher and Lieutenant Hahn of the navy the language to be used concerning the *Graf Spee*.

The German pocket battleship *Graf Spee,* displacement 12,000 tons, had been employed in raiding operations against merchantmen in the Indian Ocean and the South Atlantic when, on her return voyage to Germany, she was engaged by three British cruisers off the River Plate on December 13, 1939. In a protracted engagement the *Graf Spee* suffered severe damage and therefore entered Montevideo in the belief that she would be able to carry out repairs there. The pursuing British cruisers waited outside the three-mile limit. As shown by Fritzsche's remarks at the press conference on December 14, 1939, discussion with Goebbels seems to have led to the conclusion that the ship was not expected to accomplish her repairs in Montevideo harbour and that it was thought possible that she would allow herself to be interned. For that reason any jingoist jubilations were to be avoided in the press, so as not to aggravate public disappointment in the event of the ship's loss.

December 18, 1939

In connexion with the scuttling of the *Graf Spee* the Minister believes that it is not possible to report the bald facts alone.

It was pointed out at the press conference that the refusal to allow the battleship to remain in port until she had restored her seaworthiness represented a breach of international law and that it had therefore become necessary for the *Graf Spee* to be scuttled.

Two days previously Goebbels had thought it necessary to prepare the public for the final loss of the pocket battleship by means of false propaganda reports concerning the use of poison gas in the naval engagement of the River Plate.

After the *Graf Spee* had been scuttled by her crew in the River Plate estuary on the evening of December 17, the crew allowed themselves to be interned in pro-German Argentina. Her commander, Commodore Hans Langsdorff, shot himself in the naval arsenal of Buenos Aires after internment on December 20, 1939.

December 19, 1939

The Minister reports on the Führer's attitude to the treatment of the foreign press. The following considerations have to be applied in the following order of importance:

(a) Safeguarding our strength at home, (b) Safeguarding the strength of the Reich abroad.

For this reason there must be an absolute ban on all German-language papers which might undermine the country's strength at home.

The ban was primarily directed against the importation and distribution of Swiss newspapers and periodicals into the Reich.

December 20, 1939

The Minister opposes the slogan, which is still cropping up here and there: 'We shall never surrender!' It is to be replaced, both in pictures and print, by: 'Victory will be ours'.

The question of a smoker's card, envisaged by another authority, is discussed. The issue of such a card, it is felt, must lead to complete bewilderment. The Minister urgently advises against such a measure. Gutterer is instructed to pass this on.

Tobacco supplies remained inadequate and uncertain throughout the war. In May 1940 Goebbels demanded measures against 'the formation of queues' in front of tobacconists. (*Cf.* May 19, 1941.)

Letters from the front and conversation with soldiers suggest that there is a widespread belief at the front that the fighting on the western front is thought in the home country to be relatively easy for the troops. The propaganda companies* in the army are instructed to depict the fighting on the western front from a more serious angle.

December 23, 1939

The Minister points out that the propaganda against plutocracy in Britain is attracting notice and is beginning to be effective. He directs that this course should be maintained both in the domestic and the foreign press.

On December 20, 1939, Goebbels had instructed the press to steer an 'anti-plutocratic course' in its polemics with Britain – even at Christmas. The press campaign was to reflect the theme: the present war is a revolutionary war, an anti-plutocratic war, aiming at the destruction of British capitalism, as expressed by the government spokesman at the press conference of December 20, 1939.

* The propaganda companies in the German armed forces, set up by joint agreement between the OKW and the Ministry for Propaganda, had three tasks: (1) home propaganda, (2) frontline propaganda, (3) propaganda directed at the enemy. The first consisted of the customary work of a war correspondent, the second was concerned with stiffening the morale and 'ideological attitude' of the fighting men, and the third involved leaflets, trench loudspeakers and, later in the war, the operation of army transmitters broadcasting to the enemy's troops. In 1939 a propaganda company consisted of two 'light platoons' (each of six press correspondents and four photographers), one 'heavy platoon' (comprising correspondents, photographers, a radio section and a film section), one platoon comprising the leaflet staff, a loudspeaker section, a film projection section and the editorial staff of the army newssheet, and a fifth platoon responsible for the preparation and evaluation of the material produced. *Tr.*

10

Since then the 'anti-plutocratic course' became one of the favourite campaigns in Goebbels's propaganda repertoire, and the concept of 'plutocracy' began to be played up for the public. At the conference of February 2, 1940 Goebbels again reminded Fritzsche that 'plutocracy' was the main concept 'at which the ideological struggle will be aimed in the immediate future.'

A resumption of the *Ark Royal* question is proposed by Herr Fritzsche but is set aside by the Minister for the time being.

The subject of the *Ark Royal* had become a 'hot potato' for German propaganda, but Fritzsche evidently had not yet realized this. The repeatedly reported sinking of the British aircraft carrier *Ark Royal,* which did not agree with the facts, threatened to shake the credibility of German reporting. On September 14, 1939, a German torpedo merely exploded against the hull of the aircraft carrier. In an aerial attack on September 26, 1939 she was at best slightly damaged, but not, as the Luftwaffe assumed, wrecked. German propaganda had gradually been turning some possible damage to the *Ark Royal* into the sinking of the aircraft carrier. Meanwhile, the OKW Propaganda Department had been trying, through neutral press channels, to coax the British into divulging some details of the real condition of the carrier. This was successful. Goebbels was also notified about the result. He was not very pleased at the news. It is understandable, therefore, that at the conference of December 27, 1939, Goebbels forbade the resumption of the subject of the *Ark Royal,* without, however, giving his reasons to the participants at the conference. By October 1939 the *Ark Royal* was in action in the South Atlantic.

A few weeks later came the official announcement by the British that the *Ark Royal* was in South African waters and had entered Cape Town. When this news was mentioned at the ministerial conference Goebbels asked the representative of the navy, who was present, what he thought should be done about this 'embarrassing piece of news'. The representative replied: 'I am afraid I can't make any suggestion on this subject, Herr Reichsminister; after all, the *Ark Royal* was sunk by the Ministry for Propaganda and not by us!'

December 28, 1939
Measures to set up a pre-publication censorship of ecclesiastical pub-lications are to be taken with all possible speed. Herr Gutterer is to get in touch with the OKW and the Foreign Ministry in this connexion and subsequently to start talks with the Ministry of Church Affairs.

Goebbels's intention to clamp down on Church literature encountered rather more difficulties than he had originally expected, especially as he was anxious not to reveal publicly the real purpose of his measures. The Ministry for Propaganda had agreed with the president of the Reichspressekammer (Reich Press Chamber), Amann, that the printer or multiplier of any printed literature should generally be obliged, before any manuscript went to press, to ascertain whether the author or publisher was a member of the Reichsschrifttumskammer (Reich Chamber of Literature) – which, as a rule, the authors of religious publications were not. On March 11, 1940, the Ministry for Propaganda again urged the issuing of an order to the effect that: 'In the present lull at the front the troops are to a particular degree exposed to large quantities of such literature. Therefore, every day by which the issuing of this order is delayed represents a certain danger.' The order was issued by the Ministerial Council for Reich Defence on July 17, 1940, and published as an 'Order concerning proof of membership of the Reich Chamber of Literature'. The matter was finally clinched by a message from Keitel, Chief of the OKW, to the protestant and catholic field bishops, dated April 1942: 'In reply to my enquiry whether the publications produced by the Army Church Department (Land Forces) should be reprinted and further distributed among the army, the Führer, in his capacity as Commander-in-Chief of the Land Forces, has decided that he does not wish them distributed among his forces. In this connexion the Führer expressed the view that such literature should not be distributed among the other services either.'

December 30, 1939
The Minister instructs Herr Fritzsche to continue exploiting the *Athenia* incident and to keep it in the news.

On September 4, 1939, the U-boat *U-30,* under the command of Lieutenant Lemp, sank the British passenger liner *Athenia* which was carrying 1,000 women and children but which he thought was a British auxiliary cruiser. The High Command of the German Navy, the OKM, rule out the possibility that the *Athenia* could have been torpedoed by a German boat, especially as the *U-30* had sent no signal to this effect. Hitler nevertheless ordered that no passenger liners were to be attacked for the time being and that the *Athenia* case was to be cleared up when the U-boats returned to base. The *U-30* returned to Wilhelmshaven on September 27, 1939, and immediately reported the sinking of the *Athenia*. The very next day Hitler went to Wilhelmshaven to meet the German U-boat crews back from operations. Since, however, the German public had emphatically been told that the story of the sinking of the *Athenia* by a German naval unit was a British lie, this version was kept up so as not to arouse doubts among the German public about the credibility of the German news media. As it was felt that a simple denial would not be enough, the German media went over to a propaganda counter-attack by inventing the story of a time-bomb placed aboard the *Athenia* on Churchill's orders. Moreover, at the press conference on October 19, 1939, Reichspressechef (Reich Press Chief) Dietrich gave an 'absolute assurance' that no German U-boat had sunk the *Athenia* or been anywhere near the position of the incident, although he must almost certainly have known the truth. Finally, Goebbels himself intervened in the argument about the *Athenia* in a broadcast on October 22 and in a lengthy *Völkischer Beobachter* article on October 23, 1939, in which he presented Churchill as convincingly proved guilty of the instigation of the incident. Since the German people did not learn the truth until after the war, the *Athenia* case continued to be presented by the German war propaganda machine as the classical example of a British 'lie', although in fact the 'lie' had been deliberately manufactured by German Propaganda, turning the real events upside down.* (*Cf.* January 2, 1940.)

* See also Shirer, *Berlin Diary*, pp. 202–3 and p. 238.

'Praised be what makes us hard'

January-March 1940

January 2, 1940

The Minister speaks at length about the treatment of German cultural institutions and the German press in the Protectorate [Bohemia-Moravia]*. He holds the view that great care must be taken not to enter the arena with second-rate German forces where the Czech can show first-class quality. Anything German must always appear with the superiority which belongs to the master race.

Herr Fritzsche is instructed to continue running the *Athenia* propaganda, emphasizing the principle involved, and generally bearing in mind the fundamental principle of all propaganda, i.e. the repetition of effective arguments. (*Cf.* December 30, 1939.)

January 8, 1940

The German press is to discuss Hore-Belisha's resignation in the sense that here once again is a Jew who, having been exposed, withdraws into the background the moment a situation becomes sticky. This manner of action, which has been repeatedly in evidence over the past few years, is to be supported by the press with telling examples.

Leslie Hore-Belisha, the British Secretary for War, was replaced by Oliver Stanley on January 5, 1940. Hore-Belisha, who resigned as Minster because of disagreements with Chamberlain, remained in the Commons as an independent member from 1940 to 1945 and in Churchill's first post-war cabinet took on the Ministry of Supply.

The Minister again points out the damaging effects on the troops of listening to foreign broadcasts. Herr Berndt is instructed to draft a detailed and reasoned letter to Generaloberst Keitel.

At the conference on January 5, 1940, Goebbels had taken the view that foreign broadcasts must be listened to only by persons who were in a position

* See second footnote, p. 1.

14

to inform themselves directly about the truth. With this formulation, of course, he put in question the entire German information machinery. (*Cf.* January 11, 1940.)

As a result of Berndt's letter to Keitel, the Chief of the OKW, an order was issued to the Wehrmacht on January 26, 1940, to the effect that the ban on listening to foreign radios applied absolutely to all Wehrmacht members 'unless specifically directed by their appropriate superiors under a relevant order to listen to such broadcasts in the line of duty'. This order also includes the significant passage, undoubtedly inspired by the Ministry for Propaganda: 'Any German soldier exposing his soul and his spirit to such enemy propaganda is committing psychological self-mutilation. This is no less despicable than cowardly physical self-mutilation.' However, not even this order succeeded in putting an end to the listening in to foreign radios by members of the armed forces.

January 9, 1940

The question of the German speakers on London radio is discussed. Herr Brandt is instructed to deal with the matter.

The BBC had succeeded in imitating the voices of the German broadcasters in order to comment on what they said.

Coal supplies are on the agenda. They appear to be a difficult problem which, as Herr Gutterer explains, it will probably not be possible to solve entirely in the given situation. The Minister is of the view that a catastrophe can be avoided only by full dictatorial powers. The Minister voices most serious misgivings about the suggestion that schools, cinemas and theatres should be closed.

The coal and potato shortage was never in fact overcome, especially in Berlin. This alone was a heavy burden on the population. London, too, had a coal shortage, but there it was tackled 'by concentration of means of transport'.

January 11, 1940

The Minister rejects as too lenient the sentences passed by courts for listening to and dissemination of foreign broadcasts, and demands a few exemplary sentences. Sentences of less than four years' penitentiary are no longer to be published in the German press. Ministerialdirektor Greiner is instructed to take up this matter with Staatssekretär Freisler. Within the Wehrmacht the offence of listening to enemy radios is to be countered by a Führer's order.

15

Proposals for measures against listening to foreign broadcasts run like a red thread through the conferences of the winter of 1939–40, but even so it proved impossible to ensure complete observation of the ban by means of police or judicial measures. At the conference on January 12, 1940, Goebbels suggested a radio talk about the ban on listening to foreign broadcasts. The heavy sentences imposed recently were to be included in the talk as a deterrent.

The SD report of January 10, 1940, pointed out that although the heavy prison sentences imposed for listening to foreign broadcasts had made an appreciable impact on the public, there was still confusion about the substance of the ban. It was believed, for instance, that it did not apply to broadcasts from Switzerland, Italy or the Soviet Union, and that it did not include musical programmes from abroad. Several 'Party Comrades', moreover, had felt entitled to listen to foreign broadcasts on the grounds that the ban was directed only against the weak and the malicious.

In the preamble to the order concerning extraordinary radio measures dated September 1, 1939, it is stated: 'In a modern war the contestants use not only military weapons but also means designed to influence the nation psychologically and demoralize it. One such means is the radio. Naturally, every word which the enemy broadcasts to us is a lie and designed to harm the German people.'

January 16, 1940

Russian literature is to be treated in Germany in the same way as anti-German literature in the Soviet Union. From a report from Count von der Schulenburg it appears that a distinction will have to be made between the Soviet Union and communism, but that anti-communist literature need not completely disappear from the public eye.

After the conclusion of the Hitler-Stalin pact some circles thought that the ideological relationship towards the Soviet Union would likewise be subject to revision. National-bolshevik trends flared up, in particular, in the Party and the Schutz-Abteilung (SA; 'Brown-shirts'). Goebbels, on the other hand, evidently saw the pact from the outset for what it really was – a power-political alliance for a limited period – and therefore tried to prevent the emergence of a pro-Soviet climate of opinion. At the conference of December 20, 1939, he ordered a temporary ban on the publication of 'Russian literature': on December 28, he referred to the ban on ideological discussions of the Russians and instructed Gutterer to comb publishers' catalogues for bolshevik literature. On December 30, he gave instructions to find out whether anti-Nazi literature and films continued to be distributed in the Soviet Union. The German ambassador in Moscow was requested on January 9, 1940, to supply a detailed list of measures taken by the Russians. German measures were to be analogous. Finally, all official speakers in the Reich were to receive directives in February 1940 concerning German-Russian relations, to the effect that there must be no 'pretence of an ideological affinity with Soviet Russia'.

January 24, 1940

The subject, 'The Westphalian Peace' is to be discussed by the press in a popular form; similarly the term 'plutocracy' is to be explained, and examples are to be quoted from English history to show its meaning. The Slogan of the Week is to do likewise.

In his speech in Münster in February 1940 Goebbels explained what he wanted to be understood by 'plutocracy'. Plutocracy, he said, was the type of political and economic leadership under which a few hundred families, equipped with anything but a moral justification, ruled the world.

A denial is to be published of British reports of atrocities committed in the Government-General*. We should also oppose British reports about the sinking of neutral ships by German U-boats without warning.

The first mass executions of Jews in Polish towns took place at the beginning of 1940. In addition, deportations of Jews from Reich territory to the Government-General began at that time. These were reported in the world press. At the conference on January 27, 1940, Goebbels urged 'that something decisive should be done about the atrocity propaganda concerning the Government-General'. 'Denials by themselves are not enough; we must go over to the offensive.' On January 29, 1940, Gauleiter Greiser, the Reichsstatthalter (Reich Lieutenant) of the Warthegau,* spoke to foreign press representatives in Berlin. But this did not stop the publication of reports about German actions in the Government-General.

January 29, 1940

The radio should not allow itself to be used for experiments in the musical field; it is not a trail-blazer of new art. New music must be tried out in the Philharmonie or in the Bach Hall, but not over the radio. Care should be taken to ensure that the standards of the Request Concert are not lowered. The main purpose of the Request Concerts should be to give the people very fine music. They are not to be turned into a family affair, and all talk during the Request Concerts should therefore be cut down.

The Minister picks on the ice-hockey match lost by Germany in Prague as an example of the mistaken practice of matching oneself with colonial peoples in a field in which we are inferior. Herr Gutterer is to arrange with Herr von Tschammer und Osten, or with the Reich Sport Office, that a repetition of such incidents is made impossible.

* After the German-Russian partition of Poland in 1939, the Germans incorporated the western part of their share (which had a large German minority) into the Reich proper under the name of *Warthegau,* and designated the rest as the 'Government-General of Poland' with the status of an occupied territory. *Tr.*

17

The same view was expressed in an SD report of January 22, 1940. The ice-hockey match in question took place at the Ice Stadium in Prague on January 11, 1940, and was lost by the German team by one goal to five. The German and Czech national anthems were played at the beginning of the match. The German defeat, according to the SD report, was celebrated by the Czech players and spectators as a political triumph.

The Minister again urges the illustrated press to see to it that, in reporting political demonstrations, the speaker is not shown in a stereotype opening posture, but that lively pictures should be published, such as the audience up in the hay loft. The Minister hopes that these suggestions will now at long last be observed in connexion with the Sportspalast demonstration on Friday.

On January 30, 1940, in a speech at the Berlin Sportspalast on the 'Day of Assumption of Power', Hitler underlined his resolution to attack in the West. Speaking of Chamberlain, he said: 'Besides, every nation burns its fingers only once; only once did the children follow the Pied Piper of Hamelin, and only once did the German people follow an apostle of the international brotherhood of nations!' Hitler declared that Germany would not capitulate, 'for Germany must and will be victorious'.

January 30, 1940
Major Martin reports that, in accordance with the Führer's orders, only Alsatians, Bretons, Scots and North Africans can be accommodated in separate prisoner-of-war camps. All the rest are to be kept together. Experience has already shown that this greatly increases friction among the Allies. (*Cf.* May 3, 1940.)

Herr Bömer is authorized to inform the foreign journalists in Germany that they may listen to foreign broadcasts. However, to pass on such news is forbidden. Each foreign journalist will be given a special warrant card, made out in his name and containing precise directives.

February 1, 1940
The Minister demands that film, radio and press should launch a campaign to achieve a better relationship between sales staff and their customers. Examples are to be shown of well-intentioned people being offended by the improper behaviour of badly educated sales personnel and, on the other hand, of sales staff mitigating hardships and shortages by their tactful sympathy. The cinema, in particular, should tackle the problem by ridiculing malpractices. Herr Fritzsche is to commission a very sensitive psychological treatment of the subject, and Herr Hadamovsky is to work out interviews for radio.

Campaigns for greater courtesy in public life continued to be proposed by Goebbels in subsequent years and were also put into effect. On the other hand, towards the end of January 1941 the proprietor of a Berlin restaurant who embellished his menu poetically was threatened by Goebbels with deportation to a concentration camp unless he stopped 'his unnecessary ado'.

February 3, 1940

Herr Fritzsche reports on the hold-up in paper supplies which may make it necessary to save half the present size of the daily papers over the next four weeks. The Minister does not want to lay down details until after a conversation with Herr Rienhardt on Monday [February 5] but he lays down the principle here and now that no dailies should be allowed to fold; they should merely be reduced in size. The polyphony of the daily press is to be preserved at all costs. On the other hand, there are quite a number of unnecessary periodicals which can be discontinued.

The war-time economy measures for the supply of paper chiefly hit the periodical press. In 1939 there were 4,789 different periodicals appearing in Germany, but their number diminished during the course of the war, until it was down to 458 in 1944. At the press conference on February 5 Fritzsche announced that paper consumption must be cut by half because the paper mills were out of coal. At the conference on February 6, 1940 reference was made to a mere 25 per cent saving in paper. An economy drive in radio periodicals, planned in May–June 1940, was put off for the time being. (*Cf.* February 24, 1941.)

February 6, 1940

The Minister suggests to Herr Bömer that on a suitable occasion he might see that a foreign journalist, who has been guilty of particularly damaging and vile lies, is arrested and subjected to prolonged proceedings. This might provide a drastic check on the atrocity propaganda of certain foreign journalists.

February 7, 1940

Herr Gutterer is to inform the police that the Minister has no objection whatever to searches being made of the homes of Jews suspected of hoarding.

The Minister declares himself in agreement with the idea that more elaborate radio receivers belonging to overt enemies of the state are exchanged for small receivers, even if there is no more than justified *suspicion* that they listen to foreign broadcasts.

Goebbels's reference to 'enemies of the state' is not to the Jews, since all radios owned by Jews had already been confiscated in 1939, in a campaign directed by the Reich Propaganda Offices, and for the most part distributed to the forces. At the beginning of October 1939 Hitler had decreed that all radio receivers in the Polish occupied territories were to be confiscated from the Polish population, including the Jews.

February 12, 1940

The Minister points out that only the Party, entrusted as it is with the political and cultural leadership of the German people, is entitled to appeal to the German people at public meetings. It is therefore not permissible for aged admirals or generals to address the German people, for instance in factories, especially as they do not always have the correct approach to the people. Besides, this is in line with the wishes of the Wehrmacht itself. Herr Wächter is to see to it at once that such incidents are not repeated.

This directive was evidently designed to avoid the danger of World War One generals and admirals drawing the obvious parallels in their speeches between the two wars, and in this way giving food to the public's doubts about the outcome of the war. Goebbels took up the same theme in his first editorial article for the Nazi prestige periodical *Das Reich* of May 26,1940. Anyone 'attempting to analyse the present war by the yardstick of the last,' he pointed out in his introduction, 'runs the risk of falling victim to the worst possible political and military errors.' Further on he said: 'The Führer's outstanding, statesmanlike genius has succeeded, by dint of tireless diplomatic preparatory work, in breaking through the stranglehold or forcing it open by military means ... The Reich possesses enough raw materials to survive the war economically for an unlimited period ... Today the German Wehrmacht possesses the most up-to-date technical equipment imaginable ... Germany 'knows how to wield the weapon of truth with sovereign assurance. Her information policy is swift, skilled, clear and effective. She has developed a system of supreme perfection in the treatment of public opinion among our people and of world public opinion, down to the last deployment ... Added to this – and this is of immense importance pyschologically – the German army today carries with it the magic of invincibility and the magic of a glorious revolution ... Today it is patently obvious that one cannot conquer guns with butter, but that one can very well conquer butter with guns ...' The German people knew 'how to live in an epoch without parallel.'

February 14, 1940

The Minister fully agrees with Major Martin's observations about the debasement of army humour and formulates the principle, to be passed on to the press by Herr Fritzsche. On the subject of the soldier the press must not be any more disrespectful than it would be to a political official. All idiotic portrayals of soldiers and NCOs must disappear.

February 16, 1940
Herr Fangauf is to make a return by next Monday [February 19] of the financial losses which would result from a sudden withdrawal of American films. He is also to see to it that no World War One films are performed in the cinemas nowadays, especially from the final years of the war, showing a type of soldier not yet encountered in the present war.

On February 19, 1940, the SD was informed of the reasons why the American feature films at present showing in Germany could not be suddenly withdrawn. (*Cf.* April 10, 1940.)

February 17, 1940
On the subject of neutrality the Minister directs that the neutral states must not, of course, be threatened 'with the rifle', but that they must be gradually coerced under the terror of the new concept of neutrality as formulated by us.

Explaining his 'concept of neutrality' in his speech in Münster, Goebbels stated that he did not accept a definition to the effect that neutrality was to be understood only in the military and not in the political sense; in his opinion neutrality involved also neutrality in public utterances.

February 19, 1940
The Minister instructs the press to concentrate all its polemics on the *Altmark* incident.

On February 16, 1940, the British destroyer *Cossack* attacked the German auxiliary naval vessel *Altmark* which was lying in the Jössingford in Norway. The *Altmark* had on board British naval personnel rescued by the *Graf Spee*. Several German sailors were killed or wounded.
The British information service reported the *Altmark* incident several hours before the German, so that the major part of the world press received the British version. The German delay was due partly to differences between the German Ministry of Foreign Affairs and the Ministry for Propaganda. Hitler himself was reported to have voiced his extreme displeasure at this failure of the German information service and information policy generally.
At the press conference of February 19, 1940, the report issued the previous day, to the effect that the *Altmark* had been unarmed, was withdrawn.

21

This fact, it was said, could be stated in the press without any timidity. It was also said: 'The tone of the papers must now become sharper still: tonight the sea should boil. Even papers which habitually consider the susceptibilities of their readers must now use heavy type and large spacing. All propaganda must be focused on this single incident.'

February 26, 1940

Herr Gutterer is to see to it that the National Socialist press in southern Germany uses decent publicity methods.

On February 17, 1940 the SD report described some methods of salesmanship used by the Nazi press in Danzig, in west Prussia. There, the canvassing was done on the principle: 'Anyone not subscribing to this paper is no German.' The SD report of February 23 described canvassing methods in southern Germany, especially in Munich. There, the public were asked to fill in forms which asked whether the reader was a Party member and took the *Völkischer Beobachter*. In fact, the impression was created that the *Völkischer Beobachter* alone was permitted reading matter.

On March 21, 1940, Goebbels issued the following instruction in connexion with a case of flagrant extortion in canvassing for the Nazi press: 'If it is true that a canvasser has operated with the threat that, if the women refuse to subscribe to the National-Socialist press, their menfolk would be called up for military service, then this canvasser should be sent to a concentration camp and his punishment publicized.' In such a case, however, the German press would report only the duration of the person's detention but not the fact of his deportation to a concentration camp.

February 27, 1940

Sumner Welles, the American Secretary of State, arrived in Rome on February 25, 1940, and had talks with Mussolini and Count Ciano to explore possibilities of peace. On February 26, 1940, Goebbels threatened to have any German paper impounded which published more than the official German reports about Welles's visit.

For the duration of Welles's stay in Europe Herr Fritzsche is to remind the press repeatedly that nothing must appear about this trip in the German papers apart from the official DNB material.

March 8, 1940

Before the start of the drive for the collection of non-ferrous metal Herr Gutterer is once more to submit to the Minister all leaflets, appeals, etc. In particular, care must be taken that only such articles of daily use are collected as can in fact be replaced by the purchase of identical articles from other materials.

The 'Order for the Implementation of the Four-Year Plan Concerning the Collection of Non-Ferrous Metals' of March 15, 1940, stated: 'In order to create the stockpiles of metal required for the long-term conduct of the war' church bells of bronze were to be surrendered as well. Compensation was promised after the war.

At the conference of March 4, 1940, Goebbels had demanded measures to ensure that no works of art were destroyed in the course of this drive: metal value and artistic value must be in justifiable relation to each other. At the end of March 1940 he urged at the conferences that publicity for the collection of zinc, copper, lead, tin, etc. must not be promoted by half-measures, and that, above all, a law should speedily be issued decreeing the death sentence for anyone appropriating articles from the collection. The 'Order for the Protection of the German People's Metal Collection' was dated March 29, 1940. On April 19, 1940, Goebbels informed the conference that the result of the metal donations had already exceeded the most optimistic estimates by more than double. The exact figures, however, were not to be disclosed to the enemy, although the admirable performance of the German people was to receive the highest possible praise in the press. On April 29, 1940, Goebbels listed the total result of the metal drive as 61,000 tons but omitted to add that, measured against annual consumption, which, for copper alone was over 300,000 tons, the result was comparatively trivial. The metal collection closed a gap in supplies for a few months but certainly did not ensure the necessary stockpiles for 'a long-term conduct of the war.'

March 14, 1940

The Minister gives his approval to the tactics proposed by Herr Bömer whereby unwelcome foreign journalists are to be pushed across the frontier by the police as undesirable aliens; in this way the Foreign Press Department can be kept out of such affairs as far as possible.

For the purpose of keeping a check on foreign correspondents an extensive system of personal surveillance had been introduced. This included security police measures providing for a continuous check on the social contacts and personal behaviour of foreign correspondents. Eventually the circle of foreign correspondents in Berlin was so narrowed down by an almost invisible form of 'weeding out and selection' that, with a few exceptions, only those correspondents were left from whom no anti-German reporting was to be feared.

March 18, 1940

The foreign language service is to take up the English term 'chocolate soldier' for its future polemics, and use it over and over again.

March 19, 1940

Herr Brauweiler is to see to it that the [radio] *Talks** presuppose less on the part of the listener, that their main points are more clearly emphasized, and that they address themselves more to mass and class instincts. In this form – i.e. not as talks for intellectuals, as practised by Britain – the talks may be continued.

At the conference of March 26, 1940, Goebbels formulated his directive more precisely: 'We must always avoid the danger of the foreign language service getting too intellectual. The broadcasts must unleash anger, and not just touch the intellect of a few. Similarly, any musical framework must aim at *entertainment* and not try to re-educate the taste of other nations. Herr Dittmar is to issue appropriate directives in his "Ten Commandments for his Collaborators".'

Herr Fritzsche will assume personal control of every report from Paris or London and as a matter of principle see to it that nothing of the speculation in connexion with the Brenner meeting gets into the German press. On no account must the German public be infected by the nervous crisis on the other side, and the word 'peace' must not appear in the German press at all. The Minister emphasizes the need to adhere rigidly to the point of view: We fight on until there is complete clarity.

On March 18, 1940, Hitler and Mussolini met on the Brenner for two-and-a-half hours' conversation – but Hitler mentioned neither his planned campaign in Scandinavia nor the campaign in France. His intention was merely to impress his partner with the numerical strength of the German Wehrmacht.

The foreign language service, on the other hand, may pick up any peace rumours, etc., in so far as they seem apt to produce a demoralizing effect abroad.

An official German peace denial was issued that day and the press was instructed to make the appropriate comment. The information for the press of March 20, 1940, in this connexion contained the following passage: 'War is holding absolute sway, and no actions whatever by Germany whether of diplomatic or other character, must be seen as tactics pursuing camouflaged aims; they are of entirely concrete character and serve the sole purpose of seeing the war through to a victorious conclusion.'

March 29, 1940

Directives to the press:

    (a) The press is to point to the marked stiffening and intensification of

---

* Goebbels uses the English word. *Tr.*

the enemy's methods of warfare and war aims, noticeable since the formation of the Reynaud cabinet,* and in this connexion it must again be clearly stated that this war can end only with the crushing of international world tyranny.

(b) In connexion with certain boastful enemy remarks the press should recall that it is exactly a year since the braggards in Poland intended to conquer Berlin, and that it is now seven months since the Polish government had to leave its country. This is to be followed by words of regret for the fate of the nations who have entrusted themselves to such gamblers and now have to suffer for their deeds.

(c) In connexion with the French remark that after the end of the war the whole of Germany would have to eat from the French field kitchens, a start is to be made with the exploitation of anti-French material. The press should point out that we are not dealing here with the literary outburst of hatred by some individual, but that the same class is now at the helm as in 1918–23 and that only the faces have changed. In the interest of international understanding, it should be explained, we had in recent years allowed our public to forget what had happened a mere twenty years ago. This is to be followed up by the various papers with striking individual examples from the period of occupation.

At the conference of January 18, 1940, Goebbels had passed on a suggestion of the *Westdeutscher Beobachter* that local Party groups in the former French-occupied areas of the Rhineland should comb archives and newspapers for orders by the occupation authorities subjecting the public to hardships and chicanery. The material compiled about the occupation of the Rhineland and resistance in the Ruhr had been kept ready for instant publication since the beginning of March 1940.

March 21, 1940
Herr Gutterer reports on the subject of controlling nude shows. On the whole, there is no need for official action since not one of the night club performances criticized by other quarters contains actual obscenities. Only at the Frasquita is there a turn by what seems a very decadent dancing couple. The Minister directs that Herr Gutterer should demand from the proprietor of the Frasquita that he withdraws the couple.

The Frasquita was a well-known Berlin night club in the Hardenberg-strasse.

* The French cabinet under Daladier had resigned on March 20; Daladier refused to form another government, so Paul Reynaud (the outgoing Minister of Finance) was entrusted with the task. He completed his new government on March 21. It pledged itself to a more vigorous prosecution of the war. *Tr.*

Herr Müller is to inform the President of Police that the Minister sees no cause for intervention in the cases reported so far.

On the other hand, Herr Gutterer reports that the play *Man in the Bath-Tub,* at present running at the Theater am Schiffbauerdamm, consists of nothing but *double entendres* and that this is highly offensive and undesirable. The Minister will consider his decision on this matter.

The farce *Man in the Bath-Tub* by Friese and Felmar had its première at the Theater am Schiffbauerdamm in Berlin on March 1, 1940. In spite of Gutterer's report it was not immediately taken off.

'Epoch without parallel'

April-June 1940

April 1, 1940

In connexion with the German White Book the Minister once more issues general directives: on no account must remarks in the German press or in the foreign language service imply that we intend to interfere in internal American affairs. The aim must be to prevent Roosevelt's re-election, to make sure a re-elected Roosevelt cannot, as Wilson did in his time, agitate for the entry of the United States into the war. This aim can only be achieved if the material is allowed to speak for itself. American attempts at belittling the matter, on the other hand, may be dismissed contemptuously.

The German Foreign Ministry had published the *White Book No. 3; Polish Documents on the Period Leading up to the War*. The official German edition of the White Book ran to 120,000 copies, the popular edition to 200,000, the English edition to 40,000, the French edition to 50,000, the Spanish edition to 120,000 and the Japanese edition to 5,000. A large proportion of the White Books were distributed via Switzerland.

Herr Gutterer is to see to it with the KdF* that compères in future go in for less smutty jokes. As a general rule there may be generous exposure of the female body, but the rules concerning so-called 'jokes' must be correspondingly tighter.

Herr Gutterer will also see to it that an emphatic reminder is issued of the Minister's order forbidding compères to make any political jokes whatsoever.

Instructions went out at the same time for discussions designed to raise the level of KdF events which were threatening to degenerate into a 'veritable funfair'. As recently as March 1940 Goebbels had ordered a check on nude shows in Berlin amusement halls. Since no 'actual obscenities' were shown he could see no reason for further measures on March 21, 1940.

* NS Gemeinschaft 'Kraft durch Freude' (National Socialist 'Strength through Joy' organization). *Tr.*

27

The Secret Conferences of Dr. Goebbels

Herr Bömer reports that the Ministry of Foreign Affairs has received instructions to lodge a protest in the United States, as well as in all other countries in question, against the performance of the film *Hitler, the Beast of Berlin*, now actually showing in the United States.

The German diplomatic missions were frequently instructed to present notes of protest against the showing of anti-German films abroad – with varying success. The Belgian government, for example, at the end of January 1940 and following a German protest, banned the showing of the first British wartime propaganda film *The Lion has Wings,* but this film was at that time being shown in Italy without giving offence. At the end of May 1940 Goebbels decided to have the film shown in Berlin on the assumption that it would 'get a first-class burial in a storm of hilarity.' However, it never came to that. Before a suitable German version of the film could be completed, the RAF's bombing raids proved that the British lion did indeed have wings and that there were no longer any grounds for outbursts of hilarity.

April 3, 1940

The French periodical *l'Illustration* on its title page on March 16, 1940, published a photograph showing Sumner Welles and Paul Reynaud in front of a map of Central Europe. Into this map an appropriate German propaganda studio had touched in clearly discernible frontiers as follows: The whole course of the Rhine formed the frontier of France, and the right bank of the Oder that of Poland. Germany was divided into two states – Bavaria to the south and Prussia to the north of the Main. A Habsburg state embraced parts of southern Germany as well as the Italian provinces of Venetia and Trieste. Parts of Saxony were incorporated into Czechoslovakia. Hungary was reduced in favour of Rumania, and Belgium and the Netherlands were linked up into a uniform political entity.

It was frequently the practice with German propaganda falsifications to be first launched for publication abroad and subsequently taken over by the German press. The faked map of Europe was first published in *Regime Fascista*.

The press was instructed to present the map as cynical proof of renewed Allied intentions to annihilate Germany. 'The pot of this subject is to be kept on the boil.' Editorial offices were also instructed to work up the material on the resistance in the Ruhr and the separatist movements into an anti-French campaign. When soon afterwards Sumner Welles declared that he had not seen any such map during his conversations with Reynaud the press was instructed not to take up Sumner Welles's denial. Goebbels believed that Welles's denial had given the whole business a 'new, highly comical twist' which did not weaken the German position in the least.

The map of Europe in *l'Illustration,* which shows the re-organization of Europe after a victory of the plutocrats, is to be exploited to the full. The lesser neutral countries in particular are to be shown the kind of fate in store for them after a German defeat. The matter is to be discussed in the Topics of the Day* by Professor Grimm or some other scholar; the map is to be reproduced for the Slogan of the Week;† Herr Bömer is to arrange a lecture to the foreign press, using an enlarged map, and the foreign language service in its broadcasts to the various countries must invariably pick out in particular the country to which it addresses itself.

The Minister again objects to the nonsensical and indeed damaging flood of printed propaganda which is pouring into the neutral countries and directs once and for all that his Ministry must not in any way participate in the foolish and mistaken propaganda methods of other authorities. The basic rule of our propaganda must always be to appeal to the instincts and not to reason.

On April 5, Goebbels received the editors-in-chief of the Berlin press and the chiefs of the Berlin offices of the foreign press. His observations on the occasion were revealing in many respects. On the subject of the theory of press propaganda Goebbels said that the principle of continuous repetition of propaganda slogans once issued must be kept up at all costs; the papers had to address themselves to the broad masses and not to any narrow élite. News without comment must not be published; this meant that each report must be presented as a commentary. In order not to tie down the leadership and also to avoid alarming the common reader, the discussion of war aims was to be avoided. Only the 'section of the road' immediately ahead was to be clearly illuminated.

Goebbels's speech, moreover, intimated that a change in the conduct of the war could shortly be expected, so that the German people would be facing a test of nerves. This announcement, Goebbels said, most certainly did not represent a bluff in the war of nerves. Even though German propaganda was to aim at separating the people of the Western Powers from their governments, in the same way as during the Nazi struggle for power the electors had been split from their old Party leaderships, this was by no means a panacea for the conduct of a war. Propaganda was merely an instrument of warfare and did not render military operations unnecessary.

* 'Topics of the Day' ('Zeitgeschehen') was a daily half-hour programme on the German radio's home service, at 6.30 p.m., a peak listening period. It consisted of a series of short talks, outside broadcasts and interviews with people in the news, interspersed with music. *Tr.*

† Goebbels's ministerial conference was followed by a daily conference at the Propaganda Ministry's Press Department, at which guidelines were issued to the press. This was followed by a 'Slogan of the Day' conference in the office of Reichspressechef Dietrich. After November 4, 1940, the 'Slogan of the Day of the Reichspressechef' was issued from Dietrich's office as a concise daily directive; its introduction enabled Dietrich to tighten his grip on the German press. From then onwards the 'Slogan of the Day' conference preceded the daily press conference. In addition, the Reich Propaganda Directorate also issued 'Slogans of the Week'. *Tr.*

April 4, 1940

Herr Bömer reports about a request by the American periodical *Life* (forty million readers) that the Minister should write an original article for it. In return, the paper would undertake not to allow any anti-German sentiments to be voiced in the number in question. The Minister expresses his agreement and instructs Herr Bömer to make detailed proposals.

The project did not come off at the time. Later, in 1940, however, *Life* carried four original articles by Goebbels. These appeared on August 5 and 19, September 23 and December 30, 1940.

April 8, 1940

The main news in the press will no doubt be the British decision to mine Norwegian waters. In dealing with this complex subject it should be remarked that these matters will not bear thrashing out over a period of several days but that the German people expect action in reply.

On March 28, 1940, the Supreme Allied War Council decided to mine Norwegian waters as from April 5, and to occupy bases in Norway. On April 5 the operation was postponed until April 8 and was in fact only started that day. Work on the German deployment study *Weserübung* (Exercise Weser) envisaging the occupation of Danish and Norwegian bases, was put in hand by the OKW on January 27 and approved by Hitler on March 1. On April 2, 1940, Hitler ordered the operation to start on April 9. On April 7 the German naval units put to sea for Denmark and Norway.

April 10, 1940

For the further treatment of the measures to protect Scandinavia the Minister issues the following main directives:

(a) Germany does not need to blow her own trumpet; for that our position is too strong.

(b) On the other hand, the world and above all the British people, must be made to see as clearly as possible the humiliating position into which Britain has manoeuvred herself. The best way to do this is by printing British press comment itself, without comment.

(c) The German people must be shown clearly what has happened: that this has been the most daring and daredevil operation in modern war, one which has turned all the laws of strategy topsy-turvy.

(d) At all costs must the thesis be maintained and underlined that the operation was solely a reply to the British operations in Norwegian waters, and was only triggered off by these operations.

(e) The Minister expects of the ministry staff that they will not themselves cast any doubt on this thesis, still less ridicule it.

In view of the increasingly frequent disturbances in German cinemas by American films the Minister wishes Herr Hippler to submit a draft regulation by Friday [April 12] which would at last enable the banning in Germany of all American films by not later than Wednesday next, in order to maintain public peace and order. Herr Hippler is to consult with the Ministry of Foreign Affairs on the form of the justification of such a ban towards the United States.

Although Goebbels was evidently again ready to yield to pressure from the SD and prohibit American films, this ban was not in fact put into effect in 1940. It is not yet entirely clear to what extent Hitler himself was involved in this matter. (*Cf.* February 28, 1941.)

April 11, 1940

The Minister points out that the principal consideration in connexion with the operations in Scandinavia must be that this daring and bold operation has led to complete success. This success alone is decisive. Naturally, we shall have to expect losses. What matters are not the losses but the success which leads to victory. This alone is decisive.

At a time when the enemy is flooding the world with rumours, it is pointless for the press and radio to go in for commentaries and talks. What matters is news. If, due to a lack of communications, we have no news of our own then such news must be written up from available reports from other countries – which is what Britain and France are doing.

At the conference on April 12, 1940, Goebbels explained 'that it was absolutely necessary in critical situations to reply at once to the attacks of the enemy, but that these replies need not by any means be made in the field in which the attack had taken place. The principle must be that one must never be silent but must always have something to say. If necessary, the enemy must be compelled, instead of going on with his lies, to tie himself up in denials.'

No over-optimism must be allowed to emerge in the German people; the people must always be firmly 'supported by the corset of realism'.*

---

* The idea of the corset as a morale strengthener goes back to the old Prussian army; the corsets worn by the officers were thought to promote not only a military 'bearing' but also courage in action. The concept of the 'corset' has since been used figuratively by German military writers and, since World War One, also in the popular press. During the 1914–18 war, German military men were fond of referring to the German units sent to 'stiffen' the Austrian army as that Army's corset. *Tr.*

31

April 13, 1940

From the lies launched by the Allies during the past few days the Minister draws the conclusion that

(a) lies must be used only as a defensive measure and not for making a false show of successes;

(b) no official apparatus, news agency, etc., must ever be used for the launching of lies; the source of the latter must, as a matter of principle, be camouflaged at once;

(c) radio and press in Germany must never be saddled with such lies at all; these must only go out through the channels leading abroad.

The 'Directives for the Drafting of Tendentious and Disrupting Information' dated July 1942, which served the Ministry of Foreign Affairs as the basis of its foreign propaganda activity, similarly emphasized that the effect of a piece of misleading information depended crucially on the manner in which it was released. The way of launching such a report must always be carefully considered and must depend on the scale of distribution intended for the 'report'. 'Misleading information' could be released either as a single report or in the form of several reports. A particularly favourable way was to let it appear simultaneously or in rapid succession in a number of places.

As for our propaganda for Denmark, the Minister lays down the general rule that we should be generous in all matters which do not cost us anything.

(a) A lively cultural exchange on a reciprocal basis is to start at once.

(b) Everything should be done to help the Danes lose their inferiority complex.

Denmark is to be spared leaflets. Altogether the facts, i.e. for the main part our troops, are to speak for themselves. Generally speaking, the conviction is to be promoted among the Danes that whatever is happening now is the lesser evil. As for Norway, it is the task of our propaganda to convince the people in an unobtrusive, calm and factual tone of voice that it is lunacy for a nation of 2·9 million people to try to oppose a powerful Reich of 86 million people. The present government, it should be explained, was driving Norway into disaster by its mistaken policy, pursued for selfish reasons, since nothing could now change the fact that Norway will remain occupied by Germany for the duration of the war.

Norway was determined not to submit voluntarily, and in many places offered stubborn resistance to the German landing operations. German attempts to win over King Haakon and the Norwegian government, and to persuade them to cease resistance, misfired.

April 15, 1940
The Minister forbids the domestic press to publish any further pictures of British prisoners of war whenever such pictures reflect very good treatment.

This instruction ran counter to one issued as recently as April 10, 1940, which said that more photographs of British prisoners and the good reception they would meet with in Germany should be published abroad because of their propaganda value. Under a directive of May 29, 1940, pictures of prisoners were only to be shown when these prisoners produced an utterly dejected impression. At the beginning of September 1940 Fritzsche again reminded the press 'that reports about the good treatment of prisoners of war had a bad propaganda effect.' Goebbels evidently believed that the strict ban on contact with prisoners of war could not be enforced so long as the press carried approving reports about their good treatment. On the other hand, such reports are not likely to have met with much credence abroad. One might also point to the bitter experience of the US forces during the final years of the war when their propaganda about the good reception of German prisoners in the United States produced virtually no result.

April 16, 1940
The Minister hears a report on the question of the censorship of foreign language broadcasts by foreigners and decides that, contrary to the present practice, a script of each planned transmission is to be submitted in good time and in triplicate; this practice to take effect immediately. Censorship will be exercised by:
   (a) the Wehrmacht,
   (b) the Ministry of Foreign Affairs
   (c) the Foreign Press Department.
Attention is to be paid to the person of the speaker to make sure a harmless text is not made to produce the opposite effect by a mocking delivery. When the censors do not agree the decision will be made, not by majority vote, but by the more determined opinion.
   Herr Fritzsche is to administer a most serious reprimand to the editor of a Lippe newspaper for publicly questioning whether the transmission of the Request Concert in the afternoon was really as important as the transmission of a football match. It is to be made clear to the editor that in the event of a repetition of such insolent interference in matters of state policy he may expect to find himself in a concentration camp.

On the assumption that the international soccer match between Germany and Italy would end in favour of Germany, Goebbels at the end of April 1940 authorized the fade-in of a running commentary into the Request Concert. On May 5, 1940, however, Germany lost the international match against Italy by two goals to three. Following the transmission of the match, whose outcome could not have been foreseen, especially since the half-time score was two goals to two, Goebbels on May 6, 1940, prohibited 'sports commentaries, once and for all, being transmitted during the Request Concert.'

April 17, 1940

If our losses so far in the Norwegian operation are to be announced then the press must emphasize first of all that we have come out victorious. Anybody must have realized that the achievement of success would also demand sacrifices. It must further be pointed out that the German people may place absolute reliance in the accuracy of the Wehrmacht communiqués.

In this connexion Herr Gutterer reports a drop in public morale throughout the Reich. The Minister agrees in principle that a speedier release of news than occurred this time would be more correct.

Moreover, the figures publicized by the enemy are to be answered by counter-statistics.

The Wehrmacht communiqué of April 17, 1940, confirmed the heavy losses suffered by the German navy off Narvik. Goebbels learned these from the Wehrmacht draft communiqué submitted to him, and could not therefore know whether the events at Narvik were again being glossed over for the German public on Hitler's instructions. At any rate, considerable disquiet was spreading among the public about the lack of information.

On April 17, in a signal not passed on by the OKW, Hitler had left the German troops at Narvik with the option of internment in Sweden. But prior to the possibility of such internment an appropriate preparation for the publication of the news to the German public was indispensable.

Generally speaking, the Minister wishes all departmental heads to call more frequent departmental meetings for the purpose of giving a survey of the situation to stiffen staff morale. The Minister emphasizes that the Ministry for Propaganda must be a Nazi House from which unshakable confidence radiates out towards the population as a whole.

April 19, 1940

Instructions to the press:

(a) The Minister issues detailed instructions to Herr Fritzsche on how the German news policy since the beginning of the protection of Norway is to be justified before the public, in the shape of a kind of report from German news headquarters. It should be shown how, in order to deny information to the enemy, we were at first compelled to hold back some report or other, and how Britain exploited this period of silence by disseminating totally false reports of successes to the world at large. Now, however, the whole world is beginning to realize that the British reports were in fact nothing but lies, and, by way of contrast, the absolute credibility of the German information apparatus is again being confirmed. The German people, moreover, realize that we are in fact releasing all information as soon as military considerations make this possible.

(b) The press is to feature and emphasize comment from Italy suggesting that the latter will enter the war, without giving such reports too ostentatious a coverage.

A German military mission was just then on a visit to Italy. The news was to be published without comment, as announced at the press conference. Italy's entry into the war was by no means then definite. By pointing to this possibility Goebbels hoped to divert the Allies from the Nordic theatre of war to the danger spot in the Mediterranean. He again used this propagandist diversionary manoeuvre in May 1940, but had to pay the price of disappointment among large sections of the German people when Italy did not join the war as yet. (*Cf.* June 6, 1940.)

(c) It should be pointed out how Chamberlain, the 'good old fellow',* is suddenly losing his nerve and indulging in extravagant abuse: a man using abusive language is in the wrong.

(d) In connexion with an article in the *12 Uhr Blatt*, which, however, the Minister does not wish to be specially reprimanded, the Minister again points out that it is sounder policy to refrain from publishing anything on the subject of goods in short supply rather than publishing an account which everybody must realize does not agree with the facts.

(e) Herr Fritzsche is instructed to have harsh sentences on radio offenders published at regular intervals, perhaps every three weeks, to make sure this continuous deterrent will check a renewed growth in listening to foreign stations.

This minute clearly reveals the close links between propaganda and police measures in the Third Reich. The inadequacy of German information policy resulted in an increased listening to foreign stations and this Goebbels tried to check by deterrent sentences.

April 24, 1940

On the problem of Norway the Minister points out that up to the beginning of our invasion divergent views may well have been possible

---

* Goebbels uses the English words. *Tr.*

about Quisling's suitability, but that now, needless to say, the Führer's wish must be our command.

He does not, therefore, wish the subject of Quisling to be discussed in the Ministry in any way. The Minister emphasizes that in time of war there can be no consideration for human injustice when political justice is at stake. There can be but one task for all of us – to back the decision about the future of Norway and support it to the best of our ability.

By the decree of April 24, 1940, Hitler set up the Reichskommissariat for Norway* and simultaneously appointed Gauleiter Josef Terboven Reich Commissioner. As an executive body the Norwegian Administrative Committee was to be subordinated to him. Thus all attempts to form a Norwegian government headed by Quisling had failed for the time being.

Mention of the 'Quisling shadow government' had been forbidden to the German press by Goebbels as early as April 10, and again on April 16, 1940 because it represented only an attempt to persuade the Norwegians to cease resistance. A provisional administrative council had been set up under the chairmanship of the German ambassador in Oslo, Dr Bräuer, with Quisling as premier. A few days later a Norwegian government committee was established, headed by the president of the Norwegian Supreme Court. Quisling became a state counsellor and Minister for Demobilization of the Army. This government committee was likewise of short duration. On April 19, the German Ministry of Foreign Affairs informed the press that it would certainly become necessary to establish even stricter German governmental control in Oslo.

April 26, 1940

The Minister reports on the situation in Norway and in this connexion issues the following directive:

(a) The Quisling question is to be relegated to the background for the moment but it must be remembered that his character and national integrity are unassailable. The tendency at the moment is to get the administrative committee working and functioning, to let it carry through all the necessary unpopular measures and at the same time increasingly promote the belief among the public that Quisling would after all have been the ideal man to take over the running of the state. In this way it may be possible to reinstate Quisling on a new basis in a few weeks' time.

A Norwegian government with Quisling as premier was not in fact appointed until 1942.

* This pattern was subsequently followed in the Netherlands, *et al. Tr.*

(b) The German press must make the clearest possible distinction between those parts of Norway which are already in our possession and where the population is indeed behaving extremely loyally, and those parts which are still being fought over. It must repeatedly be emphasized that our struggle is directed solely against the government of the king and his clique of money-makers, and not against the Norwegian people.

For the treatment of Britain the Minister issues the following directives:

(a) A catastrophe for the British troops in Norway may be expected in the next few days. To make sure the effect of the final announcement is not diminished, the German papers must not now jump the gun with sporadic reports indicating the turn of events, nor must the British be told what their own prospects are.

To begin with, the very opposite happened. On April 28 the British occupied Narvik and maintained themselves there until June 8, 1940. It was stated at the press conference that no strategic overall picture of the situation in Norway must be published. The OKW, it was explained, was believed to be pursuing certain aims by deliberately inadequate reporting.

May 3, 1940

Major Martin, who reports how British prisoners of war have only with great difficulty been protected against the anger of Polish prisoners of war, is to try to trigger off a similar scene again to enable shots of it to be made for the newsreel.

At the conference of January 30, 1940, Major Martin had reported that, on Hitler's orders, only Alsatians, Bretons, Scots and North Africans had been accommodated in separate POW camps. All other prisoners had been left together because it had been found that 'in this way friction between the Allies is greatly promoted.' On May 19, 1940, Martin assured the conference that all preparations had been made to film clashes between British and Polish officer prisoners for the newsreel whenever the occasion arose.

At the conference of July 4, 1940, Goebbels demanded that 'the long-promised pictures of open hostility between British and French prisoners as well as of the animal-like meals of black prisoners of war must now be taken for the very next newsreel.'

The most important directive issued to the press on May 3 came not from Goebbels but direct from the Führer's headquarters. In future the press was to give pride of place to Britain's search for new theatres of war in the south-east and in the Mediterranean area. The neutrals, in particular, were to have their attention drawn to the alarming nature of these reports.

In this propaganda campaign Germany was in a good position to use reports in the British press which for a number of months had been speculating where and when German and Russian attacks would take place in the Balkans and in the Middle East.

Admittedly, Hitler used this propaganda campaign merely as a curtain-raiser for his offensive in the West and as a smoke screen for his immediate intentions. On May 5 he completed the 'Justification for Event Yellow' (the offensive in the West) which was to be presented to the diplomatic representatives of Belgium and the Netherlands in the form of a memorandum on May 10.

May 6, 1940

The Minister issues the directive that the press should continue to run the extension of the war as the main story, but enough scope is to be left for a possible further increase of emphasis by the middle of the week. Herr Bömer is to see to it that this plan can be buttressed by suitable information.

On the subject of 'extension of the war' it was said at the press conference that since the German revelations had produced such an unparallelled good effect abroad and the whole press up and down the continent was dominated by fear of British aggression, the German press could now confine itself for the time being to reproducing foreign comment while holding back its own. Great care was to be taken that Germany should not appear to be the originator of this fear of aggression. The world was to believe the British capable of anything, so that they should always be seen as the aggressors and the culprits, no matter what might happen in the future.

The Minister emphasizes our interest in overthrowing whatever government is in power in the enemy countries, regardless of whether this government or that may be more acceptable on points of detail. What matters is the unsettling and weakening effect of *any* change of government. Accordingly, the foreign language service must immediately do everything possible to promote mistrust of Chamberlain, and in doing so it may quite properly range itself alongside those who are championing Churchill against Chamberlain.

Herr Fritzsche is to instruct the press once more (and a similar instruction is to go to the Party and its speakers) that there must be no discussion or precise definition whatever of our war aims. The Minister emphasizes the need to present such aims in as vague a form as possible; the German war aims must therefore invariably only be formulated as: 'a just and durable peace and living space (*Lebensraum*) for the German people.'

May 9, 1940

The British House of Commons debate of May 8, on the Government's conduct of the war, included a critical speech by Lloyd George and a defence by Churchill. Although the vote of no confidence was not carried by the House, Chamberlain resigned as Prime Minister on May 10, 1940.

The whole Commons debate is to be treated rather summarily by the press. It should be emphasized that, considering the many abstentions, Chamberlain was in fact given a vote of no confidence. At the same time it should be pointed out that we are no longer interested in Chamberlain's overthrow, now that the debate has shown him in such poor light. Samuel Hoare's speech is to be briefly picked to pieces; Lloyd George's could appear in full with slight alterations; Churchill's is to be dismissed with a few witty remarks.

May 10, 1940

On May 10, 1940, at 05.35 hours, the German offensive in the West began with the invasion of the Netherlands and Belgium.

On the eve of it, as planned, Mussolini's play *Cavour* had its première in Berlin, attended by Pavolini as well as, among others, Göring and Goebbels. To celebrate the première a reception had been planned at the 'House of the Aviators' and this went on until after midnight. While Hitler boarded the 'Führer train', which had been parked on the Lehrter line north of Berlin, in order to travel by a roundabout route to the Western Front, Goebbels remained at the 'House of the Aviators' until after midnight. From there he drove to his Ministry, ordered Hans Fritzsche to join him and got him and his ADC, von Schirmeister, to read out over the radio the proclamation on the opening of the Western offensive.

Herr Fritzsche is to see to it from the very start that during the struggle in the West which is now beginning the press does not indulge in excessive optimism nor in wild panic-mongering whenever some piece of news or other appears particularly favourable or particularly unfavourable. The press must always remember that individual successes do not necessarily decide the overall outcome of the operation and that, considering the scope of the total operation, occasional reverses are unlikely to be entirely avoided.

With this directive Goebbels largely endorsed the 'Directives for the Press Reporting of the Operations in the West' issued by the Oberkommando der Heeres (Land Forces High Command) and the Oberkommando der Luftwaffe (Air Force High Command) on May 10. These pointed out that the attack on the Netherlands and Belgium could not be equated with the campaign in

39

Poland since, in the West, one was facing the most powerful fortified terrain in Europe. For that reason initial successes in the approaches to enemy territory should not be exaggerated. There could be no question of decisive operations until the offensive had encountered the bulk of the British and French armies.

The Luftwaffe similarly did not wish the numbers of aircraft shot down or lost to be emphasized. It regarded any gain of ground merely as getting nearer to the 'principal enemy', the British, and an alleviation of the situation in the Ruhr. The Luftwaffe was engaging an opponent of equal strength in the West. Enemy air raids on Reich territory were therefore to be expected, but these too were not to be given prominence since 'on orders from the Führer' no German raids must yet be made on 'open cities'.

For the time being it is the task of the press to popularize the official announcement made over the radio this morning by condensing and highlighting its essential points. Such instruction must be an explanation in a popular form, and not simply a repetition in different words of what has already been said. The entire nation must become convinced that Holland and Belgium have, in fact, violated their neutrality.

The Minister advises Herr Bömer to be particularly careful in handling the foreign press during the next few weeks. There is now no longer any point in such lax handling of censorship as hitherto. The present action must be conducted according to very sharply defined rules of censorship. On no account must it be possible for, say, panic reports from Berlin to get abroad along German wires.

May 11, 1940
The Minister formulates the principle for the immediate future that anything in enemy reports that is not correct or even anything that could be dangerous to us must immediately be denied. There is no need at all to examine whether a report is factually correct or not – the decisive point is merely whether the enemy's assertions could in any way be damaging to us. For this reason care must be taken for denials to be issued promptly. In drafting such denials the wording 'does not correspond to the facts' will probably prove too weak in a tense period; it will be necessary to make 'sweeping, wholesale' denials or, whenever enemy assertions touch upon our honour, to retort in the sharpest possible terms.

Britain and France must be told again and again, before the whole world, that it was *they* who declared war on us and that they were now having to pay the price for it. It was *their own* war which was now bursting upon them. On no account must we allow ourselves to be manoeuvred once more into the role of aggressor.

40

The foreign language service must again and again convince Holland and Belgium that any opposition to us is useless. The antagonism between Walloons and Flemings, on the other hand, should not be taken up until we have reached Flemish soil. Great care must be taken – and this applies also to the German press, to PK [Propagandakompanie] reports, etc. – that there is no hint of any intentions to annex foreign territory.

According to a directive of May 12, 1940, the subversive propaganda to be carried into the Netherlands and Belgium was to take account of 'the materialistic attitude of the Dutch' and quote Poland as an example of the pointlessness of destroying one's own country.

May 13, 1940
The radio is to make immediate recordings of the announcements by Brussels and Hilversum radios, so that the voices of the regular speakers can be used if necessary, if, in some special circumstances, we put ourselves on these enemy wavelengths.

May 14, 1940
The Minister points out that two serious psychological errors were committed by the OKW in the report it issued about reprisals in the event of German parachutists being murdered. For that reason the subject is to be taken up once more, and correctly presented this time, in connexion with Lord Halifax's speech.

The French news agency Havas reported that German parachutists had been dropped partly in Allied and partly in Dutch uniforms. On May 12 the Premier, M. Reynaud, declared that all parachutists wearing foreign uniforms were to be summarily shot at once. A protest Note presented by the German Ministry of Foreign Affairs in London, Paris, Brussels and The Hague thereupon threatened reprisals against prisoners of war.

On May 13, the OKW denied Reynaud's assertions and announced that ten French soldiers would in future be shot for every German parachutist shot. One 'psychological error' in the OKW denial was presumably the reference to the fact that the parachutists had been trained for their special task even before the beginning of the war. More important, the threat of reprisals against prisoners of war, quite apart from being in breach of international law, was a crass violation of all rules of psychological warfare, since this kind of threat invariably results in a hardening of enemy resistance.

On May 16, the DNB added a rider that the German paratroop uniform could never possibly be confused with civilian clothes. 'All the stories spread on this subject abroad are malicious inventions.'

May 17, 1940

Whereas in April the German top leaders were still divided on whether it was advisable to take up foreign reports about the activity of the German Fifth Column, the view held since mid-May 1940 was that the launching of almost entirely fictitious reports about some alleged activity by a Fifth Column would create unrest in the enemy camp and hence promote German intentions.

At the press conference of May 12 the Berlin press had been prepared for revelations about Fifth Column actions—meaning subversive work by German spies and agents—to take place abroad 'in the course of next week'. The German press was instructed not to take up such foreign reports but to leave speculation about the activity of a Fifth Column to foreign countries.

The reports launched abroad by the Ministry for Propaganda on the activity of the Fifth Column fell on exceedingly fertile soile, above all in France, where they were sensationally featured by the press. Duff Cooper reports that Henry de Kerillis, the political director of the Paris *l'Epoque,* was completely obsessed with the alleged menace of the Fifth Column. H. de Kerillis, who died in New York in 1945, was regarded as a totally committed nationalist of the Right. He went to New York on an official mission, even before the French surrender, and there worked in the Free French Movement throughout the war.

The task of the secret transmitter, from now on, is to use every means to create a mood of panic in France. To that end it must work on a wholly French platform and display the greatest indignation and alarm in protesting against the omissions of the French government. In particular, the rumours buzzing around France are to be picked up and developed. The secret transmitter must above all take up the rumours of the French government intending to flee from Paris, and Reynaud, who has denied these rumours, is to be called a liar. It must further utter an urgent warning against the dangers of a 'Fifth Column' which undoubtedly also includes all German refugees. It should point out that, in the present situation, even the Jews from Germany are nothing but German agents. Furthermore, the rumour is to be circulated that the first action of the Germans in occupied towns is invariably the confiscation of all deposits of money in the banks, so that true French patriots should withdraw their money now in all threatened regions. Finally, it should again make the most of the clash of interests resulting from the fact that Britain is interested chiefly in the defence of the coast while France wants to defend her frontiers.

May 19, 1940

A reshuffle of Reynaud's cabinet took place on May 18. The Ministry of Defence was taken over by Reynaud and the Ministry of the Interior by

Mandel. Marshal Pétain entered the cabinet as Vice-Premier. General Gamelin was replaced by General Weygand as Commander-in-Chief on May 19.

The mood in Paris and London has rallied again for the moment, which may largely be attributed to the change of government in France. A particular share in this is due to the appointment of Pétain, whose slogan 'They Will Not Pass' is still remembered from World War One. The Minister makes it the task of the press and radio – both in Germany and above all for France – to uncover the background of this political manoeuvre and to point out that a man of eighty-four is obviously in no position to change anything in the actual state of affairs. It should also be pointed out that a Jew, of all people, has been chosen as France's Minister of the Interior in order ruthlessly to suppress all signs of sound commonsense and to sacrifice the nation to save Jewish plutocracy. . . . The German press, the foreign language service and the secret transmitter should develop the subject in appropriate variations, the secret transmitter with a note of indignation that war criminals of Reynaud's type are now hiding behind the venerable figure of Marshal Pétain.

Besides, the foreign language service and the secret transmitter are to use every means to promote panic. For example, a planned attempt against the Palais Bourbon is to be 'revealed'. The Minister instructs Herren Brauweiler, Fritzsche, Dittmar and Wächter to invent further suitable false reports for the secret transmitter.

Summing up, the Minister again points out that during the next two days the French will presumably enjoy a certain period of recovery during which even local French successes may be expected. Such successes will no doubt be exploited by French propaganda with a view to boosting their morale. It is therefore particularly important to react to any such signs at once and with all possible means at the disposal of our information media. For if morale, after a short check, starts slipping again, the disruptive effect will be very much stronger than before.

May 20, 1940
The Minister points out that there is nothing in the actual situation which could explain why the mood in Britain and France has temporarily recovered. This makes it the more important to use all available information media for the launching of rumours carrying credibility and designed once more to undermine morale. Among other things it should be pointed out that Gamelin had to go because, with his sound knowledge of the situation, he had been looking for a way of coming to terms with Germany. Churchill, however, on the occasion of his visit to Paris, had again pulled Reynaud over to the British side, and the latter

had now found himself another prop in Gamelin's place. Another story to be spread more intensively than hitherto is that the French government is giving the refugees from the evacuated territories counterfeit money, that the government has privately warned foreign diplomats to be ready for a government move from Paris, and that it is exceedingly dangerous to make a change in the leadership at such a critical moment as this.

May 21, 1940

The secret transmitter must do everything in its power to step up panic-mongering. Its slogan must be: 'We are lost; let's put an end to the war.' Moreover, it must lash out at the British betrayal of France and pillory the Jew Mandel as the executioner and gaoler of the French people, a man who does not have the right to have the voice of reason mown down by his guns.

In Britain, on the other hand, fear and panic-mongering must be mobilized by pointing out that the German guns are moving ever closer to the English coast.

For tomorrow the secret transmitter is to prepare a rogation service for which Herr Gutterer will supply the sermon; the announcement of this is to be broadcast tonight.

The broadcasting of religious services or ecclesiastical morning devotions on the German radio had been banned as a matter of principle since 1939.

May 24, 1940

The Minister sharply reprimands an article in the *12 Uhr Blatt* which depicts the present state of affairs as if the final annihilation of the enemy in the Belgian theatre of war could be expected within the next few hours. The Minister points to the extraordinary damage, bordering on intellectual high treason, which might be produced by such foolish predictions, and demands a public reprimand of the *12 Uhr Blatt* at the next press conference as well as a severe warning to the editor responsible. Altogether, the press is again to be reminded that its task is merely to report about *what has happened,* and that under no circumstances are predictions permissible. In this connexion it should also be pointed out again that in the present military operations in a confined area the day-to-day fighting is marked by changeable success, so that possession or loss of one town or another is not as important as it was in World War One.

The French government is issuing a large number of denials of a number of reports allegedly put out by the German radio. Our foreign language service must refute these with emphatic counter-denials and point out that our English and French language services also observe absolute truthfulness. (The reports referred to by the French government had been put out by the secret French language transmitter.)

The secret transmitter must operate with prophecies on a big scale. The Minister refers to the prophecies of a monk, also to the legends surrounding the Heights of Loretto, and recommends that the Nostradamus leaflet should now be exploited.

Once victory in the present battle has been fully achieved the press should emphatically throw back at the British their song 'We're going to hang out our washing on the Siegfried Line.'

No predictions whatever about a German landing in England must be made in Germany, and the Minister does not, generally speaking, wish to see any bragging in the German press. These matters must be handled only by the secret transmitter.

May 25, 1940
Herr Gutterer, in collaboration with Herr Raskin, is to arrange for the production of a diary of a British prisoner of war, describing his pornographic experiences in Paris. This diary is then to be dropped over France and can perhaps also be used by the secret transmitter.

Illustrated leaflets of obscene character were simultaneously dropped over the French lines. They represented British soldiers in intimate company with Frenchwomen and were designed to arouse among the *poilus* both violent hatred for the British and strong erotic desires. A short text called on them to desert. According to Stephan, Goebbels was absolutely delighted with reports about the good effect of his 'sexual propaganda.'

May 28, 1940
Now that the Belgian army has capitulated, the secret transmitter and the foreign language service must further intensify their attacks on public opinion in France. The foreign language service for France, moreover, must now openly back the slogan 'Put an end to it!' Also, panic-mongering is to be intensified by means of detailed descriptions of French losses. The horrors of the war are to be presented to the French people in apocalyptic pictures and continually repeated descriptions.

The Belgian surrender was signed at 10.00 hours on May 28, 1940.

45

The Minister lays down the general principle that denials should only be used so long as the occasional annoying assertion is made from the other side; once the enemy develops this into a system we must immediately go over to the offensive tenfold.

Atrocity propaganda in the enemy press has now reached a level which demands that we on our part should now use all means to disseminate atrocity stories throughout the world. This task must be begun at once and must be repeated day after day; the press, too, must again and again be instructed to this effect. New enemy atrocity stories must then be dismissed as pitiful attempts to answer our atrocity stories with lies.

The foreign 'atrocity propaganda' mentioned here was largely concerned with the fact that, in the territory surrounded by German troops, convoys moving along the roads were being bombed regardless of whether they were military units or treks of fleeing civilians. At the conference of May 22, 1940, Goebbels had already instructed Fritzsche to oppose the 'atrocity propaganda' with the argument, that 'experience teaches that the hardest war is always the shortest.'

May 29, 1940

The rumour that the French might get a very cheap and just peace at this moment is to be spread further.

The press and foreign language service are to juxtapose the Belgian king and the government, showing, on the one hand, the king as the man who fought with the army and, realizing the senselessness of the struggle, has now surrendered, and on the other the government who have never smelt a whiff of powder but are corrupt war criminals and henchmen of the great plutocracies.

On May 31, 1940, Goebbels asked that the king of the Belgians should not be presented as a 'German national figure'. King Leopold III went into German captivity. The Palace of Laeken was assigned to him for his residence.

The foreign language service should try to shake the belief that Britain might still win the war. It should make a factual examination of all the fronts where Britain has already been defeated invariably after having been very boastful beforehand; from this it should be argued that the situation has now definitely become hopeless for them.

The secret transmitter is to concoct a mythical organization to which it is broadcasting code words.

Major Martin is to try to obtain the earliest possible release of German overall losses in Norway so far; these losses, according to him, still number less than 2,000 men. The press must point out that this strikingly low figure represents a success of our new fighting technique and our tactical skill in warfare.

According to official data, the German Wehrmacht suffered the following losses during the occupation of Norway and Denmark: 1,317 killed, 2,375 missing from sea transports or otherwise, and 1,604 officers, NCOs and other ranks wounded. The Luftwaffe lost 117 aircraft, and the navy one heavy and two light cruisers, 10 destroyers, one torpedo boat, six U-boat and 15 lesser craft.

May 30, 1940
The Minister points out that the most important task for the next few weeks will be to explain to the public in every possible way the need for a radical settling of accounts with France. Articles must keep on explaining in the most popular terms how the French in their relations with Germany have always pursued one aim alone – to divide Germany and then to rule her. By recalling the occupation of the Rhineland and the Ruhr the hatred of France is to be fanned afresh; it must be shown how this nation with its declining population is trying to overthrow Germany by using yellow, black and brown people from overseas, and what a monstrous crime against culture and race it committed by shamelessly bringing negroes to the Rhine. The French must be pilloried as 'niggerized sadists' and by constantly hammering away at the subject a state of affairs must be brought about, within a fortnight at the most, in which the entire German nation is consumed with anger and hatred against a France riddled with corruption and freemasonry.

The foreign press here in Berlin is to be given a categorical denial that Germany harbours any intentions whatever of a peace with France; the secret transmitter, on the other hand, should continue to encourage rumours of a separate peace and convince the French that they have only their own government to thank if nothing has so far come of it.

The Minister reports on the strengthening of the secret transmitters: Cologne is to start operating on a new wavelength tonight; Leipzig, contrary to another proposal, is likewise to operate on a new wavelength, and the Deutschlandsender is also to go over to another wavelength. Until these last two changes have been made Luxemburg must stay where it is.

This secret transmitter must operate in a revolutionary, hypernationalistic manner and, by suitable arguments about the government's weakness, oppose one government after another to the point of its downfall. The Minister desires the widest possible participation in this work.

As for the communist transmitter *Humanité,* the Minister wishes to see its scripts as Herr Brauweiler maintains that its programmes are too doctrinaire and dull. The Minister emphasizes that it must of course be the task of this transmitter to mobilize popular passions.

At the conference of June 2, 1940, Goebbels suggested that the former communist Torgler and his collaborator Maria Reese might be enlisted for the preparation of programmes for the secret transmitter *Humanité,* since the present staff of French communists were addressing themselves mainly to intellectuals while failing 'to appeal to the primitive mass instincts.' On June 8 collaboration began with the former German communist leaders Torgler and Kasper.

Ernst Torgler has asked the present editor to include the following observation about his work for the secret transmitter: he and Wilhelm Kasper 'agreed under duress, following the outbreak of the campaign in France, to supply a few drafts of appeals addressed to the French workers for the Ministry for Propaganda's secret transmitter operating against France. These called on the workers to cease resistance against a superior German enemy and avoid unnecessary bloodshed.' Torgler, however, denied that Maria Reese was also involved. Nevertheless, the fact that various agencies of the Ministry for Propaganda had enlisted Maria Reese (née Meyer) for propaganda tasks, especially during the campaign in Russia, emerges clearly from her own writings. In a letter dated June 8, 1944, she said: 'I was once enlisted for the compilation of a Goebbels speech, when I was told to supply material showing that the bolshevik statesmen had declared that they would bring about the war.' In a letter dated November 16, 1944, she further said: 'On one occasion I was to be sent to England to see Lansbury at the time when we were wooing Britain, which was Hitler's unhappy love. But Dr Taubert was of the opinion that Goebbels believed this to be impossible because Maria Reese makes her own policy.' Torgler, who was under the protection of Göring, Kasper, who was brought out of a concentration camp, and the former communist Albrecht, whose obscure activity on both sides still holds quite a few mysteries, were said subsequently to have been called up for the Propaganda Depot Detachment in Potsdam. Torgler's and Albrecht's co-operation in particular continued after the opening of the Russian campaign and evidently also met with recognition.

June 2, 1940

All available means must be used to make it clear to the world that Britain and France have suffered a defeat, not won a victory. The Minister demands that the excellent British propaganda work be countered with a list of what the British and what we proclaimed as our objectives at the start of the military operations, and what each party has in fact achieved. Our aim was: 'They will not reach the Ruhr'; instead, we have reached an objective which it would have been almost blasphemous even to think of a few weeks ago. The aim of the British was: 'We shall destroy the Germans', and the result: they are salvaging the wreck of their army from Dunkirk.

The battle of Dunkirk began on May 26, 1940, and with it the evacuation of the encircled Allied formations. 861 ships took part in the embarkation; of these 243 were sunk. Nevertheless, by June 4, when the operation was concluded, a total of 338,000 British and Allied troops had been evacuated to Britain. In his report to Parliament on June 4, 1940, Churchill said that wars were not won by evacuations, but that with this rescue the British had scored a victory that deserved to be recorded, a victory won by their air force.

We must not attack the honour of the British soldier, but our propaganda must range itself alongside the soldier against the civilians and swashbucklers of London radio. The Minister points out that it must always be the overall objective to incite the people against whatever government is in power. In our polemics with France it will also be useful – except in very special circumstances – to direct the hate campaign against the powergroups in the background rather than against individual Frenchmen.

June 4, 1940
The German air raid on Paris must be depicted as a military operation within the framework of international law, and its effect must be described as extensively as possible, in the foreign language service as well, especially for Britain and France. The secret transmitter, moreover, must point out how unprepared the defences were and how badly they functioned. It should generally be noted that the French, by stressing the fact that we attacked military objectives, are shirking the question of counter-measures, whereas Britain is calling for retribution. The foreign language service is to make it clear to the British that British airmen have been attacking civilian targets in Germany all the time and that they must now be clear about the consequences of any attempt to attack such targets deliberately.

A few papers might well discuss the atrocity problem from an ironical viewpoint, in a very superior and condescending manner, pointing out that it was downright perverse on the part of the powerful German air force systematically to pick on nothing but babes in arms and old women, on wounded persons and American cemeteries, or on British hospital ships, for their air raids and, moreover, succeeding every time while anxiously avoiding or missing all military targets.

The Secret Conferences of Dr. Goebbels

June 6, 1940

The Reynaud Cabinet was reshuffled on June 5-6, 1940. Daladier left. General de Gaulle was appointed to the Ministry of War.

The Minister lays down our attitude to the new Reynaud cabinet on the lines that it is a matter of indifference to us what new criminals have now joined the French government.

The secret transmitter is to start opposing the new government at once, pointing out that Daladier, the man now ditched, was the only person not entirely prepared to sell out France to Britain.

The Minister again points out that the Italian question must be handled with the greatest possible care at the moment.

On May 30, 1940, the Italian ambassador in Berlin handed Hitler a message from Mussolini in which the latter announced that Italy would enter the war on June 5. Hitler, apparently after consulting Goebbels, sent an immediate reply. Since an Italian intervention in the German campaign in the West formed no part of Hitler's plans, he advised the Duce to postpone his date of attack for a little while, to which the latter agreed.

The secret transmitter should not for the time being use its heavy guns, but should allow scope for further intensification so as to have enough

June 9, 1940

The German press as well as the entire foreign language service is, with a few cuts, to take up a Havas report which, in a deeply moving description, compares the tempestuous advance of the German troops with the attacking spirit of the Cimbers and Teutons. Now, if ever, the term *furor Teutonicus* finds its full justification. The *ne passeront pas,* which was still heard only a few days ago, is now to be confronted with the new reports.

The national defence film shown in France at that time, entitled *The French Army* also bore the motto *On ne passe pas.*

The Minister criticizes most sharply the publication by *Die Woche* of a picture of the record from which the radio transmits the fanfare preceding the special announcements. He wishes the press to be informed that in the event of a repetition he will have sent to a concentration camp any editor who commits the offence of disillusionment about national events, no matter whether in connexion with the cinema, the radio, etc. Herr Kurzbein, moreover, is to warn the gentlemen of the Illustrated Press Department that the Minister will not shrink from ordering the arrest of any censor who lets a similarly disillusioning picture pass another time.

The picture reportage entitled 'We are transmitting a special announcement of the radio news service,' published in *Die Woche* (Berlin) on June 5, 1940, also appeared under the same title in *Illustrierter Beobachter* (Berlin) on June 13, 1940.

The German press should go and see the excellent American anti-Soviet film *Ninotchka*.

Ninotchka, an MGM production, had its first showing in 1939. The film was directed by none other than the German-Jewish refugee Ernst Lubitsch. The leads were played by Greta Garbo and Mervyn Douglas; a major part was played by Felix Bressart, formerly a comic actor in the German UFA productions and, like Lubitsch, a refugee in the United States. Goebbels remarked to a number of prominent German actors that *Ninotchka* was the best picture he had ever seen.

June 10, 1940

The Minister issues a directive for film, press and radio to the effect that while the severity, magnitude and sacrifice of the war may be shown, any excessively realistic representation, likely to arouse a horror of the war, must be avoided at all costs.

The Wehrmacht Propaganda Department of the OKW as early as mid-May 1940 issued an instruction that pictures should not be used which 'are apt to produce fear, horror or revulsion' of the war, 'unless they acquire documentary value for this very reason.' These principles were followed by German picture reporting right to the end of the war with the result that newsreels and picture reportages never showed the war in its true frightfulness and murderous extent.

Since there has again been an instance of disregard of the repeated instructions not on any account to discuss German war aims, the Minister makes Herr Bömer and Herr Stephan responsible in future for avoiding a recurrence at all costs.

At the conferences of March 18, May 6, and June 7, 1940, Goebbels had forbidden the press to define 'clear war aims'; instead it was to confine itself to generalizations about young and old states. Both sides in the war at first were very reluctant to publicize concrete war aims, partly because they were rightly afraid of an unfavourable psychological and propagandist backlash, and partly because they well remembered the disastrous war aim debates during World War One. Hitler instead allowed the power-political realities created by him to speak for themselves.

June 12, 1940

The effects of German propaganda are beginning to be felt in Paris. From now on the foreign language service for France must be devoted wholly to disruptive propaganda, and news bulletins must retreat into the background.

(1) There must be agitation against those French circles wishing to fortify the city (Paris).

(2) There must be a call for peace demonstrations 'to avoid worse things happening.'

(3) The government must be denied the right to continue speaking in the name of France since it is no more than a tool for the British.

(4) Major Martin is to ascertain whether the military command finds it more valuable for the civilian population to remain in Paris or to stream out of the city. Accordingly, there must be calls for the one or the other.

In any event the creation of panic is now the principal task both of the secret transmitter and of the French language service. The foreign language service for the other countries (with the exception of London), on the other hand, must avoid all panic-mongering and may at most carry factual reports about the result of panic-mongering in France. For the press the moment for panic-mongering has not yet arrived. The Minister points out that the departments of his Ministry concerned are now faced with a crucial test and that it would mean the crowning of many months' work if it proved possible to trigger off a revolution in Paris.

The Minister reads out a sports report from the *Wiener Mittag* which juxtaposes 'Germans' and 'Viennese' all the way through. He instructs Herr Fritzsche to have the responsible editor struck off the professional register at once, to administer a severe reprimand to the editor-in-chief, together with a fine amounting to two months' salary, and to make it perfectly clear to the paper that if this happens again it will be permanently suspended.

June 13, 1940

The German press should practise considerable restraint with regard to Paris. Its capture should not be represented as an objective capable of realization during the next few days or hours. The secret transmitter and the foreign language service must carry appeals against the erection of barricades.

In a discussion with Major Martin and Major Wodarg the Minister clarifies the following point: There has been an increasing volume of bitter complaints in the west [of Germany] about air-raid precautions. The fact is that an alarm cannot always be given since, in the event of minor formations entering our air-space, the risk of losing a few lives must be accepted compared with the importance of the uninterrupted flow of important work in industry. Major Martin, who at first regarded a frank explanation of this kind as inappropriate, allowed himself to be convinced by the Minister that such an explanation in the press can only be for the good. An explanatory note is therefore to be drafted by military quarters, roughly to the effect that air-raid warnings can be expected only in the event of large-scale attacks which would seem to threaten the life of a city. Numerical losses from air raids so far bear no relation whatever to the paralysis of our production intended by them. For that reason, whenever only a few aircraft have entered our air space, the population must regard themselves as combatants; they should realize that they are still a lot better off than the population of, say, Warsaw or Rotterdam.

June 14, 1940

There is to be no more factual argument with Reynaud; he too is to be dismissed in the German press in the strongest possible terms as a stock-exchange fiddler and 'a lump of misfortune.' The Minister also wishes the contrast to be underlined pictorially: a photograph showing Reynaud flabby and repulsive in bathing trunks is to be juxtaposed to a picture of a wounded *poilu* still showing the horror through which he has passed.

The secret transmitter is to use all arguments to spread the slogan: 'Lay down your arms – it is all pointless.'

Generally speaking, it has become necessary for all secret transmitters to make a complete and immediate switch away from the big city and towards the peasants and *petit bourgeoisie,* since the big city has meanwhile been eliminated anyway. The communist transmitter, likewise, must no longer operate with Soviet slogans, but must put forward arguments of purely social agitation. (Everything is being smashed up; who is going to foot the bill; who guarantees our pensions; the tax burden will be crushing, etc.)

Two of the secret transmitters are to keep their 'location' in occupied territory and may put out reports such as the entry of the German troops into Paris. They are to describe with increasing benevolence how peace and order have come in the wake of the Germans.

The remaining secret transmitters, on the other hand, are to follow us into unoccupied territory.

June 15, 1940

Herr Fritzsche is to find out from the Führer's headquarters, and Major Martin from the military authorities, whether both of them agree to an announcement being suddenly launched, possibly this evening, on a wavelength not at the moment used by the French, to the effect that peace negotiations are already in progress. In view of the undoubted growth of a peace trend in France and in view of the fact that a peace party is at work even within the French government, the Minister expects such an announcement to produce catastrophic effects on French morale because the French will have to deny it willy-nilly.

June 16, 1940

Italy declared war on France on June 10, 1940, in order to ensure for herself a share in the expected booty. Not until June 19 did Italian troops attack the French Alpine fortifications – and then unsuccessfully. These fortifications yielded to pressure only when they were surrounded by German formations from the rear. In fact, neither Italy's original neutrality nor her entry into the war formed part of Hitler's plans.

The Minister makes certain fundamental observations on some political questions:

(1) Care must be taken to avoid a false idea taking hold of the German public about Italy's conduct in the war, since this might offend and discourage the Italians. For that reason – since these matters cannot be discussed in print or verbally – the skilful launching of rumours should implant in our public the conviction that the reason why Italy is not mounting an attack just yet is simply that this would be undesirable at the moment; the conviction should be encouraged that Italy will certainly attack as soon as conditions are ripe.

(2) We are not interested at the present moment in France suing for peace. Even though, in fact, France is already defeated, this is not yet obviously clear to the layman. At present, on the example of Germany's re-emergence, France would still have the possibility of attempting a national rebirth within a few years of the conclusion of peace, since she does not yet feel touched to the core of her national and military honour.

Our aim, however, must be to eliminate France once and for all as a national power of any importance in Europe. Britain can be expelled from the continent in the long run and reduced to an 'enlarged Holland' only if France, her continental sword, is smashed once and for all. For that reason France must first suffer a mortal blow to her national honour and pride. That is why the denial of German peace intentions has had to be formulated in such a ruthless manner. In everything we publish for abroad we must aim at weakening France's power of resistance, and for that reason the secret transmitter in particular must operate very flexibly along the lines that the Germans had been entirely prepared for peace negotiations until yesterday afternoon – a fact quite openly discussed in the neutral countries and in the United States.

(3) The Minister puts Roosevelt's bragging into its proper place and points out that the non-recognition of territorial gains, mentioned by Roosevelt, is a matter of complete indifference to us since what matters is the force of facts and not some measure of diplomatic recognition. The emptiness of his phrases makes it clear that no actual measures are to be expected on America's part. Besides, a future Europe would not only tolerate German leadership but call for it.

Summing up, the Minister again points out that the final decision must not be diminished for the sake of momentary success.

An appeal by Reynaud to the United States was answered by President Roosevelt in a message dated June 13, 1940.

During the winter months the press had repeatedly been instructed to hold back with attacks on the United States. This restraint towards the United States disappeared in the same measure as the German leadership's certainty of victory grew.

Paris was occupied without opposition on June 14, 1940, and Orléans was captured on June 16.

As for attempts by London and by France to dismiss the capture of Paris with the argument that while Paris may be the heart of France it is not her soul, etc., it is to be made perfectly clear that we are in no way interested in any heart or soul, but that what matters to us is the capture of *Paris*.

June 17, 1940
The Minister points out how the reshuffle of the French government in its separate phases allows it to be clearly seen that at certain moments there was already an intention of offering unconditional surrender to Germany, but that it now seems as though an attempt will be made merely to achieve an armistice. Referring to his observations of the

previous day, he explained once more that such an attempt to meet us halfway would be in our interest. For the longer capitulation is put off, the more catastrophic and demoralizing the military disaster will be once it becomes patent to everybody. For the moment, until the news of the capitulation comes from the Führer's headquarters, the German public must not in any way be acquainted with the intermediate possibilities, lest an impression be made abroad that the German people are ready for peace. For that reason the foreign language service, contrary to its line hitherto, must avoid all reports dealing with the separate phases preceding capitulation; it must now, by way of repeated appeals, concentrate its entire effort on convincing the French soldiers, especially those in the Maginot Line, that their struggle has become senseless and pointless. While Marshal Pétain should not be attacked, sharp opposition should continue to be shown to Reynaud, Daladier and Mandel, who are to be treated as a collective concept. They should be depicted as the typical parliamentarians who now want to go to ground like the cowards they are and who are now trying to put the historical responsibility for the greatest military collapse of all time on the shoulders of the aged general. Concepts like 'greatest military collapse,' 'France's crack troops facing collapse,' etc., must be used extensively in order to intensify demoralization in France. The secret transmitter should ignore Pétain for the time being, while continuing its struggle against Reynaud and his lot. Churchill and his lot are to be arraigned because they are already deciding to continue the war after a French capitulation. The German press might, moreover, raise the question of whether Britain seriously expects to improve her position by running hypocritically to church now.

After Reynaud's resignation on June 17, 1940, Marshal Pétain formed a new French government in order to offer an immediate cessation of military operations.

June 18, 1940
The Minister instructs the foreign language service, the secret transmitter and the German press to nip in the bud most emphatically all French attempts to turn a capitulation into a kind of amicable laying down of arms. It is to be stated emphatically that France attacked us without justification on September 3, that she intended to annihilate us, and that we must now see to it that a similar situation can never arise again. On no account must the real state of affairs be turned upside down now. Care must also be taken in the media addressed to the German people that the French do not come off too lightly as a result of

some false sentimentality. It should be clearly reiterated that there can be no question of negotiations, that France's army, navy and military equipment must first of all be in our hands, and that this must be the last time for the next three- to four-hundred years that France is able to attack a peaceful people without justification.

June 19, 1940

We must continue to make sure that the impression is not created among the German public that the war is already over. There are ample indications in the French and British press that resistance will continue, and this is to be exploited. France must count on very hard conditions, and it may confidently be assumed that she will at first reject the German demands. For that reason the will to victory among the German people must be further strengthened, just as its own sound instinct demands that Britain should be punished by force of arms.

The secret transmitters have the task of convincing the French and British public as before, of the uselessness of further resistance. Allowance has to be made for the fact that, for the time being, Britain is still backing the words of Churchill, whose cynicism should again be pilloried.

The German press, moreover, should not only report about [the armistice negotiations of] Compiègne but should also describe the French policy of destruction and plunder ever since the days of Richelieu and Mazarin, the repeated French pillaging campaigns, etc., and explain to the German people that an end is now being put to all that. This was not a case of satisfying any feelings of vengeance, but of making sure that such attacks can never again take place.

The French no doubt are still clinging to the hope of gradually stepping up their wishes and thus gaining for themselves enough ground so that in a few years from now they can once more pursue the encirclement of Germany under more favourable conditions and more effectively than now. There can, therefore, be no question of deviating from our clearly defined line.

June 20, 1940

The press and foreign language service should continue to ignore completely the development of negotiations and operate as if the war was being continued in the normal way. For that reason all reports are to be carried which suggest a continuation of the fighting. Moreover, examples are to be drawn from history to show that, in earlier wars too, the fighting was not immediately suspended as soon as a request for an armistice was made. It is entirely possible that the French will decline our conditions to start with and will make every effort to gain as much time as possible. Such attempts must be countered in advance.

The French, meanwhile, must be convinced of the extent to which the British have left them in the lurch. The refugee and food situation is already weighing noticeably on French public opinion, and this pressure must be further intensified by us. This pressure on public opinion must also be directed – since for the moment we lack military means of enforcement in this field – against the intention of placing the French navy and air force under the British.

June 21, 1940

The Minister explains that the momentary suspension of military operations in France is due to our interest in negotiating with a French government in power in the still-unoccupied territory, so as to lend a note of legality to any treaties that may be concluded. The negotiations at Compiègne will start at 16.00 hours.

The Minister further points out that what is happening at Compiègne is merely the act of presenting our conditions and that the decision on their acceptance or rejection is not to be expected before tomorrow or the next day. Besides, it is entirely possible that the French will decline them, unless the pressure of the hardships of the refugees compels them to accept.

The Berlin press was informed on June 21 about the expected course of the negotiations for surrender. It was disclosed that these would take place in Marshal Foch's historic coach. Hitler would say a few words by way of introduction and Keitel would then read out a three-page preamble. The conditions of surrender would be handed over without being read out.

The French delegation received these conditions on June 21, 1940, at 15.30 hours.

June 22, 1940

In the event of the German conditions being accepted, the secret transmitter should, by the middle of next week, gradually be allowed to die down on a note of increasing likelihood of a German-French understanding; it should then start broadcasting to Britain on a different frequency after a pause of a few days. In this connexion Herr Raskin reports that Lord Haw-Haw has already enlisted a number of speakers from a British prisoner-of-war camp; these come from all walks of life and are enthusiastically preparing to take up the struggle against Churchill.

The name 'Lord Haw-Haw' was given by the British to the best-known commentator of the English service of the Reichs-Rundfunk-Gesellschaft. (Reich Broadcasting Corporation). Lord Haw-Haw, whose real name was William Joyce (1906–46), was a British fascist and left his native country immediately prior to the outbreak of the war in order to fight against Britain on Hitler's side.

The Minister gives an outline of the envisaged course of the negotiations for surrender at Compiègne. The French statement is expected to be made at 11.00 hours. At present it may be expected that our conditions will be accepted, but it is still uncertain whether the French will not perhaps reject the Italian conditions. In the event of the French in fact accepting our terms, the announcement over the radio is to follow the grand ceremonial envisaged for this purpose. In case the announcement itself is couched in solemn form, the Minister reserves the decision on whether it is to be made by the Minister himself or by Herr Fritzsche. If no information is available in time for the afternoon press, the afternoon papers must certainly be prepared for war.

On June 22 at 18.50 hours the French negotiators signed the armistice conditions. These were not disclosed to the public until June 25, following the coming into effect of an armistice with Italy as well. France was occupied north and west of a line Geneva – Dôle – Tours – Mont de Marsan – Spanish frontier, so that the entire Atlantic coast was in German hands. The French army, with the exception of a volunteer army, as well as parts of the French air force and navy were demobilized, but the French naval units, a substantial number of which were stationed in North Africa, were not handed over.

German losses during the campaign in the West totalled 27,074 killed, 111,034 wounded and 18,384 missing.

June 23, 1940

The Minister points out that the England theme must now be brought to the forefront, without, however, allowing any premature signs of peace towards France to become evident for the next few days. It is still impossible to say in what form the fight against Britain will now be continued, and on no account, therefore, must the impression be created that the occupation of Britain is about to start tomorrow. On the other hand, there can be no doubt that Britain will receive the same sentence as France if she persists in closing her mind to sensible considerations.

Anti-British polemics may use as pegs Churchill's statement over the radio as well as the writings of *The Times* to the effect that Britain, allegedly, is now the last guardian of European liberty. We must now reply by pointing out that we are now the leaders in the clash between continental Europe and the plutocratic British island people. In this campaign the foreign language service must deliberately and systematically operate with slogans on the lines of 'Nations of Europe: Britain is organizing your starvation!' etc.

According to Stephan, Goebbels announced at the conference: 'Well, this week will bring the great swing [against Churchill] in Britain. Churchill, of course, can't hold on. A compromise government will be formed. We are very close to the end of the war.'

There is a danger that anti-Italian feeling in Germany may reach an undesirable degree and that, as a result of the Italians' touchy reaction to this, a regular German-Italian estrangement may come about. Much as our leading circles must on the one hand object to the tactlessness of the Italians – such as recently, in their premature announcement in *Giornale d'Italia* and *Tribuna* that the French have accepted the armistice conditions – it is vitally necessary that the press should, in a tactful manner, check the incipient anger and hatred against Italy and guide it into sensible channels. For that reason it must explain to the German people how useful Italy has been to us by holding back throughout the winter and what opportunities the Italians were offered by the Allies provided they broke with us. It will be best to pass over the military aspect altogether.

The press must also feature the Russian denial of foreign reports claiming that a shadow has fallen over the German-Russian relationship. Admittedly, certain frontier difficulties in Norway must be expected in the immediate future because some action will have to be taken against the consistent frontier violations by Russian airmen.

On June 22, 1940, Tass issued an official statement that rumours were being circulated to the effect that the entry of Soviet troops into the Baltic states meant a deterioration of German-Soviet relations. These rumours, Tass said, in no way accorded with the facts.

More alarming, on the other hand, was a Tass report of June 17, 1940, to the effect that the Soviet government saw a threat in the alliance of the Baltic states. The USSR therefore demanded an occupation of the Baltic states by Soviet troops, in identical notes, but these troops had in fact marched into Lithuania as early as June 15. (*Cf.* June 28, 1940.)

June 25, 1940
The campaign during the next few days and weeks must be fully concentrated on the creation of a continental front against Britain and

on forcing Britain off the continent in the field of polemics and ideology too.

The press was instructed on the same day not to start any clumsy attacks on Britain along such lines as 'beating the Empire into pulp'. The attacks were to be made on an 'elegant level' and directed at individuals. Germany wanted to liquidate not the British empire but only Britain's position of hegemony in Europe. This instruction bears the unmistakable stamp of Hitler.

It should be recalled that after the French Revolution some of the refugees continued for a while to 'play at monarchy' in Koblenz; from this is to be drawn a parallel with British attempts to set up a French shadow government around the British-kept General de Gaulle.

General de Gaulle proclaimed the continuation of French resistance in London on June 18. On June 27, 1940, Goebbels issued a directive that de Gaulle's name was no longer to be mentioned in the German press: only his arguments were to be refuted now. The 'Free French National Committee' set up in Britain by General de Gaulle on June 18, 1940, was recognized by Britain on June 28 as the political representative of France.

June 27, 1940
The first reports about British peace feelers, predicted by the Minister, are available. These matters are not to be dealt with by the press at all. Enquiries from abroad are to be answered by pointing out that the German press unambiguously expresses our attitude.

A few papers should also deal with the Jewish rumour that anyone who makes any sensible remark at all belongs to the Fifth Column. The Minister again comes out against any sentimental, fraternizing articles about Paris. He points out emphatically that for the next three- to four-hundred years Germany will have the importance which France has had over the last hundred-and-fifty years. In these circumstances it would be entirely mistaken for us to encourage the reputation of Paris, since naturally it will be Berlin which will now take the place of Paris. It is therefore important to boost our sense of assurance, and Paris to us can henceforth only occupy the role and significance of a provincial town. The Minister stresses the need of concerning oneself more with the ideological care of the people in the immediate future, since a sense of expectancy must be maintained even if the next few weeks prove quiet. Plans aiming at this objective are to be postponed till next week, when a clear picture of the situation will have been gained.

June 28, 1940

The Minister again points out that our propaganda for Britain must take no notice of what is happening behind the scenes, but must continue to follow its course as hitherto. It must emphasize that Britain wants this war and that she shall have it now, and it must further emphasize that Britain is governed by war criminals and that she cannot expect anything but war from us until she comes to her senses. At the same time, our propaganda must keep off precise formulations. It must not be stated that we wish to destroy the British empire, nor must there be any hint about the nature or timing of our offensive.

The Minister reports that the success of our broadcasts has now also been confirmed by German diplomatic circles as being a hundred per cent, and that the collapse in the enemy countries can overwhelmingly be attributed to their effectiveness.

The Minister intends to get in touch personally with the Führer's headquarters in order to obtain the release of at least a neutral report about the events in Rumania, since, with the exception of the German public, the whole world by now knows those events, and since it is difficult to see what harm could come of a reproduction of at least the official Rumanian and Russian announcement.

On June 28, 1940 at 14.00 hours Soviet troops marched into Bessarabia. On July 5 the Rumanian General Staff issued a final announcement that the evacuation of Bessarabia and the remainder of the Bukovina by Rumanian troops had been concluded. Incidents had occurred only where Russian troops had crossed the agreed demarcation lines.

'The hour will come...'

July-September 1940

July 3, 1940
The peace rumours, which are appearing with increasing frequency abroad, must not be mentioned in the German press by as much as a single syllable. At the same time the press must avoid precise formulations and refer neither to the date of a full-scale attack on Britain nor to our intention of smashing the British empire. For the rest, it must clearly support the continuation of our struggle with Britain.

July 4, 1940

On July 3 a French naval squadron off Oran was destroyed by British naval forces in order to prevent it from falling into German hands. Only the battleship *Strasbourg* succeeded in escaping to Toulon.

In connexion with the attack on the French fleet at Oran Churchill said that the decision was the most distasteful, unnatural and agonizing he ever had to take.

The British navy's attack on the French fleet at Oran is to be used for a detailed exposition of how Britain first dragged France into the war, how she then let France make the main preparations, how France was required to supply most of the materials, how the struggle was fought on French soil, how French divisions bled themselves white while the British carried out a 'withdrawal without losses' policy, how Britain eventually tried to force the French to continue the struggle, how the British abused them after the collapse and blamed them for the defeat, how they then set up a French pseudo-government on British soil and how, to top it all, they are now attacking the French ships – all 'in France's interest.' Here Britain has really revealed herself without her mask.

On July 5, 1940, a directive was issued to the effect that, in dealing with France, excessively favourable as well as unfavourable descriptions were to be avoided for the time being.

63

July 6, 1940

The Ministry of Foreign Affairs is to be requested to release our Note to the United States on the question of the Monroe Doctrine. The Minister deals in depth with a question by Major Martin on whether the German people are not being inadequately or too one-sidedly informed about the US attitude towards us. He explains that more important than such information is the fact that the Jews in America must not be given a chance of getting at us on the strength of a few unconsidered remarks. For that reason it is better to regard America as a negligible quantity.

The US State Department on July 5 published the German Note in reply to the US Note of June 19, 1940. The German Note rejected the warning of the United States that Germany was trying to interfere in the affairs of the western hemisphere and was aiming at territorial conquests there. If – the German reply pointed out – America expected the Monroe Doctrine to be respected then America should not interfere in European affairs.

The Minister points out that the press, the foreign language service and the information service are in a difficult position at the moment, since only the suppression of news from France can prevent an excessively francophile atmosphere from gaining ground in Germany. On the other hand it is absolutely essential to keep hatred of Britain at the same level as hitherto, while avoiding the danger that the public might at last wish to see deeds instead of accusations and threats. It is therefore necessary to mark time, since we cannot anticipate any decisions by the Führer; the mood, as far as possible, must be kept on the boil until the Führer himself has spoken.

Major Titel is to discuss in detail with the Ministry of Foreign Affairs exactly what is being expected in connexion with the welcome for the Foreign Minister, Count Ciano. He must leave no doubt about the fact that it is impossible to mobilize enough of the population to line the route all the way from the Anhalter station to the Bellevue Palace, especially as there is a very real risk that the population of Berlin might make no secret of their feelings towards Italy.

Hitler received the Italian Foreign Minister in Berlin on July 7; Count Ciano presented him with a long list of Italian requests for annexations but Hitler, engrossed in his imminent clash with Britain, did not want to know anything about them. Instead, Ciano had to listen to a victory monologue about the campaign in the West.

July 7, 1940

The Minister surveys the political situation and in this connexion again stresses the need always to attack only Churchill and his clique of plutocrats but never the British nation as such. Churchill himself had burnt all bridges behind him so that there can be no question of any arrangement with Britain so long as he is at the helm.

The Minister also points to the need of continuing to treat France as an enemy. It was unfortunately being overlooked in Germany that the circles which made and declared war on us have undergone no change whatever and that the masses of the people, who are now exhibiting a more or less sensible attitude, have never been anything other than the plaything of French politics. We must therefore go slow on anything that is too strongly in France's favour and emphasize everything that speaks against France. In particular, there should be more reports about the ill-treatment of prisoners. The whole business, however, must be done quietly, so as not to create the impression of a new anti-French campaign being launched. The general rule for all articles, in particular those against Britain, should be that the authors of the articles must not themselves get angry but must merely fan this anger – i.e. they must not lose sight of the effect.

Herr Gutterer is to instruct the police to make one or two raids on the Wannsee and the adjacent lakes to confiscate all English gramophone records as well as the gramophones themselves. As for their owners, a check should be made to see whether they are perhaps listed as 'in reserved occupations', and, where possible, they are to be employed in labour squads. The Minister describes it as a scandal that jazz music with English words should be publicly disseminated in the English language during the war. One or two such operations should be sufficient for the news of this action to spread very rapidly among the circles concerned.

July 9, 1940

The Minister again comes out against the numerous publications about France which give the German readers an erroneous picture. He points out that we have absolutely no interest in French efforts to set an authoritarian course and that it would be totally wrong to try to make the French into National Socialists now. On the contrary, our interest is in a weak and disunited France which must not even find the strength to form a front of moral resistance. It must be our aim to let France become a 'Switzerland grown obese'.

In dealing with Britain, nothing is to change in our attitude until the beginning of next week. The Minister again points out that the objective we are aiming at is not the annihilation of Britain, and that Britain therefore should be given one last chance of getting off comparatively lightly.

Since we cannot allow any of the small sovereigns ever again to turn against Germany, there is no intention of re-shaping any of the conquered countries into a dynastic state. What space we need we shall create by removing those elements which cannot be melted down. In future we shall not refer any more to the 'Government-General for the Occupied Polish Territories' but – without expressly drawing attention to this – simply to the 'Government-General'; in this way, just as is gradually happening in the Protectorate [of Bohemia-Moravia], which is now simply called the Protectorate, the situation will clarify itself automatically. The population in those territories merely has the task of making our work easier.

July 10, 1940

The Minister again urgently warns against German sentimentality being given too much scope; for centuries this has ruined the best chances in German history and is now again about to drag the Franco-German relationship on to an entirely wrong course as a result of a sickly-sweet, womanish concept of politics. The radio (by means of lectures on historical topics) and the German press (by suitable articles, among other things by utilizing Bainville*) must increasingly, though unobtrusively, lead public opinion once more into greater hostility to France.

The Minister demands a renewed directive to the press that it must not on any account ease the path of the French into a better future by giving them good advice. He quotes instances of pro-French sentiments producing the strangest flowers even in Party quarters, and he demands that even greater and sharper emphasis must in future be given to the fact that France declared this war on us and that she must now foot the bill. Pétain himself must not be honoured as a 'French Hindenburg'; indeed, there would be no harm in occasionally recalling that the French themselves demanded the extradition of Hindenburg as a war criminal. In this respect, too, therefore, a cool reserve on our part is really more than the French have a right to expect.

July 15, 1940

On dealing with the French, the Minister issues the instruction that all attempts towards a national recovery must be nipped in the bud by means of ruthless intellectual terrorizing. He describes how intelligence can overcome any obstacle invented by man, whereas lethargic apathy is the surest way of preventing any recovery. The principal task,

---

* Jacques Bainville, *France's War Aims* (in German), Hamburg, 1940. Bainville (1879–1936) belonged to the fascist Action Française. *Tr.*

therefore, is to break their morale and their will to fight; this would ensure permanent disarmament more reliably than confiscation of the weapons themselves. Dr Bömer should therefore, with immediate effect, have the French provincial press and the small local rags in the unoccupied zone continually watched for any rebellious remarks, and in any such instance we should be hypersensitive and stage violent political repercussions. Through perpetual intellectual terrorism the French are to be discouraged from the very outset, and once and for all, from ever rising against us again.

July 19, 1940
The Minister decides in detail that, as from 15.00 hours, when the Reichstag meeting has been announced in press and radio, the information may also be passed on to foreign transmitters. In the evening the opening announcement on the radio should list by name all the transmitters linked to us, to emphasize the impression that the whole world is listening.

In reproducing foreign reaction to the Führer's speech extreme care must be shown since, by Saturday morning, at the most only a partial, unofficial echo can be expected. A final foreign reaction cannot be expected before Sunday or Monday evening, especially as there will no doubt be a deep rift cutting across public opinion in Britain, and if there should be a resignation of Churchill's government then this will be preceded by major rearguard actions. The Minister emphasizes that Britain's fate will be decided this evening.

Hitler's Reichstag speech of July 19, 1940, which had been carefully prepared by German diplomatic and propaganda methods, culminated in the appeal to Britain to seek a 'peace of accommodation' with Germany, whereby Britain should acknowledge German hegemony on the continent while Hitler would leave the Empire untouched.

The press should oppose the legend, now gaining ground in France, that France collapsed under the weight of our material superiority; this must be countered with the emphatic statement that the victory was won by German troops and German leadership.

The Minister acknowledges the efficient organization of the celebrations welcoming home the Berlin division. He expects the newsreel to make a magnificent show of the coverage of the welcome itself and the public celebrations that followed it.

Herr Gutterer reports that at the time of the entry of the troops the same idle gentry could be observed in the Kurfürstendamm as always.

In this connexion the Minister announces his decision that, immediately after the end of the war, all 62,000 Jews still living in Berlin will be deported to Poland within a period of no more than eight weeks; as long as the Jews continue to live in Berlin the atmosphere in the city's West End will always be affected by them. Herr Hinkel reports about the evacuation plan already worked out with the police; it is the Minister's wish that Herr Gutterer should come in on this plan. First and foremost he is to see to it that Berlin is cleansed, because the Kurfürstendamm will continue to show its unchanged, Jewish character – even if they are no longer in evidence – until Berlin is really free from Jews. The turn of other Jewish cities (Breslau, etc.) is to come only after Berlin.

July 20, 1940

Within an hour of Hitler's Reichstag speech came a reply from the BBC: a commentary by Sefton Delmer rejected Hitler's offer. His brusque rejection, made 'without any lead whatever from His Majesty's Government' was to set the key for the attitude and tone of the British press for the next few days.

Even though some caution would be advisable after the first British reactions to the Führer's speech, there are by now so many absolutely negative and cynically rejecting opinions that to keep silent about them would promote an atmosphere of false illusions. A selection of these first comments should therefore be put out, not emphatically, but nevertheless as a first reply from Britain. It can already be pointed out that such a mass of comment, all on the same lines, could hardly be conceivable without the approval of official circles.

The foreign language service should put out the vital passages from the Führer's speech individually, each one with a commentary, repeatedly and at roughly half-hourly intervals in its broadcasts to Britain. After that it should say: 'We are now telling you what the British radio has had to say on this so far' and it should point out that, after all, for the British listeners this is a matter of life and death.

The secret transmitters, on much the same lines as before the opening of the western offensive, should make it clear what lies in store for Britain once the offensive starts. Over the *workers'* transmitter the first cautious attempts should now be made to call for the formation of action committees against Churchill. As a catchy slogan each single transmission should be prefaced by: 'The Empire is ruled by a fool; Churchill is a fool.' The *Voix de Paix* should not only demand peace but might clearly emphasize its possibility. In this connexion Herr Dr Bömer is to give Herr Raskin material about the Duke of Windsor.

Major Wodarg and Major Martin should, moreover, start working out an evacuation plan with a view to producing disastrous consequences in Britain when the offensive starts.

Furthermore, Herr Raskin is to get a Frenchman to broadcast in English, explaining what France might have been spared if she had accepted the Führer's offer in good time. Other special broadcasts should be considered, as for instance a rogation service for peace. About the Duke of Windsor it should be said that he was overthrown at the time because he wanted peace and understanding with Germany; passages from his abdication speech are to be broadcast.

King Edward VIII abdicated on December 10, 1936, because of his intended marriage to Mrs Simpson as well as earlier differences with the cabinet about his social policy plans.

In July 1940 the following secret transmitters, or 'Concordia services', were operating against Britain: the New British Broadcasting Station, which had been in existence for some time and was henceforward broadcasting over three shortwave transmitters on different frequencies. Their transmissions were directed against the government and supported a Britain 'of peace and welfare.' An amateur transmitter was operating under the name 'Caledonia', and championed ideas of Scottish independence. A third secret transmitter, Concordia 'Plan S', operated on medium waves from a mobile transmitter and used revolutionary socialist slogans in calling for action by the British working class. A secret shortwave transmitter, 'Plan W', supported Welsh separatist tendencies and a fifth Concordia transmitter, 'Plan P', was to represent a purely pacifist platform on Christian foundations.

July 22, 1940
The Minister describes the difficulties encountered by our propaganda in trying to get at the British mentality. With their totally different, un-European mentality the British are unable to believe that the offer made in the Führer's speech was not just bluff but was meant seriously. He points out that the British papers would not be commenting in such a contemptuous and off-hand manner if Britain really wanted peace, since the British press must submit to public opinion. It is our task to step up our arguments even further, and in doing so to regard British public opinion as still entirely unbreached. Britain will not see reason until she has suffered the first blows – at the moment she simply has no idea of the situation facing her.

The German press had at first been instructed to record foreign reaction to Hitler's speech in the manner demanded by Goebbels. However, that same evening the directive was fundamentally amended. The German press was instructed to give great publicity to negative British comment and to attack Britain 'with all possible might.' The rejection of Hitler's offer, it was to be said, amounted to a 'war crime'.

The question is discussed of whether the Nostradamus prophecies should be disseminated in Britain over the official foreign language service or over the secret transmitters. In view of interpretations contrary to our own it is decided to give preference to the secret transmitters. However, the secret transmitter with the biggest audience is to be chosen; this should begin by pointing to all the correct prophecies made by Nostradamus for earlier periods and should then gradually lead up to the prophecies describing the destruction of London in 1940.

July 24, 1940
The Minister defines our attitude towards Britain for the immediate future.

(1) *For the German public* the very powerful mood of militancy inherent in the people should be further buttressed and strengthened. This means that the restraint of the past few weeks must be abandoned. However, even for the German public, the British plutocracy alone is to be attacked, and not the British people as a whole. Otherwise entirely primitive arguments are to be used. It must be explained to the people that the plutocratic caste can be knocked out of its stupid and impertinent sense of superiority only by blows from our weapons.

(2) *Our official propaganda media* must make it clear to the British people that the plutocratic clique ruling them has nothing in common with them nor does it feel any ties with them. To this end arguments may also be used which could not be applied in Germany (e.g. treatment of the tax problem), since the British people have either no information or only distorted information about internal German conditions. Mistrust must be sown of the plutocratic ruling caste, and fear must be instilled of what is about to befall. All this must be laid on as thick as possible.

(3) *The secret transmitters* must on no account unmask themselves as German. They must therefore, as far as possible, begin each broadcast with attacks on the National Socialists. They must pick up and magnify the themes also tackled by our official transmitters; in addition, they are to invent political incidents on the home front in clubs and nightclubs and protest against these on behalf of the British people. In particular, they must now spread horror by putting out British eye-witness reports from Warsaw, Dunkirk, etc., and they must now use

every conceivable means to make sure the very first blows against Britain fall on psychologically well-prepared ground.

The secret transmitters, in particular, must conjure up the danger of inflation. They should call on the public to hoard whatever foodstuffs it can, withdraw its money from the banks, and buy jewellery and articles of lasting value.

July 25, 1940

It is the particular task of the secret transmitters to arouse alarm and fear among the British people. But since the German propaganda behind this campaign must not be apparent, they must wrap up their real intentions in moral tales and good advice. Among other things, they should now put out expertly prepared ARP (air raid precaution) classes of which all details must be so accurately described that the civilian population is seized with horror from the start.

July 26, 1940

Herr Hadamovsky is to examine from every angle whether it seems more to the point to jam enemy transmissions or to use them as a source of information, since frequently they are the only source of news available to us.

July 31, 1940

A Potsdam priest is reported to have said in a sermon: 'Lord, have mercy upon our young people who go through life without a purpose'. If this report is correct, Herr Gutterer is to make it clear to that priest, beyond any possibility of doubt, that in the event of a repetition he will find himself in a concentration camp.

August 3, 1940

The report – spread especially in America – that Hamburg has been 'pulverized' by British air raids is to be taken up in a big way. Herr Dr Bömer is to see to it that foreign correspondents can immediately convince themselves on the spot of the mendacious nature of the report. All possible counter-measures should be launched at once in collaboration with the German press, the radio, the Air Ministry, and the weekly newsreel. Arrangements should further be made to ensure that, on their way back from Hamburg, the foreign journalists are shown the effects of a British air raid on a lonely farmstead in the province of Hanover.

71

Moreover, all transmitters should take up the incident and use it as an opportunity for pillorying the mendacious character of the British news services.

The foreign journalists' visit to Hamburg is described by Shirer in *Berlin Diary*, pp. 463–5. A farmstead had been set on fire in the Borken district.

The Minister criticizes that, whenever the press reports receptions at foreign embassies, etc., the gentlemen of the Ministry for Propaganda are invariably mentioned right at the end of the visitors listed by name.

August 5, 1940

Propaganda against Britain must be stepped up over the next few days even more than in the past, and the secret transmitters in particular must try to achieve the maximum effect. In this connexion the Minister praises the ARP transmissions to date and suggests that gas defence instruction programmes should now be broadcast, and fear promoted of accidents in connexion with ARP classes. For instance, when the manufacture of home-made Molotov cocktails has been represented as a national duty, extreme nervousness must be aroused a few days later among all owners of such grenades that their devices might blow up at any moment.

Such broadcasts were repeated several times at Goebbels's suggestion.

In connexion with directives for the treatment of a speech by Cardinal Hinsley as well as one by Duff Cooper, the Minister again makes it clear that although he has no objections to the occasional use of invectives, these must subsequently be made to appear justified by sound argument, so as to avoid on the part of the reader an impression of mere insult. As for increasingly frequent British assertions that the responsibility for the famine now certainly threatening Europe lies with no one but the Führer, indeed that 'General Hunger' was identical with Adolf Hitler, this should immediately be countered by the question of who it was who started the blockade in the first place. The Minister, moreover, reports that Mussolini has expressed his admiration for the magnificent manner in which the German press is standing up to the present momentary period of stagnation.

August 7, 1940

An article by the former editor of the *Daily Herald* contains very useful material for replying to *The Times* article mentioned yesterday. This should be thoroughly exploited, in particular by the foreign language service and the secret transmitter; examples from our Winter Relief Scheme and the collection for the German Red Cross should be used in this context.

On August 6, 1940, the German press had been warned that British papers, in particular *The Times,* would try 'to take over National Socialist slogans' and make various promises of a social nature. The German press was directed to represent such attempts by British papers as 'snares for the gullible,' designed to make the war popular with the British masses. The social problem was likewise touched on by Percy Cudlipp in an article, 'To those who work today', in the *Daily Herald* of August 5, 1940. (*Cf.* August 8, 1940.)

On the subject of leaflet propaganda, the Minister declares that he does not expect much from a leaflet campaign in Britain, since the effort involved would be quite out of proportion with the result. The British masses can be reached much more easily by radio. If Britain for her part is operating with leaflets in Germany, then this is due to the fact that Britain cannot reach the German listener by radio to any appreciable extent. Besides, the spoken word has a more magnetic effect than the written word. The Minister admits that the leaflets most recently dropped by the British are a little more dangerous than the earlier ones. He wishes to be informed at once about any new publication, and its exact wording.

(*Cf.* May 5, 1942.)

August 8, 1940
The Minister refers to an article in *The Economist* about 'Dynamic Democracy', on the same lines as a recent article in *The Times,* and demands the strongest possible refutation, especially in the foreign-language service. He explains that the British are, no doubt, above all hoping to gain time; by October, they hope, the worst will be over. The spectre of famine is already being painted large in the hope that this will bring with it revolutionary development and that the states attracted by Germany will abandon her again. It is essential that we should knock this theoretical speculating out of the hands of the British at once. That this can be done was first shown at the beginning of the war when the British were trying to operate with entirely different slogans, but, under the pressure of our counter-measures, had to change their tune.

Moreover, our greatest efforts must be directed at attacking the repeated English attempts at distorting the apparent shortage of food supplies. It cannot be made too clear that responsibility for any possible shortages does not lie with *us,* but that Britain's blockade alone is to blame if foodstuffs from the United States do not reach the countries occupied by us. To the occupied countries it must also be pointed out that we are not responsible for their food supplies, and that our food reserves are not for feeding the defeated nations which now simply have to bear the consequences of the war which they themselves forced upon us. Besides – contrary to an allegation maliciously spread by Britain – the Führer did not say that we have safeguarded *Europe*'s food supplies; he merely spoke about the food supplies for the *German* people.

Goebbels is referring to the article 'England's Example' in *The Economist* of July 20, 1940. The relevant quotation from Hitler's speech of July 19, 1940, runs: 'Food supplies also have been safeguarded, thanks to measures taken in good time, no matter how long the war may last.'

Herr Raskin is to keep handy for the secret transmitter a British report to the effect that 100,000 British uniforms fell into German hands at Dunkirk. At the right moment the secret transmitters should then put out the story that parachutists have been dropped over Britain wearing these uniforms.

It is thought that the secret transmitters on August 14, 1940, first put out the report that parachutists in British uniforms and civilian clothes had been dropped over northern England and were being hidden by members of the Fifth Column. Britain seemed to be in the grip of a paratroop psychosis, but the success of the campaign was foiled by the British papers the following morning when they announced that, although parachutes had been found, these had been un-manned since there had been no tracks whatever leading out of the cornfields and away from the other places where the parachutes had come down.

At the conference of August 20, 1940, Goebbels ordered that British reports about the existence of German parachutists in Britain were to be officially denied, while the secret transmitters should continue to nourish fears of further parachute drops. The secret transmitters reported, among other things, that the parachutists would be protected by Fifth Columnists. On August 20 and 22, 1940, Goebbels suggested a repetition of the parachute operation over Britain since British press comment revealed 'very considerable disquiet among the public.'

August 9, 1940
Yesterday afternoon's *single* German special announcement about an air victory over the Channel, with 34 enemy aircraft shot down, was met by the British with 14 separate reports culminating, after a dramatic crescendo, in the allegation that altogether 53 German aircraft had been

shot down. In a detailed discussion it is pointed out that, with the method at present practised by us, of issuing an entirely sober OKW communiqué, we are bound to be defeated in the propaganda field. The Minister made the point that enemy lies, comparatively speaking, have not represented much of a danger so long as they have dealt with military operations on the ground, since the gain of territory, at least in the long run, cannot be concealed. Matters, however, are entirely different in the war in the air since the accuracy of a report cannot be proved here in the same clear-cut manner. The tactics already used by the British clearly suggest that in the event of a really large-scale German operation against Britain the British will claim enormous German losses and, unless our own tactics are changed, will also find credence for their reports. It is high time it was realized that we are about to change our information policy dramatically; unless we realize this fact there is a danger that we may lose the battle in the field of information.

In a detailed discussion a number of the reasons have been clarified why it was possible for a delay of several hours to arise between the first British report and the German special announcement. Both Major Wodarg and Herr Fritzsche consider it necessary for the Minister to get the Führer's permission to issue partial reports independently on future occasions, without previously submitting them to him.

The OKW announced on August 9, 1940, that 49 British aircraft had been shot down in aerial combat over the Channel, while German losses had only been 10 aircraft. In the evening of August 9 the British Air Ministry, in a final report, listed German losses as 53 aircraft and stated that 16 British aircraft were missing.

August 12, 1940
The Minister points out that the news reporting in connexion with the German victory in the air over Portland on Sunday was carried out exceedingly well; he adds to this the demand that the same speed of work should be displayed on all future occasions. Reports for abroad should always be given priority, and only when a number of reports have been broadcast to foreign audiences should arrangements be made for the first comprehensive report for home listeners. As for the ceremonial to be given to such special announcements on the German radio, the Minister stipulates that the full ceremonial should be reserved, as a matter of principle, for OKW communiqués. However, in the event of such great aerial victories as yesterday's, some ceremonial is necessary if only to make the German people realize the magnitude of the success and its significance.

As for the mendacious British reports, the Minister points out that the German figures are in fact as accurate as the most conscientious checking can ensure. In our polemics concerning British allegations we must continue to point out – quoting specific examples – that Britain has been systematically lying ever since the beginning of the war and that, in point of fact, she has no other alternative but lies, unless she wants to give up her case as lost from the start. Listeners should also be reminded of Churchill's admission that, in World War One, Britain had also lied her way out of more than one desperate situation.

For the sake of speedy reporting of German news an occasional slight error is entirely acceptable in future.

Commodore Hahn is to ascertain whether it might be possible to station a foreign journalist so near the Channel that he would be in a position to give eye-witness reports of future engagements.

The OKW communiqué gave British losses in the aerial battle over Portland as 90 aircraft. (*Cf.* August 13, 1940.)

Concerning the press photograph of the Russian exhibition at the Königsberg Fair, which shows Stalin's head, the Minister criticizes those circles which are still desperately trying to establish some inner ties between National Socialism and bolshevism. With reference, for instance, to the Russian film *Assault on the Mannerheim Line* and the Zoshchenko book *Sleep Faster, Comrade,* the Minister points out how mistaken are the attempts of pro-bolshevik circles to prove an inner ideological affinity between National Socialism and bolshevism, and he calls on Herr Gutterer not to allow any bolshevik tendencies and attitudes into Germany. Our relations with Russia are guided purely by power-political expediency.

August 13, 1940

The press should not display our reports of successes during the past few days in a way which suggests that the great blow against Britain is now beginning to be struck. As a general rule it must proceed from the view that the war against Britain is in progress and, although it has now intensified, it is not possible to define any fixed points in it.

On August 12, Göring ordered that the air battle over England ('Offensive Eagle') should be opened with the aim of gaining aerial superiority over Britain.

August 14, 1940

The Minister points to the necessity for a continued, systematic undermining of the credibility of British reports about the results of the air war. In the United States, too, the suspicion is growing that Britain is simply falsifying the figures, since the divergence between the German and British reports can no longer be explained in any other way. In fact, the figures issued by us are absolutely correct and the confidence placed in the German reports is therefore fully justified. It is altogether necessary to discuss the systematic character of British polemics, quoting examples. The German people are following this information battle with intense interest, since it is widely thought that the outcome of the fighting now developing will allow conclusions to be drawn on whether the war will last through the winter or whether it will end in the late autumn; and the British figures, which of course cannot be kept entirely secret, are therefore closely compared with ours.

The *foreign language service* must continue, by means of numerous individual reports, to present an unvarnished picture of the real situation, whereas the *secret transmitters* must above all depict for the British public the devastating effect and frightful circumstances of aerial bombardment. In addition, the press should some time compile a list of all the lies put out by our opponents during the offensives against France and Poland in connexion with the results of German aerial warfare, and compare these with the real state of affairs, or rather the final outcome.

Herr Dr Bömer reports on the departure by air of eight foreign journalists whose flight to the Channel coast meant overcoming considerable difficulties first. In this connexion the Minister appeals to the liaison officers present to help get rid of bureaucracy in the various Wehrmacht departments as far as possible. Shortly after the outbreak of the war he himself had to overcome the most determined opposition of the relevant military authorities in arranging for the American journalist Lochner to visit Czestochowa, although in doing so he nipped in the bud the first great lie of the war.* Since then he has repeatedly been able to employ foreign journalists for the refutation of enemy lies, each time, however, running into stubborn opposition. Each time, needless to say, those quarters which first offered resistance have subsequently applauded him on his success. Surely the time has come for everybody

---

* Soon after the start of the campaign in Poland the big American news agencies denied a false report from Paris (where the canard is reported to have been planted by the Nazis themselves to discredit French and Polish credibility) regarding the destruction of Czestochowa and its famous, venerated, miracle-working painting of the 'Black Virgin'. Bömer had on that occasion arranged the journey of an American correspondent, Louis J. Lochner, who was chosen by lot, to Czestochowa.

to realize what a useful weapon the American press representatives in Germany are in the neutralization of enemy lies.

At the conference of August 13, 1940, Goebbels had applied for the stationing of foreign journalists on the Channel coast. (*Cf.* August 18, 1940.)

August 17, 1940

The Minister points out that the military events in Britain have been handled very well both in our domestic and foreign news media and that our press commentary has also tackled the matter in the right way. The important thing now is to intensify as far as possible the mood of panic which is undoubtedly slowly gaining ground in Britain. The secret transmitters and the foreign language service in particular now have the task of painting a picture of the magnitude and volume of our attack for that part of the British population which has not yet experienced the frightful effects of our air raids. The Minister again emphasizes the value of American comment; without any doubt reports by the London correspondents of these papers are already reflecting an incipient change of mood in Britain. We must continue to emphasize that even the present attacks are a mere foretaste of what is yet to come. It should, moreover, be pointed out that fog and mist are in no way to be regarded as allies of the British, since all these can do is affect the accurate aim of the German bombers, so that their bombs must then be expected to drop more frequently on areas adjacent to the targets. The secret transmitters, in particular, should marshal witnesses who must give horrifying accounts of the destruction they have seen with their own eyes. However, the last stops of panic-mongering are not yet to be pulled out. Nevertheless, the severity of the war must now be reflected in full and, as a general principle at least, the pillorying of ridiculous features should cease. If at all possible, the Luftwaffe Operations Staff should continue to provide such extensive and colourful accounts as during the past few days; this kind of reporting has been magnificently successful and public opinion in the United States, in particular, is entirely spellbound by these reports.

The problem of American correspondents was touched upon in a letter by the British Premier to the Secretary for Air a few days later. On August 21, 1940 Churchill wrote to him, among other things: '. . . how far the American correspondents and the American public are convinced of our victory or of the accuracy of our figures is far less important . . . There is something repulsive about taking reporters out to air crews so that they can assure the American public that they neither brag with their figures nor lie. Surely we could afford to display a little coolness and calm in these matters. . . .'

The Minister expects that sooner or later the British will abandon their present tactics of belittling, and supplant them by new tactics which will play the humanitarian tune in order to 'arouse the world's conscience.' For this foreseeable event, when they will be trotting out their numbers of women killed, expectant mothers, old men, etc., Herr Fritzsche and Herr Bömer are to have material handy so that they can at short notice supply pictures of the children killed in Freiburg,* etc., and also reports about British air attacks in India, etc. Herr Braeckow, moreover, is to keep the departments concerned currently informed about British air raids, so that any suitable material can be recorded on photograph and film. In reply to a question by Herr Hadamovsky, the Minister decides that the time has not yet come for our big transmitter facilities to be made available to the secret transmitters. The facilities of the foreign language service, on the other hand, should be extended. The Minister approves a suggestion by Herr Brauweiler that the secret transmitter should put out frequent air raid alarms, using the British air raid warning signal. The assertion that Hitler intends to get Britain down on her knees by using the Luftwaffe alone and dispensing with an invasion, is not to be spread either at home or abroad.

August 18, 1940
Herr Raskin is to continue inserting mysterious-sounding but well thought-out messages in German into our official foreign language service, thereby keeping alive the suspicion that we are getting in touch with members of the Fifth Column in Britain.

No measures were to be taken against 'nonsensical' articles appearing in the American press about the Fifth Column, 'so that the existence of the Fifth Column is left open to doubt'. At the beginning of August two Berlin dailies were instructed to carry articles on the fact 'that in the enemy countries the most convenient method of dealing with a political opponent is now to label him as a member or leader of the Fifth Column.'

Developing a proposal by Herr Glasmeier, the Minister gives instructions that one Italian and three American journalists, accompanied by a member of the Ministry and at least one officer, as well as three broadcasters for the South American short-wave transmitter and one or two broadcasters for the North American transmitter should travel to the Channel coast on Tuesday August 20 in order to report from there. In connexion with the employment of the

* On May 10, 1940, Freiburg in the Breisgau was heavily bombed, not by French or British aircraft, but by German bombers in error. This fact was, of course, kept secret from the public.

Americans, the Minister points out that the American press has undoubtedly revealed a certain change of tune recently, in that Germany's prospects of victory are being emphasized far more objectively than in the past. Even though this new editorial policy has in part been created to bolster the interventionist forces before the presidential election by depicting Britain's position in the darkest possible way, there is nevertheless a great need, even in the Jewish press, to prepare their readers for a way out of the severe crisis of confidence which would arise if Britain were to collapse suddenly.

August 20, 1940
Against the opposition of the Ministry of the Interior, all Jews living in Berlin are having their telephones taken away as from the end of this month.

August 21, 1940
In further dealing with Churchill's speech on Tuesday the papers are to employ their best writers. Herr Fritzsche is to release the speech to the press for general criticism, but with the proviso that some passages must not be quoted by us textually but that only the gist of them must be reproduced.

In his speech to the Commons on August 20, 1940 Churchill first announced British losses to date as totalling 92,000 killed, prisoners and missing, including civilians. On the war in the air, which had just begun, he said it was obvious that Hitler could not admit the failure of his air offensive against Great Britain without incurring grave damage.

The Minister praises the work of 'Lord Haw-Haw', which is so effective because it is based so entirely on the British point of view and operates with British arguments. Herr Dr Naumann is instructed, in response to a request from 'Lord Haw-Haw', to present him with a few cases of very good cigars as a token of the Minister's recognition.

(*Cf.* June 22, 1940.)

For the time being no explanation is to be given for the closing down of transmitters as early as 23.00 hours since it is intended, first of all, as a try-out over the next few days, until Monday. In reply to questions Herr Dr Bömer should meanwhile explain to the foreign journalists that this is a military secret which must not be discussed.

Göring had ordered the closing down of all radio transmitters (long and medium-wave) from 23.00 to 03.00 hours until August 26. This applied also to the Reich transmitters employed as radio beacons for the German Luftwaffe. The purpose was to deprive the RAF of a convenient system of orientation, a point of particular urgency now that the Reich territory was almost entirely stripped of Luftwaffe protection, as the squadrons were intended for operational use over Britain.

At Germany's request a radio shut-down was also introduced in Italy and later in the Balkans from 22.00 hours onwards. The measure, however, failed to produce the expected result. The curtailment of broadcasting proved of considerable disadvantage to the effectiveness of propaganda. (*Cf.* October 7, 1940.)

The Minister instructs Major Wodarg to propose to the Luftwaffe Operations Staff that the parachutes used by airmen baling out in an emergency should be differentiated from those used by paratroops. Only if such a visual distinction is possible can action be taken in the event of the British firing at descending airmen while still in the air.

August 23, 1940
The Reich Propaganda Offices are to be reminded once more that local reports about air raids must be in conformity with the facts. It is nonsense to distort facts which have taken place in front of everybody's eyes.

August 24, 1940
The foreign language service is to issue an emphatic denial of British allegations that the New British Broadcasting Station is a German transmitter. The British government, it should be said, is trying to saddle German propaganda with broadcasts for which, in our view, it is itself responsible. Besides, it is a cheap way of dealing with an opposition by ascribing it simply to the Germans.

(*Cf.* July 20, 1940.)

August 28, 1940
Since even in Berlin itself the wildest rumours are circulating about the overflying of Berlin by British aircraft during the night of August 25 and 26, a precise statement should be issued once more – in conjunction with a totally distorted New York report – setting out the damage actually caused by the British raiders. (As against the fact that a

summerhouse was burnt down, the foreign reports actually claim that extensive destruction was caused in the most various parts of the city, to industrial installations, etc.)

Unofficial measures are to be taken by way of the Party to ensure that rumour-mongers from among the decent circles of the population are dealt with rigorously and on occasion, if necessary, can even be roughed up.

Stop-press reports should carry purely factual accounts from London, showing how Londoners were forced to spend six hours on end and more in the air raid shelters; this kind of report will make it clear to the population of Berlin that the discomforts they had to undergo are as nothing compared with conditions in London. Similarly, a report that South Wales has now had its one-hundredth air raid should be commented on for western Germany on the lines that the west German people are not the only ones who have to make special sacrifices at this moment – quite apart from the different results of air raids on the two sides.

As for the air-raid warning on Wednesday morning, it should be stated that this was a false alarm; a few sentences should be added to explain how this kind of thing can happen. The overall picture of the situation in Britain, to be published again by the press today, should always include a few aspects which are unfavourable to us, so as to prevent the impression that Britain is already knocked out. Possibilities of further intensification must always be kept open, and at some future date it should be possible, from our reports on the situation in Britain, to gain a truthful picture of the real development.

August 30, 1940
It has been shown that the Reich Marshal's decree whereby the public in Berlin need not necessarily take to the air-raid shelters whenever an air-raid alarm is given fails to get at the heart of this problem in the capital. The correct way of posing the question is *when* air-raid warnings ought to be given for Berlin. But once an alarm has been sounded everybody must go to the shelters. This view is to be spread by the Party by word of mouth, and the view that taking to air-raid shelters reflects a lack of courage is to be opposed.

Not until the end of September 1940 did Hitler issue a ruling which made it obligatory to go to air-raid shelters once the alarm had been sounded. Goebbels still believed that an alarm should not be given every time British aircraft flew in; he still believed that the loss of life was more acceptable than the loss of production which would arise from the invariable stoppages due to air-raid warnings.

August 31, 1940

In connexion with the air raid on Berlin during the night of Friday to Saturday there is no reason why one should not say that, for instance, two small fires were started at Siemensstadt. The damage in fact is so insignificant that a frank admission will make a better impression than keeping silent about it. To point out the difference between the attacks on Berlin and those on London, the British figures are to be used which state that 700 German aircraft were simultaneously employed in our raids, as compared to only 15 [British] aircraft over Berlin. This comparison will make the difference in effect obvious to anybody.

It should further be emphasized in the reports that this time only three persons were injured – due to the fact that, after the experiences of the last raid, the population displayed superb discipline in going to the air-raid shelters.

At the press conference Major Wodarg is to repeat his reports on the exemplary attitude of the population of Berlin. Immediately after the raid he visited the air-raid shelters where bombs had dropped, and watched the population put out fires, etc.; he has the highest praise for the disciplined, matter-of-fact attitude shown in particular by the workers who, working without complaint or emotion, made an absolutely exemplary impression. The Minister wishes the press to report these matters untendentiously and without dramatizing them.

He expects that this kind of report, far more than instructions or appeals, will produce among the public a kind of rivalry to do equally well in the event of a recurrence. Altogether, reports of raids should not be so extensive in future or go into quite such detail as after the last raid, which merited particular publicity as an incident for window dressing.

On the subject of the funeral of the victims of the last air raid the Minister directs that this should not be turned into a gala event, since the treatment given to the first such ceremony will have to be kept up for future casualties, and a continuous re-enactment of a great state ceremony is not possible. It should also be remembered that it would make a bad impression in the provinces if Berlin were to give quite such prominence to its victims. What the Minister has in mind is a solemn funeral, to be attended by the appropriate Kreisleiter with the local Ortsgruppenleiters.*

The second British air raid on Berlin was made on the night of August 28–29, 1940. High explosive and incendiary bombs were dropped on residential districts in the east of the city, killing and injuring numerous civilians. Military targets were not damaged.

* See the list of Nazi Party ranks, p. 348.

September 3, 1940

The Minister makes some fundamental observations about the likely further course of the war against Britain. Views differ on whether the war in the air alone can achieve the final result, and reports on the effects so far achieved are likewise contradictory. There is no doubt that these effects are considerably greater than the British have so far disclosed. There is no doubt that a nation which is really determined to defend its freedom can be forced to its knees only in hand-to-hand fighting. It is quite another question, however, and one open to doubt, whether Britain has this firm determination. Britain, after all, is waging this war to get rid of a troublesome German competitor – not in order to present a shining example of her love of freedom. It may therefore be expected that some sensible circles will perhaps intervene in time. In order to get a really clear picture one will have to await the development of the next few weeks.

The German press, meanwhile, must only publish truly authentic reports about Britain. Fantasies must be avoided, and foreign comment which at the moment seems too favourable to us had better also be omitted.

W. V. Oven describes the impressions brought back by Goebbels in the summer of 1940 from a visit to General Sperrle's Luftwaffe headquarters. Goebbels, Oven reports, returned to Berlin from Deauville with the worst possible impression. It may well be largely due to this visit that he was from then on clearly no longer convinced of an imminent, overwhelming defeat of the RAF by the German Luftwaffe, or of Britain's early collapse.

It is not certain whether the torpedoing of a British steamer carrying children to Canada is true or a hoax. In any case, however, the foreign language service should retaliate. It should emphasize the irresponsibility of allowing children to sail through the danger zone.

As early as July 18, 1940, Churchill in a letter to the British Home Secretary had sharply condemned any evacuation by sea. After September 17, 1940, the evacuation of children to America was suspended.

September 4, 1940

A simultaneous announcement in London and Washington on September 3, 1940, stated that the United States and Great Britain were planning a deal whereby the United States would put fifty destroyers at the disposal of the British navy in exchange for naval and air bases in the western hemisphere.

The Führer's decision on the treatment of the Anglo-American

Agreement has not yet been received. The Minister points out that it is the more necessary to inform the German public as some preparation is needed in the event that the United States, as now seems likely, will enter the war in the course of the winter unless operations have come to an end before then. In practice such a step would be of very little importance, but the people must be prepared for it. Besides, the Anglo-American Agreement and all that goes with it is evidence of Britain's exceedingly weak military position and is generally seen in that light throughout the world.

The British Home Office had introduced a new air-raid warning system on September 1, 1940, to avoid work in the undamaged armaments factories being interrupted. In future only in the event of an immediate attack was the alarm to be given and the staff sent to the shelters.

On September 7, 1940, Goebbels instructed the secret transmitters to employ socialist arguments in inciting the British workers against staying at their posts during air raids. Reports were to be invented that a factory had been levelled to the ground with 800 workers in it merely because half an hour's production was to be saved by not sounding the air-raid warning.

The foreign language service and the secret transmitters should between them broadcast the fact that the British want to abolish air-raid warnings for their industrial areas. It should be explained to the British workers that they are now doubly and trebly exposed to the risk of bombing while the English lords are sitting in air-raid shelters, having taken their families to places of safety. The Minister of Information, in particular, who has sent his daughter to the United States, is a fine person to call on the workers to stay put in their factories. In this way the British measure should be divested of its patriotic meaning and given a plutocratic character.

September 5, 1940

Major Wodarg transmits a request from the Luftwaffe that all pictures of destruction to buildings, etc., by RAF bombs should be banned immediately, as the British would be bound to discover from these photographs that their fuse settings were totally wrong. The ban is to take immediate effect.

It appears that the ban was in force only for a short time.

September 6, 1940

On September 1, 2 and 3, 1940, demonstrations against the acceptance of the Second Vienna Arbitration Award took place in the Rumanian territories to be ceded to Hungary as well as in Bucharest itself. The demonstrations were suppressed on the instructions of the Rumanian government. On September 4 King Carol II of Rumania (1893–1953) appointed General Antonescu his premier and instructed him to form a new government.

As a result of the Second Vienna Arbitration, King Carol found himself compelled to renounce the Rumanian throne in favour of his son Michael. The abdication took place on September 6, 1940 at 06.00 hours. A few hours later the news was put out over the radio. King Carol's dramatic flight by special train across the Rumanian frontier began the following Saturday. After a number of intermediate stops it ended in Portugal. Carol was accompanied by his faithful woman friend and later wife, Mme Helene (Magda) Lupescu and the Minister of the Royal Household, Ernest Urdarianu, who was an intimate friend of the king's mistress but was not married to her. Mme Lupescu was of Jewish extraction and was said to have been originally called Wolf (Rumanianized to Lupescu). It was she who had tried to check the anti-Jewish excesses in Rumania.

Now that the Rumanian king has abdicated and the need for consideration no longer exists, at least some of the more radical papers in Germany should try to spotlight the character of this decadent monarch, and state quite clearly that it was he who ordered the Rumanian patriots to be shot. Moreover, his affair with Mme Wolf-Lupescu is to be publicized, as well as the fact that he got his mistress married to his court minister so that he could live with her under one roof, and that he then wanted to put this court minister in charge of the anti-Jewish movement.

The Minister is also in favour of the news of the torpedoing of a 12,000 ton troop-transport ship being released to the home public, as otherwise it will only encourage rumours to spread.

In this connexion he suggests to the Luftwaffe in particular that, should the daily number of aircraft shot down for once be to our disadvantage, this fact should be made known to the public without any glossing over, since this more than anything else would underline the credibility of the German OKW communiqués.

On September 2, 1940, the m.v. *Perseus* was sunk by the British while sailing in a German convoy bound for Norway.

Herr Hinkel reports about the expulsion of the Jews from Vienna and Berlin. In Vienna there are 47,000 Jews left out of 180,000, two-thirds of them women and about 300 men between 20 and 35. In spite of the war it has been possible to transport a total of 17,000 Jews to the south-east. Berlin still numbers 71,800 Jews; in future about 500 Jews are to be sent to the south-east each month.

Herr Hinkel reports that all preparations have been made for removing 60,000 Jews from Berlin within a period of four months, mainly to the east, as soon as transport is again available after the end of the war. The remaining 12,000 will likewise have disappeared within a further four weeks.

A few days later Goebbels had this to say on the Jewish question: 'That we were opponents of the Jews was generally known throughout the world, even before 1933. We have, therefore, in any case reaped the disadvantages of anti-Semitism in world propaganda; hence we can afford to enjoy the advantages too, and displace the Jews. Since we are being opposed and calumniated throughout the world as enemies of the Jews, why should we derive only the disadvantages and not also the advantages, i.e. the elimination of the Jews from the theatre, the cinema, public life and administration. If we are then still attacked as enemies of the Jews we shall at least be able to say with a clear conscience: It was worth it, we have benefited from it.'

September 7, 1940

The Minister reports that, contrary to expectations, last night's air raid on Berlin has not produced the effects which are necessary for us to justify to the world, with a howl of indignation, a massive intensification of our attacks on London. It must be understood that the destruction of London would probably represent the greatest human catastrophe in history; this step, therefore, would have to have some justification before the eyes of the world. It is therefore to be hoped that such an opportunity will be provided as soon as possible by a British air raid. In line with the Minister's predictions, the British press is now increasingly churning out humanitarian sentiments (bombed churches, hospitals, women, children, etc.). These tactics are to be countered in good time by pointing out at once that it is easy to feel sorry for the poor English working-class children now that the plutocrats have got their own children away to safety. But no one in Britain had shown pity for the poor mothers in Germany who, as once before, would have fallen victim to the British hunger blockade, and no one would have mentioned the poor German children if they had pitifully starved to death.

Since the German Luftwaffe did not confine itself to attacks on military targets in Britain, Churchill, in spite of all representations of a moral and technical nature, urged that the RAF should make reprisal raids on Germany on one or two nights each month, and thus score against German morale, since wherever the RAF had not been the Germans were told that the German defences were invincible.

The Reich Marshal desires most of the transmitters to be put on the same wavelength from 21.00 hours, which means in practice that one single, Reich-wide programme alone can be put out during the evening. The Minister wants the public to be instructed as promptly as possible about the reasons for this measure.

Major Wodarg remarks in this connexion that penetration into Germany by British bombers will stop anyway the moment our operations, at present directed against the British fighters, can be shifted to the bombers.

September 8, 1940

The Minister issues directives for the press treatment of the full-scale attack on London which will be kept up for a few more days.

(1) Great care should always be taken to maintain our assertion that our attacks are aimed solely at military installations. If civilian targets are hit as well, then this is due to the fact that many military targets are situated in the middle of the built-up area of London.

(2) Such cynical turns of speech, frequently found in British reports, as 'British airmen managed to get a little bombing practice over Nuremberg' should be prominently featured by way of justification for our reprisal measures.

(3) Even though greater speed is important at present, the psychological point of view must not be lost sight of. It is wrong, therefore, to speak in advance of the heavy casualities which our attacks will cause; we must only refer either to very slight casualties or to precise figures. Likewise, it is out of the question even to concede the possibility that German airmen may have aimed their bombs at anything other than military targets. The Minister points out that once a small, partial admission is made by us, much more extensive conclusions would immediately be drawn abroad.

On September 7 there began the second phase of the air war against Britain, designed to destroy Britain's economic potential and demoralize the British population. According to the OKW report on the air situation, about 8,100 high explosive and incendiary bombs of a total weight of 1,500 tons were dropped on London, *et al.*, between September 7 and 11. Aerial photographs, however, showed only about 400 bomb explosions outside gutted buildings. The actual effect, however, was estimated to be greater than revealed by the aerial photographs.

Conducted tours of Berlin for foreign journalists after enemy air raids have lately not produced the hoped-for results abroad. The reports sent abroad have either been distorted, or else the journalists misrepresented the real scale here in Berlin because they were unable to judge accurately the insignificant ratio between the individual bomb incident and a city of millions like Berlin. The Minister agrees that absolutely reliable foreign journalists, such as Spaniards, Italians and Japanese, may continue to be shown around; as for the doubtful journalists, however, they are to be shown a model of Berlin and instructed that the damage about which they are making so much fuss is of no account whatever considering Berlin's size. As an experiment, conducted tours for them are to stop for the time being.

At the end of September 1940 conducted tours for foreign journalists after air raids were banned by the Reich Chancellery. This resulted in anxiety at the Ministry for Propaganda that the diplomatic missions might now start working as news sources for foreign countries.

The destruction of the Church of Our Lady in Hamm by bombing should be featured in a big way in order to keep hatred of the British alive among the German people.

September 10, 1940
The air raids on Berlin and Hamburg during the night of Monday to Tuesday are to be featured prominently with all details inflated as much as possible in order to buttress before the world the justification of our retaliatory measures. Material from the past few months should also be more thoroughly exploited than hitherto in order thus to demonstrate clearly the justification of our measures.

Since, as expected, the British are stepping up their atrocity propaganda, our press and our foreign language service should now emphatically point out that it was Britain who wanted and declared the war, and that whatever is happening now was provoked by Britain in disregard of all our repeated warnings. Besides, it must be emphasized again and again that, unlike the British, we attack only military targets and that the British now have only themselves to blame if, now that the war is rebounding on them, civilians must suffer as well. This argument should by no means be only defensive; it is important that the British system should be exposed time and again.

The foreign language service must always keep in mind that the population of London represents only one-third of the total population of Britain and that it is therefore as important as ever to demoralize the hinterland as well. For a change, Lord Haw-Haw should refer today to the Nostradamus prophecies which seem to be on the point of fulfilment.

The Secret Conferences of Dr. Goebbels

September 11, 1940

In the British air raid on Berlin during the night of September 10–11 damage was caused to, among other buildings, the Brandenburg Gate and the Reichstag building.

The British raid on Berlin during the night of Tuesday to Wednesday is to be castigated by the press with burning indignation as an attack on our national symbols. As a general rule, however, in the interests of good coverage, the press should not publish a complete spread until the morning papers, unless, of course, individual papers have done enough groundwork on their own and not just followed the lead given at the press conference.

Moreover, the casualties of British air raids are to be listed again, and it should be pointed out that the British have lied inasmuch as they have represented the number of *children* killed in Germany as the *total number* of persons killed. Herr Braeckow should, therefore, also find out the number of adults killed and pass it on to the press.

On September 11 the press was informed that during the period from May 10 to September 10, 1940, British air raids on Reich territory caused the death not of 1,500 but only of 617 people. This figure, however, was not to be published since the same number of people were being killed in London by German air raids every day.

On September 11, 1940, before an audience of 'Czech cultural workers and journalists,' Goebbels delivered a speech which was quite typical of his propaganda technique. With a skilful mixture of threats and persuasion he disclosed a few prospects of the future 'new order in Europe.' To this new order the Czechs would have to submit like everyone else. Goebbels said: 'For that reason, gentlemen – and I am now speaking in terms of realistic politics without any appeal to sentiment – whether you approve of this state of affairs or not is of no account; whether you welcome it in your heart or not is irrelevant; you will not change the actual state of affairs. Now I believe that if one cannot change a state of affairs and if in any event one has to accept the very real, existing disadvantages of such a state of affairs, it would be foolish not to try to profit also from its advantages ... This is a thing which you and which the Czech people must decide. Don't tell me the Czech people want this or that. I think I may claim a certain experience in the field of public-opinion guidance. A people thinks as its intelligentsia teaches it to think; it always holds the views which its intellectual leaders hold ... As I have said, we offer you the opportunity of collaboration ... I invite you, therefore, to speak to the Czech people along these lines. If *we* were to do so the Czech people would not believe us. ...'

September 12, 1940

We should refrain from reports which might convey the impression that London will be finished in the next few days. It is also in our military interest to represent the resistance of the British people as being, for the moment, undaunted. Appropriate comment from neutral sources should be continually interspersed with the German reports. In doing so, of course, the monumental character of our attacks on London must continue to stand out clearly.

The press had been instructed by teleprinter on September 11 to be more careful with foreign reports suggesting that London had had enough or that the morale of the population was undermined, or that British resistance had suffered. For the next few days an intensification of the air raids could be expected, but such an intensification would not make sense if an impression were created prematurely that the enemy was already reeling under Germany's blows.

The anti-Semitic 'documentary film' *Der Ewige Jude* (*The Eternal Jew*) had its première in Berlin on November 28, 1940. Dr Fritz Hippler was responsible for producing the film. The script was by Dr Eberhard Taubert.

Since in the view of the Deputy Gauleiter, the Police President and numerous journalists the Jewish film in its present version is suitable only for people with strong nerves, two versions are to be produced, the milder one intended for women and juveniles. The version which includes the ritual slaughter scenes is to be shown by the Party in closed performances, but maybe *one* of the daily performances in the cinemas could show this more graphic version provided the public has been accurately instructed on the subject in the press beforehand.

September 15, 1940

Destruction caused to Buckingham Palace by German bombs had been given much publicity in the London press, both in reports and pictures.

Major Wodarg is to ascertain whether there are any military targets in the vicinity of Buckingham Palace; if not, it should be asserted, in the event of foreign agitation being further stepped up, that secret military stores are concealed in its immediate neighbourhood. No details are to be published about the damage.

September 16, 1940

As for the British attempts to present Sunday as a great British victory, with figures inflated even by British standards (allegedly 185 aircraft shot down), the press should reply that the effect of our raid on London that day was presumably particularly heavy so that the British must now appease their public with this kind of lie. The foreign language service must in particular counter the suggestion that this was a British victory.

The report of September 16, 1940, on the German air situation stated that aerial combat over London on September 15 had not been as successful as usual. There had been inadequate fighter cover. German losses, it claimed, had been 50 aircraft; enemy losses had been 79.

The British Air Ministry announced on September 16 that 175 German aircraft had been shot down in an air battle over the Kentish coast. The OKW communiqué put German losses at 43 aircraft.

September 17, 1940

The Minister describes it as a grave insult to decency that the Swedes, following an official special session to investigate the anti-German articles in the *Göteborgs Handels- och Sjöfarts Tidning,* should have merely decided to withdraw on the 17th the issue of the 13th, which contained an anti-German article. In practice this measure is nothing but a grave mockery of the German point of view. Dr Bömer is to make it clear to the Swedish press attaché that the only adequate amends would have been an immediate ban on the paper, and Herr Fritzsche is to authorize a few papers to deal in the strongest possible terms with this shameless provocation.

Herr Hinkel reports about the age breakdown of the 72,327 Jews still in Berlin:

Under 18	3,900 men	4,000 women
18 to 45	7,000 men	11,000 women
45 to 60	9,000 men	14,000 women
60 and over	11,000 men	15,000 women

In addition, 15,727 Jews from the Old Reich [Germany within her pre-Anschluss frontiers] have been deported via south-east Europe during the period from 1.9.1939 to 1.9.1940, in spite of the war and closed frontiers.

Altogether the following totals are present:

Old Reich, including newly-acquired eastern provinces	743,000 Jews
Government-General [of Poland]	2,300,000

Protectorate of Bohemia:		
Moravia		77,000
Belgium		80,000
Holland		160,000
Luxemburg		2,500
France		270,000
Total	approx.	4,000,000

The Madagascar project, which has been approved, provides for the deportation within about eighteen months from the end of the war of about 3,500,000 Jews from the above total.

The project for the deportation of all Jews to Madagascar after the war was first considered by Hitler about October-November 1938. In doing so he appears to have taken up a demand raised in Poland in connexion with anti-Semitic excesses. The project envisaged the setting up of an autonomous Jewish reservation in Madagascar under a German police commander. The project increasingly became a piece of fiction as the war continued, and was officially abandoned in February 1942. It is believed that Hitler dropped the idea immediately after the capitulation of France and at that time ordered Himmler to pursue the accelerated annihilation of European Jewry by other means.

September 18, 1940
The Minister wishes a good deal of prominence to be given to a comparison of aircraft shot down on both sides since the beginning of the battle of London. The prominence should be such that the foreign press, too, will be induced to take up the story.

According to the OKW communiqués the RAF lost a total of 2,096 machines during August and the first two weeks of September. Goebbels did not, of course, realize the full implications of German and British reports of aircraft losses; in particular, he could not know that the German Luftwaffe was altogether in no position to conduct a strategic bombing or air war against Britain.

On the subject of the *Göteborgs Handels- och Sjöfarts Tidning* Herr Dr Bömer and Herr Fritzsche report that the Ministry of Foreign Affairs has asked that no verbal attacks should be made for the time being; negotiations are at present in progress to discover whether the king, who has full understanding for the German point of view, might simply override the restrictions imposed on him by the Swedish constitution and take action himself. The Minister directs that in the circumstances the Ministry of Foreign Affairs should be informed that we would wait another week; if, however, the *Göteborgs Handels- och Sjöfarts Tidning* should make any more false moves then the German press will hit back most vigorously without prior consultation.

September 19, 1940

The press is again to be reminded that it may attack British policy and in particular British air-force policy in whatever sharp terms it chooses; but it must not abuse individual pilots as cowards (or similar) when they are doing exactly the same as our own airmen.

Since August 1940 the German press repeatedly carried banner headlines about the British 'air pirates', etc. The British press, when referring to the German Luftwaffe, for its part employed similar terms, with an increasingly frequent use of the term 'terror bomber' which subsequently found its way into the German media. However, on September 16, 1940, the German press was forbidden to use the term 'air pirates' in headlines. Other prohibited terms were 'air gangsters' and 'flying mercenaries'.

September 20, 1940

Very considerable prominence should be given to the report that British censorship has been tightened up so that virtually no report will now be allowed out of the country unless Herr Churchill wants it. On the other hand we should avoid creating the impression, on the strength of the few reports at our disposal, that London has already had its vital nerve hit. The Minister emphasizes that this moment has not yet come. Altogether, he wants to play it safe, and for that reason the British collapse must come *before* the date which will be considered likely in Germany on the strength of our publications, and not afterwards. In no event is this collapse merely a matter of days.

On September 3, 1940, the German press received a strictly confidential background report on the situation in Britain. This stated that Hitler had not yet decided on a date for the landing. British air raids on German installations along the Channel coast would certainly be 'uncomfortable', but would not change anything decisively. The aim of the German air raids had been to paralyse London and destroy the country's main communications and economic centres. In spite of successes achieved, however, it had not so far been possible to realize the hope nurtured by certain people that the invasion might be altogether avoided with air attacks alone. The British air force was not yet smashed. That was true for the bombers and also for the fighter force which the British would wish to preserve for the event of an invasion. Altogether, the invasion depended on the weather, and in particular on the sea, especially as the bulk of the craft used for the landing would be flat-bottomed. The postponement of the invasion, however, could also be due to political reasons, since Germany was preparing a 'great colonial campaign'. 'Surely it is well known that the Führer has never undertaken two major actions at the same time.'

The foreign language service is to start its English transmissions in future with the sentence: 'British people, don't forget: Lord Derby said you'll have a delightful war!* How delightful this war is, we will now show you in our news bulletin.'

In this connexion the Minister rules that daily polemics with the German transmissions of the British radio are not desirable since these transmissions are not being listened to in Germany and are unknown to the British anyway.

September 24, 1940

On the subject of the Anglo-French incident at Dakar the Minister directs that the press must not report this in a form which might trigger off a new wave of sympathy for France.

British naval units on September 23, 1940, attacked the French North African fortress of Dakar in order to seize the harbour and land General de Gaulle's troops. The operation was foiled by the opposition of French formations loyal to Vichy. The French air force, moreover, made a reprisal raid on Gibraltar.

In reply to a question by Herr Direktor Dittmar about the best way of releasing information, the Minister decides that information had best be so issued that it appears to be without comment but instead bears a built-in bias. That there *must* be bias in our news handling is obvious; but it had best remain invisible.

As Lord Derby's alleged remarks about the 'delightful war' cannot be attested, the foreign language service had better stop exploiting it as a slogan. On the other hand, there is no reason why it should not continue to be used by the German press or as an occasional quotation.

(*Cf.* September 20, 1940.)

* Although this quotation from Lord Derby was not reliably attested (*cf.* Sept. 24, 1940), Goebbels continued to work it hard. In his editorial article in *Das Reich* (Dec. 22, 1940), he said that Lord Derby had welcomed Australian units in Britain with the words: 'You'll have a delightful war!'

September 25, 1940

Last night's air raid on Berlin should again be given much prominence, but care should be taken not to reveal any details which could provide the British with important information. Moreover, the incident must not be so inflated as to allow Churchill to exploit the German reports for creating the impression among the British public that our raids on London and the British raids on Germany are roughly balancing out.

September 27, 1940

The solemn ceremony at which the Tripartite Pact between Germany, Italy and Japan was signed took place on September 27, 1940.

The press must be dominated entirely by the events of mid-day; it is the task of both the press and the radio to explain the exceptional importance of the pact and to show what a heavy blow it is to Britain.

'The Home Front does not complain . . .'
October–December 1940

October 2, 1940

The Minister points out that an unmistakable wave of optimism and make-believe is at present being spread by London over the whole of Britain and possibly also over the world as a whole. A counter-offensive is to be mounted at once; this too should, if possible, get a hold on world opinion. In particular, the methods of the British should be unmasked by a systematic campaign; it should be shown, on the example of the foundation of the 'Iron Front'* (which likewise reflected no real gain in strength) that hollow phrases without any substance behind them are intended to deceive the world and that this entire manoeuvre is possible only because outwardly Britain still possesses some power. It should further be pointed out that Britain now represents as an outstanding victory the fact that she was not smashed in September.

October 3, 1940

Major Wodarg should look into the question of why SHD men† have again been employed in the disposal of time bombs; six of these men were killed in the process. The Minister recalls his earlier suggestion that Polish prisoners should be used for this work; similarly, convicts could be employed on this job, but on no account should valuable German people be needlessly exposed to danger.

Shirer, *Berlin Diary*, p. 494, reports that concentration camp inmates were largely used for defusing unexploded bombs.

The Minister points out that it continues to be virtually impossible to

---

* Formed in 1932 from the 'Black, Red and Gold Reichsbanner', the fighting organization of the Social Democrats and the trade unions. The new organization had great propaganda appeal. *Tr.*

† Sicherheits- und Hilfsdienst (Safety and Auxiliary Service), a voluntary organization composed largely of elderly people, rather like the ARP in Britain. *Tr.*

form a clear picture of real conditions in London. It has lately become known that the American embassy in London has sent back to the United States some quite catastrophic reports, but that these are contradicted by reports from other observers. In any case, the illusion at present cultivated would suggest that London considers it necessary to do something for public morale. That is why the campaign against this make-believe must be continued. The secret transmitter should in this connexion take up the allegation spread by the British that German aircraft losses were now so great that 5,000 Italian aircraft had to be switched to the French coast. The transmitter should point out that surely this report gives no cause for joy; on the contrary, it proves that the British Mediterranean fleet is not even able to tie down Italian forces there.

The report that the British are planning to employ the Gibraltar Barbary apes in operations against the Axis Powers is to be killed, since this is all too obviously a joke.

On the subject of the British cabinet change, the Minister desires the sharpest possible commentaries – to the effect that the two greatest warmongers, Daladier and Chamberlain, have been forced to resign, with Chamberlain now similarly accompanied by the curses of his own people. Chamberlain is to be pilloried as the man who found the most honeyed words for peace but in fact had been agitating for war in every possible way.

Chamberlain left the British cabinet because of ill health. Morrison took over the Home Office while Anderson became Lord President of the Council responsible for Home Affairs. Chamberlain died at his country home in Hampshire on November 9, 1940.

In connexion with the evacuation of children cases are reported when officials are said to have declared that although this was described to the public as a voluntary evacuation it was in fact a compulsory evacuation *after all.* Party Comrade Böker is to inform the Kreisleiters immediately that the Minister will hold them personally responsible to see that such cases do not occur again; should the Minister come to hear of a similar case then the person spreading such rumours must expect to find himself in a concentration camp. In this connexion Major Martin reports that the OKW has forestalled the possible effect of rumours about compulsory evacuation among servicemen at the front by sending telegraphic instructions for these rumours to be officially contradicted. At the Minister's request, the announcement authorized by him is also to be published in all frontline newspapers.

The evacuation of children came as a shock to the German population; it gave rise to the worst possible anxiety about the war in the air. The public quite naturally noted the discrepancy between the evacuation of the children and the propaganda claims about German air superiority.

Herr Dr Bömer reports the case of an officer allegedly having spread the rumour by telephone that the British would make a gas attack. The Minister directs that Herr Dr Bömer should pass on his information to Major Martin for investigation; he proposes that, in the event of the information being confirmed, the report must be widely published that the man in question has been arrested. As a general rule the Minister lays it down that at a time when the public is already very nervous because it has to readjust itself to the possibility of a second winter of war, measures against panic-mongering must be doubly brutal, and ruthless examples must be made wherever proved instances of rumour-mongering are ascertained.

October 7, 1940
The Minister wishes the anti-illusion campaign to be conducted in the same way as was done on Sunday afternoon and Monday morning. He points out that Britain is now faced with the choice of either surrendering or, by way of ruthless lies and bluff, pretending that there are still good prospects for the future. He recalls that Britain was on the brink of capitulation in World War One and merely cheated her way out of a difficult situation by bluff. This time, Germany must show the world that she does not dream of being caught by the British bluff and that she remains unimpressed by anything except facts. What these facts look like can be gauged from the circumstance that some 23 tons of high-explosive bombs have so far been dropped on Berlin, whereas 7,000 tons have been dropped on London. If one realizes the meaning of these figures one can gain a picture of what really lies behind the British illusionist reports. For this reason the German press must ceaselessly endeavour to paralyse the British campaign, regardless of whether the press finds this boring or not. Naturally, in doing so it should not create the impression that Britain is on the verge of collapse; nevertheless it should describe Britain's hopeless position each day and show how every report coming from Britain reflects Churchill's policy of bluff. Until the Minister countermands this order the press is to keep up this campaign.

The Minister's attention has been drawn by Herr Berndt to the danger that with the continuing suspension of our broadcasts the British news service is gaining a dominant position. In point of fact, British news is already being broadcast in German eight times a day. Herr Gutterer is therefore to make serious representations to the Luftwaffe Operations Staff, emphasizing the great danger, especially during the winter months when the population can perhaps no longer go to the cinema or the theatre because air raids will start earlier with the earlier onset of darkness. Under these circumstances the radio will be indispensable as an instrument of guidance; likewise we cannot allow this most acute weapon, where foreign countries are concerned, to be knocked out of our hands. The question should therefore be re-examined of whether the dangers of a further curtailment of our broadcasts may not be greater than the advantage derived.

October 8, 1940

The British air raid on Berlin during the night of Monday–Tuesday was the heaviest Berlin has experienced so far: twenty-five people were killed and fifty injured. While only slight damage was caused to industrial and military installations, three hospitals were hit, as well as a cemetery chapel, a maternity home and forty residential buildings. The press must make a big splash about how the whole world can now see the real nature of the 'carefully selected targets' of the British. The foreign journalists resident in Berlin should be conducted round the non-military targets in particular, to gain an impression of the scale of the attack on the civilian population.

Moreover, the Minister rules that foreign journalists are henceforth forbidden to send out reports either about the timing or about the duration of air raids.

In the British air raid on Berlin during the night of October 7–8, 1940, between 02.00 and 03.00, the Robert Koch Hospital was hit. Direct hits were also scored on the Army Clothing Office, an army equipment store, the Stettiner railway station and the Moabit goods station. According to the German report on the air situation, two persons were killed by flak shells detonating on the ground.

The Minister points out that the first Reich street collection this year has shown a slight decline compared to last year's collection. Herr Gutterer, however, demonstrates that this decline is not due to morale but solely to the fact that last year the collection was organized by the DAF [Deutsche Arbeitsfront – German Labour Front] with all its great facilities, whereas this year it was run by youth sports organizations. This year's result, therefore, represents the net collection result without those additional amounts which the DAF is able to provide.

The Minister points out that the collection results are more important indications of the mood of the population than an election, and that notice would certainly have to be taken of a more marked and well-founded decline. He agrees with the view of Herr Hinkel that sports [organizations] must not in future be made solely responsible for a collection.

Since Goebbels invariably saw the results of WHW [Winterhilfswerk – Winter Relief Scheme] and Red Cross collections as a barometer of public morale, he usually feared that a drop in the collection result reflected a drop in morale – which in fact was frequently the case. He first revealed his alarm in August 1940 when the collection result in Berlin for the German Red Cross was appreciably lower than that in Munich. The Red Cross collection in May 1941 also produced far less than in the preceding year. Nevertheless the published figures showed 'donations' increasing year after year.

October 9, 1940
The Minister discusses the question of whether we can continue to accept without contradiction British allegations that power stations and other important targets in Berlin or in other parts of Germany have been destroyed by air raids. The effect of such reports in Britain, he points out, must be to give the British the impression that the war is being waged with approximately equal results on both sides and that it is therefore only a question of who has the longer arm and who can stand the attacks longer. It is thus no longer possible to give defeatist propaganda sufficient scope. It would now be far more effective to convince the British again and again that, although they are hitting civilian targets in Germany – and even those only on a scale totally inadequate for Britain compared with what we are doing to the British – they have hit virtually no military targets at all. It is therefore necessary for the Luftwaffe Operations Staff to examine once more whether a further undermining of British morale is not considerably more impor- tant than the reasons which the Luftwaffe Operations Staff adduces in support of the tactics demanded by it. It is, moreover, doubtful whether the British would really not order any further bombing of military targets which they have once reported as hit – just as the British airmen are quite patently still able to penetrate to Berlin even after the transmitters have been switched off. The Minister again emphasizes the danger that we are voluntarily surrendering an effective weapon in two fields, just before the onset of winter. We are voluntarily surrendering the ether and we are voluntarily waiving our chance of refuting British propaganda lies.
On the subject of the new SD report the Minister observes that,

although the account of the drop in public morale seems to him rather too pessimistic, he too regards it as necessary for the press to do more than in the past to see that interest in military matters does not decline any further.

On September 26, 1940, it was reported that public morale continued to be good. The public expected Britain's defeat but hardly hoped that this would come about before the beginning of winter. The SD report of October 7, 1940 showed that interest in military developments had declined and that the public was unenthusiastically and reluctantly reconciling itself to the idea of a second winter of war. Daily worries were becoming more important. An exceptionally large number of Germans, moreover, were grumbling about the monotony of the information supplied by the daily press.

October 11, 1940

The Minister points emphatically to the need for the public opinion-moulding media to avoid more than ever anything that might further depress an already nervous public. During the summer months and the great events that occurred in them propaganda was able to work more in the manner of a woodcut, and the individual omission or slip-up was not then very important. Now, however, psychological mistakes must be avoided at all costs, since even trivial occurrences would be unfavourably exploited by grumblers.

Thus the problem of air-raid shelters, for example, must at all costs be kept out of the press. On other issues, such as coal supplies, the population is urgently demanding information, and Herr Fritzsche must therefore see to it that the people are at long last told something about the matter in the near future. In these matters the Ministry must not submit to what are called the given circumstances; it must not, for example, reconcile itself to the fact that the Commissioner for Coal will not make an announcement until he has spoken to the Reich Marshal, but we must insist that the necessary statement is made at the moment the Ministry considers right. Whereas in the summer our propaganda, as it were, was running on its own momentum, it will undoubtedly again have to receive priority during the coming winter. For that reason it must vigorously enforce its point of view wherever it feels this is necessary. As in the past winter, this will frequently entail painstaking treatment of what may appear to be trivialities. One must not lose sight of the fact that the people no longer go for grand phrases such as 'Just wait and see! Now comes our retribution!' but want factual arguments.

In particular, the propaganda struggle must now be waged vigorously against British attempts at undermining German morale. The major papers should now openly take up this question.

Until the end of October 1940 there was 'some confusion' in Germany about the air-raid precautions to be taken. It was widely believed that air-raid shelters did not provide adequate protection. At the conference of October 23, 1940, Goebbels reported on the results of an investigation on whether it was any safer to take to an air-raid shelter than to remain in the street. In Berlin so far, 32 persons had been killed in the streets and 33 in shelters; it would be absurd, he said, to interpret these figures as showing that the degree of safety was about the same in both places. After all, there was at most one-tenth of the population in the streets whereas ninety per cent were in the shelters. Besides, there was no longer any need to argue the point since the Führer had meanwhile issued an order which made it obligatory to go to the shelters in the event of an air-raid warning.

On October 23, 1940, the Reich Commissioner for Coal, Walther, delivered his long-delayed address to representatives of the German press; this was by no means favourably received by everyone. He declared that gaps in coal supplies, which had occurred in the east of the Reich, would be closed during the next few weeks. He said: 'By introducing compulsory rationing we have achieved, probably for the first time, a state of affairs when, with very slight exceptions, every German household possesses an adequate coal supply.' He added, however: 'For the duration of the war every German must tell himself that every quintel of coal he saves will be saved in the interest of Germany.' The Reich Commissioner for Coal was over-optimistic. On March 10, 1941, it was observed at the conference that there was no guarantee of future coal supplies. There was even a danger, it was said, that certain industrial plants might have to be closed down because of a coal shortage.

Since the OKW has now released the appropriate figures, the following juxtapositions are to be made: the course of events in Berlin and in London over the past fortnight, the amounts of high explosives dropped to date over the two cities, and the number of dead and wounded in London and in Berlin. By no means, however, should the impression be created that this is a race for the greatest number of civilians killed; on the contrary, we should display extreme indignation even over low figures of persons killed, and in this way ruin the effect which Churchill is aiming at among the British: 'Of course things are bad, but the Germans are no better off, and because we British are tougher we shall win the war.'

We must eliminate the view that the effects of the war are imposing about the same degree of strain on both countries; this must be countered by pointing to the hopeless situation which must inevitably lead to the destruction of London. The British must, moreover, be convinced that even if they succeeded in bringing their air force to the same numerical strength as the German air force, London, because of the German Luftwaffe's shorter approach flight, would still have to expect ten times the weight of bombs compared with Berlin.

The foreign language service alone had until then been allowed to contradict British reports of 1,700 people allegedly killed by the bombing of Berlin, by quoting the real figure of (until then) 77 victims. At the end of October, when London reports eventually spoke of 2,871 killed in Berlin, although their total had only increased by 12, Goebbels's demand for a concrete 'balance-sheet' on the effects of the air raids on London and Berlin was still not approved by the Führer's headquarters. There it was rightly feared that such a balance-sheet might all too strikingly, in the eyes of the world, contradict the German propaganda claim that the Luftwaffe attacks were aimed exclusively at military targets. The fact that it was Germany which had started the large-scale bombing of civilian targets was by then no longer to be denied.

Major Martin is to compare the prisoners-of-war figure contained in the British casualty list with the actual number. If the figure claimed by the British proves false, then press and radio should brand the mendacious British assertion as a standard lie and exploit this fact on the largest possible scale and with all means at our disposal.

According to a presumably unofficial AP report from London about the total losses of the British army since the outbreak of the war, 1,770 British servicemen were in German or Italian captivity. Yet, according to the official British casualty list of November 30, 1940, their total came to 32,219. It was claimed that more than 38,000 British prisoners had been counted in German camps, as reported in the *Völkischer Beobachter* on December 5, 1940.

October 14, 1940

The Minister points out that a certain sagging of morale has at present occurred in the Reich because the people have now got to reconcile themselves to the probability of another winter of war whereas until now, due partly to some clumsy measures – there was a hope that the war might be finished before the end of this year. While it should not be said in so many words that the war will, after all, now run on into next year, this must nevertheless be made clear by various measures. It is the more important that everything be avoided which might in any way promote grumbling. This presupposes an exceedingly sensitive handling of press policy and it is therefore not acceptable that the Ministry of Foreign Affairs should try to turn the press exclusively into a servant of diplomacy.

October 21, 1940

The Minister relates how, on his visit to France, he has been able personally to convince himself of the precision and thoroughness with which the air war is being conducted on the German side, and what an excellent impression he has gained above all of the men who are waging this struggle. He has become even more convinced that London is presenting the world with the most grandiose bluff imaginable, and that real conditions must be infinitely worse than is admitted by the British communiqués. It should be borne in mind that Britain's collapse will probably occur without prolonged preliminary warning; a number of brittle points already exist but the real collapse will come suddenly. Needless to say, in a gigantic contest between two gigantic empires one cannot expect one contestant to remain entirely unscathed while the other is being beaten to pulp.

The press, the foreign language service and our entire propaganda machine should explain these considerations more fully than hitherto, but in a cautious manner. They should show that the daily attacks on London are by no means a 'boring spectacle' but that they are part of a military operation of grand design. The papers should also give more publicity than in the past to the type of German airman who with modesty and with contempt for death wages this struggle against Britain. The German people should realize the respect they owe these men.

The historic character of what is happening at this moment should be made quite clear to the German people; there must be no doubt left that one day this struggle will be decided finally and unequivocally in our favour.

From October 17 to 19, 1940, Goebbels made a tour of the occupied French territories and also visited Luftwaffe units stationed on the Channel coast. Shortly before his flight out to the Luftwaffe bases in France the Luftwaffe liaison officer, Wodarg, had warned him: 'Herr Reichsminister, London will be our Verdun in the air.' By the end of October 1940 the Luftwaffe had lost 1,733 aircraft in the Battle of Britain, while British aircraft losses totalled 915. Within roughly two and a half months from mid-August, the Luftwaffe therefore lost about three-quarters of the fighters and bombers on its operational strength.

October 22, 1940

From an exhaustive discussion of the question of why the British do not come over on certain nights when an attack on Berlin would technically be possible, it emerges that even the Luftwaffe itself does not know the reasons for this behaviour. From the experience of World War One and also from the experience made by the NSDAP at the time of its struggle for power, the Minister concludes that we should avoid reading too much into our opponents' actions. The systematic character which marks our own work is totally unknown in other countries, he explains;

there a great deal is done by improvization. In 1918, too, there was total chaos in Britain and the unfortunate outcome of the war was due solely to that fact that we lost our nerve prematurely.

October 24, 1940
Field Marshal Milch [Inspector-General of the Luftwaffe] has made a request, setting out his reasons at some length, that no independent reporting about air raids should be permitted in the future. Herr Fritzsche is to study these instructions and pass them on to the press. If on some point or another he feels that the ruling may do more harm than good he is to get in touch with the Luftwaffe Operations Staff with a view to a possible relaxation. Generally speaking, however, the Minister considers the instruction correct and appropriate.

In a letter of October 23, 1940, Milch, acting on Göring's orders, informed the Ministry for Propaganda as follows: 'I request you to see to it, by immediate instruction to all officials concerned within your sphere, that in future there is no independent reporting whatever about enemy air raids which have taken place, or about their effects. In view of the intensification of the air war it is unacceptable in future that the enemy should be able to draw any important conclusions whatever from German publications about the effectiveness of his methods of attack or about the extent of damage caused. This was to apply also to air raids on Berlin, where in each individual case the appropriate report was to be discussed between the Ministry for Propaganda and the Commander-in-Chief of the Luftwaffe. Any officially-guided reporting beyond the OKW communiqué would be considered only in cases when the population had suffered particularly heavily as a result of air raids or when 'an exaggeration of the damage caused is expressly desired for propaganda purposes by the highest quarters.'

The Minister voices a reproof that his numerous suggestions for the press have remained ignored, above all by the *Berliner Börsen-Zeitung,* and that, instead, this paper has certainly not published any more interesting reports or articles of its own. The Minister points out that we must forcibly get the press back to the conditions of last winter. During the uneventful months ahead nothing can be achieved by featuring news alone. It is urgently necessary to take up the sharpest polemics once more, in the old familiar way, as public hostility to Britain is quite undoubtedly beginning to weaken and indeed a certain respect for the stubbornness of the British is being encountered instead. Herr Fritzsche maintains that even so the BBZ is more compliant than the *DAZ* [*Deutsche Allgemeine Zeitung*]. The Minister directs that Herr Fritzsche should summon the leading papers to a special conference some time, when he should explain to them calmly and factually that it is their task to supply some amusing and good substitute for all those things which cannot at the moment be offered to the reader. It is certainly not easy, but the attempt must be made again and again to captivate the public. There is no doubt that at present the papers are no longer sufficiently interesting. Indeed, with some papers, on has the clear impression that they are boring because they are prevented for the moment from discussing a number of topics. The reader, however, must at all costs be given an opportunity of finding at least some subjects to get his teeth into. A gingering up of the papers is therefore again urgently needed.

October 28, 1940

On the strength of observations made on his trips to Danzig and Vienna the Minister presents a picture of the mood among the German people. He expresses the view that the slight depression in morale which had been noticeable over the past few weeks could rapidly be shaken off again. In his speeches in Danzig and Vienna he used the arguments which have been put forward for comment at the ministerial conference over the past few weeks. The arguments, which to a small circle of propaganda experts have already seemed outdated, have produced such tumultuous applause at public meetings as he can hardly remember from the period of the Party's struggle for power. The Minister believes that the depression in the morale of the German people can in a very short period of time be shaken off by suitable means and by the application of suitable arguments. He directs that banner headlines representing military events in a glaring manner must disappear at once. It is bound to be repulsive in the long run if day after day the press creates the impression: tomorrow Britain will collapse. The German people are prepared to fight stubbornly for their victory and they can therefore be told quite calmly that a worldwide empire, such as the British, does not collapse in a matter of weeks. In other words, military reports and political arguments should be balanced in the papers. Sound, well-balanced polemics should alternate with reports of military successes. The German press should embark on a subtly mounted campaign of clever, convincing arguments against Britain. Needless to say, military reports of great importance must continue to be given appropriate treatment. The Minister's criticism is aimed merely at the tendency to let political arguments slip into the background compared to the daily reports of the bombing of London.

October 30, 1940

At the conference of October 28, 1940, Goebbels had instructed Gutterer to get in touch with Freisler and to request him 'to pass on to him for publication during the next fortnight details of a number of heavy sentences of penal servitude up to terms of seven or eight years.'

The Minister instructs Ministerialdirektor Gutterer to make further representations with State Secretary Freisler on the subject of heavy sentences of penal servitude for radio offenders. Ministerialdirektor Gutterer is to point out to the SD and the police that the enemy radio is again being listened to on an increasing scale. The Minister demands heavy sentences for radio offenders because, at this decisive phase of the war, every German must be clear in his mind that listening in to these broadcasts represents an act of serious sabotage.

The Roman Catholic Bishop of Speyer attributes Germany's victory over France to 'the favour of the Holy Virgin' and calls on his believers to give financial support to the building of a new church, so that they shall be protected against enemy air raids. Ministerialdirektor Gutterer and Major Martin are to make it perfectly clear to the German bishops that in this day and age it is no longer possible to attribute the military victories of our Wehrmacht to religious glorification.

November 1, 1940
The Minister announces the Führer's instructions that the greatest possible reserve is to be shown by the media in dealing with France. Neither should positive features be underlined nor negative ones criticized; until further notice they should confine themselves to factual reports.

Hitler had met Marshal Pétain at Montoire on October 24, 1940, but his hopes of persuading France to enter the war against Britain were in no way fulfilled.

The Minister directs that, at the next suitable opportunity, the following considerations should be put before the German people: The British are saying: Napoleon could not defeat us. Against this it should be pointed out that Napoleon had set up a tyrannical rule in Europe and that this had been opposed, in varying alliances, by three of the great powers of the day – Russia, Prussia and Austria. Today Britain has no continental sword left anywhere in Europe.

The Soviet Foreign Minister Molotov visited Berlin from November 12 to 14, 1940 and discussed political issues with Hitler, Göring and Ribbentrop. The conversations with Hitler did not lead to any agreement and in fact ended in failure, since the Russians would neither let themselves be induced to move against Britain nor relinquish in Germany's favour their spheres of interest in the Balkans and the Black Sea.

On November 10, 1940, the press received the following directive: 'In connexion with Molotov's imminent visit to Berlin attention should be drawn to the development of German-Russian relations since last year, with reference to Ribbentrop's visits to Moscow and the agreements then arrived at. The non-aggression pact between Germany and the Soviet Union then marked the climax and crowning conclusion of those negotiations. In this connexion mention should be made of British attempts at interference which were then, and still are, designed to drive a wedge between Germany and Russia. . . .'

On November 11, 1940, the following directive was issued: 'Molotov's visit is to be evaluated as a political event. Presentation must be based on factual points and we must not create the impression in the world that we are rubbing our hands with glee at the visit. Without indulging in speculations about Molotov's talks in Berlin the visit must be assessed as a political factor in German-Russian relations. In a historical review it may then be pointed out that both Germany and Russia have always benefited from an alignment, whereas any clash has always harmed them . . . Attention should also be drawn to futile British attempts at spreading, not only illusions about military successes, but also about political successes, such as the attempt to present Russia as a political friend of Britain. This is something which Britain would like the United States, in particular, to believe.'

On November 14, 1940, according to the Slogan of the Day, Molotov's departure from Berlin was to provide the lead for the press, with the joint final communiqué to be the central feature. Molotov's visit, the communiqué said, had again served the 'renewal and deepening' of friendly relations between Germany and the USSR. It continued: 'Topical questions of interest to the two countries were examined in personal conversations between the Führer and Herr Molotov, and in detailed and friendly conversations between the Foreign Minister and Herr Molotov, and it was found that agreement exists between the two governments in their assessment of all important questions. Germany regards the policy embarked upon last year as a firm and durable basis for collaboration. . . .'

November 15, 1940

The Minister informs the conference of the exceptional success of a large-scale German air raid on the British aircraft armaments centre of Coventry. This operation should be given a great deal of prominence in the press.

About 500 German aircraft attacked Coventry on November 14, 1940. The city centre was wrecked and some 400 persons were killed. However, Coventry's aero-engine and machine-tool factories were not put out of action.

November 26, 1940

We don't want to have a sentimental Christmas atmosphere created just yet, from the beginning of Advent. This must be confined exclusively to Christmas Eve and Christmas Day. Even then the feast of Christmas itself should be fitted into the framework of present-day happenings. A sloppy Christmas tree atmosphere lasting several weeks is out of tune with the militant mood of the German people.

Next year the press will not take so much notice of the long string of traditional Christian holidays in November. All this blubbing and mourning throughout November is unsoldierly and un-German. Only November 9 is dedicated to the remembrance of the dead.

December 2, 1940

On the attitude of our press the Minister makes the following observation: reports coming from Britain at the moment reflect rather pessimistically and in considerable detail the effect produced by the large-scale attacks of the German Luftwaffe on British provincial towns. The German press should not give too much space to reaction from various sources to these attacks, although these comments may be utilized fully in working for the foreign readership. The Minister believes that it would be a mistake to bring to the knowledge of the German people this 'pessimistic wave' in Britain. For if it turns out to be no more than a temporary mood of crisis, then the broad mass of people in Germany will have been excited needlessly.

As a general rule the Minister directs that reports published in the German press may reflect in full the extent of the destruction, while strictly avoiding the drawing of any political conclusions from the scale of the present attacks.

The Minister points out that the present pessimistic note in the British press may very well be designed to induce America to take a more active part in the war. For that reason alone caution is advisable.

The press had already been given a confidential hint at the press conference of November 29, 1940, that foreign reports on the effect of German air raids were greatly exaggerated. The British seemed to be handling their censorship less rigorously, so that the reports now produced a false picture. For that reason the publication of foreign reports about German air raids would in future be forbidden unless confirmation was available from German quarters.

December 3, 1940

Large-scale propaganda by word of mouth should be applied to persuade the public that, just because there have been few or no British raids recently, they should not draw the false conclusion that the danger from the air has now become less serious. This propaganda should point out that British raids may be expected again with improved weather.

The press was similarly informed on the same day that the take-off of bomber aircraft had been encountering great difficulties in Britain because of ground haze and that for this reason only few penetrations into Reich territory had been made during the previous few nights.

In this connexion the Minister demands that the effect of the evacuation of children, which had not been handled very happily in the past, should be guided back into proper channels. The request, encountered here and there, that the children should be allowed to return to their homes must be opposed for the above reasons.

In January 1941 the population of the big cities was again alarmed by the rumour that the compulsory evacuation of children from air-raid danger areas was planned – which was in fact the case. When the thousandth train of evacuee children left Berlin on March 31, 1941, this event was therefore allowed to pass without any publicity. The evacuation of children continued to represent a problem for German domestic policy.

In August 1941 it was decided to bring back all juveniles who had already spent six months or more away from their families in air-safe camps; this was in response to the wishes of the majority of parents. But this transport home could not in fact be carried out at the beginning of summer, since nearly all means of transport were required for military purposes. As a result, the children only got back to Berlin at a time when hardly a night passed without air-raid warnings. Another children's evacuation campaign was therefore started, envisaged for a period of nine months at least. During that time the children would be allowed back home only in the event of death or grave illness of the parents. In the meantime the press published accounts of the good reception given to the children in the camps.

December 4, 1940
The Minister again explains why the present pessimistic press comment from Britain must be handled with care. He believes that not even the city businessmen in Britain are now championing a continuation of the war. It is only the Jews who are afraid of being driven from the continent. Naturally there are also the men whose names are linked with the outbreak of the war – Churchill, Eden, etc. For them the continuation of the war is a desperate matter.

The Minister authorizes Herr Fritzsche to illustrate Britain's present situation as that of a gambler in a casino. The gambler who has lost

900,000 Mark of the million he has stacked will go on believing that with the 100,000 Mark left he can recover his loss.

On December 4, 1940, the papers received the following directive: 'Over the past fortnight the German press has repeatedly received directives not to arouse in the German people any false or exaggerated hopes through the reproduction of foreign press comment. Although the German press has met these requests by the Ministry, it appears nevertheless that, in spite of the cautious attitude of the press, the flood of pessimistic reports has resulted in a marked degree of optimism which, in some parts of the country, has even produced a belief in revolution in Britain. It is, however, a fact that the British politicians are gamblers who will continue playing until they have nothing left to stake. For that reason when reproducing reports on the situation the papers now have the task of omitting anything that might suggest the idea that peace, an armistice, or even a revolution in Britain could be expected in the near future. It is true, of course, that the German air raids on Britain have had disastrous effects on her economy and on the morale of the population. But with the mentality of the British, revolution is out of the question in spite of this state of affairs. Britain's collapse will come only when the ruling stratum of the City realizes that Britain's position is hopeless and that no help can be expected from America.'

December 5, 1940
No strip dancers are to perform in rural areas, in small towns, or in front of soldiers.

Ministerialdirektor Gutterer is to submit for the Minister's approval a circular addressed to all compères. The circular is to be in the form of a categorical final warning, forbidding compères to make political wisecracks or to use lewd erotic jokes in their performances. The Minister points out that this directive has nothing to do with 'a dose of morality.' He explains that it is equally embarrassing for a man or woman to be subjected to this kind of dirty innuendo.

(*Cf.* January 14, 1941.)

December 12, 1940
The Minister points out that the British are now beginning to deal with the arguments in the Führer's speech. They are putting their labour leaders forward in order to deal, above all, with the Führer's social-political arguments. German propaganda must give a clear reply to these moves.

In his speech to the workers of the Borsig Works in Berlin on December 10, 1940, Hitler promised that after Germany's victory he would create a social-political 'people's state' on a grand design.

The point can be made that until the beginning of the war Britain had absolute power to reorganize Europe. The question should be asked what Britain did to organize Europe along sensible lines after her victorious war of 1914–18. Nothing was done then. Europe was atomized at Versailles according to the laws of political unreason. Britain has been a poor guardian of the great European cause. She has made a whole continent unhappy. Indeed that was what led to the war.

Yet the same British who from 1919 to 1939 demonstrated their incompetence now have the effrontery of addressing Europe and declaring: 'If we win the war, just you wait and see what social accomplishments we shall achieve, how we shall reorganize Europe both politically and economically.'

Morrison should be asked why, in that case, Britain, in token of her newly-discovered social leanings, is not prepared to reduce armament dividends during the present war. Our propaganda should emphasize that in Britain the opposition is paid by the government so that there can be no question of a clash of opinion on political matters. The Minister compares the state of the Anglo-German dispute with the situation encountered by National Socialism shortly before its assumption of power. Those then in power also tried to parade in front of the people with National Socialist slogans in order thus to take the wind out of the Party's sails. Then, too, the most effective argument with which to confront the ordinary member of the public was the one that should now be used towards Britain: 'You had the power – why then did you not act that way long ago?'

December 13, 1940

The Minister directs that the successful air raid on Sheffield should be featured prominently by the press. Leading articles, however, should provide a counter-weight to the impression that this has brought the end of the war any nearer. The leading articles should point out that the destruction of one city or another cannot mean the end of the war. What is at stake is more than a mere destruction of a few cities. Two worlds are locked in combat. At the same time, the press should draw comparisons between the present day and the seemingly endless period of waiting between August 1932 and January 1933 before the enemy on the home front was finally beaten into submission. This is precisely the situation with regard to Britain today.

Sheffield, the centre of the British armament industry, had its first German air raid during the night of December 12–13, when 336 bombers dropped 335 tons of high-explosive bombs on the city.

December 16, 1940

British propaganda is increasingly exploiting the low morale in Italy. It operates mainly with the assertion that an anti-Italian attitude is beginning to appear among the German public and that, in the event of an outbreak of unrest in Italy, Germany would occupy Italy. The Minister directs the German press to be exceedingly careful with regard to Italy. Such resentment as there is among the German public must never in any way appear in the press or on the radio.

The press conference was informed on the same day that the British press had published reports of disorders in Italy, a possible fascist counter-revolution, the movement of German troops over the Brenner, and the employment of German commissars and Gestapo agents in Italy.

December 19, 1940

Lately British propaganda has been increasingly trying to incite Germany against Italy and Italy against Germany. The Minister therefore desires that the Italians should be given moral support at every opportunity. Press and radio should quote anything the Italians are putting forward to strengthen their psychological position. Each news-paper and every radio bulletin should ceaselessly emphasize [Italian] loyalty to the German alliance and the concept of the Axis, even though this is unpopular at the moment. Simultaneously, more prominence should be given to the great services which Italy has rendered to the conduct of the war and which she is still rendering us by tying down large forces in the Mediterranean.

This instruction also applies to the foreign language service. For the reasons given the papers should counter the *Times* leader on Italy. These commentaries must aggressively express the view: these then are the British, those cowards, whose sole aim is to drive a wedge between nations. They are now talking nonsense about the danger of a revolution in Italy, just as they were talking nonsense about a revolution in Germany when we had suffered a slight reverse at Narvik. They believe that when a strategic retreat has to be made a revolution must break out at once. They do not comprehend the strength of fascism just as they have never comprehended the strength of National Socialism.

114

The Times on December 18, 1940 had an article headed "No Respite for the Italians".

December 20, 1940

The catholic and the protestant Churches are deliberately falsifying the concept of the 'Führer'; they have lately been particularly fond of applying it to Christ. The Minister instructs Ministerialdirektor Gutterer to get in touch for that purpose with one authorized representative each of the two Churches, plus one representative each of the Ministry of Church Affairs and the Gestapo.

The concept 'Führer' had never been applied to Christ until it was created by the Party. Unless a very rigorous halt is called to this falsification of concepts, the Churches would be in a position to devalue every single German political concept with transparent perfidiousness. The state does not steal the slogans of the Church. The Church, therefore, will kindly keep its hands off our slogans. Anyone offending in this manner against the hallowed concepts of the state will be called to account. Ministerialdirektor Gutterer is to inform the representatives of the Churches that henceforward any periodical or any book which falsifies our concepts will immediately be confiscated. Exceedingly high fines will see to it that those thus punished will not become martyrs.

The previous year, the *Essener Nationalzeitung* had been reprimanded for a Christmas article in which Hitler was likened to Christ and alleged similarities were discussed in detail. The editor-in-chief, Count Schwerin, was informed that Hitler himself did not desire any such comparisons although Goebbels personally had been fond of making them.

December 27, 1940

The Minister again emphatically points out that a wave of Axis friendship must radiate from the Ministry for Propaganda. Any mockery or jibes at Italy must cease. This attitude must be adopted not only towards the Italians but also towards the leading German political and economic circles. It is an old historical weakness of the Germans that they allow their foreign policy to be influenced by personal feelings. This must be opposed with all possible vigour. We can only win together or perish together.

'How dare Churchill presume?'

January-March 1941

January 6, 1941

The Minister again points out that the large-scale German attacks on Britain must not be presented by the press too blatantly. Otherwise the impression might too easily be given that British resistance is about to collapse.

January 7, 1941

The Minister points to the great danger resulting from German troops listening in to British transmitters. There are indications that British broadcasts, which are now being put out daily from London for the German Wehrmacht, are being listened to on an increasing scale by members of the Wehrmacht in the occupied territories. There is a real danger of contamination by these enemy broadcasts.

The Minister refers to the example of France, which at the moment of decision had already been totally broken in her morale by German radio transmissions. The Minister instructs Major Martin to see to it that a categorical order is issued by the Chief of the High Command of the Wehrmacht, on behalf of the Führer, prohibiting once again as a matter of general principle the listening to enemy radios by members of the forces on pain of heavy penalties.

At the end of February 1941 the Ministry for Propaganda agreed with the Wehrmacht Propaganda Department of the OKW to have all radio sets fitted with a reminder notice from the Wehrmacht, reading as follows: 'Listening in to foreign transmitters is an offence against the national security of our people. By order of the Führer such listening in will be punished by long terms of penal servitude. Remember this, soldiers!' The notice, however, was not very effective.

January 13, 1941

The Minister sharply criticizes the presentation of the Sunday afternoon papers which, contrary to his express instruction, have again given much prominence to neutral comment on the raids on London. To dramatize the incidents of the air war by huge headlines means giving dangerous support to the illusions held by the public. How, if it goes on like this, will the press pay appropriate tribute to final victory over Britain when it comes? The Minister sees a danger in the fact that, if the fighting continues to be thus dramatized, our people will accept Britain's capitulation as something that might really have been expected a long time ago.

The Minister recalls the psychological mistake made by the radio when it put out the final OKW communiqué about the campaign in Norway. At that time the German people had been so worked up into a state of tense anticipation by continuous preliminary reports that the final announcement, when it was made, no longer came up to the expectations of the man in the street.

The Minister suggests that the illusions harboured among wide circles of our public about the situation in Britain should be skilfully checked in the following way: when the occasion arises for the publication of a very favourable report from Britain this should be followed by a critical assessment by way of commentary. This commentary should then point out that the German people do not allow the sensational reports of a few journalists to dim their realistic view of the situation in the British Isles.

January 14, 1941

Various reports from Reich propaganda offices suggest that political cracks are again being given much prominence in cabarets in spite of the ban. Measures must be taken at all costs to see that this does not turn into a camouflaged form of political sabotage, for instance against Italy.

The records list the following anti-Italian joke told by a compère at the Berlin Kabarett der Komiker in January 1941: 'Who wears a feather but isn't a cockerel? Who wears a steel helmet and isn't a soldier? Who keeps going backwards and isn't a crab? Whereupon the audience replied in unison: 'The Italians!' In September 1940 complaints had been made about the low standard of variety performances. 'The Party should let Berlin have the names of those compères, and particularly women compères, who endeavour to conceal their artistic inadequacy behind dirty jokes,' Goebbels had ordered on October 11, 'so that these pseudo-artists can be excluded from the Reich Chamber of Culture.'

February 1, 1941

The Minister defines his attitude on the question of jazz music on the

German radio and rules that the following is forbidden as a matter of principle:

(1) music with distorted rhythms,
(2) music with an atonal melodic line and
(3) the use of so-called muted horns.

This regulation is henceforward to be binding on performances of any kind of dance music.

Since the official ban on jazz was by no means universally accepted, Goebbels justified his negative attitude about a year later: 'If by jazz music we understand a kind of music which, under total disregard or even derision of the melodic element, aims only at rhythm, and in which the rhythm too is manifested mainly by a cacophonous squeaking of instruments which offends the ears, then we can only reject this out of hand.'

February 5, 1941

The Minister believes that the hectic string of invasion stories in the press is merely designed as a pretext to allow Britain after a little while to accuse Germany once more of not having kept to her invasion date. No reference whatever should be made in the German press to these invasion reports.

Today's news from Britain contains a number of statements which put the allegedly social endeavours of the plutocrats in their proper light:

(1) The findings, now published in book form, of a British commission of enquiry into the living conditions of the British working people.

The Oxford Institute of Statistics had outlined a plan for a new taxation system which would guarantee a fixed standard of living.

(2) A remark by Lord Queensborough, recommending that after the war the British people return to a simple way of life, and abolish cocktails, sloppy films, dance halls and road houses.

(3) A report in the *Göteborgs Posten* to the effect that boys from the poorer circles are now to be accepted on scholarships even into the public schools.

These three British reports, which should be dealt with in the German press, provide an excellent opportunity for extensive polemics, spread over several days, against the pseudo-socialism of the British plutocrats. The lying nature of the social promises now being made by leading figures in Britain is to be exposed with the aid of the description of social conditions in the report of the commission of enquiry. In this connexion the Minister intends to mount a major German press and radio campaign which would teach the British once and for all not to make any social promises for after the war.

In reply to questions the Minister emphasizes that the German people now hold a proper attitude to the question of the United States' possible entry into the war. No-one in Germany is viewing such an event frivolously, but the people have the assurance that the Führer is prepared for all eventualities.

This way of viewing the political situation is very different from that during World War One. At that time our people were whipped up into a mood of delirious enthusiasm marked by the motto: 'Hand in your declarations of war here!'

In this connexion, at the conference of March 17, 1941, Goebbels further directed that the press should point out more frequently that the state of armament of the United States was not such as to justify anxiety among the public.

February 7, 1941

It has been found that pictures and reports of the British royal couple inspecting air-raid danger areas in Britain have not created anti-British sentiments among the German public but have, on the contrary, often produced a reaction unfavourable to ourselves. For this reason it would be advisable in future for the German press not to take any notice of the King and Queen of England, except in special cases.

In view of the highly probable intensification of enemy air activity in the coming spring it is necessary to familiarize the German people with the harsh side of the war, which invariably entails losses on one's own side too. One means to this end is the unvarnished publication of casualty figures after enemy air raids.

February 13, 1941

Having studied data concerning the compulsory employment of women, the Minister declares that he has given his approval in principle that all childless women and girls in the age group 14 to 40 must compulsorily register at labour offices.

The practical importance of such a measure is obvious, if only in view of the considerable manpower shortage in the Reich. But there is also a psychological side to the compulsory labour service for women, since this is likely greatly to raise the morale of those women who have been employed in German armament factories for months or years. Moreover, it is an effective means of fully overcoming an outdated class attitude, traces of which are still to be found, especially among the better classes.

119

After some initial difficulties there can be no doubt that all women enlisted, especially among the higher strata of the population, will devote themselves to their novel activity with zeal and with a certain sporting enthusiasm.

On March 15, 1941, the Reich Propaganda Directorate (Department for the Training of Speakers) issued the instruction that a campaign 'German women work for victory' should be started during the period of March 23–29, 1941; this campaign was inaugurated by Rudolf Hess. Its objective was to get women and girls who were not following an occupation, or those who were only looking after their own households, to make themselves available for employment in factories vital to the war effort or for other important war work.

The campaign did not produce the hoped-for result and the number of women among industrial workers in fact declined during the spring and summer of 1941. This was by no means due simply to the fact that Party propaganda for many years had consistently supported the idea that a woman's place was in her home and that her employment in industry was biologically detrimental to the race. According to statistical data the number of women employed in German industry on May 31, 1939 was 2.62 million; on May 31, 1941, it was 2.61 million, and on May 31, 1942 it was 2.58 million.

February 24, 1941

In accordance with an order by the Chairman of the Ministerial Council for Reich Defence, 30,000 employees of the printing trade will shortly have to be released for the armaments industry. This entails the need for a considerable curtailment of printed matter in the entire Reich territory. The principle in this, the Minister points out, must be that printed matter of importance to the national interest must on no account be curtailed, but that the saving of manpower must be achieved in less important sections of the printing trade. Whatever happens, the daily press must be maintained on its present scale, whereas a large amount of less important printed matter of all kinds can be discontinued without danger.

As a necessary consequence, therefore, any new publication of periodicals is prohibited as a matter of principle with immediate effect.

The Minister points out that here is a good opportunity to abolish and ban the entire Church press.

At the end of May 1941 the Reich Press Chamber instructed some 540 daily papers to cease publication. This measure was justified by the demands of the war to save paper, printing lead and manpower.

On March 28, 1941, Goebbels informed the Reich Minister for Church Affairs that he had 'given instructions that the entire denominational press, with the exception of papers published by official order, is to be suspended with immediate effect until further notice.'

In August 1941 Goebbels set out in detail his attitude on the ban of the denominational press, as indeed his attitude to the Church generally, in a conversation with Tiessler, his liaison man at the Führer's headquarters. According to a note by Bormann, Goebbels took the view that 'in his judgement it would have been better not to challenge the Churches while the war was on but to try as far as possible to guide them into line with our intentions. . . . Much as he would have been in favour – unlike certain other Reich leaders – of banning the Church press . . . he nevertheless believed that it would have been more correct to preserve appearances towards the Churches generally so long as the war was on. One should never attack an opponent until one was able to retort suitably in the event of a decisive counter-attack by him. But this was exceedingly difficult or even impossible in the event of a counter-attack by the Church while the war was still on. One should never indulge in hot-blooded vengeance; one should remain cool. In politics one must be able to wait; this was something the Führer had again very clearly shown in the case of Russia. If he had had his way one would have treated the Churches during the war as though one wished to collaborate with them loyally. But once the war was over, the Führer, when announcing his great social measures, would also have announced that the entire property of the Churches now belonged to the German people. . . .' (*Cf.* February 17, 1942.)

February 26, 1941
The Minister has before him an examination of the regulations of international law concerning the responsibility of a conqueror state for the food situation in the territories occupied by it. International law does not lay down any such responsibility but indeed concedes to the conqueror state the explicit right to confiscate food supplies, cash, stores, and indeed any other mobile property of the country.

When an English commentary pointed out the following day that hunger in the German-occupied territories must have a detrimental effect on Germany since hungry workers could not adequately work for the German armaments industry, Goebbels demanded 'that this blatant British cynicism should be nailed in the way it deserves.'

The Minister has pronounced certain measures which have to be taken immediately by the German side in connexion with a strike in Amsterdam. The Minister instructs Ministerialdirektor Gutterer to get in touch with the Ministry's departments in The Hague to ensure that radical means are used to suppress the Amsterdam strike and any possible spreading of it.

A suitable measure would be the suspension of trams, the closure of cinemas and theatres, a general curfew after 18.00 hours and the imposition of a heavy fine on the city of Amsterdam. Immediate measures must be taken to separate the circles advocating and agitating for a strike from the rest of the population, so that the anger of the inconvenienced population will very quickly begin to turn against these elements.

Since Jewish circles, above all, are behind this strike, deterrent measures against Jews would produce a markedly calming effect.

In connexion with the strike in the Netherlands from February 24 to 26, 1941, the first major act of rebellion against the German occupation, which was preceded on February 15 by a demonstration organized chiefly by communist workers, a German official announcement of February 27 stated that clashes had taken place in Amsterdam in the course of police measures designed to uncover the organizers of a night ambush of a police patrol and the members of a secret Jewish club; several persons had been killed and wounded. A considerable number of arrests had been made.

At the press conference of February 26, 1941, on the other hand, it was stated that the rebellion had been triggered off by propaganda campaigns of Dutch SA members. The rebellion had so far cost 75 lives.

An occasion for ironical polemics in the German press and the foreign language service is provided by a remark in the British House of Commons that the British public must not take the wording of the Air Ministry communiqués too seriously, since information about damage should only be understood relatively. Such unique opportunities for an effective exposure of the enemy must not be missed by the German press.

February 27, 1941

In reply to a question Herr Gutterer reports that by this morning he has not had any further news about the strike in Holland. Herr Fritzsche requests that a short news report should be authorized for publication in the German press about the events known so far. The Minister points out in this connexion that news of the Amsterdam incident is bound to leak out to the German public anyway by way of the *Deutsche Zeitung in den Niederlanden*. Besides, a short report had already been released for abroad. The Minister therefore directs that Herr Fritzsche should get authorization from the Obersalzberg* for a brief report.

The Minister also points out that the Amsterdam incidents are a classical example demonstrating the correctness of the views he has

---

* The hill overlooking Berchtesgaden where Hitler had his villa. He first rented it (or rather his half-sister Angela Raubal rented it in her name and there kept house for Hitler) in 1925. *Tr.*

always held – that any attempt at disturbances or demonstrations must *immediately* be opposed by small measures if one wishes to avoid the need for the application of considerably greater measures later.

On February 28, 1941, Gutterer reported at the conference that conditions in Holland appeared to be 'slowly getting back to normal.' At the conference of March 4, 1941, Goebbels objected to what he felt to be an excessively lenient handling of the rebellious elements in the Netherlands. He said it was not tolerable that Jewish gangs who committed offences against German troops every day should be sentenced to prison or penal servitude while in Germany theft committed during the black-out was now being punished by death.

He further instructed Gutterer to see to it that severe penalties were imposed in future. At the conference of March 7, 1941, Goebbels was able to report that, as a result of representations by the Ministry for Propaganda, death sentences were now carried out in Amsterdam.

February 28, 1941
Major Hoffmann reports on the present strength of the RAF. According to this information, which comes from a reliable source, Britain at present possesses:
70 fighter squadrons with a total of 700 machines,
65 to 70 bomber squadrons with a total of 1,100 machines,
30 squadrons of long-range reconnaissance aircraft with a total of 400 machines,
25 to 30 squadrons of close-range reconnaissance aircraft with 350 to 400 machines.

From the above it appears that competent German quarters assessed the strength of the RAF higher than it really was. At the end of September 1940 the RAF had at its disposal 569 bomber aircraft and 665 operational fighters (Churchill, *Second World War,* ii/2, pp. 452–4). At the end of December 1940 the Luftwaffe had 1,956 operational aircraft, while its nominal strength consisted of 3,050 combat aircraft (bombers and fighters).

President Roosevelt has made a speech at an American film banquet in which he has dared to assert that Germany has banned American films from her cinemas for fear of the truth.

The Minister recommends that this vile lie should be suitably pilloried both over the shortwave transmitter and in the German press, maybe under the slogan 'The US President's love of truth.' In fact, the American film-Jews have for years been engaged in furious agitation against the showing of German films in the United States and have eventually made all exports to America impossible. In consequence,

Germany has found herself compelled to exclude all American films from the German market.

The ban on American films in Germany had now become a reality one year after Himmler's first agitations to have them withdrawn.

March 5, 1941

The Italian paper *Piccolo* has been talking about our alleged promises to Bulgaria to get her to join the Tripartite Pact. *La Stampa* has similarly stepped out of line with such a story. The Minister again brands the indiscipline of the Italian press.

The palpable advantages which Bulgaria would gain from Hitler's 'New Order' in Europe, which among other things assigned Yugoslav Macedonia to Bulgaria, induced the Bulgarian government to accede to the Tripartite Pact.

It has been ascertained that about half the foreign students are in lodgings with Jews. The Minister points out that in this way the foreigners are being turned into counter-propagandists. He demands that an end be put at once to this state of affairs; where suitable accommodation cannot be found in any other way, the question should be examined of whether a number of hitherto Jewish flats could be vacated. The Minister directs that Herr Gutterer should see to it that henceforward Jews are only permitted to let rooms to other Jews.

The SD reports that the behaviour of foreign students towards girls of German blood is often assuming undesirable forms. The Minister comments that it is probably more the behaviour of the girls of German blood towards these foreigners that is deserving of criticism.

March 6, 1941

The present efforts of the British to reorientate their industry to wartime requirements must not be treated with contemptuous condescension by the German press. The German people do not see this as a discreditable measure but instead see in it a reflection of Britain's firm resolution to hold out under all circumstances.

The periodical *Daheim* has published an article on 'Strategy and Tactics' which, in a camouflaged form, might be described as the most vicious and vile defamation of the Führer's genius of generalship. The article is said to have been written by a Major Dr Hense of Osnabrück. The Minister instructs Ministerialdirigent Fritzsche to ascertain the background of the article and to take appropriate measures against those responsible.

The article referred to stated that strategy and tactics could 'never tolerate such a thing as dilettantism.' Strategy and tactics 'can be mastered only after thorough study and many years of peacetime or wartime experience in the service of military establishments, preferably in command of troops, at the Military Academy, on the General Staff, just as one would learn a real craft or a science. Once a foundation of craftsmanship or scientific knowledge is laid, skill or intuition or genius may raise them to a higher level.' In consequence, not everyone was a general who had himself commonly so described. Even Scharnhorst, the 'creator of the Wehrmacht' or 'the moulder of our military strength' could not be regarded as a general; 'nor of course can anyone claim to be a general in the true meaning of the word who, as "Supreme War Lord" merely gets the responsible commanders-in-chief to "make their report" to him, who "issues directives", or who, in Ludendorff's words, "sweeps across the General Staff map with an elegant gesture of his hand" and, as it were, "wages war between meals". . . .'

The Minister objects to the summer and autumn fashions for women, described and reproduced in all fashion magazines, which envisage long and full dresses and are therefore in total disregard of the necessities of the war and entirely fail to take account of the need for economy measures. Fashion must now be attuned to the war and must not be created by a few aloof and detached artists.

The Minister instructs Ministerialdirektor Gutterer to see to it that the intended excesses of the forthcoming fashions are subjected in good time to a revision appropriate to present-day conditions.

On May 29, 1941, Goebbels, by way of contrast, praised the shortening of skirts in Britain to save cloth.

March 7, 1941

Whenever fantasies appear in the British press about alleged new German weapons these should never be contradicted, not even in the foreign language service, since rumours about new German weapons can only produce anxiety and fear in Britain.

The foreign language service should also take up British comment suggesting that the British have in fact forgotten nothing and learned nothing since World War One, so that in the event of our losing the war, we could only fare worse than in 1919.

March 17, 1941

The Minister deals with the negative psychological reactions produced among the public by the too frequent quoting of figures in reports about transport of Italian workers to Germany. The mood is such that the public is asking why we should have our soldiers fighting in Libya when the Italians still have hundreds of thousands of workers to spare who, after all, might just as well be in the forces. It is therefore more appropriate to look after these workers than to keep praising them in the press.

March 20, 1941

The Minister suggests that the German press should juxtaposé the British reports about the German air raids on Manchester and Glasgow and the subsequent figures of British losses. Whereas the first official reports described casualties and damage as light, the British Air Ministry, a full five days later, now feels obliged to reveal the real scale of the loss of life. This discrepancy should be exploited polemically again and again in future, whenever casualties and damage following German air raids are described as slight or insignificant by British sources.

The Minister thinks it psychologically wrong that those men in the Reich whose duties frequently involve harsh and brutal action against enemies of the state, Jews, Poles, etc., should have their names linked with the execution of the measures or punishments authorized by them.

The deterrent effect of the execution of death sentences, which they are frequently compelled to witness, can only be detrimental to the further consistent performance of their judicial and political duties.

From this directive of Goebbels it would seem likely that Goebbels and the participants in the ministerial conference, though not the general public, were informed about the execution squads of the SS Totenkopf units and their tasks.

The Minister comments on the proposed closing of the United Press bureau in Berlin and emphasizes that this closure must not be broadcast abroad as a reprisal against the measures taken against Transocean in New York, because otherwise the editorial staff of United Press would needlessly be turned into martyrs. Dr Bömer adds that the evidence available against the American journalist Hottelet has after all now been found to be more serious than originally assumed. It may be expected that he will have to be sentenced to several years of penal servitude at least if not, indeed, to death.

Bömer confirmed at the conference of March 14, 1941, that appropriate counter-measures had been taken against American journalists and agencies. With Hitler's approval the first such measures would be directed against the United Press Agency and its member Hottelet.

126

Richard C. Hottelet was arrested by the Gestapo in the early morning of March 15, 1941. His arrest was evidently directly connected with measures taken against two German correspondents of the Transocean Agency in New York and Washington. The latter were, however, not arrested until May 7, 1941.

After having been interrogated on the most diverse topics during some six months of detention at the Berlin-Alexanderplatz Prison, Hottelet, whose anti-Nazi views were well known, was suddenly released at the beginning of July 1941. An exchange had meanwhile been arranged for the two German correspondents arrested in the United States.

March 21, 1941

The papers may deal at length with a characterization of the Germans published in the *Daily Mirror,* in which the Germans are represented as an inferior race of pot-bellied and crooked-legged Huns. It may be pointed out in this connexion that these pot-bellied Huns have certainly made the straight-legged British run like rabbits on land, sea and in the air.

Goebbels was presumably referring to the article 'Nazi Spring' in the *Daily Mirror* of March 7, 1941. The Germans at that time were referred to as Huns not only in the British press but even in official speeches. This defamation was not confined to Nazis alone but was applied to the German people as a whole, and proved to have some lasting effect.

The length to which the British press occasionally went is shown in a *Daily Sketch* article of October 1940 which said that the Germans were lower 'than the lowest forms of life in the darkest crevices of a tropical swamp' and that they found 'orgiastic bliss in the murder of children and sick people.'

The Minister draws Herr Dr Bömer's attention to the increasing number of complaints that the Moscow journalists are acting as panic-mongers in Germany. Dr Bömer reports that, on the contrary, the Soviet ambassador has already lodged a complaint with State Secretary Weizsäcker that the Tass representatives are being treated badly by us. The Minister directs that the Russian journalists are to be treated very coolly and should be carefully watched.

Speaking more generally, the Minister again explains that weeks, and perhaps months, may yet pass before the first cracks appear in Britain. It will be impossible for our press to keep up its present volume over such a long period if it gives too much prominence now to our attacks on London, etc. For that reason yesterday's publicity for the devastation in London is to be regarded as a special case and, generally speaking, even major attacks on Britain should, for the time being, be featured only on the second page and on a muted note.

March 24, 1941

The Minister emphasizes that even greater publicity than in the past should be given to the fact that the 7,000 billion credit which the United States is granting Britain is in fact not going to Britain at all but straight into the pockets of the American capitalists. The press must emphasize that the American people now have to raise 7,000 billion which will profit no-one except the big industrialists. It should, moreover, be pointed out again and again that Britain has not yet paid off even her World War One debts and that she is not therefore likely to set about repaying her gigantic debts from this war once the conflict is over. The starting point for our propaganda must be: the ordinary American citizen and working man must now shell out his money so that wealthy, plutocratic Britain can wage war.

March 26, 1941

The Minister expresses his acknowledgment to the German press for the way it has handled Yugoslavia's accession to the Tripartite Pact. The contrast between the enemy's campaign of make-believe over the past few days and weeks and the reality created in Vienna yesterday has come out particularly well. A number of British reactions today clearly reflect the rude awakening of the British after their fruitless attempts at interference; in consequence, there is ample material for continuing our polemic. In some respects the Anglo-American commentaries are so contradictory that here, too, quite a few points may be found for effective rejoinders.

Several reports, chiefly from British sources, have come in about alleged unrest and anti-Axis demonstrations in Yugoslavia. The Minister directs that the background of these rumours should be investigated, but does not wish the German press to discuss the matter.

On March 28 and 31, 1941, Goebbels issued instructions that the 'unfavourable' reports from Yugoslavia, which by then had been confirmed, were to be reported as straight news 'without comment and without showing our hand'.

March 28, 1941

The Minister reports that Churchill in a speech yesterday touched on the subject of 'war aims'. Britain, in order to cover herself on all sides, is trying to dodge all discussion of war aims. The real war aim, i.e. to smash Germany and reinstate British plutocracy into its rightful place, cannot at present be mentioned in Britain, while on the other hand it does not seem advisable to British politicians to proclaim some new

'Wilson's Points'.* Faced with this dilemma Churchill now declares that one cannot at this moment make any statement on the subject. German press polemics with Churchill's speech must proceed from this most salient point.

On March 27, 1941, Churchill made a speech to trade unionists and said, among other things: 'as for the future, I have always been a bit shy of defining war aims, but if these great communities, now struggling not only for their own lives but for the freedom and progress of the world, emerge victorious there will be an electric atmosphere in the world which may render possible an advance towards a greater and broader social unity and justice than could otherwise have been achieved in peace-time in a score of years.'

* Woodrow Wilson formulated his Fourteen Points on January 8, 1918, incorporating his ideas for the post-war settlement, emphasizing the principle of self-determination of nations. *Tr.*

'A thing like this must show in the long run'
April-May 1941

April 1, 1941
The Minister comments on broadcasts by the Vatican radio and states that this transmitter has lately been strikingly unfriendly and at time positively aggressive towards us. The Vatican radio has now taken up a speech said to have been made by Cardinal Faulhaber in Munich on March 9. The radio is using quotations from that speech for most shameless agitation against Germany.

The Minister requests Ministerialdirektor Gutterer to investigate, in cooperation with the Gestapo, whether Cardinal Faulhaber did in fact make such a speech since, in the text available, it comes within the legal definition of high treason.

April 3, 1941
British propaganda keeps on trying to palm off the responsibility for attacks on the civilian population on to the German Luftwaffe by claiming that it was Germany who first started bombing civilian objectives.

Against this, the German news media must never weary of emphasizing that it was the RAF which in fact committed the first act of war against the civilian population by its raid on Sylt.

The British government's exceedingly difficult position with regard to the definition of its war aims must time and again be emphasized and strongly underlined by the press and the radio. The British government must constantly be faced with the embarrassing question of the Why and Wherefore of this war. What makes our polemics particularly effective is the fact that Britain, in spite of certain propaganda needs, cannot make any declaration of her war aims before the end of the war – for if she tried to satisfy the British public then the other side, the German people, none other, would be outraged. On the other hand, if Churchill were now to hand out a sedative to the German people he would be in danger of running against public opinion in Britain. Churchill, moreover, out of consideration for the United States must play down this issue in order not to trigger off, as a result of a discussion of British war aims, an unpleasant reaction which might do grave harm to British politics.

April 4, 1941
The British have coined the term 'quislings' for the politicians of other countries who are prepared to collaborate loyally with Germany, and have thereby given this term a compromising character. The Minister requests that a generic term should be found to describe all those politicians who, against their better knowledge and probably bribed, have hurled their country into disaster on Britain's command – the most recent instance being the Yugoslav government. However, this should not be done by generalizing a proper name since such a name would make its bearer too popular.

April 6, 1941

The German attack on Yugoslavia and Greece began on April 6, 1941, at 05.15 hours. The same day Hitler issued a 'Proclamation to the German People' and an 'Order of the Day to the Soldiers of the South-East Front.'

This night has seen the triggering off of the event which we have been expecting for days or weeks. During the next few days or hours a similar process will unroll as witnessed by us, not during the offensive in the West, but during that against Norway. It would be a great mistake to think that this will be just a stroll to Belgrade or Athens. There can be no question of that. Not that particularly tough military resistance is to be expected – but the geographical and road conditions facing us are of exceptional difficulty. The Führer himself estimates the duration of the whole operation at about two months. I personally believe that it will probably be shorter. In any case, we would be wise in all our calculations and in our entire presentation of the situation – although of course we shall not say so in so many words – to start with the supposition that it will be two months. The first few obstacles, in particular, are difficult to overcome because in the mountainous regions we shall probably encounter very tough and perhaps savage partisan resistance, although – the Führer is firmly determined to do this – this is to be crushed with the most brutal measures, similar to those used in Poland. It is also to be expected that the massive air raids

131

which have already been made on Belgrade this morning and which will, in particular, be made on a very large scale on Belgrade this evening and during the night will have a profound effect on the morale of the Serb population. But regardless of all this we must, as I have said, be prepared for this generals' clique to offer resistance as long as possible – this clique whom one can no longer credit with any human reason or sound common sense. I think we do these gentlemen too much honour in judging them by our yardsticks of sound common sense; I am convinced that no statesman or general can be so stupid as Herr Simovic has just been, or as those gentlemen Hambro and Koht and Rydz-Smigly and Beck were last year, and that these are all individuals bought by the British. They did exactly the same in the Boer War. Wherever the British appear on the scene they naturally try to apply the cheapest means; i.e., by means of bribery to buy the responsible leaders of those nations they want to use for their own ends and whose blood they want to stake for British interests.

It would be wise to be prepared from the outset for the operation to be hard and attended by great difficulties, but it will lead to the desired result in six to eight weeks. All in all, we can be very pleased that things have happened the way they have. For if the stupidity of the Serb government had not given us the opportunity of making a clean sweep in the Balkans now, the latter would have remained the powder-keg of Europe, and Britain – we must not judge this by the present power relations but by the state of affairs in ten, fifteen or twenty years' time; i.e., a span of time which is insignificant on a historical scale – would always have been in a position to thrust the torch into the hands of a few daring *comitadji* so that they might once more blow up that powder-keg. It therefore suits us quite well to use this opportunity, backed by the best moral and psychological convictions, to clean up the Balkans now, good and proper.

For your own reassurance, although I shall not put anything down on the subject, I would like to answer a question which naturally disturbs everybody just now – the question of Russia. It is not just that we here have been turning over this idea 'Russia'; the idea 'Russia' has of course been under consideration in the responsible quarters, and above all by the Führer himself, for weeks and months. Nor are we particularly surprised by any treaty of friendship, or of support, or of neutrality which Russia may have concluded or may yet conclude. On the contrary, I may tell you in confidence that probably nothing would suit us better at this moment than Russia's intervention in the present situation. She would suffer a military fiasco in no time at all.

132

The Soviet Union had concluded a Treaty of Friendship and Non-Aggression with Yugoslavia on April 5, 1941.

There is no doubt at all that Russia will be very careful not to get her fingers burnt in this fire; she will stand aside, with clenched fists, watching further developments. You all know the Führer's method. In the course of this very day and the coming night such retribution will burst upon Belgrade that over a radius of a thousand kilometres everyone will be saying: 'Hands off! Don't interfere!' And that is, after all, the purpose of the exercise. The entire operation is based on the fact that it will come off even if suddenly everything east and south of Vienna should rise against us. Hence there is no trace of danger or risk in this calculation. Nevertheless, as I have said, we must expect nature to put certain difficulties in our way. We must also be clear on the point that the Serbs, needless to say, are good soldiers and that, provided the state does in fact put up military resistance – which, to my mind, is by no means certain yet – we shall probably have to expect rather different soldierly virtues than, say, in Norway or Holland or Belgium. But I am nevertheless convinced that the whole operation will be concluded by about the end of May. Nor is it certain that this will be the only operation. Only last year we witnessed the western offensive bursting into the Norwegian campaign, each offensive making the other more flexible and giving it a greater chance of success. Whatever happens – although I'm not shouting this from the rooftops – we may remain entirely calm in our minds about this whole operation. There will be critical phases in this operation, there will be some unfortunate days which will not bring us great successes, there will be critical trials of a psychological and military character; but I believe that we have experienced such crises so often in the rise of the Party and the National Socialist state, and above all in the course of this war, that we shall see them through easily. Therefore, now that we have been let off the leash, we shall get down to our own particular tasks and I am convinced that in no time at all we shall have laid here a sound, psychological basis which will somewhat facilitate the execution of the operation for our military leaders, if only by keeping the world neutral.

Propaganda line for our information service at home: This line is fully defined by the Führer's proclamation; this contains all the arguments which we may put forward to the German people.

It must therefore be the task of the German press firstly to print the proclamation in full and then to expatiate on it. When the Führer talks about the damnable assassination of Sarajevo then this is a concrete concept for us, but to the younger generation it means nothing. The German press must, therefore, on its political pages, insofar as these are not taken up by polemics, describe during the next few days for the German people this Serbian criminal clique and explain to them: What do we mean by 'the Balkans'? Of what nations is the Yugoslav state composed? How did it come about in the first place? How did those gangsters gain possession of this state? Each paper should pick out a few sentences from the Führer's proclamation and comment on them: What is this Sarajevo? What do we mean by Serbs? Where do the Serbs live? What race are they? What national peculiarities do they have? What religious views? What are Slovenes? What is a Croat? What is the relationship between those nations and us? What are Party conditions like in Croatia? What are the economic conditions like? By what does the country live? What is its geo-political make-up? How high are the mountains? What is the Balkan Range? How did the name 'Yugoslavia' come about?

In our polemics we must no longer speak of Yugoslavs or of the Yugoslav people – there is no such thing. (The Führer's proclamation only refers to the Yugoslav state.) The name must be made to disappear more and more, and we must speak only of Serbs, Croats and Slovenes. (Parallel to Czecho-Slovakia!)

Propaganda line for the neutral and the enemy world: For Britain it is quite clear. We must emphasize again and again: 'We are knocking the south-east and the Balkans out of your hands. We are going to prove it to you – here, in the south-east, we shall not tolerate a single Briton, any more than we tolerated him in Scandinavia or in western Europe. We tolerate no Briton on the continent, no matter where he appears. Perhaps we may wait a little while, but in the end we kick him out. No Briton has any business on the European mainland. We'll now demonstrate it to you once more. Whether you come in on secret service or with your tanks – no matter, you'll be kicked out!'

Propaganda line for the Serbs: Here we are pursuing a line similar to the one we followed with the Poles. The Serbs must be told:

For all that is happening now you have the management of a clique of generals to thank. You might have been the quietest, the safest and the most peaceful country in the world today if this clique had not overthrown a government which, on behalf of its nation, had tied itself by the most solemn signature to the Tripartite Pact. We never compelled you to join it: you acceded to the Pact of your own free will. And now this generals' clique has led you into this madness. Just look what these 17- or 18-year-old schoolboys, those immature, snotty louts, have done for you. They staged a few demonstrations – that's cheap enough. You were triumphant and you felt great and powerful because you smashed up our tourist office, because you booed the German minister and because you injured the German military attaché. What's happening to you now you owe to the generals' clique. They first ordered the street demonstrations so as to give themselves a certain political floor-space at home. For in reality this revolution was staged by twenty or thirty people. Now you have a young man of 17, who doesn't know what's what, as your king, and he is to lead you now in a situation in which you have no idea what to do next, in which you are militarily encircled on all sides. What kind of government is that which starts a war, which stages such provocation against the strongest military power in the world! You only need to look at the map to realize that you are encircled on all sides, that you can no longer breathe, that you can no longer move. You will simply get under Germany's steam-roller. For that you can thank the generals' clique, that criminal clique which started the First World War!

We think it unnecessary, dear Serbs, to prove to you that British help will remain a piece of paper. The most recent past proves that the British have no intention whatever of helping you. Not only have they no intention of doing so but they are in no position either. How are they to bring you equipment and troops? Where should they land? That same Britain which this morning pompously declared: 'Official circles announced on Sunday morning that Yugoslavia will be granted unlimited support by the British Empire' – that same Britain has nothing left for herself. Aren't the British crying across to America: 'Can't you let us have a few old scrapped ships? Or a few aircraft? We don't have this or that,' In other words, the same Britain which is already on the brink of starvation, the Britain for which Lloyd George has predicted famine, which is crying out to America for help with equipment – that same Britain declares grandiloquently: 'We shall grant Yugoslavia all help!' This help will be just like the help which Britain granted Poland, which she granted Norway, which she granted Holland and Belgium, and which she granted France. We must systematically get out all suitable material on how the British left the French in the lurch at the decisive moment, how they would not dream of employing their fighter and bomber squadrons in support of the French; how Daladier and Reynaud addressed calls for help to Churchill: 'Give us at least one air squadron,' and how they were cynically, brutally and impertinently turned down. We must keep telling the Serbs: British help is so much poppy-cock, you can't expect anything at all from that quarter. And if, being Slavs, you are perhaps relying on Russian help, then you will be left in the lurch good and proper; the Russians won't dream of helping you. They have concluded a pact of benevolent neutrality with you. A lot of good this benevolent neutrality will do you Serbs! Now, all over your country, wherever you think of offering resistance, your villages will be laid waste, your cities will be reduced to rubble and cinder. Look at Holland, Belgium, Norway – there the whole show only took three or four days in some places, or a fortnight to three weeks at the most.

Offer no resistance! For wherever you offer resistance you will only be repaid by having your villages and cities destroyed. Look at Belgrade! Herr Simovic's theatrical putsch has been paid for dearly by a ruined capital!

(Skilful psychological use must be made of the Serb mentality. It must not be forgotten that we are dealing with a Slav people. A typical characteristic of Slav peoples is megalomania, and when certain events then occur this whole Slav megalomania collapses. We have seen this with the Poles. This experience must be borne in mind!)

The Serbs must be clearly told: Your generals are responsible.

(For a small people it is always very popular to agitate against the generals, especially when things go wrong; we experienced the same thing even with the most soldierly people of all, the Germans. When a war goes wrong and demands frightful sacrifices it is not difficult to incite a people against the generals.)

We must not attack the generals as generals, but solely as generals meddling in politics, the bloody dilettantism with which those politico-generals have hurled the Yugoslav state into this frightful disaster. Slogans must be stressed again and again, such as: Belgrade destroyed – that's what you owe to that dilettante general named Simovic! If the old government had remained in office this would not have happened, you would now be the safest country in Europe. Again and again point out: We desired nothing beyond what it says in the Tripartite Pact. We merely wanted the present constellation to be preserved, so you should be rid of your anxieties that Hungary or Bulgaria might one day come to you with fresh demands. Juxtapose: What would your country be like today if you had remained in the Tripartite Pact, and what does it look like today, now that you are being ruled by a boy of 17 of whom the British have written that, strictly speaking, he ought already to be called Peter the Great.

One of the most important arguments is that the government has left Belgrade. If tomorrow morning Belgrade is in flames we must say: 'Serbs, please note: the members of your government, having provoked this war, have now been careful to leave Belgrade complete with their families and have left you in the soup. That's what you owe to the 17-year-old schoolboys, headed by a 17-year-old king, and to those corrupt generals. (Slogan: corrupt, dilettantish generals.) That's what they have let you in for. Go now and look at your splendid avenues in Belgrade and then go and thank the gentleman who was kind enough last Saturday, before the conflict broke out, to inform you that the government has left the capital 'in order to maintain its freedom of action'! A fundamental rule of propaganda even for the Serbs: never attack people but invariably only governments. The whole argument is to be formulated with a view to making the Serbian people more or less our ally. The propaganda must always be an appeal to the Serb people against the generals' clique.

Propaganda line for the Croats: In the official service the distinction between Croats and Serbs should not yet be made too clearly, or at least not too noticeably, because if our intention is too obvious it will give offence. The propaganda line for the Croats is really contained in the Führer's proclamation: 'We have nothing against you – in fact we have nothing even against the Serbian people; we are only against the Serbian generals' clique. We have nothing against the Croats – on the contrary, we find you particularly likable. We don't find the Serbs quite as likable, but we have nothing against them either.'

In dealing with the Croats the official service can begin quite gently to use the line – but this should be done more in the style of a scholarly exposition on the strength of the past and of experience since World War One – : 'What advantage, in fact, did you derive from your alliance with the Serbs? You were oppressed. You were barred from becoming officials, you had no chance of advancement. The state was run by the Serbs, just as the Czechs used to run their state.' For the *secret transmitter* (this subject must not be touched upon in the German press or on the German radio): pull out all stops, using all means of demagogic persuasion. The only limit here is the credibility of what we say. Repeat again and again, at considerable length, what the Croats had to suffer at the hands of the Serbs, how they used to be oppressed. (Material on this point from Macek's parliamentary speeches, etc.) As soon as the first crisis arises, perhaps after the first severe test for Belgrade tomorrow morning: 'Our moment has now come. If we are ever to have an independent state, now is the time. We are convinced the Germans will do this for us. Look at Slovakia. The Slovaks have autonomy. They seized their chance at the moment when the artificial Czechoslovak state found itself in a crisis. The result: They have their own state president, their own parliament, their own armed forces; no-one is meddling in their internal affairs; we have never heard of the Germans interfering in Slovakia's internal affairs. Nothing of what was predicted along these lines took place. The Germans have not appointed a governor. They merely have a minister.' Here again, argument must be focused on the Serb generals' clique. It must be made clear: 'We are totally defenceless – quite apart from the purely practical considerations which we are setting forth, it would be senseless to offer any resistance. Slogan: Do not resist. Begin amongst yourselves to form the future

F

autonomous Croat state now! Set up action committees! In each village, in each town a new commune council (or choose some other appropriate term!) must be set up.' ('The village elders are getting together' or some such phrase.) 'If you are real men then you will make use of the present situation! Ever since 1919 you have been clamouring for your autonomous state. If you don't seize the present moment then you might as well get yourselves buried; then everything will have been only shadow boxing. Don't make any speeches now, just act. If you don't achieve your autonomous state now you will never get it. Now is the moment! The Germans are looking for friends. They can now give us autonomy. What does "betraying the fatherland" mean now? This is not betraying our fatherland at all. This Serb state was not our fatherland. It was the tyranny of the Serbs who forced us into this artificial state. We are not deserting a state. One cannot desert from something into which one was press-ganged. For us, this state was merely an instrument of oppression. After all, we have always emphasized that at the first suitable opportunity we would escape from this oppression. Now the moment has come.'

Propaganda line for Greece: Here too the basic line is contained in the Führer's proclamation. No agitation yet against the government; first wait and see how the Greeks are going to behave towards us. 'We have nothing against you, really. The British must get out – apart from that we don't want anything from you.' The issue should not be made too rigid, but we should point out the hopelessness of the situation. The Greeks must understand that we cannot tolerate the British repeating the experiment of World War One. 'That's got to be cleared up – the moment that's cleared up we shall have no quarrel with anything in Greece.'

Propaganda line for the Slovenes: Halfway between the lines for the Serbs and Croats – not to be treated quite so gently as the Croats, whom we can directly assure of our friendship, but not to be handled as roughly as the Serbs. Here too, we must say: 'What did you get out of the Serbs? You were always against the Serbs.' Similarly: 'The generals' clique', etc.

April 7, 1941
The Minister emphasizes the need to divide our tactics and propaganda concerning British aid to Yugoslavia. For our domestic propaganda, for the imminent enhancement of the glory of our Wehrmacht and also for the better psychological and moral justification of the attack, we must highlight all information showing that the British have in fact been in Greece with strong forces for a long time. However, when speaking to

the nations whom we want to undermine we must emphatically point out that British aid is inadequate and must therefore remain ineffective. Since the British are pursuing a very conflicting news policy it is not difficult to find the necessary arguments for this propaganda. The British are in fact helping along our propaganda efforts by their own magniloquent pronouncements that they had been transporting large amounts of war material to Greece for some weeks. In this context the Minister quotes British reports to the effect that: 'We have been in Greece for a number of weeks' or, 'troops sent to Greece from Benghazi' or, 'direct military contact between British troops and the Germans on the continent of Europe.'

British propaganda is fond of operating with the slogan that Hitler is now forced to fight on two or even three fronts, and that this will inevitably lead to a considerable weakening of the German war potential.

This argument, the Minister points out, is of considerable importance in polemics with abroad. We must devote special attention to its refutation. This British manoeuvre might be foiled by pointing out that the British would immediately extend their front to Norway, Holland, Belgium and northern France if only they saw the shadow of a possibility of doing so. It may also be pointed out that our million-strong army has been waiting all winter to go into action again, somewhere and somehow. In this connexion one might point to a popular British propaganda slogan, frequently quoted by the British radio during the past winter: 'Hitler has a few million unemployed troops; they will constitute the nucleus of the coming revolution.'

In order to meet their immediate requirements the British are now once again rushing into an unimaginable psychological bankruptcy. They are grandiloquently stressing their massive engagement in the Balkans and the resulting hopes of a British victory over the German army.

With an eye to later polemics the Minister desires all this comment to be accurately recorded because the time will soon come when Britain is driven out of the south-east. At that moment the comment from Britain will be: 'After all, we had only relatively weak forces stationed in Yugoslavia and Greece.' Besides, use may already be made of British and American observations to the effect that it was naturally not possible to send the Serb, Croat, Slovene and Greek people as much aid as one would have liked, because 'possibilities of such aid are restricted since the United States must hand over all available war material to Great Britain.'

The Minister desires that the name of Sefton Delmer, at present a broadcaster in London and at one time correspondent in Berlin, is not to be mentioned again either in the German press or on the foreign language service. With his accurate knowledge of German conditions Delmer tries to invest his very rude insults with an air of great verisimilitude and endeavours to inflate beyond all measure such disagreements as he may have accidentally got wind of and thus to play off one leading German figure against another.

April 8, 1941

The Minister states that complaints have been coming in from various quarters about the new radio announcer, on the grounds that he has too strong an Austrian accent. The radio, the Minister says, must speak the purest, clearest and most dialect-free German because it speaks to the whole nation. As a matter of principle, there must be a certain standard language just as there is a standard orthography. What Luther's translation of the Bible has done for written German, we on the radio must do for German speech: fix a standard language which, even if it does not sweep away the dialects, is valid throughout the Reich.

April 9, 1941

The Minister explains that it is the Führer's wish that as little as possible should be said at the moment about the military successes we have achieved in Yugoslavia and Greece. If, however, the outside world puts out certain reports or tries to belittle events, we must of course argue the matter out. It is our intention that reports of our successes, once we issue them, must immediately so burst upon our opponents that an enormous moral effect is achieved. The reports about Derna, Salonika, Uesküb must therefore be published in the German press only when the High Command communiqué mentions them. In reply to a question on the attitude to be adopted towards foreign press representatives, the Minister points out that in that respect we are in a magnificent position. One might perhaps say to them: 'We have so many victories; I really can't tell you any details at the moment, we shall announce everything in a collective report when the time comes. We have no reason to turn defeats into victories; on the contrary, we do not even list our victories. Besides, we predicted all this. We do not report every single town we have taken; we leave it to the British to list every town they have to evacuate.'

On April 9, the OKW reported that mobile troops had thrust into the Uesküb Basin to a depth of over sixty miles and that formations of the German Afrika-Korps in Cyrenaica had reached Derna on April 7.

British statements that they are not particularly affected by the military developments because these had been expected, as well as the observation that the Greeks must now themselves defend Salonika and hold their positions at all costs must be strongly and prominently featured in the foreign language service, in particular also in speaking to the smaller countries. The German press, on the other hand, must take them up only in so far as the OKW communiqué provides support for them. If the British say that they now intend to give up eastern Libya and to concentrate their forces in the Balkans; that they will turn the extraordinary heat, the waterless desert, etc., into their allies, then we should comment on these British efforts in our foreign language service by pointing out that in addition to General Fog, General Winter, and such like, they are now creating new 'allies' for themselves.

April 11, 1941

The Minister emphasizes our present exceedingly favourable position which enables us to carry out not only a military exposure but also an absolute propagandist and political unmasking of the British. The fact that Britain's prestige is rapidly declining is largely due to our full exploitation of the incipient catastrophe. The greater part of the German press has brought out these points with great skill.

Today we again have a number of observations which we can make good use of. Provided the present tactics are consistently continued and the British are given no respite – after all, they must on the one hand save face towards us and on the other they must get their own people gradually used to the idea of a defeat in the South-East – then we shall get them into a similar situation as in June last year, at Dunkirk.

Our air raids on Britain should at present be featured with greater prominence than usual, to prevent the German people from gaining the impression that while we are winning victories in the South-East, German cities are being destroyed by the RAF without German counter-measures. Reports such as yesterday's British announcement that Britain has altogether lost about 40,000 people killed in air raids should be published with particular prominence in those cities where there have been numerous fatal casualties – i.e. not only in Kiel or Bremen themselves, but throughout the north-western region. The Minister instructs Major Titel to have a list of fatal casualties compiled for the various German Gaue.

Goebbels announced the percentage casualty figures for the various Gaue at the conference of April 16, 1941 and demanded better welfare measures for the most badly affected cities.

Persons killed per 10,000 inhabitants: Hamburg 1.5; Weser-Ems 1.43; Essen 1.18; South Hanover-Brunswick 0.81; Cologne-Aachen 0.75; Düsseldorf 0.73; Westphalia-North 0.67; Berlin 0.61.

The number of British civilians killed by air-raid action alone during World War Two, according to official statistics, totalled 51,509, not including seriously wounded. By the end of the war the number of German civilian air-raid victims was more than ten times that figure. Goebbels's intermediate balance-sheet therefore merely proves that Britain experienced the horrors of the air war mainly during 1940–1, while the German civilian population had the full extent of them still to come to them.

April 14, 1941

The Minister begins by stating that the great sensation of the day, of course, is the signing of the Russian-Japanese Friendship Pact and the dramatic send-off for Matsuoka [the Japanese Foreign Minister] in Moscow. For certain reasons, however, we for our part must report these events only in a small way at home and in the foreign language service. Sensational reporting, therefore, is not permitted; the affair is to be noted only by way of dutifully recording it. What must not be recorded is the exceptionally cordial send-off for Matsuoka and, above all also, the German military attaché being embraced by Stalin. For that reason there can be no argument with the conflicting American reports, much as they invite comment, claiming as they do on the one hand that the pact has not caused any surprise and, on the other, that the news has produced in America the profoundest shock for many months. Only the Japanese press may be quoted briefly.

A Japanese-Soviet non-aggression agreement was signed on April 13, 1941. This had been preceded by Matsuoka's visit to Berlin.

There is a report by the American, Dr Herbert Spencer, about German POW camps which, in spite of a favourable introduction, goes on to list only unfavourable observations. The Minister instructs Lieutenant-Commander Hahn to find out from OKW how Spencer managed to get into the POW camps. The Minister emphasizes: 'We National Socialists have always refused to allow matters which concern only ourselves to be investigated by international commissions.' From the very first day the Führer has declared that he would not dream of allowing any experts into our concentration camps or admitting any 'appraisers' to the Reichstag-fire trial, who would then work as 'disruptive reporters'. If Spencer got into the prisoner-of-war camps through the Red Cross then one cannot do anything about it; if, however, this was a case of journalists then an end must be put to it.

April 15, 1941

The main task for today and the next few days, the Minister explains, is the discrediting of Britain in her attempt to abandon Greece. Admittedly this attempt has not yet been made on the scale on which we are presenting it, but we must nevertheless begin straight away to give it much space in order to goad the British into making a reply. They are already declaring that they have merely taken up rearward positions and that they have no intention of leaving the country. The entire press must now be concentrated on discrediting the British, and what is more in the strongest terms they can find. In talking to the neutral world we must use a tone which reflects the peak of accusation and castigation. Churchill should be pilloried as a gambler, as a character more at home at the tables in Monte Carlo than in the seat of a British prime minister. A typical gambler's nature – cynical, ruthless, brutal, staking the blood of other nations in order to save British blood, riding roughshod over the national destinies of small states. We must then point out that we did our best to preserve the nations of the Balkans from a similar fate, but that evidently the cruel lessons which history dealt out last year were not sufficient for them, since they were evidently bent on experiencing for themselves what it was like to accept British promises of help in order to be left in the lurch by her when things got tricky. This gentleman who, when he received the news that Simovic had made a putsch in Belgrade, told the Conservative Party: 'I bring you good tidings', this gentleman who was jubilant when he heard that Yugoslavia had joined battle, the man who said: 'Our troops are itching to cross swords with the Germans; now we are there, we British are now moving into firm positions,' this gentleman who is now trying to talk his way out of it with rotten phrases such as: 'We are no longer in reserve, but standing to arms,' is now ordering his 'troops itching to cross swords with the Germans' to make for the ships helter-skelter and to beat it as fast as they can.

Above all, the point should be made with savage scorn that the slogan is now beginning to come true: 'Instead of butter – Benghazi; instead of Benghazi – Greece; instead of Greece – nothing.' This then is the end.

April 16, 1941

The Minister points out that our persistent propaganda has now at last succeeded in getting the British out into the open: they are now reacting and denying our reports of their flight. These denials must be refuted and branded as impertinent lies. We might present to them, above all, the observation of *The New York Times* which says it is entirely possible that the British are now giving up the Greek operation and are 'temporarily abandoning' Greece. We must now ask the question: 'How can these statements be reconciled? On the one hand the British are saying: There is not a grain of truth in the German reports; on the other hand the American papers, running ahead of British admissions and taking account of actual facts, are reporting that the British are not only considering the idea but carrying it into practice. As for the British declarations, we attach no importance to them whatever. The British made exactly the same boastful noises before fleeing from Dunkirk; indeed, when they got part of their invasion army back to England they even represented this as some special trick by which they had brilliantly out-manoeuvred us. This time we are going to tear the mask off their face; we know very well that they are fleeing and leaving the Greeks to their fate.' As for the Transocean report 'Britain is heading for a disaster of the first order' (threat to the Suez Canal), the Minister explains that this is not to be used in the German press for the time being, but only in the foreign language service, and then only as a quotation of a British comment, without comment of our own. The Minister emphasizes that on the subject of Africa we do not want to speak of our intentions at all, but only of what we have achieved. Our whole news policy has been distinguished by the fact that, quite unlike the British, we have never had to retract anything. The flood of incoming material and victory reports at the moment is so great that we do not depend on such optimistic forecasts but can confine ourselves to actual facts.

The observations of the Reuters diplomatic correspondent on the loss of Bardia can also be very profitably taken up. (Bardia, he says, lacks water during the hot months and cannot therefore be held.) One might remark, for instance: 'The British, as of course everyone knows, can manage without water. They don't drink water, only the Germans drink water. Therefore the Germans cannot hold Bardia whereas the British, if they had wanted to, would of course have held on to it. One is reminded of the story of the fox and the grapes.' (Also for the foreign language service.)

April 17, 1941

Reports on the very heavy German air raids on London, very effectively describing their devastating effects, are to be extensively reproduced in the German press (and of course also in the foreign language service), especially in the air-raid danger areas. A report from Kiel indicates that morale in Kiel is rather low; it is reported, among other things, that hundreds and thousands are leaving the city each night in order to camp in tents outside. In those areas, in particular, it is important to list the figures of persons killed on the enemy side, since this provides them with a boost to morale.

The Minister states that there is an impression that public opinion in Britain is at present on a rapid downward slide, although it cannot be said for certain whether it will lead to a crisis. There are two possibilities – on the one hand, an opposition to Churchill may indeed develop in the press and in the circles behind the press, but this seems rather unlikely at the moment; the other possibility, and this looks more probable, is that owing to the campaign of make-believe, followed by disappointment, a profound malaise is now sweeping the British public. It is possible that the British press's criticism of the government and its measures is in fact being practised at Churchill's direct request; it might be compared with the opening of a valve to prevent a boiler exploding. The Minister does not think it right to derive from this crisis of morale any hopes of a collapse of British resistance.

As for the cynical American remark that 'America can now no longer offer any aid to the Balkans – this was only a gesture in the form of cheques and a few ambulances,' this should be given a good deal of prominence, preferably without much comment, simply in the form of a juxtaposition, for instance with Roosevelt's telegram to King Peter at the beginning of hostilities.

The Minister instructs Herr Fritzsche to see to it that no remarks whatever about any sign of British readiness to come to an agreement should reach the public by way of the press. The foreign language service, likewise, should not take any notice of such comment.

In this connexion the Minister explains that we should be clear on the point that the campaign in the Balkans had not been so popular as the campaign in the West, and that naturally our people's enthusiasm for military developments must flag a little as time goes by. It has been reported, among other things, that military events were viewed more objectively when the last newsreel was shown, and no longer with the wild enthusiasm met during the campaign in the West. Fortunately the new weekly newsreel, which is just being issued, is quite exemplary, one of the best newsreels ever brought out.

In reply to a question Herr Gutterer reports that the Vatican radio has been transmitting its news bulletin twice daily since April 15. Herr Dr Bömer states that material about this is now being compiled. The Minister wishes to use this material by way of Ambassador Alfieri and the nuncio, without ourselves making an appearance at all. He thinks it possible to silence the Vatican radio. This would be highly desirable since the Vatican radio is more troublesome than, say, a communist transmitter (which in Germany has no class to address itself to) simply because it addresses itself to forty million catholics who do not consider it a crime to listen to the Vatican radio since most catholics believe it to be a religious institution.

At the end of April a compilation of material about the Vatican radio was passed on to the Italian ambassador in Berlin. The ambassador was to draw the nuncio's attention to it in an entirely informal way and, as it were, 'only as a piece of friendly advice'.

April 18, 1941

Herr Fritzsche asks whether a celebration should take place on the radio at 12.00 hours today at the moment of the coming into force of the armistice; he himself does not consider this necessary. The Minister explains that the German people view the Serbo-Greek war as one whole; any celebration therefore would be more suitably postponed until the end of the Balkan campaign as a whole. Lieutenant-Colonel Martin recommends that tribute should be paid to the significance of the event by drawing attention once more, in retrospect, to its difficulties and above all to the very different situation compared with 1915. Then, a large part of the Serbian army had succeeded in escaping; this time not a single Yugoslav soldier got away.

The Yugoslav army capitulated on April 17, 1941. Hostilities ceased at 12.00 hours on April 18, 1941.

The Minister refers to A.P. reports about heavy German losses in the Balkans. The German press should not counter these, but the entire external service should do so, and so should Herr Bömer for the foreign press. Our comment could be something like: 'These reports are no surprise to us. They are the obligatory claims. We remind you that, when Norway was being occupied, it was said that the whole Skagerrak was covered with the corpses of German troops; afterwards it turned out that the entire Norwegian campaign cost us about 3,000 killed.' The Minister does not desire a formal denial; it should simply be said: 'We know those methods, they are nothing new to us.'

The total losses of the German Wehrmacht during the Balkan campaign were 2,559 killed, 5,820 wounded and 3,169 missing.

Prior to the official release of German casualty figures the press and radio had mostly been obliged to use the British casualty reports as a basis for their polemics. Later too, it appeared to have been a principle of British information policy to counter reports of German victories by figures of German losses; this practice gave Goebbels a good deal of trouble.

April 19, 1941

The Minister next remarks that he has seen a PK* report this morning

* See footnote on p. 10.

about Greece in which the Greeks were referred to in a somewhat derogatory manner. The Minister does not believe that this is right. It is not to the liking of the German people, nor to that of the Führer. Nor is it true that Athens was attacked yesterday. The Führer has issued express orders that Athens should not be bombed, not even if it is strategically necessary. All that happened was that the *Piraeus* was mined. All possible care should be taken not to offend the Greeks in any way. Herr Stephan is instructed to see to this. Turns of phrase such as: 'Now the Greeks are really on the run' are out of place. Besides, this is not even correct; on the contrary, in most of the captured bunkers only dead troops were found.

April 20, 1941

The foreign language service must deal with the British assertion, which has cropped up again, that the Austrian troops have no particularly high morale. When addressing Britain, in particular, it should be suggested that it is time the British thought of something new for a change. Surely it was boring to hear again and again of the same mountains of dead bodies, of incinerators for the corpses of soldiers and of the lacking fighting spirit of the 'Austrian troops'. Surely it would make a bit of a change for once to say that the Saxon or Württemberg troops had mutinied, just to add a little colour to the affair. (The subject is to be treated in a very condescending manner.)

Commander Fletcher has declared that if Hitler continues to lose his nerve and wastes the strength of his Luftwaffe on raids on London this can only suit the British. To this one might reply: 'If we attack London with exceedingly strong Luftwaffe forces this is seen as proof that Hitler has lost his forces, or rather his nerve, and is wasting his forces. If we expand our forces in North Africa then these are 'peripheral successes'. If we employ them in the Balkans it is said: 'Hitler is opening another front and dissipating his forces.' What then are we supposed to do with the Luftwaffe? After all, we've got it. Perhaps the British could give us some good advice? On what we should do so as not to open a new front, not to dissipate our forces and not to waste them. Perhaps we should attack our own cities?'

According to an official British report of May 23, 1941, the German Luftwaffe lost about 10,000 aircraft during the preceding 21 months, whereas the RAF lost only 227 machines. According to the figures of the German Quartermaster General, German aircraft losses during that period amounted to barely 5,000 machines, including aircraft with as little as 10 per cent damage.

Lieutenant-Colonel Martin reports that information from a source regarded as reliable shows that there has been a certain drop in morale in Britain. In particular, an argument hitherto heard only in certain leading circles – that Britain, even if she won the war, could not actually gain anything, so that the war was in effect being lost by Britain – was gaining ground among the people. The slogan is going the rounds – and perhaps this could be used by the secret transmitter – 'Britain cannot win anything by winning the war.'

The Minister states that he too is of the opinion that the morale of the British people is low. The press invariably reflects public opinion. If Churchill has now opened the valve of press criticism he has done so only because there was a need for it; if, however, the press has really 'gone wild' then this too could not have happened unless the mood among the public was the same. Generally speaking, he believes that the British are not only deliberately dishonest, but in part genuinely believe that the damage they have caused in Germany is more frightful than destruction in Britain. People are encouraging each other – just as the opponents of National Socialism once did in the internal political struggle – each tells the other only the favourable news, and the result is a make-believe picture without realistic basis. Only with extremely heavy blows are these illusions then shattered. If our present victories were to be followed by a period of calm, then the whole business would be checked within four weeks; only by ceaseless and repeated blows can success be achieved. We could not have overcome France on the propaganda front if this had not been combined with crushing military blows – blows, moreover, which meant the gain of space and territory. We cannot, at present, claim such gains from Britain. But in the one place where, for the first time, we are getting near British property, where we are standing at the gates of Egypt, one can suddenly see the full implication. Air raids cannot achieve what can only be achieved by territorial gain.

April 21, 1941

On the subject of Greece the Minister states that, following the Greek appeal put out over the radio, the king too (but not the royal house) should now be attacked. Over the secret transmitter, for instance, it should be said: 'Has it anything to do with Greek honour that, merely for the sake of offering resistance for another 24 hours, we should let all our bridges be smashed and all our oil depots be burnt? Patriots, we call on you! Has this king any right to speak any longer on behalf of the Greek people? This king, who has already had the Greek crown jewels shipped to Egypt, whose ministers are on the point of flying off to

Istanbul and who, as soon as the German troops appear within a hundred kilometres of Athens, will board his aircraft to escape.'

The secret transmitter 'Fatherland', aimed at Greece and masquerading as an independent patriotic voice of Hellas, operated by a secret political organization, started transmitting on April 18, 1941. On April 19 it reported that the British had poisoned the drinking water with typhoid baccili; on the 20th it called for the arrest of anglophiles and demanded the confiscation of British military vehicles and the looting of food stores; on the 21st it reported that the British would hold the families of Greek seamen as hostages and related scandals from Athens high society; transmissions on April 23 were concerned chiefly with berating the Greek king who was an 'adventurer' leaving 'nothing but catastrophe' to the Greek peole.

The Minister comments as follows on Sullivan's* observations: We can again take up the theme 'America will fight to the last Englishman.' It is perfectly obvious what Roosevelt wants; he wants to step into the British position of power in the world, and for that purpose he does not care whether Britain wins or loses the war. If Britain wins the war she will be so weakened that Roosevelt without any difficulty will be able to claim a whole series of British power positions; if she loses the war, Roosevelt can anyway claim for himself Britain's possessions in the western hemisphere. Roosevelt has no serious intention of supplying material to Britain – and even if he wanted to do so he would not be able to, since the American armaments industry is in no position to do so. He has only one interest – to prolong the war, so that the empire is weakened and made ripe for American legacy-hunting. That is also the purpose behind all Roosevelt's efforts to drag other countries into the war. In each case Roosevelt declared: 'We'll send aircraft, we'll send ships!' But he never had any intention of sending a single item of material. The classical example is again Greece and Yugoslavia. Even the Americans are beginning to reproach Roosevelt with this. These points of view should be brought out clearly over the English transmitters.

The Minister next reports that it has been proposed to him that a badge should be introduced for the Jews in Berlin – whom we cannot at the moment evict because they are indispensable as manpower. The Minister agrees that this is desirable and instructs Gutterer to carry out this measure.

At the end of August 1941 Goebbels, after a visit to the Führer's headquarters, noted in his diary that he was starting at once to bestir himself on the Jewish question, for Hitler had authorized him to introduce a

* Frank Sullivan was the Berlin correspondent of the *New York Herald Tribune* syndicate. *Tr.*

badge for the Jews. This was to be a large yellow Star of David, but its wearing was not to be made obligatory by way of a public decree.

April 23, 1941

The Minister remarks that everywhere among the German public one can now hear the offensive phrase: 'The British are tougher than us! Just suppose we had to go through what the British are now standing up to.' It is shameless impertinence to claim anything of the sort. The British today have not yet experienced or suffered even a fraction of what the German people suffered during World War One. Then, throughout four years Germany proved that she was tough at taking it – and not only at the front but also in the homeland. The homeland would not have collapsed, even in November 1918, if we had not had leaders hopeless beyond all description. What gives the German philistine the right to say: 'The British are tougher than us'? The philistine also finds it 'admirable' if Churchill gets up and, in reply to an MP's remarks about unrest among the people says: 'I refuse to answer that one – I know nothing about any unrest among the British public.' This is anything but admirable. Churchill unmasks himself here as a brazen liar.

The Minister announces that in a leading article early next week he will hold up to the German people the shameless and humiliating nature of such a remark about the so-called greater toughness of the British; upon this shot from the starter's pistol the entire German press must take up the subject. We must oppose such an attitude in the press, mobilize the Party, and, if anyone comes up again with such a phrase, say to him: 'So you find it admirable that such a rascal should come along and try to annihilate our people?'

April 24, 1941

At a mass meeting on April 24, 1941, Colonel Lindbergh made a speech in which he pointed out that the United States was not in a position to win the war for Britain. (*Cf.* April 26, 1941.)

The Minister instructs Herr Fritzsche to get in touch with the Ministry of Foreign Affairs concerning the treatment of the Lindbergh speech. The Minister has the impression that the United States is just now 'on the brink' and that, provided the matter is skilfully handled, it may be possible to change the mood there considerably. He recommends that the essential part of the speech should be carried on the second page, without dramatizing it, and that in particular it should be extensively reproduced in the foreign language service. It would then speak for itself. Altogether Lindbergh really seems to be a courageous fellow, making this kind of statement in the face of a Jewish public.

US press comment sensationalizing the British failure should be muted a little; in particular, we should delete from it the observation that discontented elements are also strongly represented in the House of Commons and that this will create serious difficulties for the British cabinet. Nor do we want to gloat over the fact that a swing in the popular mood has taken place in the United States. Such an observation would, if anything, impede it. We want to publish facts – one such fact, for instance, is Lindbergh's speech – but without drawing conclusions, and without reproducing any conclusions drawn by the US press. The same ruling applies to the sort of vocabulary used concerning events in Britain.

Herr Dr Bömer next reports that Stefani* has published full details of the armistice terms for the Greek Northern Army. The Minister believes that, allowing for conditions in Italy, we should not be too strict about the behaviour of the Italians after the victory in the Balkans.

The Greek Twelfth Army signed its capitulation on April 21, 1941. At Mussolini's insistence the signing was repeated in Salonika on April 23, 1941, with the Italians participating this time. Italian reports presented the Greek surrender as if it were a success for the Italians alone.

Throughout the Balkan campaign, German propaganda had to tread a difficult course between the resentment and capricious information policy of Germany's Italian comrades-in-arms on the one hand and the anti-Italian sentiments of the German troops and the German population. At the very beginning of the campaign the Italians complained that their achievements in Yugoslavia were not being adequately publicized. Goebbels demanded greater forbearance to prevent the 'anti-Italian wave' getting out of hand. The SD report of April 10, 1941 stated: 'The more successful the Germans are in those theatres of war where until now the Italians have been fighting, the more does public indignation and dislike of the Italians grow. The question is being asked everywhere, and with a certain bitterness, of what the Italian troops were doing throughout those long months. In most conversations among Germans the difference in the standard of armament of the German and Italian troops is not mentioned, and indeed it is almost universally unknown.'

Lieutenant-Colonel Martin passes on a report about the effect of German propaganda in Britain. This begins by saying that the effect of German air raids on Britain is being impaired by the firm conviction of the British that their air force is causing equally extensive devastation in Germany. It then points out that the broadcasts intended for Britain fail to make adequate allowance for the psychological make-up of the British working class. One of the biggest mistakes of the German radio is its

* The official Italian news agency. *Tr.*

tendency to ridicule British reports as a matter of principle, instead of dealing with them seriously. The British public is entirely accessible to reasoned arguments, but these must be put forward calmly and factually. German propaganda misses its purpose and becomes downright counter-productive if it claims that all British radio and newspaper reports are invariably lies.

April 25, 1941

The Minister states that we are now at a certain turning point in our foreign propaganda – both with regard to Britain and also to America.

(a) *Britain:* British public opinion is at present quite unmistakably passing through a profound shock, brought about on the one hand by the serious military failures suffered by the British Empire and on the other by Churchill's persistent silence in the face of mounting criticism in Britain.

A whole series of intelligence reports reveal clearly that our air raids have caused very heavy devastation, not only in the cities but also in British public opinion. In such a situation heavily loaded polemics are not as effective as an entirely sober, realistic presentation of facts. When a person has suffered some very heavy blows and you then step in front of him and say: 'It's all your own fault because you wouldn't listen,' then his reaction will be annoyance. But if one allows the facts to speak calmly and without any polemical overtones, then this will impress him far more. For this reason we must now as far as possible completely eliminate in our foreign services addressed to the British public (not only in the mother country but also in the Empire) all condescending, ironical and in part even cynical polemics, and instead confine ourselves to the quoting of press comment, remarks by Lindbergh or Wheeler, to reporting what *The New York Times,* the Athens press, the Turkish press are writing, talk about the high morale in Germany, contradict that Berlin has been attacked, etc.

(b) *America:* There can be no doubt that opposition to Roosevelt is now growing in America from hour to hour. This, too, is due to the serious military failures of the British in the Balkans and in North Africa. Under the pressure of public opinion, Roosevelt now has to drag his feet in pursuing his interventionist policy. There can be no doubt that he would have got very much further today if the British had not suffered such serious military failures in recent weeks. We must now make every effort to eliminate the hysteria from American public opinion. Roosevelt would not be able to do anything at all if he did not pretend that we are in fact planning to attack the United States once we have defeated Britain.

We should not now ridicule this mood or make such comparisons as: 'Why, the Martians are just as likely to come as us!' We must let the facts speak: (1) point to the distances involved; (2) demonstrate that we have no need to make such an attack; (3) quote what the Führer has said about our relations with America, why we do not want anything from the United States, why we have no interest in America; that anything now happening in Britain is an expression of German self-defence. All these arguments are to be presented in the immediate future without any feigned intellectual superiority. It is all right to show one's intellectual superiority when the military weapons are silent. But while these have an absolute superiority one can afford, in the sphere of polemics and psychological argument, to waive this feigned intellectual superiority and let nothing but the facts speak. If we now pursue this path consistently, i.e. if we describe our military victories rather than use them as pegs for sarcastic commentaries, then we shall impress both American and British public opinion much more strongly than if we adopted the opposite road. I shall try to get the Führer and [the American journalist] Cudahy together and I hope that the Führer will make a statement to him. If so, I am firmly convinced that at this moment, when a very severe crisis for the interventionists has arisen in American public opinion, we shall be able to add that two per cent in order to increase the percentage of non-interventionists from 49 to 51.

All offensive turns of phrase must now be avoided by the foreign language services. The German press may well reflect a little of this new line, but basically there is no need for it to change its attitude.

John Cudahy, the American ambassador in Brussels at the outbreak of the war and a leading isolationist, was working at the time as a correspondent for *Life;* he was granted his interview with Hitler at the Obersalzberg on May 23, 1941, as arranged by Goebbels. On that occasion Hitler first of all rejected as total nonsense all claims by American circles that Germany was planning a military invasion of the American continent. Questions about his intended political and economic "New Order in Europe", Hitler very largely dodged. Cudahy first published the interview in *The New York Times* on June 6, 1941 and in *Life* on September 25, 1941. The interview gave rise to some discussion in the American press in which Cudahy repeatedly advocated an isolationist foreign policy for the United States.

April 26, 1941

President Roosevelt at a White House press conference on April 25, 1941, announced that, because of his political views, Colonel Lindbergh was not being recalled for active service with the US army. On April 28, 1941, Lindbergh resigned his commission as an officer in the US air force reserve. In a letter to the President he explained that he was taking 'this step with greatest regret.' But he would continue to 'serve my country to the best of my ability as a private person.'

At the conference of April 29, 1941, Goebbels declared that this 'classic' letter from Colonel Lindbergh to Roosevelt could not possibly be passed over by the German press, even though one of Lindbergh's intimates had conveyed the request that reserve should be shown in reports on Lindbergh since any publicity in Germany would only harm him in the United States.

Roosevelt's measures and remarks against Lindbergh should be commented on something like this: 'So that's what is called democracy! That's what the democracies are fighting for! For the sake of this sort of thing Germany has been challenged to war! That's how they are defending the freedom of opinion, the freedom of conscience! Just because Lindbergh took the view that Britain cannot win the war, and supported it with entirely clear evidence, he is not now called up for active service and is described as a defeatist.' This is to be confronted by the fact that the great American press (Hearst) is unreservedly backing Lindbergh.

In connexion with a *Suisse* report of a speech made in Switzerland by Professor Barth, the Minister desires the *Börsenzeitung* to carry the following reply by Megerle on Sunday morning: The *Suisse* correspondent writes that in the course of a six-months' stay in France, i.e. a belligerent country, he had never heard such incredibly sharp sallies against the Reich as in this speech made by a theologian in neutral Switzerland under the protection of the public and the state. In view of Switzerland's neutral stand the paper must decline to reproduce the speech.

This must be commented on as follows: 'That is how things started in Prague, in Warsaw, in Paris and in Belgrade. We want to point out that a government is responsible for the attitude of public opinion; examples prove that otherwise the attitude of the public can precipitate a government into adventures which will eventually lead to the annihilation of that state. We were on the best of terms with Belgrade – then came the gutter scum and made speeches, and it ended with bombs falling. Eighteen months ago we had discussions with the Swiss press about neutrality of the mind. We have no need to chew the same things over forever. We warn the Swiss government not to continue watching inactively this culpable and criminal activity of the gutter. Bismarck once said: "The nations have to foot the bill for the windows which the press has smashed." '

April 28, 1941

The Minister issues the following directives for commenting on Churchill's speech which, however, should not be given too much publicity in the German press but should, on the other hand, be run extensively in the foreign language service, especially to Britain, America and Australia: 'Churchill is one of those hippopotamus types who, after inspecting destruction in Britain, return to London not merely reassured but even refreshed.' We must bring out that whole cynicism with which Churchill declares that the British people are pervaded by a 'joyous serenity'. In connexion with a further remark by Churchill it should be said: First he drove the Greeks and Serbs into the war. Did he tell them in advance that his forces were not sufficient to protect these countries? On the contrary, he declared: 'I bring you good tidings,' and expressly declared that it was possible to protect the Balkans and cleanse them of the Germans. Now that matters have taken the opposite turn and, against all British expectations, the British have been driven from the continent, they are suddenly saying: 'We knew from the start that Greece and Serbia could not be held, but our honour demanded. . .' Now, did Churchill tell the Serbs and Greeks in advance, 'we know very well that we cannot protect you, that our forces are insufficient for that – but our honour demands it' ? Before it all happened, were they talking about honour or about the possibility of defeating Germany?

If Churchill now goes on to declare: 'Thus a large part of the mobile army of the Nile was sent to Greece in order to meet our obligations. It so happens that the available formations . . . came from New Zealand and Australia' – we must comment: Indeed, it so happened! It invariably 'so happens' that the British are in the rear; it always so happens that they are in retreat. It so happened that the British had no share in the casualties. It so happened that the greatest sacrifices during the offensive in the West were made by the French, the Belgians and the Dutch. It so happened that the Norwegians had to provide cover for the British flooding back from Norway. And it now so happens, since no one else is available any longer, that troops from the empire have taken over this task. The Australians are now available, but not the British, because they have to be kept busy as secret service agents in the Middle East with bombs and poison plots. A further piece of impertinence is Churchill's assertion: 'The Germans are trying to cause friction between Australia and the mother country.' We never said a word about this at all! On the contrary, this news came to us from Australia. This is really the last straw – Churchill suddenly attributing to German propaganda any friction that may arise between him and the members of the empire. If Churchill now actually suggests: 'Let Australia reply,' we may point out: she *has* replied already. She has recalled Menzies.

The German press at the time reported that there were stormy demonstrations against Britain in the Australian parliament when a telegram was read out from the Prime Minister, Mr Menzies, in London to the effect that, for reasons of security, he had been unable to get Parliament's approval for the despatch of Australian troops to the Middle East. Although Churchill had expected Mr Menzies to stop in London for some time with a view to closer contact between the British and Australian governments, he left London to return to Australia via New York. Fierce clashes between Indian and Australian troops were also reported from Singapore.

Churchill now declares: 'Of course we knew very well that the forces we were sending to Greece would not by themselves be enough to stem the flood of German invaders.' This cardsharper has always pursued the same tactics, starting at Gallipoli and Zeebrügge, and continuing with his sham participation in Poland, the operations in Norway and one in the West – a criminal, dilettante policy which results in whole nations bleeding to death so that Britain should subsequently be able to ramble on about 'honour'. As for Churchill's remark: 'When at last the Yugoslav nation rose spontaneously it saved its soul and the future of its country,' we should ask the question: Did Herr Churchill really, when the Yugoslav nation rose spontaneously – though of course there was no question of that at all, since no more than a dozen generals triggered off the disaster – did he then tell the Serbs: 'Gentlemen, of course I cannot help you, but why don't you at least save your souls' ? Did Churchill say to Simovic and 'Peter the Great': 'Gentlemen, there is no prospect of our sending you equipment!' ? Or did Roosevelt cable: 'We cannot send you any equipment, but do at least save your souls!' ? Or did he not instead cable: 'With our entire fighting strength and with all our material means we stand by your side.' ?

At the very start we must emphasize: It is typical that Churchill three days ago dodged all questions in the Commons. There, he might have been challenged after his speech, and awkward questions might have been asked – whereas now, at the microphone, he could not hear the interjections for one thing, and for another no questions could be put to him.

On April 27, 1941, Churchill made a broadcast on the war situation. Goebbels sustained his polemics against Churchill in his *Reich* article of May 4, 1941, entitled 'Bad Marks for Application.'

Churchill's speech contained these words: 'No prudent and far-seeing man can doubt that the eventual and total defeat of Hitler and Mussolini is certain in view of the respective declared resolves of the British and American democracies. There are less than seventy million malignant Huns, some of whom are curable and some killable, and most of whom are already engaged in holding down Austrians, Czechs, Poles, and many other ancient races they now bully and pillage.

The people of the British empire and the United States number nearly two hundred million in their homelands and in the British Dominions alone. They possess the unchallengeable command of the ocean, and will soon obtain decisive superiority in the air. They have more wealth, more technical resources, and they make more steel than the rest of the world put together. They are determined that the course of freedom shall not be trampled down nor the tide of world progress be turned back by the criminal dictators.'

April 29, 1941

On May 10, 1941, Hitler signed the euthanasia decree, which was back-dated to September 1, 1939. The decree states: 'Reichsleiter Bouhler and Dr med. Brandt are instructed and held personally responsible to extend the authority of physicians to be listed by name in such a way as to authorize euthanasia for persons who, to the best of human judgment and after the most careful assessment of their condition, are incurably sick.'

For the first time yesterday an argument appeared in British propaganda about which we need not do anything for the moment, but which, in the event of repetition, must be vigorously repudiated. The British are claiming that the Germans, who, as is well known, sterilize or even kill all their mental defectives and hereditary sick, would also after the war kill all their war disabled because they were of no more use to the community. The Minister points out that the subject of 'euthanasia' must on no account be touched upon at present. The issue of the mentally defective and hereditary sick must likewise not be taken up at all in this context. In case a systematic campaign is developed against us on the subject of the war disabled, we should merely say: 'British propaganda shamelessly alleges that the Germans are intending to kill off the war disabled after the war,' and this claim should then be opposed by all that we have done for the war disabled, and how much better off they are in Germany than in other countries. It might be pointed out that Churchill is making the dependants of British sailors killed in action return their excess pay. Herr Braeckow is instructed to obtain from the OKW data about our welfare measures for war disabled and – only for information, not for use – also data concerning the issue of euthanasia.

May 3, 1941

A *coup d'état* by Rashid Ali el Kailani led to the installation of a pro-Axis government in Iraq: on May 2, 1941, it ordered the British airfields of Habbaniya to be attacked. Iraq's rebellion against Britain greatly promoted German intentions, and plans for a 'New Order' in greater Arabia were seriously considered.

On May 23, 1941, Hitler issued his Directive No. 30 which laid down the measures to be taken in support of the Iraqi rebellion. Although German aircraft arrived in Iraq to support Rashid Ali, no effective military help was possible. The attempt collapsed on May 30, 1941. Rashid Ali had fled to Iran at the beginning of May; from there he fled to Turkey and eventually arrived in Germany by air.

The Minister points out that the clash between Britain and Iraq provides a good field of exploitation for our Arabic transmissions. We must now take up this conflict in the foreign language service on an increased scale, regardless of how we are treating it in the German press, since the foreign language service is not, after all, regarded as much of a yardstick of our official point of view. We must try to mobilize Arab instincts, which were so very successfully mobilized by Britain for her purposes in World War One, for our purposes now.

A report from Dr Schlosser states that the city commandant has informed the proprietor of the Frasquita that his dancing beauties are a threat to discipline and that, unless they are dropped, the Frasquita will have to be declared out of bounds for the Wehrmacht. The proprietor thereupon cut these dancing beauties from the programme. Herr Hinkel is to get in touch with the city commandant and convey to him the Minister's request that such measures should be discussed with his Ministry beforehand, instead of a *fait accompli* being presented.

The dancing beauties performing at the Frasquita from 21.00 onwards were a highly popular feature during the war. (*Cf.* March 21, 1940.)

In another context Goebbels remarked, on April 8, 1942, that a city of millions of inhabitants such as Berlin could not avoid having a brothel.

May 5, 1941
Hahn reports about the military situation and gives a preliminary numerical breakdown of British prisoners into Britons, Australians and New Zealanders. According to this, the roughly 9,000 prisoners consist of 7,000 New Zealanders and Australians and 2,000 Britons – but even these 2,000 are really only ground staff and rear communications personnel. The frontline troops, therefore, consist almost exclusively of Australians and New Zealanders.

Gutterer asks for other precise figures to be ascertained as far as possible, as these are very important for our foreign language services.

May 7, 1941
The Minister states that neither the German press nor the foreign

language service should carry commentaries on Stalin's assumption of the premiership. Besides, it is not yet possible to gain a picture of the reasons behind this measure, although it is probably correct to assume that it reflects a strengthening of authority in Russia, above all also in view of impending events.

The press was instructed on the same day not to carry any commentaries about the Soviet cabinet change, although this was featured as a sensation in the world press. The former Russian Premier Kerensky said in an interview in *The New York Times* that Stalin's assumption of the premiership certainly meant Soviet participation in the war on the German side. The German press was instructed to treat this remark with caution.

May 8, 1941

In his speech in the Commons on May 7, 1941, which was pervaded by restrained optimism, Churchill characterized the military situation and above all dealt with remarks by MPs. He said: '1943, even if we should still be at war then, will perhaps present us with less difficult problems.' This marked the beginning of the increasingly frequent argument of foreign news media that Hitler was engaged in a race against time.

On the subject of Churchill's speech the Minister declares:

Churchill's entire polemic is based on two foundations: (1) You must give me a vote of confidence, since otherwise you give joy to the enemy; (2) I cannot tell you anything, because information would be given to the enemy. With these two arguments Churchill successfully avoids being called to account at all. The Balkan operation with its huge losses of equipment, with its frightful loss of prestige for the British empire, is simply set aside, without any further ado, merely because Churchill says: 'You must not overthrow me or else you will give joy to the Germans, and I cannot tell you anything or else the Germans will learn something.' How, by way of contrast, does the German policy come out? The Führer yesterday gave an entirely unequivocal, clear, precise account of the events in the Balkans, furnished with most exact figures. We should be delighted if Churchill had done something similar. The Führer, however, who has kept nothing concealed, is being attacked because he has offered 'nothing new'. Churchill was not even in the position of doing as much as the Führer. We have nothing to hide in these matters. If in the Commons debate a British MP, Lloyd George, for the first time touches on matters which the whole world is discussing – and it isn't as if he had unjustly attacked the British government, he merely stated what the whole world knows – then Churchill says: 'This

159

is not the kind of speech one would expect from a statesman.' The main emphasis in our polemic about Churchill's speech should therefore be put on Churchill's evasion of all criticism.

The Minister further mentions a whole list of points from Churchill's speech on which our polemics can seize upon. Thus, if Churchill asserts that by bringing Greece and Yugoslavia under their control the Germans have gained no advantage, we can reply that nevertheless this represents an undoubted increase of power. We can point out in detail how much copper, iron and additional manpower we have gained for ourselves.

When Churchill alludes to Napoleon and says: 'It should at least be remembered that Napoleon's armies carried with them the spirit of freedom and equality of the French Revolution,' we may retort by saying: 'That was precisely why Britain fought Napoleon.'

As for his 'explanations' of events in Cyrenaica, we should observe: 'So Churchill at this moment still lacks all information of what has happened at El Agheila. The German armoured forces, which the British were 'going to cut through like cheese' and which were present in the şame numbers as the British, were able at any rate to chase the British out of Cyrenaica.'

For future use we shall make a note of the sentence: 'We are determined to defend our offensive outposts of Crete and Tobruk unto death, without a thought of retreat.'

May 12, 1941

The Minister begins by making the following fundamental remarks about our general propaganda concerning the war in the air: 'I have lately made the following observations on an increasing scale. We, who have to handle air raid reports day after day, are running the risk that topics which to the public are matters of life and death are gradually becoming routine matters to us. This applies to the troops even more than it does to us. It is natural that a serviceman who, at the age of 23 or 24, makes repeated flights over to England, smashes up the Tower or with a well-aimed bomb reduces Westminster Abbey to ruins, should have a totally different attitude to things from a person at the receiving end of the bombs.

In soldiers' language – but not in the language of the public – the Channel is known as 'the brook'. A serviceman does not say: 'We have made a heavy bombing raid' but 'That was a neat job.' The public does not feel it that way. On the contrary – for the greater part they now see the air war as a necessary and unavoidable but nevertheless frightful disaster. This is so not only among our people but also in Britain. It is highly typical that in a recent opinion poll in Britain on whether reprisal raids should be made against German civilian targets, the lowest figures in favour came from Coventry, Birmingham and Bristol. – i.e., the cities which have suffered most. Only 10 to 15 per cent of those asked there were in favour of reprisal raids, whereas such raids were demanded in areas of the north where no aircraft had ever approached and where, therefore, tap-room strategy was practised most.

I had a word with Gauleiter Kaufmann yesterday. There can be no question of the population of Hamburg having been softened up. But equally there can be no question of them saying now: 'Wonderful! Let's have more bombs!' When a city has lost 200 persons killed in two nights, when its town hall and several railway stations have been smashed, when the trams are no longer running and when civilian houses in the city centre are in ruins, then it will stick in the citizen's gullet when he reads a phrase like: 'That was a neat job last night' or 'That was a good punch we landed on the British.'

Of course I don't want us suddenly to develop fits of pacificism or to be too shy to call a spade a spade – but I do want those rather dashing and swaggering expressions, coined by 22- and 23-year-olds, to be left out of the discussions, so that our reporting is serious, factual and appropriate to the severity and tragedy of these events.

In this way we shall best meet the mood in cities like Hamburg and Bremen. I am, moreover, firmly convinced of one thing: it is fortunate for us that the bombing raids on German Reich territory are made in the north of the Reich and not in the south, so that these hard trials of endurance are faced by unspent Frisians and nordic men.

May 13, 1941

Rudolf Hess, Hitler's deputy, succeeded on May 10, 1941 – after three earlier but abortive attempts – in taking off from Augsburg in a converted Me – 110, reaching Scotland unscathed, and there landing by parachute.

It was not until 06.00 hours on May 13, that the British radio announced that Hess was in Britain. A few hours later the Nationalsozialistische Parteikorrespondenz, the Party information service, issued a communiqué which emphasized that Hess, physically sick, had 'lived under a delusion' that by contacting former British friends he might be able to bring about an understanding between Germany and Britain at this late hour.

The Minister comments as follows on the Hess incident: 'I am not allowed to give you any details at the moment about the background of the dramatic events of yesterday and last night. I only want to give you a few hints on your attitude before I am off to the Obersalzberg.

Our job for the moment is to keep a stiff upper lip, not to react, not to explain anything, not to enter into polemics. The affair will be fully cleared up in the course of the afternoon and I shall issue detailed instructions from the Obersalzberg this afternoon.

I do not regard the whole incident as so serious that it could shake our task – there can be no question of that at all. I am convinced that the military events of the next few weeks will make it possible to wipe out the whole affair easily and in a relatively short space of time.

History knows a great many similar examples, when people lost their nerve at the last moment and then did things which were perhaps extremely well intended but nevertheless did harm to their country. At some future date this will be seen as a dramatic episode in a great historic struggle, even though, naturally, it is not pleasant at the moment. However, there are no grounds for letting our wings droop in any way or for thinking that we shall never live this down. We have lived down quite different things in the Party and also in the state!

During the next 48 hours we really must move in with all we've got so as to divert public attention, to some extent at least, away from this painful incident.

The Minister further observes that his attention has been drawn to the fact that British transmitters are being listened to on a growing scale in the Wehrmacht, above all by the Luftwaffe – not for the sake of their spoken programmes but because of their jazz music. Herr Martin points out that during the day the men usually tune in to Radio Calais (a German transmitter) which puts out that kind of music. The Minister directs that Herren Glasmeier and Diewerge should discuss the matter with the gentlemen from the OKW; arrangements should be made for one or two transmitters to be made available for the broadcasting of light jazz dance music after 8.15 in the evening. The Minister emphatically sticks to the view that listening to foreign transmitters must be ruthlessly stopped, even in the Wehrmacht. It must be impossible for an air-force officer – even if he bears the Ritterkreuz* – to boast of listening in to foreign transmitters – i.e., of committing a crime which the Führer has threatened he will punish by penal servitude. Either this law must be revoked for the Luftwaffe – and that of course is impossible – or else it must be enforced. To let it stand without enforcing it is dangerous.

---

* *The Ritterkreuz (full official designation 'Ritterkreuz des Eisernen Kreuzes' – Knight's Cross of the Iron Cross) was a new super-grade, instituted by Hitler in World War* ii, *above the* EK1 (Iron Cross First Class). It was awarded for outstanding operational achievements rather than bravery – e.g. to U-boat commanders, or for the capture of major fortifications, etc. Subsequently Hitler instituted further grades for those already holding the Knight's Cross: the 'Oak Leaves to the Knight's Cross' (awarded rather like a 'bar', i.e. a second Knight's Cross) and the 'Diamonds and Swords', the highest Nazi military decoration, awarded to senior commanders in the field for the victorious conclusion of a campaign or a major victory. *Tr.*

May 15, 1941

The Minister states: 'In spite of a good deal of urging from many quarters I do not want to take up the Hess issue in our internal propaganda, or at least not just yet, but I first want to be clear about British intentions. So far no clear line is discernible among the welter of news and reports. True, an A.P. report is just coming in to the effect that the British will now try to make us jittery 'by unparalleled broadcasting propaganda.' That, in my opinion, would be the shrewdest thing the British could do – to fire off the wildest reports so that this schoolboy prank will after all cost us dear. Nevertheless I would like to wait and hear what Churchill has to say this afternoon. Certainly there is no need for us to put on our armour and strike out just yet. Once the business is touched on it will of course have to be treated exhaustively. Once touched on it cannot be dismissed in a few lines. One might, for instance, have to publish the full text of the letters. But one cannot take such a far-reaching decision until one has a clear picture of what the British are up to – are they planning to be mysterious about the affair and bombard us with atrocity stories, or do they intend to tackle the hub of the matter, or do they intend, since it involves the opening of peace talks, even though in a crazy manner, to let the whole business die down gradually? Up to this moment nothing has emerged yet that would entitle us to say: we are heading for danger.

The important thing now, as I said yesterday, is to preserve calm and composure. In a week from now the business will look different. Let me remind you of the Röhm* precedent. Then we took the lid off everything, and for years the business was a topic of conversation among the public. The British are trying to draw us out into the open. For the moment we will ignore the affair. Besides, something is shortly going to happen in the military field which will enable us to divert attention away from the Hess issue to other things.'

The Minister further declares: 'As far as the documents are concerned, you've got to be careful. Hess set out his whole plans in a long letter to the Führer. They include a peace programme which he drafted as long ago as last October. The main letter is dated October last year, and Hess disregards the fact that in the meantime the situation has fundamentally altered and that we are now able to demand a great deal more than we could then. That peace programme was made off his own bat, by rule of thumb, without consulting the Führer. Now Hess has cut out those points from the letter and had them translated by Herr Bohle

---

* Captain Ernst Röhm, co-founder of the Nazi Party, the leader of the SA, was shot at Hitler's orders, together with about 150 top SA leaders, in the 'blood purge' of July 1934. The breaking of the power of the SA was the price the Wehrmacht demanded for its support of Hitler.

one by one, so that his plan should not be discovered. Bohle innocently translated it all, in the belief that these were some leaflets which we were going to drop over Britain; each point was translated separately. I assume that Hess pocketed these sheets and took them with him, in order to make them the basis of his talks.

If the British government publishes what Hess has said or written then there is no danger for us at all, and indeed it may turn out to our advantage. But if the British government is determined – and if I were in their place I should be – to apply the principle: "Right or wrong, my country!"* then the business is dangerous. If they put out falsified statements about the raw materials or food situation, or the Führer's intentions, which after all they can fabricate at will, maybe even with faked signatures, then we must be prepared for a drubbing.'

In reply to an A.P. despatch we must point out that the British should not think they can rattle us with that kind of childish trick. What Hess wanted to say he put down very precisely in his letters. If anything else is now put in his mouth, beyond those intentions, then it must be a falsification. After all, we know Churchill's methods. And besides, we know that wars are decided not by phrases but by realities. And these realities have not changed in the least since last Monday [May 12]. We have not lost a single tank, a single Stuka, a single soldier or a single machine-gun, nor have we had to clear out of a single country; we are in Europe, bristling with arms, bristling with troops. The rest will look after itself.

We might also point out that every major blow and every historic success of the Führer's has been preceded by a similar event in Germany – just as if fate was trying to put us through some final test.

We were on the point of attaining power when Strasser's defection from the Party took place.† We can still hear our opponents' howls of triumph in November and December 1932, when they declared that Hitler was now a fallen star, a 'back number'. Eight weeks later we were in power.

Another example: When the Blomberg affair‡ burst, rumours were spread that the Wehrmacht was against the SS and the SS against the Party; there was wild talk of fighting in government quarters and of guns having moved into position. Four weeks later we had annexed

---

* Quoted by Goebbels in English. *Tr.*

† Gregor Strasser, probably the most important of Hitler's collaborators, who separated from him in protest against his opportunist policies, was killed in the blood purge of June 1934. *Tr.*

‡ General von Blomberg, Hitler's Defence Minister, was deposed (or 'resigned') in 1938 because he wanted to marry a whore – Wanda Sterzlmayer. The SS intervened by showing Hitler the police dossier on Miss Sterzlmayer's activities as a prostitute, declared that the officers' corps would not stand for it, and that, moreover, the Rassenamt (the Race Office) must strenuously oppose such a liaison. *Tr.*

Austria. Then, too, those illusion-mongering gentlemen on the other side believed they could wipe out realities with phrases.

The same thing is happening now. Just as the Reich is on the point of snatching victory, this business must happen. It is the last hard test of our character and of our staying power, and we feel entirely up to such a trial sent to us by fate. As for those illusion-mongers in London, those tellers of fairy-tales and inventors of atrocity stories, we shall talk to them again in a few weeks, when the guns will speak out. Then we shall see which is harder – the paper in London or the guns in Germany.

For foreign audiences there is no harm now in occasionally using arguments which we must not normally use during the war but which we used a good deal in the past: 'We believe in the Führer's powers of divination. We know that anything which now seems to be going against us will turn out to be most fortunate for us in the end.'

May 19, 1941

The Minister begins by stating: 'I believe we may now regard the Hess affair as closed as far as we are concerned, both for abroad and at home. At home the business has largely died down. Of course people are still talking about it, and we shall also feel certain effects of it for some time to come. But the public has reconciled itself to the fact; I have, altogether, got the impression that National Socialism among our people could be shaken only by the Führer and by no other person or event. I have just been among the people in the Oberdonau Gau, at Aussee, among quite ordinary peasants and wood-cutters, and all one can say is: To them the Hess affair is merely like a razor-cut on the face of the German people. I believe, therefore, that our tactics of passing it over in silence were right. Abroad, by the nature of the thing, a counter-wave has come into being, so that the Hess affair is no longer in the spotlight over there either. At any rate, the British have not done what I was at first afraid of. I must confess to you today that I had a few sleepless nights when I pictured to myself what the British might make of the incident and what serious damage might be done to our international prestige. Characteristically, the British have let a golden opportunity go by, and have again proved themselves clumsy and shortsighted. I believe the business has now more or less gone cold. We will not, therefore, mention the subject when talking to foreign listeners.'

The Minister desires the tobacco question to be taken up now with greater energy. The working people are complaining that they are getting less tobacco than anyone, because most of the time when they finish work the tobacconists are already closed. There are also complaints that certain firms are placing bulk orders for tobacco for their canteens, so that their own staff can buy there as many cigarettes as they wish. Suggestions are being made that consumer cards for tobacco should be introduced, although at one time this was found not to be necessary. Herr Gutterer reports that a commission is at present in Greece to arrange for purchases of tobacco. It is likely that the desperate shortage will be over by July. Besides, this is not just a question of tobacco supplies, but also of manpower and of coal supplies for the factories, many of which still hold major stocks of tobacco. Total production of cigarettes is fifty per cent above the peacetime level. Lieutenant-Colonel Martin points out that the Wehrmacht is beginning to economize: cigarettes are now being issued only to smokers who must instead go without chocolate. The Minister makes the point that in no case must matters be allowed simply to go on as at present. Useful as a universal stopping of smoking may be from a health point of view, at the present moment it would be highly inappropriate. The Minister instructs Herr Gutterer to convene a commission to examine how the problem could be solved.

The only thing Goebbels achieved for the moment was an improvement in cigarette supplies for Berlin in June 1941. By 1942, however, the introduction of a Smoker's Ration Card had become unavoidable.

The Minister states: 'Since the day before yesterday a full-scale atrocity campaign has been waged in the entire foreign press. It is claimed that photographs have been found which show how harshly the population is being treated in Poland, the Protectorate [of Bohemia-Moravia], etc. These stories are to be firmly refuted in the foreign language service, with reminders about the atrocity propaganda of World War One with those hacked-off children's hands, etc. By way of comment we may say: "We know that tune; the British have nothing left in their propaganda arsenal." In the German press, on the other hand, the subject must only be briefly touched upon.'

The Minister directs that as from today only light entertainment music is to be transmitted on the radio after 20.15 hours. He instructs Herr Fischer to work out a circular to RPAs [Reichspropagandaämter – Reich Propaganda Offices], the Party and its branches, etc., along the following lines:

In response to an urgent request from all military authorities, from the OKW down to our air squadrons, as well as from broad sections of our working population whose entire nervous energy is expended during the day's burdens and labours, the German radio has now decided to switch its evening programme through the summer months to gaiety, relaxation and entertainment. We know that there are a good many grumblers who cannot bear the idea, and who instead believe that we could see the war through more efficiently in sackcloth and ashes than with gaiety, good cheer and inner contentment. We also know that these people write more assiduously than those calling for merriment. These matters have received mature consideration and have been examined from all angles. The pros and cons are well known. We ask, therefore, that such letters should no longer be passed on; they cannot deflect us from our decision to introduce this innovation. Instead, we ask that the writers of such letters be acquainted with the arguments which have induced us to adopt it. The specific entertainment transmitter, Herr Glasmeier points out, can go into operation the moment the starter's pistol is fired. The type of music to be broadcast will be determined by the Minister himself.

The Minister instructs Herr Tiessler to discuss the matter with Herr Bormann and to tell him that it is important to prevent really serious damage. In connexion with the Hess affair the public has again been listening in to British transmitters on an increasing scale; they must again be weaned of the habit.

The plan was for three Reich programmes to be transmitted in future. A so-called 'Beethoven Transmitter' was to offer serious music; a 'Johann Strauss Transmitter' was to provide light music and entertainment, and a so-called 'Goethe Transmitter' was to be concerned with the spoken word, from political information and propaganda to poetry. The 'Goethe Transmitter', however, does not appear to have seemed to Goebbels to be a suitable medium for propaganda and was not, therefore, followed through in the way envisaged.

The German radio programme after May 23, 1941, nevertheless consisted of three programmes. There was, first of all, a 'Reich programme', broadcast from 5 in the morning until 2 at night; secondly, a light entertainment programme, carried by the transmitters Luxemburg, Weichsel [Vistula] and Alpen from 20.15 to 22.00 hours; and thirdly, a more serious music programme, carried by the Deutschlandsender during the evening hours and consisting of orchestral, operatic and chamber music.

May 26, 1941
The Minister begins by referring to the eminently usable American comment on the sinking of the *Hood,* which we must of course continue to publicize. British claims that they have been pursuing the *Bismarck* should be refuted, but of course without mentioning the aerial torpedo which the British claim to have dropped on a German ship.

During an exchange of fire on May 24, 1941, the *Hood* was hit by a salvo from the *Bismarck* and sank after a tremendous explosion. The *Bismarck* was damaged.

We must join issue with Vernon Bartlett's speech because there is a

167

risk that the next trick of British propaganda will be: 'Hitler is winning all the battles, but Britain is winning the war.' British logic therefore claims: 'Our victory consists of defeats.' The Minister further refers to a passage in the speech to the effect that the British retreats are sending the whole world into delirious transports of delight while it is taking no notice whatever of German victories.

Charles Vernon Bartlett was a Member of Parliament, correspondent of the *News Chronicle* and publisher of the *World Review*.

The Minister declares that numerous active servicemen who have had extensive contacts with the British are time and again pointing out that the front does not understand or approve of any frivolous belittling of the British on our part. There is, they say, no justification for this since the British are very tough, brave and devoted fighters. True, they will send the others in first and make them pay the first toll of blood, but if things get really tough they will fight with tremendous courage and daring. Besides, the Minister continues, we ourselves should be deriving no advantage from such reports, since it is no honour to us to fight and defeat a cowardly enemy who is forever retreating. The Minister therefore desires that, while not expressly giving the British a testimonial of particular Germanic courage, we should on the other hand avoid accusing them of special cowardice.

The Minister points out that it is a mistake to give the German people a drastic picture of the toughness of the struggle at particularly critical moments. Certainly it would be a mistake in a week when the German people are being told about such a tricky and dangerous operation as the occupation of Crete. The people are in a tremendous state of suspense as it is. The Cretan operation has undoubtedly stirred the German nation to its very depths. It would not be right in such a situation to point to its inherent dangers.

May 27, 1941

In view of the still uncertain outcome of the engagement of the battleship *Bismarck* with superior enemy forces the Minister considers it advisable not to touch too closely just yet on the *Bismarck* and *Hood* issue. Both in the foreign language service and in the German press the whole discussion of naval matters must be switched again to the Mediterranean. There is magnificent material available for that purpose. The Minister issues a few hints in this connexion. Particularly notable is the admission of the American paper *PM** that the British have

---

* A left-wing New York paper which ceased publication in 1948. *Tr.*

lost at least twelve cruisers in the Mediterranean. For the foreign language service the Reuter report about the 'heroism' of the British troops in Crete is very useful. Once the British start talking about 'tribute to the heroism of their troops' things are invariably in a bad way for them.

From among American reports to the effect that the successes of the Axis are of paramount interest in the United States, the reports on Crete should be featured. Remarks about the *Bismarck* should be left out. Herr Fischer is to instruct the press that phrases such as 'the battleship *Bismarck* is safe' must be avoided at all costs.

The 53,000 ton battleship *Bismarck,* launched in April 1939, was sunk by numerous artillery and several torpedo hits on May 27, 1941, while on her way to Brest, after having been crippled by damage done to her steering gear.

The British Mediterranean fleet lost three cruisers and six destroyers in the fight for Crete. Three battleships, one aircraft carrier, six cruisers and five destroyers were damaged. According to official German data, altogether one battle cruiser, seven cruisers, eleven destroyers, seven motor torpedo boats, three auxiliary cruisers, four submarines and six patrol boats of the British fleet were sunk by German air and naval forces in May 1941; five cruisers, one destroyer and two submarines were sunk by Italian units.

May 29, 1941

According to the SD report, foreign radio stations are again being listened to on a major scale. For that reason a few deterrent court sentences must again be published tomorrow or the next day. German listeners to foreign broadcasts fall into three categories: first, there are the deliberate enemies of the state, secondly there are the curious, and thirdly the philistines. A large proportion of the two last-named groups are deterred from listening in to foreign broadcasts by the publication of sentences.

Lieutenant-Colonel Martin reports that there has been some discussion in military circles on whether it is advisable to try to balance unfavourable news with good news on the same day. The view has been expressed that if, for instance, the announcement of Prien's death is released simultaneously with a report of the sinking of 110,000 tons, then the public at home and abroad see only the report of Prien's death and do not absorb the success story; it would therefore be better not to publish the report of our success until the following day: in this way a certain psychological low is allowed to spread and the next day our success is reported and boosted and the overall effect neutralized.

The Minister points out that this may be true for those people who look at things analytically, but not for the masses. Nor should one, when considering such questions, draw one's conclusions merely from the masses in Berlin, which are known to be particularly 'clever', but from the broad cross-section of the German people. Surely it is a most primitive form of consolation to draw the attention of a sorrowing person to something positive.

U-47, commanded by Lieutenant-Commander Prien (1908–41), was sunk in the course of a convoy engagement on May 8, 1941. The boat sank with her entire crew. On May 24, 1941, the press was instructed to 'give a good spread' to the Order of the Day of the U-boat service announcing the death of Commander Prien.

May 30, 1941

By June 1, 1941, Crete had been cleared of all British and Greek troops.

On the subject of Crete the Minister directs: the material which we have collected about Crete can now be exploited. True, we must not yet say that Crete is now in our hands, but we may start to talk in a way which assumes that we shall certainly seize Crete and that no reverse is possible any longer. We can now rub Herr Churchill's nose in what he himself declared on the first day of the operation and compare his remarks then with his present admissions and draw our conclusions. Then the slogan was: 'We shall defend Crete with the entire strength of our empire; Crete must not be lost.' Today: 'Oh, Crete is not really important; we only wanted to hold up the Germans!' In exactly the same way the British said: 'Norway is not really so important, we merely wanted to tie down the Germans in Norway for a while so that they should not be able to attack in the West', and in just the same way they said: 'France is not really all that important, we merely wanted to use France as an intercepting position so we could make our preparations in the British mother country.'

In speaking to foreign audiences and also to the British troops one should say: 'The British are bad losers. One always hears praise of the "gentlemanly spirit" of this nation and of the importance they attach to being sporting and fair. But we have not been able to discover anything of these qualities in their presentation of the war. They have never once said: "We have suffered a reverse." It must sicken a soldier, the way they try to turn retreats into victories, defeats into stages on the way to their final triumph, and the brazen way in which, in turn, they represent German victories as stages on the road to Germany's ultimate collapse. The British soldier, in fairness, does not deserve such poor propaganda.

It would help his reputation far more if London were to admit calmly: "True, we tried to hold Crete, and we defended it bravely. We did not succeed, we've suffered a reverse, and of course it is a great pity." In that case the whole world would say: "Bravo, that's the spirit!"

'Strictly speaking, every British serviceman should object to those braggards on the London radio saying: "We are cutting through the German tanks like cheese," while in fact the British troops are then obliged to retreat in the face of these allegedly rubbishy German tanks. If British propaganda had said: "The German tanks are invincible, there is nothing human strength can do against them," then a necessary retreat would be far less humiliating for their troops.'

A similar line, but of course with a few variations, should also be used in the German press.

In connexion with the report sent from Alexandria by the U.P. correspondent McMillan, about frightful atrocities committed by the Maoris in the fighting in Crete, the Minister states that this report is the crudest and most unambiguous admission ever made about such matters by the enemy side. Surely the political effect to be achieved with this report is greater than the disadvantage resulting from the anxiety caused to the next-of kin of the troops engaged in Crete. Herr Fritzsche is to get in touch with the Berghof* and point out the importance of this report.

Lieutenant Colonel Martin reports that the Chilean chargé d'affaires has notified his ambassador that, if the ambassador wishes to present his letters of credence to the King of England, he had better hurry up and come soon as it is being said, with an increasing degree of certainty, that the English Court will shortly move to Canada. The move is being opposed – so it is said – chiefly by the Queen and by Churchill, both of whom would presumably remain in England even if the King and the government were to leave the country. The Queen, it is said, has very much gained in popularity and is regarded by many as the true personification of the British people. The foreign diplomats are now housed some 50 kilometres [30 miles] from London, in accommodation built 6 metres [20 feet] below ground, in limestone. They are about the only Londoners who still receive petrol for journeys between London and their places of residence. Food supplies are getting more difficult all the time. Wealthy Englishmen are trying to cash cheques with New York banks, at a high premium, in order to pay for their passage should an opportunity of leaving the country present itself. This report could be used, in certain circumstances, on the secret transmitters.

The question of the radio music programme is discussed once again. The Minister directs that, even for the light entertainment transmitter,

* Hitler's HQ at Berchtesgaden in Bavaria. *Tr.*

everything of Jewish origin, or with English words, or with no melody and only rhythm, must be eradicated. Besides, measures should be taken to make sure that records with English words (also of American manufacture) are no longer on sale in record shops.

(*Cf.* May 21, 1941.)

May 31, 1941

Wilhelm II (1859–1941), German Emperor and King of Prussia (1888–1918), died at Doorn in Holland on June 4. The Reich Commissioner for the Occupied Netherlands, Seyss-Inquart, laid a wreath from Hitler at the Kaiser's grave, at Doorn on June 9, 1941. A Wehrmacht funeral cortège in regimental strength was also provided.

The Minister reports that the ex-Kaiser is dying and announces the ceremonial for the event of his death. The German press is not to make too much of the news of the death (one column on the bottom of the front page). The funeral ceremony may be described. The Minister gives the following hints for comment: 'It is not in the nature of National Socialism to revile former exponents of the Reich idea or to speak ill of them after death. There is no doubt that the Kaiser had the best intentions, but neither his régime nor his person offered any assurance that the interests of the Reich would be championed in a way which today's National-Socialist State both demands and guarantees. The decisive factor in history is not goodwill but great ability. Besides, the present period, when we are engaged in our struggle of destiny, is not the moment for a final historical assessment; that will be the task of future historians.' It should be expressly emphasized that we decline to revile such a man in death or to say anything hurtful about him. Besides, we are no iconoclasts; unlike the Marxists we have not removed the monuments of the monarchy; in our view all this is part of German history. Comment, the Minister points out, must be so devised as not to offend either a Nazi who is anti-monarchic or a good German who is monarchic. No paeans of praise but no condemnation either. 'The decision about the German state leadership has long been made by the victory of the National-Socialist movement, and from our secure position as a well-established national régime we may now pass calm and factual judgement.'

Herr Fritzsche is instructed to clear with the Berghof the presentation and commentary of the news when it comes through.

On May 29, 1941, the *Neue Zürcher Zeitung* published a major article by

Dr Urs Schwarz (b. 1905, Berlin correspondent, 1940–1) headed 'The Atmosphere in Berlin' and dated May 23. The article dealt with the after-effects of the air war and the preparations for it; it touched on the excitement caused by the Hess affair; it then spoke of the queues outside tobacconists' and the restrictions on the sale of beer; and it dealt extensively with the shortage of manpower and the measures designed to cope with this problem.

The Minister presents excerpts from the report by the Berlin correspondent of the *Neue Zürcher Zeitung,* Dr Schwarz, and points out that it is a piece of impertinence. He instructs Herr Dr Brauweiler to inform Herr Schwarz – not at the foreign press conference – that we strongly object to such ill-mannered insults. It is bad manners for a member of such a small country to try to sermonize us with such condescension. That kind of thing will no longer be tolerated; if it occurs again he will be expelled. Herr Fritzsche remarks in this connexion that the foreign journalists in Germany are altogether no longer serving any useful purpose; opinions abroad are now so crystallized that there is little point in chasing along after a few foreign journalists and organizing costly trips to the Balkans for them. The time for that has passed. Foreign reaction to Schwarz's report is bound to be: 'If that got through the German censorship then of course things are much worse still in reality.' The Minister points out that he has hardly ever seen a report by a foreign journalist which describes Germany's internal situation favourably. The Minister is of the opinion that one should take tougher measures against unfavourable reports by the foreign press representatives in Berlin. Herr Hunke points out that he has the impression that foreigners are being treated much too softly. That includes the foreign workers.

Nevertheless, no warning appears to have been administered to Dr Schwarz.

'The veil drops'

June-October 1941

June 5, 1941

The Minister remarks that it is now necessary to instruct the conference about the military and political situation which will arise in the near future. The Führer has decided that the war cannot be brought to an end without an invasion of Britain. Operations planned in the East have therefore been cancelled. He cannot give any detailed dates, but one thing is certain: The invasion of Britain will start in three, or perhaps five weeks.

By way of such and similar statements at the conferences in early June 1941 Goebbels tried to counteract the numerous speculations which were circulating about an imminent attack on the Soviet Union. He believed, moreover, that he had to deceive and mislead the participants at his conference. He also instructed his departmental heads to make certain preparations for an invasion of Britain. With the aid of the Party, rumours were systematically spread about an imminent visit of Stalin to Germany and about a ninety-nine-year lease of the Ukraine to Germany. In 1942 Werner Wächter, Chief of Staff of the Reich Propaganda Directorate, gave some of the secrets away at a private meeting. Since one was living in 'the age of whispering propaganda', he explained, the preparations for the campaign in Russia had been accompanied by so many rumours 'all of which were equally credible, so that in the end there wasn't a bugger left who had any idea of what was really up.' We now know that Stalin himself was deceived by German propaganda because he evidently placed more trust in his secret intelligence sources, which had been fooled by Goebbels, than in the first German defectors on the Bug.

Finally, in May–June 1941, some commentaries in the British press led Goebbels to stage a propaganda trick. On June 13, 1941, the Berlin edition of *Völkischer Beobachter* alone carried his leading article entitled 'The Parallel of Crete' which did not in fact go beyond what British press comment had already begun to be nervous about. The article became a sensation only when the edition concerned, having been first put on the street, was subsequently seized by the police during the early hours of the morning. All this, however, had been planned and staged by Goebbels in advance, in order to create the impression that he had given away the news of the imminent invasion of Britain.

174

In this article Goebbels wrote: 'And if the Cretan incident is today being hotly and passionately discussed in Britain, all one has to do is to read Britain for Crete to know what is meant.' He concluded with the prophecy: 'And if one were to tell him [Churchill] today what will happen in two months' time he would probably laugh again, and when two months were up he would, as before, be the loser.'

June 22, 1941

On June 22, 1941, at 03.15 hours the German offensive against the Soviet Union began without any previous declaration of war. German preparations for an attack on the Soviet Union had been going ahead at full speed ever since the 'Führer's Directive' No. 21 ('Barbarossa') of December 18, 1940; only the date of the offensive had to be postponed because of the Balkan campaign. On June 22, 1941, the German and Rumanian armies encountered an opponent who was prepared neither for an offensive nor a defensive war and was almost completely taken by surprise. However, not only Hitler but the entire German General Staff were convinced, on the basis of incorrect 'intelligence reports', that the Red Army was deployed along the western frontiers of Russia for an attack on the Reich, that such an attack was imminent and that it had to be anticipated by a preventive war.

On June 22, 1941, Hitler addressed a 'Proclamation to the German People' which put all the blame on the 'conspiracy between the Jewish-Anglo-Saxon warmongers and the equally Jewish rulers of the Moscow centre of bolshevism.' The Reich, he said, was now compelled to take over the protection and salvation of Europe. Simultaneously, Hitler issued an 'Order of the Day to the Troops of the Eastern Front,' along the same lines, but, significantly, he omitted to address himself in a proclamation to the 'peoples of the Soviet Union.'

The criminal, bolshevik double game which has triggered off the overwhelming deployment of the million-strong German army from the North Cape to the Black Sea is to be made the subject of extensive publicity in the German press during the next few days, in order to explain to the German people in impressive terms the meaning and historic significance of this struggle, as set out in the Führer's proclamation, in the special directives issued by the Reichspressechef, and in every other available form.

The outcome of the struggle is clear to us. It can end only with victory for German weapons. It is now the decisive task of the press so to guide the hearts and sentiments of the homeland that the front can again rely on it. This task is of vital importance because – in the interest of military operations – the German people have not been prepared to face this turn of events.

175

The German people are at present asking two questions:

(a) How is this war with the Soviet Union to be reconciled with hopes of an early end to the war?

(b) After years of anti-bolshevik struggle we concluded a pact with Moscow – so how did this second switch come about?

(a) Here the most important argument is emphasis on the fact that a full deployment of the German Wehrmacht in the West was impossible so long as an unknown, treacherous quantity stood ranged [against us] in the East. The presentation of this argument is decisive in shaping the psychological attitude of the entire German nation in this struggle, and must therefore be handled particularly well.

(b) Here it must be pointed out that this is not simply a straight-forward about-turn. National Socialism started as a movement in the struggle against bolshevism. As such it conquered and recreated the Reich. Once these tasks were accomplished, the struggle against bolshevism was set aside for nearly two years in what seemed to be a truce. Now that the Führer has unmasked the treachery of the bolshevik rulers, National Socialism, and hence the German people, are reverting to the principles which first impelled them – the struggle against plutocracy and bolshevism.

The Minister points out: 'The Führer says this will take four months. But I tell you it will take only eight weeks. For just as the essence of National Socialism towers head and shoulders above that of communism, so its enormous superiority is bound to prove itself on the battlefield in an exceedingly short period of time.'

Semler reported that Goebbels telephoned the Führer's headquarters on July 1, 1941, and was told by Hitler that he expected the campaign in the East to last three months. Nothing of this, of course, was to be mentioned publicly; instead, the German press was directed to stall public opinion on the likelihood of a rapid military victory. According to the SD report of June 1941 the German people's first reaction to the attack on the Soviet Union was partly bewilderment and partly 'sober confidence'. The first reports of victories dispelled what initial unease there had been.

June 27, 1941
Reports from all over the world reveal that we are experiencing a rising of the whole of Europe against bolshevism on a scale never seen before. Europe is on the march against the common enemy with unique singleness of purpose and is rising, as it were, against the suppressor of all human culture and civilization. The hour of the birth of the new Europe has arrived without pressure or compulsion from Germany.

With the proclamation of 'Europe's crusade against Bolshevism' the German press was reacting to suggestions from the Ministry of Foreign Affairs. In this crusade, according to the German diplomatic and political information service, Germany would with her allies, Italy, Finland, Rumania, Hungary and Slovakia and with fascist volunteers from all countries, discharge a European mandate. Goebbels, on the other hand, did not wish to see the word 'crusade' used too often in this context since the mediaeval crusades, in which rivers of blood had been shed, had never brought complete success and, in his opinion, would therefore give rise to pessimistic comparisons.

On June 29, 1941, the CPSU Central Committee in Moscow declared the defensive struggle as a 'Patriotic War'. In his broadcast of July 3, 1941, Stalin described the offensive against the Soviet Union as a 'treacherous' attack and announced that 'the best divisions of the enemy and the best units of his air force are already smashed.' The war, however, was not to be regarded as an ordinary war, not as a war between two armies, but as a patriotic People's War on a grand scale, whose end was to help all peoples of Europe 'now groaning under the yoke of German fascism.' It was a war of liberation, in which the Soviet Union had 'loyal allies in the nations of Europe and America.' 'Our war for the liberation of our fatherland will blend with the struggle of the nations of Europe and America for their independence, for democratic freedom,' Stalin declared.

July 5, 1941

Germany's squaring of accounts with Moscow is now uncovering and unmasking the greatest Jewish swindle of all times. The 'workers' paradise' is now revealed to the world as a gigantic system of cheats and exploiters, in which the workers are compelled by the most bloody terrorization to live an indescribably pitiful existence in inhuman conditions. This system where Jews, capitalists and bolsheviks work hand in glove, has created a quite inconceivable degree of human depravity. What millions of German troops are seeing there today is a picture of the lowest possible social living standard – from the pitiful hovels and lice-ridden homes, neglected roads and filthy villages, to the bestial drabness of their entire existence. By means of their diabolical system of bolshevism, the Jews have cast the people of the Soviet Union into this unspeakable condition of deepest human misery. The mask has now been torn off this greatest confidence trick ever practised in the history of mankind. The struggle in the East means the liberation of mankind from this crime.

It will therefore be the task of the German press to present these views in an effective campaign of enlightenment, by means of fundamental comment of its own, by the presentation of written and pictorial evidence and by striking lay-out. A particular role will have to be played in this by an impressive juxtaposition of inhuman conditions in the

177

Soviet Union on the one hand and the social progress, the high cultural standard and the healthy *Lebensfreude* of the working man in National Socialist Germany. A good choice of pictures, contrasting the bestialized bolshevik types with the free and open gaze of the German worker, filthy Soviet hutments with German workers' settlements, muddy tracks with the German Reich highways, etc., will be of particular importance in this connexion. This must be reinforced by pictures of GPU crimes, some of which are already available from Lemberg* and which the papers must not be squeamish about using.

The signal for the start of this press campaign was given by Goebbels himself with his *Reich* article of July 6, 1941, 'The Veil Drops'. His article ended with the words: 'The Führer's marching order issued to the German Wehrmacht during the night of June 21–22 was a historic act on a global scale. It will probably go down as the decisive moment in the history of this war. The troops now marching in accordance with that order are in fact saving European culture and civilization against the threat from a political underworld. Germany's sons have again gone into action to assume, not only the defence of their own country, but also that of the whole civilized world. Schooled and strengthened by the teachings of National Socialism, they are moving towards the East, a huge host, ripping the veil off the greatest political confidence trick of all time, thereby enabling their own people and the world at large to see what is happening now, and to see what will happen in the future.'

August 2, 1941

By August 1941 the Southern Army Group had reached the Dnieper, the Centre Army Group had been victorious in the battles of Smolensk and Rosslavl, while the Northern Army Group had crossed the Dvina and captured Estonia. A strictly confidential report sent to a press agency on August 2, 1941, describes the situation on the Eastern Front, principally on the basis of information received from competent persons and authorities in the Ministry for Propaganda. The report reads as follows:

The question of Soviet reserves has become of topical interest with the public since, more than a fortnight ago, the OKW communiqué reported baldly: 'Stalin is throwing his last reserves into the battle.' This OKW communiqué had a profound political purpose. It was to have an effect on the Japanese who were in the middle of the Matsuoka crisis† and

* Polish: Lwow; Russian: Lvov. *Tr.*

† Yosuke Matsuoka was Japan's Foreign Minister. He was a staunch friend of Nazi Germany and tried to push Japan into an even more pro-German course. But when Hitler deliberately misled him about Germany's plans to attack Russia and in consequence he failed to warn the Japanese government that this was about to happen, he was forced to resign. He was arrested as a war criminal by the Americans in 1945. *Tr.*

were in need of a boost. It is possible that the expected *political* effect of the OKW communiqué has in fact been achieved.

On July 26, 1941, all Japanese deposits in the United States were frozen. President Roosevelt decreed an oil embargo against Japan. The Japanese Premier, Prince Konoye, tried to alleviate Japanese-American tensions by calling a conference with Roosevelt. But before such a conference could even be discussed Roosevelt stipulated that Japan should abjure the Tripartite Pact. This it was unable to do. Goebbels gained the impression from a lengthy conversation he had with Hitler at the latter's headquarters towards the end of August 1941, that Hitler very much hoped, and had recently come firmly to believe, that Japan would intervene in the war against the Soviet Union, but that the realization of these hopes would depend on whether the Germans got to Moscow.

After their heavy losses in the battle of Minsk and Bialystok the Soviets were in fact obliged to use reserves, but these were not thrown into the battle hastily or without a plan, nor had they been brought up from far away; they represented the regular replacements for the various divisions. There can be no question of the Soviets being at the end of their military reserves of manpower. They still have enormous numbers of troops at their disposal and the question is merely whether they also have sufficient officers and leaders and enough heavy equipment available. The Soviet Union has about 190 million inhabitants, and the trained troops alone must certainly comprise a contingent of 12 million. The bolshevik system, moreover, is in a position, as a dictatorship, to mobilize a great many more male and also female forces, since all that is needed for this is a signature on the dotted line.

After the first lost frontier battles and the siege of Minsk it was up to Voroshilov, Timoshenko and Budennyy to reorganize Soviet resistance and rally their forces. In this they succeeded. Timoshenko, above all, had enough active divisions at his disposal to turn the battle of Smolensk into one of the fiercest battles ever. Only on very rare occasions was the Soviet army compelled to improvise. This happened in one case on the Leningrad front, where, in order to fill a gap, Leningrad factory militia were moved up to the front line for a day or two. They were, however, very quickly relieved by units on active service. Another Soviet army of five million men is believed to be standing by beyond the Volga; further major contingents are certainly stationed in the Caucasus, and beyond the Urals is the wholly unscarred Far Eastern Army. So far the Soviets have not drawn on these contingents at all. They are still feeding the battles with the huge numbers of troops from the various western Russian military districts.

The heavy armament at the disposal of the Soviet Union is likewise enormously plentiful. They have, moreover, still more than enough tanks, and it is becoming increasingly obvious that the low standard of living enforced by the system and the not inconsiderable labour efforts of the individual over the past twenty years have resulted in an unprecedented supply of armaments for the Soviets; this must have been known to our General Staff even though it was a closed book to the general public. Nor is it correct to say that the Soviet soldiers are fighting to the finish only because their commissars would otherwise shoot them. The active divisions consist of active bolsheviks who regard their system as paradise; men who, as a result of being cut off from the outside world for years on end, have never known anything else and have therefore been grateful for even the slightest token of advance in cultural standards. All this, needless to say, cannot yet be stated in so many words to the German public, even though it would go a long way towards a better understanding of the situation.

On the occasion of his first visit to the Führer's headquarters since the beginning of the campaign in Russia, towards the end of August 1941, Goebbels mentioned, among other things, the Soviet armies' power of resistance. Hitler explained to him that the German leadership had underestimated the Soviet striking power and above all the equipment of the Soviet armies. The number of Soviet tanks had been estimated at no more than 5,000, although in fact it was nearly 20,000. The same was true of the number of aircraft, which had been estimated at about 10,000 whereas in fact the Russians had over 20,000 at their disposal. In reply to Goebbels's question of whether, if he had known the exact numbers, Hitler would have shied away from an attack on the Soviet Union, Hitler allowed it to be understood that in that case his decision would have been much more difficult. (Hitler's figures were, in fact, vastly exaggerated.)

Because of this underrating of the Soviet armies the German Military Command, Hitler added, had found itself in a serious crisis in early August, but was now hoping to thrust beyond Moscow before the onset of winter. Perhaps, Hitler suggested in his conversation with Goebbels, the moment would then come for Stalin to sue for peace. Hitler would be prepared to accept capitulation provided he received extensive territorial safeguards and provided the Red Army were smashed to the last rifle.

The stubbornness of bolshevik resistance was taken into consideration in the German calculations, since one always allows for maximum difficulties and acts accordingly. Nevertheless, this stubbornness, like a lot of other things, comes as something of a surprise to the German people, so that PK reports, newsreels, etc., must now enlighten and instruct them about the facts.

No dates can be given for the capture of large cities. The view is being voiced that the occupation of Soviet territory as far as the Urals might not, in certain circumstances, be achieved until Christmas this year, but this speculation too is totally irrelevant and any discussion of this point is virtually impossible. In a war there must be surprises both positive and negative, and in a campaign against the Soviets such surprises can be discounted even less. According to authoritative official information everything so far has gone according to plan and we are in many respects relieved that the Russians have already engaged us with massive numbers at this early stage.

In an editorial article on August 3, 1941, Goebbels stated: 'The course of the war against the Soviet Union has so far confirmed all our predictions . . . The German people have every reason to look ahead with confidence and with the absolute certainty of victory . . . At the moment we are wrestling for the supreme decision. With it, the cardinal problem facing our continent will be resolved. The whole world is watching this dramatic event with bated breath. The enemy is still hopeful. But he hopes in vain. The German Wehrmacht is on the point of shattering his last illusions for ever.'

September 5, 1941

On September 5, 1941, Hans Fritzsche – very probably on Goebbels's instructions – conveyed to a small circle of Berlin press representatives a confidential picture of the situation on the Eastern Front, based on information from military sources. A record of his exposé contains the following passage:

The most important part of the front is *at the centre, roughly in the Smolensk-Gomel-Chernigov-Bryansk area.* At the *beginning of August* the Russians mounted a strong counter-offensive which carried them past Smolensk through *Yelnya* and across the Berezina to the Pripet Marshes. In the course of this initially successful big *breakthrough movement* the Russians succeeded in recapturing Bobruysk. The threat to the flank of Bock's armies was obvious. A counter-blow had therefore to be struck, and there followed the great battle of *Gomel* whose course is known from the Wehrmacht communiqués (mid-August). No sooner had this threat passed than the Soviets opened a new counter-offensive, this time from the *Bryansk* area in a two-fold direction – one thrust towards Gomel and the other in the direction of Smolensk. The Russians made a quite exceptional effort and are probably still doing so at this moment. It has been established that *two new Soviet divisions* are sent into action almost every day, or at least every other day. Former World-War-One officers reported a few days ago that the severity of the fighting was worse than in the most violent days of fighting on the

Chemin des Dames. The operations are still in progress. It can, however, be said that neither Smolensk nor Gomel is immediately threatened. On the contrary, in a certain sector the operation of the Soviets has provided us with an important strategic opportunity in the *Chernigov* area. We succeeded in crossing the *Desna* there and in taking the city of Chernigov itself a few days back. One cannot make any prophecies, but it is entirely possible that, striking from *Chernigov,* we may gain the road to *Kharkov.* This development would threaten the eastern Ukraine too and would enable us to attack Budennyy's army from the rear. This operation certainly could lead to a decision in this area.

The intention of the Soviets in these two major counter-offensives was the recapture of Smolensk (the key to Moscow) and Gomel. German supplies are reaching Smolensk in complete safety. They have at their disposal a four-track railway, right into the city of Smolensk, and, what is more, of German gauge – undoubtedly one of the most astonishing achievements of the German railway engineers. From Smolensk, however, it is not possible to mount a direct operation against *Moscow.* Timoshenko still has very substantial defensive forces stationed in the *Vyazma-Moscow* region. The town of Vyazma has never been in German hands.

Not until September 26, 1941, did Hitler give the Centre Army Group the order to mount the attack which would open the battle of Moscow.

After discussing the various operational sectors, Fritzsche makes a few observations about the *fighting strength of the Soviets:* the stubbornness of the fighting and of their opposition continues to be the same as on the first day of the Eastern campaign. True, on less important sectors of the front one has noticed that Soviet troop replacements are now of poorer quality. Occasionally untrained or badly equipped contingents are encountered. The number of deserters is also increasing. But none of this applies to the main sectors of the fighting. The number and quality of heavy equipment is decreasing on several sectors of the front, but the German heavy equipment is likewise over-stretched and has frequently to be withdrawn. There is an appreciable weakening of the Soviet air force. The OKW claims that the Russians have only 2,000 combat aircraft – i.e. bombers and fighters – left and that these cover principally the European front. This relatively small number is being switched from one front-line sector to another, so as to achieve some sort of air protection where it is most urgently needed. This figure of 2,000 cannot of course include the machines currently produced by the Soviets, dating roughly from the beginning of the war. There are also

182

occasional signs of a shortage of tanks. A few Siberian tanks have already been identified. This is regarded as most welcome, since the withdrawal of men and equipment from the Soviet Far Eastern Army is obviously of interest not only to ourselves but above all to the Japanese, who are believed to be accurately informed about this. Nevertheless it is surprising to see time and again how many tanks the Soviets still have left and are able to bring into action.

September 18, 1941
In their reporting of the campaign in the East the British and the bolsheviks, in contrast to their earlier optimistic accounts, have lately been indulging in excessive pessimism. They are now predicting targets for Germany's advance which are greatly in excess of what can be reached during the next few days. They are pursuing these tactics with the intention of subsequently belittling the German successes. Thus, certain time-tables and definite dates are put up again and again (such as reaching the Caucasus in six weeks). The German press has an opportunity here of consistently pointing out that these dates are falsely attributed to us by the British.

Although Soviet propaganda at the end of September 1941 was stressing the danger represented to the Soviets by a further advance of the German armies, it added that ultimately the winter would 'crush the fascist marauders'. Soviet propaganda, moreover, invariably claimed: 'Our reserves are unlimited.'

On September 30, 1941, Goebbels, in a leader in *Das Reich,* said: 'What London thinks about us or what value it deigns to assign to us is entirely irrelevant. At dramatic moments only realities count. And these cannot be swept away by phrases or illusions but only by even harder realities. These, however, are not at Britain's disposal – and that is why she will fall. Her fate is sealed. No power on earth can avert it. We shall live through great and eventful days yet. At the end of them Germany will stand victorious. It will be the culmination of the united efforts of all our people. It will mark the end of a total operation aimed at a total objective and achieved with the employment of total means – the triumph of a war and of a policy aimed at and achieving totality.'

October 4, 1941
In commenting on the Führer's speech, in particular his remarks about Moscow, we are requested by military quarters not to go beyond what the Führer himself actually said. Any further comment may let it be understood that new operations are now in progress and that, in the now familiar way, nothing is being said about these operations until the

desired objectives or successes have been attained. As for the end of the war, it is important now to make the point that what matters is not so much when the war will end as how it will end. There is also the opportunity of commenting on the Führer's remarks on speeches and deeds in such a way as to emphasize that ever since the beginning of the war the initiative has not for a single day slipped from Germany's hands.

There are no objections to drawing up figures and data about our successes in the East to date, in order to support the commentaries. Finally, it is in every respect desirable for our commentaries to contain an appeal to people to be prepared to make sacrifices; in this way it may be pointed out that in overcoming bolshevism Germany has overcome a crisis of life-and-death, and that bolshevik resistance is now broken.

The great German offensive against Moscow began on October 2, 1941. During the night of October 1–2 Hitler issued a proclamation to the troops on the Eastern Front, in which he declared that 'conditions are at last ripe for the final mighty blow which is to shatter this enemy even before the onset of winter.'

In the afternoon of October 3 Hitler made a speech at the Berlin Sportspalast at the opening rally of the War Winter Relief Campaign. In it he declared that the Soviet Union was 'already broken' and would 'never rise again.' This was certainly not reflected in the despatches from the front. Nevertheless, from the time of Hitler's speech of October 3, German propaganda was, for the next few weeks, governed by the slogan: 'The war in the East has been decided, even though the struggle is not yet over.' A press statement by Reichspressechef Dr Dietrich on October 9, 1941, emphasized Hitler's remarks that the outcome of the Eastern campaign had been decided 'with the smashing of Timoshenko's Army Group.' The *Völkischer Beobachter* stated on October 10: 'Stalin's armies have vanished from the surface of the earth.'

Dietrich subsequently added: 'Hitler told me – I am repeating this by way of summarizing the contents – that, after everything that has gone before, the two last great battles of annihilation [Kiev and Vyazma/Bryansk] have, numerically alone, so tremendously weakened the enemy, both in the field and in his war material, that he no longer possesses the strength to resist the victorious German Panzer armies with any prospect of success. Even though a number of more or less difficult operations still lie ahead before the enemy's total defeat, the German armies nevertheless have turned the corner, and the outcome of the Eastern campaign has now, for practical purposes, been decided. Our enemies' dream of a war on two fronts is over.

At this moment Hitler was firmly convinced that the whole war was won and he expressed this conviction to me in an emotional outburst although, of course, at my press conference I did not go as far as to inform the public of this. But I had no reason to doubt what the war leader and supreme commander told me at his headquarters in such a spontaneous manner and with a view to publication.'

October 13, 1941

In the evening of October 13, 1941, Hans Fritzsche, 'undoubtedly on higher instructions', addressed the Berlin Foreign Press Association on a number of fundamental ideas concerning future political plans. The political content of his observations is quoted here from a record dated October 14, 1941:

Militarily this war has already been decided. All that remains to be done is of predominantly political character both at home and abroad. The German armies in the East will come to a halt at some point, and we shall draw up a frontier there which will act as a bulwark against the East for Europe and for the European power bloc under German leadership. It is possible that military tensions and perhaps even small-scale military conflicts may continue for *eight or ten years,* but such a situation – and this is the will of the German leadership – will not prevent the reconstruction and organization of the European continent along the lines laid down by Germany. Certainly this will be a 'Europe behind barbed wire', but this Europe will be entirely self-sufficient economically, industrially and agriculturally, and it will be basically *unassailable* militarily.

The German state leadership has no intention of pursuing Britain and America into the wilderness in order to engage them in battle. This would be of no profit to Europe, and the expenditure in men and material would be out of proportion to the advantage to be derived. Things are different with regard to the island territory of Britain. The very massive German denial, issued on Monday, of alleged peace feelers by the Reich towards Britain and the United States has already revealed the political line we are now following. It is out of the question that, after the outcome in the East, we should approach Britain over any negotiation of terms – it is at most conceivable that Britain, at the moment of her total military defeat, should approach us with a view to receiving a place assigned to her by us as an outer island within the framework of the new Europe. In this connexion it is irrelevant whether Britain is to be attacked and occupied very shortly – or in the spring of next year, or in the summer, or whenever. Such a military operation would be carried out and completed by only a small portion of our total Wehrmacht. Germany will now lead a well-protected and secure European continent towards reconstruction, even though behind barbed wire and ever ready to defend herself. We do not desire to conquer boundless distances but instead to concentrate on the vast European tasks of the future. Should we be disturbed in this by enemy bombing or by attacks on the eastern frontier, or in some other frontier regions, then retribution will inevitably be frightful – until such actions by the enemy are stopped. As for the nations dominated by us, our language to them will become very much freer and colder. There will, of course, be no question of some crummy little state obstructing European peace by some special requests or special demands – in such an event it would get a sharp reminder of its task in Europe. In consequence, whenever the status of a peaceful Europe is proclaimed in future, the German press will be able to be very much freer in its treatment of the European nations and small countries. No censorship will then be necessary any longer since the imperial instinct will probably be sufficient to assert the German point of view at every opportunity.

If, therefore, the military aspect recedes – since the war as a chain of military operations will have been substantially concluded – the *political* one moves the more emphatically to the fore. This is where the papers are of enormous importance, and become the decisive instrument for guiding the people. The German people, then, are to be guided towards the imperial European idea, towards the realization that a state of tension will persist for many years and that this represents a natural order of world events for our European future. Just as the British are continually having skirmishes in India, on their north-east [*sic:* should be north-west] frontier, Germany too will perhaps have to engage in some fighting or skirmishes in the East or on other frontiers. This will strengthen the fighting spirit and the training of the young men of the Reich. It will be possible to reduce the great armies of the Reich automatically, perhaps to three-quarters of a million or one million or one-and-a-half million men. True, one will probably need a powerful air fleet, but no longer a ten-million man army. In the opinion of the German state leadership, the South has become an absolutely secondary theatre of war as a result of the military outcome in the East, which the Soviets can never again reverse.

Once the German people have in their own minds reconciled themselves to the fact that a war of this nature, naturally on a smaller scale than the present one, will persist for ten years, then nine of those years will virtually have been mastered. It is now the task of the German press to pursue this enlightenment during the coming winter, following up certain cues – and for psychological reasons this is, needless to say, a *highly political task*. The German people's *staying power* must be strengthened; when that is done the rest will follow of its own accord, so that, within a very short space of time, no one will notice that no peace has been concluded at all. This may sound odd at first sight, but it must be remembered that very considerable relaxations will be introduced in the near future as indeed they must as part of our European task; moreover, in extensive regions of the Reich, above all in the east, the south and the centre, the blackout will be partially lifted so that the entire labour effort of the people will now concentrate on production targets more in line with peacetime; also, within a foreseeable time, foodstuff supplies from the East, etc., will begin to function again – in short, the hardships of the war will disappear. Perhaps not at one blow but by and by, an enormous working rhythm will begin, with earnings and land gain and big transactions. Bombing raids, in the opinion of the state leadership, will also gradually lessen, simply because the subsequent German reprisals will make it seem inadvisable to the enemy to intimidate the German people in *this* way. The press will become much more flexible, it will be able to touch on much wider issues, and it will be able to operate politically in a sovereign manner where in the past it was tied to the most petty directives. For this purpose, of course, newsprint will be necessary, and during the course of this winter allocations of newsprint will become available in ever more generous quantities, since this is a decision by the Führer. If, however, this has for the moment to be preceded by a further restriction of newsprint allocation, then the German press should not despair of the task which, almost by a natural law, will shortly have to be assigned to it on an increasing scale. Even if the papers have to come out as leaflets, these leaflets will already have such validity in the European context that their repercussions will be greater than those of some impotent and obese periodical.

The outcome of this war has been decided. After so many years of hardships and of discipline German journalism will soon have a chance of collecting its reward. It will continue to be *the* instrument of guidance, before which the radio, the People's Assembly and every Gauleiter and Reichskommissar have to fall silent.

Although the official statements about the by now certain outcome of the Eastern campaign encountered a good deal of opposition with the army stationed there, and although the situation at the front did not justify any talk of an imminent collapse of Soviet resistance, opinion at the Führer's headquarters during the first half of October undoubtedly supported the official view – and not only in order to draw Japan into the war or reassure her in her dispute with the United States by means of premature reports of victories. The front, in mid-October 1941, reported fierce Soviet defensive and offensive fighting from south to north. Moreover, the German advance was slowed down as the roads became muddy and as continuous snowfalls resulted in three-foot drifts.

As for the allegedly imminent Germany victory, it was believed that this was suggested by 'intelligence reports'. According to 'unanimous statements by prisoners' in early October, only largely untrained NKVD and military formations without artillery and with little heavy equipment were then available for the defence of Moscow. Hitler already saw himself in Moscow and therefore, on October 7, 1941, forbade the acceptance of the expected capitulation of the city. On October 10, moreover, came the news of the evacuation of Moscow and the transfer of industrial enterprises from Stalingrad, Kharkov and Kursk to the Urals. When, on October 11, an appeal was issued in Moscow which called upon the last available forces to be mobilized for the defence of the city and ordered all Soviet troops to look after their weapons, it was believed at the Führer's headquarters that Soviet reserves of manpower and equipment were now exhausted.

There is no doubt that Fritzsche had Goebbels's full authority to disclose to the Berlin press the political plan on which Hitler was presumably engaged at that time; hints of this occur repeatedly in Hitler's table talk from November 8 to 10, 1941. Because of this faulty assessment of the military situation, Goebbels, in a letter of September 30, 1941, to Reichsleiter* Bormann, requested him to get Hitler's authority for the release of indispensable propaganda experts from the Wehrmacht even before the onset of the winter. On October 18, 1941, Keitel, the chief of the OKW, informed him in a reply from the Führer's headquarters that Hitler had made the following decision: 'With the conclusion of operations in the East, propaganda will again become a focal point of the German war effort. For that reason the Führer has agreed in principle to your demands, and he desires that within the framework of the exigencies of the continuation of the war, manpower indispensable for propaganda should be released wherever possible. . . .'

October 14, 1941

The vastly increased number of prisoners (the topping of the three-million mark will be reported in the course of the day) is an opportunity for the German press to discuss fully the collapse of the Soviet army and the enormous achievements of the German troops and their leaders, as well as the significance of the military accomplishments in the East. In addition, it is the task of the German press currently to dismiss the ludicrous reports and accounts by the enemy's so-called military experts and to confront the childish lies from London and Moscow with the actual outcome of these historic events.

In order to grasp the full significance of the number of prisoners taken in the eastern campaign it is necessary to know, and to compare it with, the total number of prisoners in World War One, which came to 2,520,983. Of these 1,434,529 were Russian, 535,411 French and 185,329 British. It is further necessary to add to these the number of Soviet soldiers killed, as well as the other casualties in order to realize that by far the greatest armed force in the world has been annihilated in manpower and material.

Since Germany's opponents had expected an early fall of Moscow, which did not however materialize, the British press in particular, during the second

---

* The highest rank of office in the National Socialist Party. A Reichsleiter was the Party equivalent of a Reich Minister and similarly concerned with a 'department'. *Tr.*

half of October, pointed out that German propaganda was desperately trying to mesmerize the German people into believing in its victory over the Soviet Union; this was being done both by special announcements creating the impression that something had happened, and also by the publication of figures to which a string of noughts had been added, giving the total number of prisoners and designed to prove that there were no Soviet armies left. It is believed that in October Goebbels protested to Hitler against Dietrich's news policy which, he said, was depriving German propaganda of all credibility, but he clearly did not suspect that this was directly inspired by Hitler himself.

'A war without crisis is no war'
November 1941-March 1942

November 17, 1941

On November 17, 1941, the press carried the announcement that Hitler had set up a civilian administration for the restoration of public order in the occupied eastern territories where military operations had come to an end. Reichsleiter Alfred Rosenberg (1893–1946, the son of a shoemaker in Reval) was appointed 'Reich Minister for the Occupied Eastern Territories' with headquarters in Berlin; Gauleiter Dr Alfred Meyer was appointed his permanent deputy. Gauleiter Hinrich Lohse was appointed 'Reich Commissioner for Eastland' (Byelorussia and the three Baltic countries) and Gauleiter Erich Koch was appointed 'Reich Commissioner for the Ukraine'. Reich Commissioners were also envisaged for the Caucasus and for Moscow.

From the very start, Hitler's intention to turn the occupied eastern territories into a big German colony could not remain hidden. Nor was it possible to conceal it by directives to the press such as that of December 21, 1941: 'Nothing is to be said for the time being about final intentions concerning the administration of the eastern territories. In particular, it is undesirable to use the term "colonies" or "colonial methods" in discussing the problems of the East.' Even less was information about the executions which preceded the introduction of the 'New Order' allowed to reach the public.

The military feats of the German army are now being succeeded by a generous new order whose importance must be suitably appreciated. The concept 'Eastland' is to feature prominently, without, however, circumscribing the boundaries of this territory in any way. Reference is made to DNB material which pays tribute to the pioneering work done by, above all, the new Reich Minister and his collaborators Meyer, Lohse and Koch. The appointment of Reich Minister Rosenberg with special duties for the reconstruction and reshaping of the Eastern Areas is the Führer's token of appreciation of him as a statesman. Commentaries should not make any predictions on the sort of areas these will in future become. What must be highlighted is the fact that this

190

appointment will serve to restore order in the occupied territories which for so many years suffered under bolshevik misrule. In paying tribute to Rosenberg's personality as a fighter, and in particular to his refutation of bolshevism, which he has actively been engaged in since 1918, care must be taken that the statement of June 22, 1941, on responsibility for the war is not shaken.

November 18, 1941

About the supply of *winter equipment* for the troops in the East it is stated: the winter clothing necessary for the troops (furs, drivers' coats, warm underwear, etc.) was organized as early as last summer. It is stored at railway terminals, ready for issue to the troops. Up to a point, distribution of the clothes has already begun. There is some hold-up because of the transport situation, so that a certain delay is unavoidable. It is therefore undesirable to refer just yet to winter equipment for the troops even though this in itself might be desirable with a view to calming the public. The result would only be that, having read about it in the press, the soldiers would then write to their families to say they have not yet received their winter clothing. In consequence, trust in the German information media would be shaken on a vital point. Particular care must therefore be taken when selecting PK pictures to avoid publication of pictures which might suggest that our troops have not yet received any winter clothing. (Undesirable, for instance, are pictures showing a column of enemy prisoners in greatcoats, while their German escorts are marching along without coats. This danger exists, in particular, with older pictures.)

The first preliminary talks about supplies of winter clothing for the troops were held about the end of July and the beginning of August. About mid-September the Quartermaster General reported to the Chief of General Staff about the latter's request for measures to be taken for 'winter preparations'. But by the time that winter had set in in Russia the troops had neither been supplied with the necessary winter clothes, nor were these available on the requisite scale in the army stores. To meet the urgent demand, the 'Wool Collection Drive' was launched at the beginning of December 1941, although Goebbels had proposed this as early as August. At that time, however, General Jodl had declined his offer to organize a 'national collection' of winter clothing because it was feared that both the men at the front and the people at home, believing as they did that the campaign in the East would be over before the onset of the winter, might be shocked.

Goebbels subsequently related that he had again approached General Jodl on the subject of winter clothing in October 1941, and that Jodl had replied condescendingly: 'In winter? But we'll be sitting in warm quarters in Leningrad and Moscow. You leave us to worry about that.' Meanwhile General Wagner, the Quartermaster General who took his own life after July 20, 1944, had organized an exhibition in Smolensk of winter equipment for the troops on the Eastern Front. Pictures of this appeared in the newsreels. Goebbels commented on this as follows: 'It turned out that General Wagner's exhibition and the assurances he had given me and the Führer were nothing but swindle. He had scarcely more winter equipment than he needed for himself and for his exhibition. In my newsreel I showed our people the Potemkin village of the winter exhibition in Smolensk, even though it was General Wagner who had built it. Naturally, the people held me responsible. Now you can see, they were saying, how that man Goebbels is lying.' But he lied again when on November 18, 1941, a press directive was issued stating that the army in the East had been supplied with winter clothing.

The British military mission in Moscow has repeatedly advised the Soviets to cease resistance in the Moscow area, to withdraw towards the Urals and to reorganize the Soviet armies without interference from the enemy. It is undesirable that the same advice is given to the Soviets in the German press.

The second phase of the battle of Moscow began about mid-November and from this, on December 5–6, developed the Soviet counter-offensive which finally halted the German offensive and forced the units which had advanced almost to the outskirts of Moscow to retreat. The Führer Directive No. 39 of December 8, 1941, ordered: 'Immediate suspension of all offensive operations and transition to defence.' On December 16 followed Hitler's order to hold-on. On December 1, 1941, Goebbels declared in the Great Hall of Berlin University: 'Militarily unassailable and economically secure, this continent, though in the middle of a war, can now organize its New Order just as if the forces of the past no longer existed.'

December 7, 1941
On the strength of the impressions he gained in Vienna the Minister makes a few fundamental observations:

Our propaganda so far has made the basic mistake of making the German people over-sensitive about any possible temporary reverses by withholding from them all unpleasant news. The public itself generally knows more about the overall situation than what emerges merely from the press, and it can take unpalatable truths and indeed demands them. Churchill did the right thing when shortly after the beginning of the war he promised the British 'blood, sweat and tears'. German propaganda, though of course it must always make justified optimism about the outcome of the war its fundamental attitude, must in future be kept more realistic in all its branches. As an example the Minister quotes that the public may be told quite frankly that the overall situation generally rules out Christmas presents, and that the travel restrictions – and this must be suitably explained – are expected to last, not just a few days, but some length of time, and so forth.

The Minister touches upon the question of how the resistance of the Russian troops and the Russian population should be explained. He points out that the Russians are used to very much greater hardships than the Germans. In the Russian army, for instance, neither the institution of a field post nor the notification of next-of-kin of those killed is known. Germany defeated France because the Germans were tougher than the French; now the Germans must become tougher still in order to gain that inner superiority over the Russians as well.

December 11, 1941

The Minister states that there is deep depression in Britain because of her heavy shipping losses. German propaganda, however, must not now make the mistake of emphasizing this depression too much. As was seen after Dunkirk, any such excessive publicity is apt to produce entirely false ideas among the German public. It should also be remembered that British propaganda, whenever reverses occur, skilfully allows morale to slump heavily in order to let it flick over into well-founded optimism very soon afterwards on the grounds that 'things are not as bad as all that,'

On December 7, 1941, Japanese naval and air force units attacked the American base of Pearl Harbour in Hawaii; 19 US ships were sunk or put out of action because of heavy damage. The United States and Britain thereupon declared war on Japan on December 8.

In his speech to the Reichstag on December 11, 1941, Hitler announced his declaration of war on the United States. He read out three articles in which the German, Italian and Japanese governments agreed 'jointly to wage the war forced upon them by the United States of America and Britain, with all means at their disposal, until its victorious conclusion.'

The Minister refers to public opinion in Germany which continues to compare Japanese and Italian achievements, with the result that the already poor opinion of the Italians is further worsened. In these circumstances it would be better not to quote Italian comment too much to the German public, even when it describes events in the Far East in a favourable light; any such Italian opinion would only encourage criticism of the Italians among German readers.

The Secret Conferences of Dr. Goebbels

December 12, 1941
The Minister directs that internal propaganda should not produce any excessive euphoria on the strength of military events in the Far East because it would be difficult to sustain this for any length of time. On the other hand, needless to say, the Japanese military successes must not be handled in a way unwelcome to Japan, let alone be ignored. German propaganda media must find the right path between these two points of view.

Japan's surprise victories in the Far East nevertheless remained the leading topic in the German press during the winter of 1941–2, especially since there were hardly any successes to report from the German side. The information media found this therefore a welcome opportunity of glossing over the crisis on the Eastern Front. Japan's entry into the war, Goebbels declared on February 18, 1942, had been 'a real godsend' for Germany. It was principally due to Japan 'that we got out of our severest crisis. . . .'

The British colony of Hong Kong surrendered on December 25, 1941. On December 27 the Japanese captured the American base of Manila in the Philippines and simultaneously reported their first successes in the island war in Oceania.

The conference of December 18, 1941, discussed the introduction of a Japanese fanfare to herald reports of Japanese victories on the German radio. The objection that this might offend the Italians was countered with the argument 'that an appropriate Italian fanfare is envisaged in the event of an Italian victory.'

December 16, 1941
The Minister demands the following propaganda measures against the United States:

(1) Preparation of pamphlets addressed to the German intelligentsia and proving by objective argument that the United States possesses virtually no culture of her own and that her cultural products are essentially derived from European achievements. In this context there should also be critical reviews of the American cinema.

(2) Alongside with this, some very popular pamphlets are to be issued which will address themselves to the broad masses in Germany, and in particular to the young people, and which are to point out that the uncritical acceptance of certain American measures, as also, for instance, of jazz music, etc., represents a lack of culture. Reference should be made, among other things, to the grotesque distortions represented, for instance, in the transformation of music by Bach into jazz.

(3) This German domestic propaganda should be prepared im-

mediately. It is not, however, intended for use at the present moment because, for the time being, there is a considerable wave of profound rejection of the United States evident in Germany. With the German leanings towards objectivity, however, the Minister points out, this wave must be expected to die down after a certain lapse of time and to give way to a more friendly assessment of the Americans – as had happened with the British at various times during the war. The material referred to is to be kept ready for the moment that this reversal of the public attitude occurs.

A great many brochures about the United States were in fact published, for instance by the Party-owned Eher-Verlag and by the Nibelungen-Verlag, the regular publisher of the Ministry for Propaganda. Goebbels, at the conference of September 9, 1942, criticized the America brochure published by the Eher-Verlag and already distributed in an edition of half a million copies. It contained pictures, he said, which, in spite of their unfavourable captions, produced a propaganda effect favourable to America. Captions, generally speaking, could never undo the publicity value of a picture.

December 19, 1941
The Minister makes some fundamental observations about internal German propaganda: there is no cause to dramatize the military, political or supply situation. At the same time, however, it has been found correct and necessary to present to the German people the reality of our overall situation clearly and brutally and to acquaint them with the necessities arising from it. The propaganda of 'realistic optimism' is necessary both with regard to the relations between homeland and front and to the domestic mood of the homeland. The Gauleiters, who have recently received appropriate directives of a fundamental nature, are unanimously reporting that this clear line is being welcomed enthusiastically by them because the stuffy atmosphere in which German enlightenment and propaganda work was conducted in the past has become intolerable in view of the actual situation.

Field Marshal von Brauchitsch, the Commander-in-Chief of Land Forces, had first offered Hitler his resignation on December 7 because he no longer enjoyed his confidence. On December 17 Brauchitsch repeated his offer which Hitler accepted on December 19. In a proclamation to the army and the Waffen-SS* of the same date Hitler announced the change in the Supreme

* The Waffen-SS was one of the branches of the SS, forming a separate army in the field, additional to the army proper (Heer). Before the war, men were volunteers, 6 ft tall, 'pure Aryans' and reliable National Socialists (like all SS personnel they swore a personal oath of loyalty to Hitler). In the final years of the war recruitment was progressively on the same lines as

Command and his own assumption of the Oberkommando des Heeres (High Command of Land Forces).

On December 22, 1941, the press received the following instructions: 'The Führer's assumption of command of the OKH, which is an impressive sign of the concentration of all forces on the front and at home, of the universal determination to make even greater efforts, and of the magnitude of the trust in him, is not to be commented on in any way, but should be taken by the papers as an occasion for deepening their own attitude of militancy and for redoubling their own efforts.'

The crisis on the Eastern Front had meanwhile become more acute. On December 17 the OKW communiqué first used a vocabulary which was to provide the propaganda 'cover' for military retreat until the end of the war. It spoke of 'improvements of the front line and shortening of the front according to plan.'

The Minister defines the aim of this propaganda as the toughening-up of the German people and the conveying to them of the impression that the government demands toughness but in return guides its people with firmness and justice. In this connexion it is entirely mistaken to describe whatever the homeland makes available for use at the front as sacrifices. It is no sacrifice if someone has to wait longer for public transport than in peacetime, or if he makes gramophone records, woollens or such like available. These are inconveniences, perhaps even deprivations and natural acts of help, but not sacrifices. What the soldier at the front is going through, the way in which, frequently without adequate clothing, with no fur coat, with insufficient ammunition and without adequate food, he faces a perfectly equipped, fresh, newly deployed enemy, the way he holds on to his position even though he may read in the paper that some society reception has just been held at some place or other in Berlin – that deserves the name of sacrifice. German propaganda, therefore, the Minister points out, must avoid indiscriminately using expressions, concepts and words which are suitable only for one particular situation. A differentiation must be made in our diction, in line with the real situation, between what the front is accomplishing and what the homeland is doing.

The Minister points out that in particular the woollens collection already ordered for the Christmas holidays must be presented to the public correctly and along these lines. The German people do not wish

for army units, with transfers from the army. SS ranks corresponded with army ones, but had different designations. Several colonels and generals held at the same time commissions in the SS, the Waffen–SS and the police – showing the close connection between these services, deliberately fostered by Himmler. The Waffen-SS looked upon themselves as élite units, employed for the political and ideological stiffening of the regular army. In the early stages of the war they were invariably the first to be pulled out of the line, to keep losses as low as possible. *Tr.*

to know anything about 'sacrifices' in this context; they will donate and collect gladly and generously if it is explained to them, first of all, that there is a grave shortage of warm things at the front and if, secondly, arrangements are made to get the collected articles to the front promptly and reliably.

In a broadcast address on December 21, 1941, Goebbels called for a collection of winter clothing for the front. He declared: 'I should like, therefore, to call the collection, which will open on December 27, 1941, and close on January 4, 1942, a Christmas present from the German people to the Eastern Front . . . We cannot yet give our soldiers back their homeland itself.'

The picture of the overall situation presented to the German public must at all costs be in line with the real situation. Only then is it possible to keep quiet about details the knowledge of which might induce the public to draw premature or false conclusions. We must make sure, therefore, that such details as are not disclosed to the general public but which, through other channels, will not remain hidden from a few people here and there, must fit into the overall picture presented by German propaganda.

As for the German supply situation, there is a prospect that the bread ration will be cut by 250 grams from February. The Minister points out that the correct way, once this fact has to be announced to the public, is to justify it simply and clearly. There is no reason why the public should not be told that these cuts have become necessary because of German deliveries to our Finnish allies fighting heroically and suffering a severe shortage. Disclosure of this fact can only have a desirable effect both at home and abroad.

(*Cf.* February 3, 1942.)

The Minister further points out that although in the past German domestic propaganda has always taken into consideration the effect it produces abroad, this point of view is now outdated. It was undoubtedly right, prior to Japan's entry into the war, not to allow Germany's situation to appear in an unfavourable light in German propaganda. But now every nation has taken up its position. Considerations of this kind, therefore, are no longer necessary.

The Minister points out in conclusion that these directives concern the basic line of German domestic propaganda for the next three months. These three months have to be viewed as a critical period which will automatically come to an end with the onset of spring. Just as, according to Clausewitz's dictum, a battle without a crisis is no battle

197

but merely an engagement, so, quite naturally, a war without a crisis is no war. It is the task of propaganda, by way of its fundamental attitude, deliberately to make the German people crisis-proof.

December 21-22, 1941
Care must be taken in internal German propaganda to avoid any discussion of the race issue cropping up in connexion with German-Japanese collaboration. The Minister points out that it may be assumed that, once the first major successes of the Japanese lie behind us and a calmer examination and assessment of events has begun, many a German will ask himself this question. Efforts must be made as far as possible to avoid a polemic arising in Germany which might offend Japan. For that reason the entire complex of questions had best be excluded from internal German discussion in the press, on the radio, in the cinema, etc.

In his further observations the Minister points out that the creation of the Greater East Asian Sphere by Japan has of course, in the long run, a dangerous side to it for the all-European sphere. Europe, and hence primarily Germany, has a high standard of living which is to be further raised. In future, however, it will sooner or later be brought face to face in East Asia with a bloc of 500 million people of yellow race whose average standard of living is very low and cannot therefore remain without effect on Europe. In mentioning these considerations the Minister adds that naturally this question must not be touched upon in any form.

Goebbels made a broadcast on Christmas Eve 1941. He took this opportunity to prepare the people for the new propaganda line and to point out that the front and the homeland would in future have to undergo more sacrifices, hardships and privations. He said: 'We must bear the necessities of the war. Life is hard. The war has made it harder still. We cannot master it by sentimentality. We must be brave and permanently at the ready. Victory will not come to us as a gift; we can only earn it.'

December 28, 1941
After presenting a detailed picture of the situation on the Eastern Front, the Minister points out that the moment has now come for the fortitude inherent in the German people to be made evident. People must be made to realize that our thesis of the superiority of the German people over the Russians must now be put to the test since we cannot otherwise maintain our fundamental claims. The Minister recalls November

1932, when the NSDAP lost 40 of its 230 seats: if the Führer had then paid attention to the low morale within the Party then a collapse of the Party could indeed not have been avoided. Similarly it is now the task of the leadership to inform the German people of the realities of the situation, and also to get them used to the idea that a reverse on one front is of no real importance whatever within the context of the overall situation.

The Minister requests those who may receive reports from the front not to give general currency to any unfavourable accounts these may contain.

The Minister points out that the Japanese in their propaganda are now evidently putting out not only facts but also forecasts. He requests that German domestic propaganda should confine itself to the reporting of facts.

Goebbels repeatedly directed that exaggerated Japanese forecasts should not be recorded. Such propaganda mistakes as the Japanese were committing, he said were 'the eggshells of the early phase of a war'; the Japanese were still unskilled in this art. They would, Goebbels argued, only do harm to their own cause if they declared – as a Tokyo naval spokesman had done – that they intended to land on the American continent and to march into Washington.

Goebbel's 'New Year's Message' for 1942 was addressed, presumably because of his anxiety about the military situation, to the troops at the front. In it he said: 'No one knows how long the war will last. But everybody knows that we shall win it – and that, moreover, is what the front is fighting for and the homeland working for.'

January 1-2, 1942

The Minister points out: the small European countries, and in particular the ones occupied by us, must be systematically persuaded by German propaganda that Britain has now finally decided to surrender the European continent to bolshevism. This fact, to be supported by British press comment and statements, is to be emphasized in particular to the leading classes of the small countries. In this way they must be made to realize that a common European defensive front is necessary against bolshevism and against the traitors of European culture.

In the German propaganda exploitation of the results of the collection of woollens and winter clothing it should be remembered that foreign countries will be very much more impressed by Germany's extra-ordinary and, what is more, successful efforts than by seeing a people which, while engaged in a struggle of life and death, continues to play at peace or to pretend the existence of peacetime conditions at home. Just as we are impressed by the enormous military efforts of the Japanese, while reports of a continuation of normal amusements and entertainment in Japanese cities would leave us entirely cold, so German propaganda must be clear that foreign countries, and that means our allies as well as neutrals, and even enemy countries, have more respect for massive achievements than for a mistaken playing at peace. By comparison, the argument used by enemy propaganda that Germany has to resort to such desperate measures as launching a public collection of woollens, is of no importance whatever, since enemy propaganda would interpret *any* German measure unfavourably.

The Minister points out that in future the Party will have to rely even more than in the past on improvizing major drives. Naturally, the planning of such 'mobilization campaigns' is easier, but is in no way adequate to periods like the present. Besides, the gramophone record collection and the woollens collection have again confirmed his old thesis that the people want to tackle practical tasks. All political lecturing is quite useless really, and merely depresses morale; if, on the other hand, the public is given concrete tasks which demand from them an effort and work, then morale immediately improves. The Minister expresses the view that morale among the public at large, in spite of increased restrictions, is better now in the third winter of the war than it was during the first.

The winter clothing collection was undoubtedly blown up by Goebbels into a political campaign of the first order. The press had been instructed to comment on the final result of the collection, which had been extended by a few days, as 'a vote of confidence by the German people for the Wehrmacht and the state leadership.' On January 15, 1942, Goebbels announced the final result of the collection. It was said to have produced over 67 million items.

January 11, 1942
As a reply to persistent stories about a revolt of German generals it is proposed to spread a report via Sweden or some other neutral information source, and also in the foreign language service, to the effect that a mood of crisis is reigning in London. London, it should be said, is now trying to cover up various crisis reports from the Empire by spreading big stories about the situation inside Germany. This news offensive by the British is best met by a counter-offensive. The German domestic press must not publish any of the reports about symptoms of breakdown in British government circles. The Minister explains that the British are 'raising a smokescreen' in order to conceal the signs of their crisis.

As far as can be established, a Washington despatch first reported on

January 7, 1942, that, in connexion with the winter crisis, German officers were planning to depose Hitler.

January 12, 1942
The Minister believes that there is in fact a crisis atmosphere in London at the moment. He is curious to see British reaction to last night's reports in the foreign language service about tension in London.

When the German press took up reports about disagreements in the British government, Goebbels, on January 15, 1942, directed that propaganda reports originating in the Reich and launched abroad must not be reported in the German press.

At home a campaign against barter and black market trade is being prepared.

The planned drive was approved by Hitler, although he first demanded a definition of what would be permitted and what forbidden in the future.

Goebbels tried to get the penal provisions of the war economy decrees made tougher. On March 25, 1942, a new 'Decree Supplementing the War Economy Order' was issued, signed by Göring, Frick, Funk, Lammers, Keitel and Bormann. This envisaged the death penalty only in serious cases, such as forgery of vouchers. Goebbels regarded this order as too lenient and intended to convey his views to Hitler once more. He believed that the ministerial bureaucrats had thrown 'a spanner into the works' of his efforts to convey ' the radical climate of the war.'

January 13, 1942
Complaints are made about the reporting of the [Vichy] French news agency OFI which has lately been putting out unfriendly military reports. The question is asked whether appropriate pressure might be applied to the French government at a suitable moment. For the time being the agency's reporting is to be watched.

On January 15, 1942, Goebbels instructed that, in view of the persistently unfriendly reporting by the French OFI news agency, steps should be taken in the appropriate quarters. The Ministry of Foreign Affairs was to protest in Vichy and perhaps threaten and even apply reprisals. In his diaries Goebbels recalls that German policy towards France had more or less foundered. Peace was being made although no peace had been concluded.

In future there are to be no more references to Anglo-Saxons but only to Anglo-American plutocracy. The concept 'Anglo-Saxon' suggests too

H

much their German descent and is not at the present moment suitable as a concept for our enemies.

January 14, 1942

The Minister believes that the German press is going too far in its examination of the British colonial question, and is giving rise to mistaken ideas among the German public. Signs of crisis and of food shortages in Britain must not be used in German propaganda when we are ourselves about to introduce restrictions. Such British conditions prove nothing except that they too have to tighten their belts. The Minister does not believe that the war can be ended by the moral collapse of a people but only by a military decision or a compromise. In our propaganda for abroad, however, these aspects of breakdown in Britain may be used quite legitimately.

In domestic politics the Minister demands a full-scale drive to organize untapped manpower among the German bourgeoisie. A bottle-neck has arisen in the armaments industry owing to a shortage of labour. This shortage can undoubtedly be redressed by using labour forces from our own country.

At nearly every meeting with Hitler Goebbels tried to get him to approve the introduction of compulsory labour for women, but until early 1943 he was almost invariably told that the latter had fundamental misgivings about the introduction of general labour duty, especially for women from the higher social orders. He was afraid that such compulsory work would lead to a dangerous blurring of class distinctions. The number of German women in employment declined by 147,000 between 1939 and the beginning of 1943.

January 16, 1942

In discussing the Rio Conference the German press should exercise the greatest reserve. The more reserved German press comment is, the better.

A conference of the Foreign Ministers of twenty-one American republics was held at Rio de Janeiro from January 15 to 21, 1942, to discuss the co-ordination of measures for the defence of the western hemisphere. The conference was called at the initiative of Roosevelt whose hope it was to persuade the South American countries to break off diplomatic relations with Japan, Germany and Italy.

The conference adopted a resolution consisting of four articles; the third of these, however, was amended at Argentina's request, to include the reservation that the rupture of diplomatic relations with the Axis Powers would merely be recommended to the individual states. Goebbels was jubilant when the conference ended with this compromise, even though only four of the 21 countries continued to maintain their diplomatic relations with the Axis Powers. In the case of Chile, Japanese pressure had played some part, and in that of Argentina Germany had exerted hers.

The Minister complains about a report in the *Göteborgs Handels- och Sjöfarts Tidning* which affronts the reputation of the German Reich in a shameless manner. He requests that the Ministry of Foreign Affairs should be asked to lodge a vigorous protest with the Swedish government against this article. In his view it is necessary to act against such vulgar offences, even if only to ensure an alibi [sic] for the future. He himself was overcome with wrath when he read this report.

At the end of January 1942 Goebbels received a report from the Ministry of Foreign Affairs about German relations with Sweden. This said that, especially in the war against the Soviet Union, Sweden had done more for the German war effort than was generally assumed.

The report also made it clear that Professor Segerstedt, the publisher of the *Göteborgs Handels- och Sjöfarts Tidning,* was a person against whom 'it is rather difficult to take any action.' Nevertheless, the paper was repeatedly confiscated in Sweden as a result of German protests. According to German information, the King of Sweden eventually called for Segerstedt to see him and asked him if it was his intention to drive Sweden into war with Germany. When Segerstedt did not deny this, the King is said to have drawn his attention to the fact that in that case neither he nor the former Pastor of Göteborg would be sitting in their seats a fortnight later. Segerstedt thereupon showed more restraint in his paper for the next few weeks.

January 24, 1942
The Führer now has before him a compilation of British comment on the hopes of the offensive in North Africa. This optimistic assessment [of theirs] will possibly be published during the next few days, when the Führer has given his approval, to be compared later with the actual situation.

The British offensive in western Cyrenaica, mounted in November 1941, ground to a halt at Agedabia in January 1942. On January 21 Rommel opened his counter-offensive for the recapture of Cyrenaica. The German-Italian forces, which had been encircled for weeks at Sollum and at the Halfaya Pass on the Egyptian frontier, had to surrender on January 17. On January 20 the German press announced that the Italians were defending the mountain position at Halfaya 'to the last round'.

On January 29, however, German-Italian troops again occupied Benghazi, the capital of Cyrenaica – an event which the Italians immediately recorded in a 'documentary film'. The film *Benghazi* had its first performance at the Venice Biennale in September 1942, two months after the final loss of Benghazi. Goebbels did not attend the performance because in his opinion the film was a 'falsification of history,' but on the other hand, he was anxious to 'show the strictest reserve' so as 'not to upset' the Italians. When the film was to be shown in Germany about the end of October 1942 he refused his authorization. In a note to the Ministry of Foreign Affairs he justified his ban on the grounds 'that a large number of German troops are familiar with the actual developments at Benghazi and that a showing in the Reich might therefore lead to undesirable comment about Italians. Besides, it might be pointed out to the Italians that not a single German soldier is to be seen in the whole film, a circumstance which might likewise produce an unfavourable effect on the public mood.'

Australia's serious worries should be greatly emphasized. The Australians could now be greatly stirred up by focusing attention on British neglect of Australia's defences.

Japanese propaganda to the oppressed peoples in East Asia should be supported. The Indians, in that case, would regard us as far more objective than the Japanese and our attitude, therefore, is of particular importance.

The domestic press is instructed to give more prominence to Italian military operations. Something has got to be done at long last in the domestic press to tone down the bad feeling towards Italy. We must keep the Italians on our side at all costs, and it is necessary therefore to give them some publicity.

Now and again the world press publishes peace plans by various individuals. These peace plans are to be passed over in silence as a matter of principle.

January 26, 1942
The Minister criticizes the Wehrmacht censorship in exceptionally sharp terms. Any photographs likely to popularize German generals are being ruled out by the Wehrmacht as a matter of principle. Pictures from Reichenau's life, for instance, are not allowed to be published. The Minister says: 'One feels like slapping those censors' faces!' Evidently a few superiors in the Wehrmacht would feel inferior to their subordinates. Rivalry and envy in the Wehrmacht seem to end only with death. Certain persons are evidently being plagued by the fear that some generals might become too popular.

The Minister mentions the fact that, among other things, the Wehrmacht censorship altogether forbade the German press to mention

General Rommel's fiftieth birthday, while that of some unknown Luftwaffe general who holds some administrative and technical post in the provinces, is allowed prominent treatment.

Goebbels's diaries of those days are full of praise for Rommel. In them, Goebbels also criticized the poor organization of von Reichenau's state funeral.* Nevertheless, the press did record Rommel's fiftieth birthday on November 15, 1941. The *Stuttgarter NS-Kurier,* for instance, carried a two-column article with a picture.

On January 20, 1942, Hitler awarded Rommel the Oak Leaves to the Knight's Cross with Swords for his 'defensive victory' in Cyrenaica. On January 29 he promoted him to Generaloberst for his recapture of Benghazi. On both occasions the press published the pictures customary on such occasions. The ban on the publication of anecdotes from the lives of German generals was relaxed on January 24, 1942.

January 29, 1942

The Minister states that, according to reports from numerous sources, morale in the Reich has reached a low ebb, or seems to have passed through it already. In particular, the German public now appears to have gained the conviction that there can no longer be a question of a disastrous turn of events but that, on the contrary, the front is being stabilized.

There was violent criticism among the public of the German information media. At the ministerial conference of January 19, 1942, it had been pointed out that the German public no longer placed any credence in the majority of reports. The reason for this was the inadequate information given to the press. On January 24 Goebbels decreed rigorous measures against defeatist comment from 'certain circles'.

The Minister directs that internal German propaganda must carefully see to it that no false hopes are raised on any military matter. This applies, for instance, to the development in Libya which, though very favourable in itself, must not be presented as though we intended to reconquer Cyrenaica.

Rommel's thrust into Libya petered out in early February.

January 30, 1942

The Minister announces that the Führer yesterday again gave him the task and the full power to decide who shall receive foreign news reports

---

* He had died of a stroke on January 17, 1942. *Tr.*

of any kind (DNB, TO, Europapress, the Seehaus monitoring reports, the Johannsen service etc.). The Führer has expressly named the few Reich Ministers and Reichsleiters who may receive these, and he has issued instructions that others, even those in the highest positions, regardless of rank or influence, are not to be supplied with them, and that the very strictest yardstick is to be applied in every respect.

In early December 1941, when a Reich Minister shocked Hitler by uncritically quoting foreign reports which he had taken from the secret DNB service, Hitler ordered 'that foreign transmissions and reports are to be made accessible even to the highest-placed persons only to the extent to which these persons absolutely need them for their actual work.' Moreover, Goebbels discovered that confidential and strictly secret information bulletins and situation reports sent out by various authorities were being used by many people to satisfy their 'hunger for news'. The Seehaus service in particular, i.e. the reports of the Ministry of Foreign Affairs' radio monitoring centre, had become a source of 'defeatism'.

On January 15, 1942, Hitler issued a directive whereby only Göring, Ribbentrop, Keitel, the commanders-in-chief of the three Wehrmacht services, Lammers, Frick, Goebbels and Ohnsorge were entitled to listen to foreign transmitters, whereas the remaining Reich Ministers required Hitler's authority to do so. Ministers so authorized were entitled in turn to issue listening permits within their official sphere, but were to confine these to a small circle of persons. Persons authorized to listen were issued with a special warrant card.

Dealing with the general situation, the Minister points out that, if we view the events of the past few months from a slight distance, we shall find that it is on the whole more favourable than one is apt to assume when dealing with the day-to-day events on the Eastern Front. The Russian attempts at a breakthrough did not, as one may now point out, come off. The British attempt to roll up Tripoli has boomeranged, and events in East Asia also make the overall situation in Europe and North Africa appear in an entirely different light from that of a few months ago. The Minister points out that this basic interpretation may also be conveyed to the German public without adding any false embellishments. For the rest, he refers to the imminent speech by the Führer.

In his speech at the Berlin Sportspalast on January 30, 1942, Hitler predicted that 1942 would 'again be a year of great victories.'

February 1-2, 1942
The Minister directs that the changes in Norway are not to be discussed

with the foreign public and that, generally speaking, there should therefore be no argument with foreign criticism of Quisling. In our internal propaganda the terms 'Führer' and 'Reich', applied in today's *Völkischer Beobachter* and elsewhere to Quisling and the Norwegian state, are not to be used.

Quisling's appointment to the post of premier of Norway on February 1, 1942, gave rise to highly critical comment in the foreign press. Goebbels felt that he had to support Quisling, who was despised in all civilized countries as the prototype of a venal political traitor, but at the same time he wanted to keep the terms 'Führer' and 'Reich' for Hitler and the German Reich alone.

The Minister points out that whenever Britain has suffered a military defeat anywhere, British propaganda has invariably argued that Britain had been inferior in material and equipment at that particular moment. By means of collecting together such British statements, German propaganda should remark that it is difficult to understand where, in that case, Churchill found the impertinence to declare war on Germany. The fact that we are dealing not with a defensive war but with the British war of aggression must of course be suitably high-lighted.

The Minister directs that, within the framework of the propaganda drive for greater efficiency scheduled for the month of February, the theme of 'courtesy' should also be clearly dealt with. The public must be supported against the impertinent tone of certain shopkeepers, public transport employees, etc., even though this is frequently due to nervousness or to presumptuousness.

(*Cf.* April 12, 1942.)

In connexion with the order given him by the Führer of strictly defining who is to receive the secret information material, the Minister directs that proposals should be submitted to him on how to ensure that the recipients will not, for their part, allow such material to pass through a great number of other hands. He has noticed that the recipients themselves frequently do not in fact receive the material but that, instead, a large number of male and female staff, and frequently also technical auxiliaries, deal with the material in detail as a matter of routine.

There were about a hundred confidential or secret information bulletins in existence in Germany at the time, published in up to 4,000 copies. On February 3, 1942, Goebbels declared that only information bulletins 'which are expressly acknowledged to be vital to the war' could be allowed to continue.

February 3, 1942

The Minister directs that the dissemination of all reports about Russian acts of terrorism in a few localities recaptured by them must be stopped at all costs: we must not let the local population in the territories occupied by us learn about this lest it should induce them to restrict their collaboration with us.

Ministerialdirektor Berndt (Department for Propaganda) reports that the Führer has authorized a cut in food rations starting with the rationing period from the beginning of April. The bread ration is expected to be cut from 2,250 grams to 2,000 grams, the meat ration from 400 grams to 300 grams, and the fat ration also: no precise figure was given for the last named. The reduction in bread consumption is entirely due to our aid to Finland, whereas the remaining reductions are only partially caused by that measure. The Minister points to the special need to keep this information secret.

Food conditions in Finland were positively alarming. German grain deliveries enabled the bread ration to be raised. But it was in Greece that famine had become an 'epidemic'. In Athens people died of starvation by the thousand. (*Cf.* March 18, 1942.)

February 4, 1942

The Minister directs that the speech of the Finnish Premier, Ryti, is to be given particular prominence.

The Finnish Premier, Risto Heiki Ryti, in his address denied rumours circulating about an intended separate peace between Finland and the Soviet Union. Nevertheless, rumours about Finnish hopes of a separate peace continued. In December 1942 it was decided at the conference: 'Nothing is to be said from our side about renewed reports of Finnish hopes of a separate peace since on this topic the Finns should be allowed to decide.'

In connexion with the sequestration of church bells some disagreeable scenes occurred in a few localities. Propaganda is instructed to draw the public's attention to the fact that church bells had to be surrendered in World War One too.

The confiscation of church bells, especially of those of historical value, produced a very unfavourable response at home and abroad. The sequestration drive was also in part to be extended to the occupied territories, Denmark alone being spared. In Norway and Holland the bells were taken down, but in Norway the result was very slight because – in the words of a report of the Ministry of Foreign Affairs – 'the Norwegian bells were only the size of good-sized cow bells.' In Belgium and France the bells were allowed to remain where they were, but instead, in accordance with a decision by Hitler, France and Belgium were made to deliver the same quantity of metal as 'would have been obtained from a seizure of the bells.'

According to an OKW report the number of troops with frostbite totalled 50,000 by January 20. Of these 46,000 were of first and second degree, and 4,000 of third degree; among these 1,856 amputations had to be carried out. These figures may be released by word of mouth.

Men suffering from first-degree frostbite remained with their units and were treated locally. The above figures agree with those in the Goebbels diaries.

February 5, 1942
The Minister points out that we must on no account yield to a mood of euphoria about the successes in Africa or in the event of a future offensive in the East. The situation must be represented in the press calmly and factually. We must not make the mistake of putting up targets before the public which we cannot afterwards reach. Thus, in connexion with the recapture of Cyrenaica he decrees that the words 'Suez Canal' are not to be mentioned in the press at all. Churchill is for ever putting up targets for us which we never set ourselves, and afterwards argues that it is proof of a British victory if we have not reached the targets which only he has set us.
According to an official OKW report there have been 4,119 cases of typhus in the army in the East; of these 685 were fatal.

The incidence of typhus continued to reach an alarming scale during the next few months too. Thus, 2,301 new cases were recorded during the first ten days of May. Not until the summer was the disease brought under control.

February 9, 1942
British comment on the death of Reich Minister Todt is to be dismissed with a few contemptuous words. If the British cannot stop their calumnies even at a man's grave then this shows how far the Jewish contamination of the British people has progressed.

Dr Todt, the Reich Minister for Armaments and Munitions, was killed in an air crash on February 8, 1942, immediately after a visit to the Führer's headquarters. In his diaries Goebbels notes with satisfaction that the British had praised Todt's 'genius for organization'.
Todt was succeeded by Professor Speer.

Sir Stafford Cripps's speech should be given much publicity in our polemics. The toll of British lives should be compared with that of the troops from the Empire, and it should be disputed vigorously that the British are making sacrifices on a similar scale in the defence of the Empire. Cripps claims that the British are not even doing their best in terms of work. How then – this is how we should put it – can they properly judge how many lives must be staked in the present situation?

Cripps's remarks that the British have not yet understood the urgency of the situation are to be ascribed to Churchill. The liar Churchill – it should be said – has simply concealed from the people the gravity of Britain's position. The Minister suggests that we should say to our foreign audiences: You see how right we were in portraying Britain's difficult position. Sir Stafford Cripps has now confirmed it.

Sir Richard Stafford Cripps (1889–1951), frequently described by Goebbels as a 'drawing-room bolshevik', had been British ambassador in Moscow from 1940 to 1942. Upon his return to London he made a number of often sensational speeches on the war situation, both in the Commons and in public. Immediately after his arrival he claimed that the German spring offensive represented one of the most critical phases of the war.

February 13, 1942

On February 11, 1942, the Japanese captured the British fortress of Singapore with astonishing speed, attacking from the landward side. Some 60,000 British were taken prisoner. The news of the fall of Singapore came as a shock to the British public. The British press made comparisons with Dunkirk and Crete.

The Minister directs: In our propaganda about the fall of Singapore the argument should be emphasized that the British did not want Danzig to become German; because of that they are now apparently prepared to surrender Singapore.

The Minister proposes that all broadcasts for abroad should again and again emphasize the argument that the British are letting all other nations fight for them while declining to shed any blood themselves.

In the opinion of the Minister, Cripps has become the 'darling' of German propaganda. He must not, however, be represented as an outsider in Britain but must be made into a representative of the British people. Even though he is in opposition to Churchill, he must not be championed by us since this would discredit him.

Cripps declared in an interview: 'After the victory of the Allies the Soviet Union will without any question be the strongest European power; they will end the war and probably settle in Berlin.'

The German press received the following instruction on February 10, 1942: 'The fact that Ambassador Cripps has announced a bolshevik government for Berlin must be given great prominence; the resulting dangers for the East European countries generally and the whole of Europe in particular can be shown up in this context. The same applies to Cripps's admission that Stalin took the decision to attack Germany as long ago as 1939, which was why he ordered the armaments industry to be developed to its maximum. But quite apart from all this, Cripps's observations once more furnish proof that in the event of victory Britain intends to surrender Europe to bolshevism. Cripps has returned to London as Stalin's exponent in order to promote the radicalization of the masses in all fields, including internal politics. That is why he was not prepared to enter Churchill's cabinet as a minister when that cabinet was reshuffled, because he does not believe that the moment has yet come for him. Before leaving Moscow he received clear instructions from Stalin and he is now letting some of these out of the bag. This is being done in agreement with Churchill. Proof of this is the fact that the broadcaster Elliot pointed out yesterday that after the war the Soviets must play a fundamental role in Europe. The *News Chronicle,* moreover, yesterday publicly thanked Cripps for championing the Soviets so manfully. Cripps, the *News Chronicle* pointed out, had done the nation a valuable service by drawing the attention of the British to the need to meet the Soviets half-way. But if the press and radio are allowed to carry such reflections then this proves that Churchill is an accessory. Cripps is regarded as Churchill's heir presumptive. Nevertheless it would be a mistake to put the whole responsibility solely on Cripps's shoulders since this would merely relieve Churchill and we should merely be giving Churchill an alibi for his bolshevik policy.'

February 14, 1942

The Minister points out that the loss of Singapore and the breakthrough of the German naval forces are not nearly enough to bring about Churchill's departure. He compares Britain's situation with that of the SPD prior to the [National Socialist] assumption of power in Germany. In spite of all the heavy blows suffered by it, the SPD was not then broken, though its striking power steadily declined before the assumption of power, and that in itself was important. Things are probably much the same today with regard to the British Empire. He does not believe in a dramatic turn in British politics. For that reason no great hopes should be raised among the German people.

On February 12, 1942, the battleships *Scharnhorst* and *Gneisenau,* as well as the heavy cruiser *Prinz Eugen,* sailed up the Channel from Brest. *The Times* described the event as 'the most humiliating incident suffered by Britain since the seventeenth century.'

The Minister suggests that broadcasts to Britain should not sneer but should be sham-objective and say: 'It is not for us to talk about your losses, but you yourselves always said how important Singapore was.' Churchill is a man of blunders, and if I were British I would not place much confidence now in the whole policy of the government. There should be just a shade of regret in our arguments and we should add that we, the Japanese and the Italians have always been prepared to reach agreement with the British, but they of course forced this war on us.

February 16, 1942

On the subject of criticism of Churchill's speech the Minister points out that it must be emphasized that Churchill has no British argument left to advance. He merely relies on Russia, the United States and China, and he is hoping that these will bring about a decisive turn in the war. This must be countered in our propaganda by showing up the impertinence of Churchill calmly relying on his allies now, although it was he who had provoked and brought on the war. References to the speech in which Churchill promised blood, sweat and tears can be attacked with the remark that a physician who can never predict anything but a further aggravation of the disease, or even death, is a bad physician.

The unconditional surrender of Singapore would be a superb opportunity for us to go back to Churchill's old speeches in which he attacked Belgium, Holland and France for their capitulation, which as a matter of principle he represented as dishonourable.

In his broadcast address of February 15, 1942, Churchill emphasized 'two tremendous fundamental facts which will in the end dominate the world situation and make victory possible in a form never possible before.' These facts were, first, the entry of the United States into the war on the side of the British Commonwealth, and secondly, the fact that it had not been possible to defeat or destroy the Soviet armies. In conclusion he emphasized: 'We must remember that we are no longer alone. We are in the midst of a great company. Three-quarters of the human race are now moving with us.'

February 17, 1942

The Minister directs that the sharp comments on Churchill made by the [British] opposition should not be publicized, to avoid false hopes being raised. Churchill has succeeded in once more rallying the most reluctant elements behind him. The events in Britain must not be dramatized.

The Bishop of Berlin, Count Preysing, has issued an impertinent pastoral letter to which the Minister objects in the strongest terms. In his pastoral letter the bishop has raised nothing but complaints and accusations against the Reich and its leadership, without devoting even a single word to the German soldiers fighting in the East.

Goebbels at first toyed with the idea of summoning the bishop 'for a carpeting'. However, he decided not to pursue the matter, and instead to postpone his clash with the episcopate until after the war.

The first time the German leaders were faced with the question of 'making an example' was in August 1941 when the Bishop of Münster, Count von Galen, in a speech opposed euthanasia in strong terms. However, they decided to take no action because it did not seem advisable 'at a critical period of the war' either to challenge the Church or to trigger off a discussion on euthanasia. At the end of May 1942 Hitler again assured Goebbels of his determination 'to destroy the Christian Churches after victory'. The moment his hands were free, he declared, the Churches would feel his power. (*Cf.* February 24, 1941.)

February 19, 1942

In connexion with the publication of the Kleffens documents the Minister points out: The publication of such stories must, in his opinion, be cleared with him first. Words like revolution, rebellion, attempts on the life of the Führer will always produce major repercussions in Germany and must cause considerable anxiety among a large part of the public. The words 'attempted assassination', in connexion with the Führer produce a mesmerizing effect on wide circles.

The press had published a diplomatic report from the former French Minister at The Hague to Daladier, which connected the former Dutch Foreign Minister Kleffens with a somewhat vague plan to assassinate Hitler and Ribbentrop about the end of 1939.

The German press is still publishing biographies, pictures and stories of Churchill which are too favourable and tend to make Churchill popular among the German people. The Minister therefore places pictures connected with Churchill under censorship with immediate effect. Churchill must be described as a liar in the German press, his disreputable family relationships must be described, and his amateurish way of waging war highlighted.

February 23, 1942

The Minister bans the words 'spring offensive' as far as the German press is concerned. This is not to say that there will be no spring offensive but one does not want to tie oneself down in any way. Similarly, objectives of an offensive must no longer be named. The situation in the East is to be viewed optimistically but realistically.

(*Cf.* March 26, 1942.)

In the characterization of certain leading British figures it must not be said that they support social trends or are active in the social field, but they must be presented to the German people as bolsheviks and Stalinists.

February 26, 1942
The Minister directs that polemics against Cripps must not argue that he intends to act against the plutocrats. Such an approach would only earn Cripps sympathy. Cripps's entry into the War Cabinet must be presented to the German people as the beginning of a spiritual and ideological bolshevization process in Britain.

In a reshuffle the British War Cabinet was reduced to seven members. Lord Beaverbrook left the cabinet. Sir Stafford Cripps was included as leader of the House of Commons. The Slogan of the Day of the Reichspressechef of February 20 ran:
'The reshuffle of the British War Cabinet is to be exposed as a wild bluff, as a new attempt at deception designed to chloroform the British public, which is gradually beginning to realize the seriousness of the situation; it is an incredible cardsharper's trick, devised by that past-master of disasters and that bad loser, Churchill. Instead of at least giving up the Defence Ministry, seeing that he alone is guilty of the endless chain of military defeats, this man on the contrary manages to shirk his duty of answering to the House of Commons for his rotten strategy, in order to gain even more time for his disastrous military adventures. This truly Churchillian deception of the public and parliamentary swindle of pompously staged and ridiculous government reshuffles, which he has used so often before at critical moments, must be unmasked by references to the cabinet comedy so far.'

February 27, 1942
So as not to make the Russian partisans needlessly popular and so as not to invest them with the halo of heroism, the Minister directs that new names are constantly to be given them in the press and on the radio.

The Soviet partisan formations had become an increasingly serious danger to the rear of the German Eastern Front. The German press had been instructed on February 23, 1942, not to use the term 'partisan' in future. To avoid a glorification of the partisans the words to be used were 'gangs' or *franc-tireurs*. The term 'rifle hag', familiar from the campaign in Poland, again became a current expression.

On the subject of Cripps the Minister again points out that Cripps certainly

(a) does not wish a bolshevization of Britain;

(b) regards bolshevism in Europe as desirable only in as far as the German leading caste will be exterminated by communism.

Cripps no doubt believes that bolshevism would be a good thing for the German people for a few months, since it would eliminate them for all time as competitors.

The Minister believes that Cripps undoubtedly means an intensification of the war effort in Britain. He is Stalin's outpost in Europe and as such he would be the best target for German propaganda.

March 1, 1942

During the night of February 27–28, 1942, British parachutists, supported by a Polish exile detachment, landed close to a Luftwaffe radar station near Bruneval (north of Le Havre), overpowered the guards, removed the most important parts of the so-called Würzburg instrument and withdrew without loss to motor torpedo boats standing by inshore. The possession of the German aircraft location device enabled the British to develop effective means for disrupting the German aircraft tracking system.

The Minister directs that the landing of parachute troops in northern France should be compared to a highwaymen's operation without military significance. It is quite obvious that with a long front, reaching from Kirkcness down to the Spanish frontier, there will always be a gap here or there which cannot be closely guarded.

March 2, 1942

The Minister announces that he is having a compilation made of the British news service from yesterday until today in order to ascertain, on the basis of the report, what the British technique is in camouflaging unfavourable news. Reports about heavy Japanese losses near Java are merely intended as the sugar coating to conceal the bitter taste of the occupation of Java. The British information service has once again been twisting and squirming, revealing its whole embarrassment.

The crushing Japanese victory in the naval battle in the Java Sea, which lasted from February 27 until March 1, 1942, and resulted in the sinking of the entire Allied naval forces there numbering five cruisers, six destroyers and one sloop, cleared the road for Japan's occupation of Java (Netherlands East Indies). The Dutch troops on Java surrendered on March 8.

March 4, 1942

British bombers made an air raid on Paris during the night of March 3–4, 1942. According to definitive French reports 340 people were killed and about 600 wounded. At the conference of March 6, 1942, Goebbels ordered that the funeral ceremonies in Paris were to be turned into a first-rate anti-British demonstration. 'The population of Paris must be whipped up into unprecedented fury and they must be made to realize that their anger is also the best air defence against the British.'

The following points are to be highlighted:

(1) Throughout our entire offensive in the West we never attacked Paris; only the operational airfields of the French air force in the vicinity of Paris were bombed.

(2) The British, more than anyone else, have always presented an attack on Paris as cultural barbarism of the first degree. Now they are attacking their former ally and do not shrink from raiding the city which they themselves described as the centre of culture.

The German Reich suffered hardly any damage from the bombing of Paris, but instead some innocent civilians had to suffer.

Transmissions for Holland should point out that the same bombers which attacked Paris were missing in Java.

March 7, 1942

The Minister requests the OKW representative to obtain authorization for the Russian reports of the capture of Orel to be published, so that the German people and the world can be shown the mendacity of Russian information. At Orel, which lies 100 km behind the front, there is absolute quiet.

At Orel, which had in fact become a frontline city, heavy defensive fighting had been going on since January 1942. Throughout March and April there was continuous anxiety that Orel might be overwhelmed by a Russian offensive any day. As a means of countering the often premature Soviet reports of successes, which were usually taken up by the foreign press, Orel was certainly not the most suitable example. Another proposal by Goebbels, made on March 21, 1942, concerned the Eighteenth Army. which had gone over to positional warfare outside Leningrad: 'The enemy powers have repeatedly reported first the annihilation of this army, then its encirclement and its relief. Juxtaposition of these reports would provide a good picture of the mendacity of the enemy news media.'

March 8, 1942

The Minister directs that the creeping crisis in Britain must be presented again and again. However, no false hopes must be linked with it. We must not commit ourselves to any dates. We must repeat time and again that England is in the grip of a disease which is so serious that it must end fatally. The crisis would at one time appear to be at home and at another time abroad. Our propaganda must adopt the role of an objective critic of history.

Some press comment seems to suggest to the Minister that certain circles desire Churchill's overthrow. However, no hopes must be linked with this. The public must be told that Churchill's departure would probably get Cripps into power and that this would mean an intensification of the war.

American press despatches first speculated about an overthrow of Churchill. At the Berlin press conference of March 8, 1942, the following was said on this subject: 'Criticism of Churchill is undoubtedly again very much on the increase, and it is by no means impossible that Churchill may yet be forced to resign. This may happen quite soon or it may take a long while. If the German press continues to take no notice whatever of such possibilities, then, in the event of Churchill's resignation occurring some day, the impression might be created among the German people that the war was over. Of course, that would not be so, since Churchill's critics accuse him of not conducting Britain's war effort with sufficient energy any longer. The people who would like to overthrow Churchill want to make even greater efforts for the war. This must always underlie our reporting. In other words, from now onward, we can cautiously begin to refer to Churchill's threatened position, perhaps under the slogan "the creeping crisis".'

March 10, 1942

The subject of the 'yellow peril' must on no account be even touched upon.

At the conference of March 6, 1942, Goebbels had given directions for a circular to be issued to all Gauleitungen referring to 'the disastrous effect of all that twaddle about the yellow peril.' The subject was again discussed at the conferences throughout March. The Japanese Embassy, moreover, complained that 'there is frequent talk in the Reich about a "yellow peril".' The Minister requested that the matter should be put to the Ministry of Foreign Affairs and that it should be pointed out that he himself had most strictly forbidden all discussion of the concept. Nevertheless, there was no concealing the fact that the subject was being widely discussed. In the Minister's opinion it was quite impossible to raise the issue publicly because enemy propaganda would at once eagerly join the debate.

The Minister proposed that the Ministry of Foreign Affairs should be asked whether one might not prevail on Ambassador Oshima or some other gentleman from the Japanese Embassy to give an interview. It would be desirable to point out in such an interview that the Japanese do not intend to use the raw materials of their conquests in East Asia in a capitalist and plutocratic way, for themselves alone. The conquest of those territories was not intended as an act of isolation against the Axis partners, but should, on the contrary, be of some economic benefit to them.

Such and similar public statements, as also for instance the one a few days ago about a conversation with a Japanese lieutenant-colonel, would – without the concept of the 'yellow peril' being spelt out at all – let public discussion of this unwelcome subject gradually die down.

In future, Jews will be forbidden to use public transport in Berlin. Those Jews who are employed in industries essential to war – whose number runs to about 17,000 – will receive a special red pass authorizing them to use public transport.

On January 12, 1942, Goebbels had demanded that no newspapers should be sold to Jews either by way of subscription or at newspaper kiosks. On February 17, 1942, the order was issued, chiefly at Goebbels's instigation, that Jews were no longer to be supplied with newspapers, periodicals, etc. On April 24, 1942, came the ban on the use of public transport; on May 15, 1942, the ban on the keeping of pets; on May 29, 1942, the ban on Jews using any kind of hairdressers' services; on June 11, 1942, the decree forbidding Jews to purchase any tobacco, and on September 18, 1942, the decree stopping the supply to Jews of all foodstuffs available only on ration cards.

With these and similar measures Goebbels pursued his own special campaign to make Berlin a city 'clear of Jews'.

March 18, 1942

The Minister directs that commentaries on food cuts must on no account ascribe these to the success of the British blockade. It must be pointed out that Britain is suffering the same difficulties as we are. In any war, owing to a reorientation of the economy and the withdrawal of manpower, there must always be restrictions. This point should be made with particular emphasis.

On March 22, 1942, came a directive that the food cuts, justified by food supplies to the occupied territories, should be explained by the argument that these territories were making manpower available to the Reich. The rations for normal consumers were reduced as follows from April 6, 1942: meat from 400 grams to 300 grams per week, butter from 150 grams to 125 grams, margarine from 96.87 grams to 65.62 grams and bread from 2,250 grams to 2,000 grams.

March 26, 1942

At the request of the OKW all official statements, radio transmissions and the press are to avoid any references to spring at the present moment. Not until spring has arrived in Russia too is this season to be given publicity again.

The Minister believes that this ban can no longer be applied quite so rigorously since better weather has now arrived in the East too.

On March 29, 1942, another ban was issued on the use of the word 'offensive' in the German press. The Führer's Directive No. 41 for the summer offensive of 1942 is dated April 5, 1942. The German offensive began on May 8 with the opening moves in the reconquest of the Kerch Peninsula.

The Minister then speaks about British propaganda and expresses the opinion that had enemy propaganda consistently and repeatedly, throughout the two and a half years of the war, claimed that the Allies were fighting not against the German people but solely against Hitler, then, even though this would have produced no results at first, it might very well have tricked a few people in the long run. At the moment it seems that this subject is being taken up again by the propaganda of the United States of America. The Minister directs that this should not be countered, but that instead all comment should be published which refers to the annihilation of the entire German race. Speeches such as that by Vansittart* are the best method of immunizing the German people against any propaganda that aims at driving a wedge between the people and their National Socialist leaders.

March 28, 1942

During the night of March 28, 1942, the British mounted a landing operation at St Nazaire with the aim of destroying the German U-boat base and its installations. The operation had to be called off at dawn after no more

---

* Baron Vansittart was Chief Diplomatic Adviser to the British Foreign Secretary from 1938 to 1941. He was the principal exponent during the war of an uncompromising anti-German attitude, opposed to all differentiation between German moderates and Nazis. *Tr.*

than partial success had been achieved. Germany's only large dock on the Atlantic coast capable of receiving the battleship *Tirpitz* was destroyed.

On the Minister's instructions the attempted British landing at St Nazaire is to be described as a Maisky offensive.* Our commentaries are to deal with the matter in a condescending manner and cordially invite the British to continue mounting such operations.

The Minister warns against criticism in the German press of the possible plan to reorganize the House of Lords by replacing hereditary membership by free election. This might suggest to some people that there are progressive views in Britain.

In December 1940 Pétain had dismissed Laval, until then his deputy, from his post and ordered his detention. Shortly afterwards Laval was brought to Paris by the Germans. Admiral Darlan was Premier of the Vichy government from 1941 to April 1942.

The Pétain-Laval meeting cannot very well be reported since for the German people Laval is still the French Premier and it is surely not feasible to say now that Pétain and Laval have had a clandestine meeting somewhere.

March 29, 1942

The campaign against profiteers and black-marketeers has not yet been taken up by the British. The Minister directs that our propaganda should ask why the British do not see this measure as a sign of decay of the German people, as they are wont to with every other campaign. The British, the Minister believes, are in a dilemma: if they publicize our campaign the question may be asked in Britain why this is not being done in Britain also?

When the subject of the decree on the black market was raised at the conference of March 21, 1942, Goebbels demanded that the situation should be depicted in the sense 'that there are only very few scoundrels and enemies, and that it is not as if everyone was profiteering.'

On April 27, 1942, came the directive that heavy sentences on profiteers and usurers should be given greater publicity in the domestic press and radio. Goebbels still did not think it sufficient that about the end of March and the beginning of April 1942 death sentences passed on 'black marketeers' were reported in the German papers nearly every day. At that time it was chiefly 'black slaughterers' who were sentenced to death in all parts of Germany. The

---

* i.e. an offensive to placate the Soviet ambassador in London, Ivan Maisky, who kept accusing the Allies of dragging their feet on the question of a Second Front. *Tr.*

black market itself was naturally not stamped out. Already by the end of 1941 people were paying twenty Marks for a kilogram of butter and up to one Mark for an egg.

March 30, 1942

The Führer has given the Minister full powers concerning supplies to the population in the event of British air raids. After yesterday's air raid on Lübeck the authorities concerned were so tied up in legal clauses and questions of competence that they never got around to any concrete aid.

Complaints have been made that such heavy bombing as that on Lübeck was dismissed in the Wehrmacht communiqué in a few words. The Minister requests the OKW representatives to see to it that the severity of the bombing of Lübeck is emphasized, even if after the event, in the new Wehrmacht communiqué, so that public confidence in the latter should not be shaken. The Minister expresses his agreement that the German press should give the greatest possible prominence to the bombing of art treasures, as has happened in Lübeck.

On March 31, 1941, Goebbels ordered that art experts should go to Lübeck to form an impression of the extent of the destruction of Lübeck's cultural monuments and that they should report on this to the foreign press.

Lübeck suffered a heavy British air raid during the night of March 28-29, 1942, when the heaviest type of bombs were dropped. Two hundred and thirty-four bombers dropped three hundred tons of incendiary and high-explosive bombs on the city. Destruction was on a devastating scale and conditions after the raid were chaotic. The first-aid measures organized by Goebbels got going during the night of March 30. On April 4, 1942, he expressed concern that a continuation of British air attacks on the same scale over a number of weeks might 'certainly produce a demoralizing effect on the German public.' According to an official final announcement, altogether 298 people were killed in the attack on Lübeck. There were several hundreds of wounded and a slightly smaller number of missing.

The OKW communiqué of March 29, 1942, stated laconically: 'During the night, British bombers attacked a few localities in the north German coastal area, principally the city of Lübeck. There were some casualties among the civilian population.'

'Superior leadership'

April - June 1942

April 1, 1942
The Minister directs that the atrocity stories of the Russians should be taken up and commented on in the German papers. There is no objection to dealing with such implausible reports, but he requests that, for obvious reasons, stories of food supply disruptions should not be published.

The day before Goebbels had already ruled that Moscow reports about hunger demonstrations in German towns must not be taken up in any way. On February 25, 1942, Moscow radio had declared, with every assurance, that during the first twenty days of February the inhabitants of the town of Warne in Mecklenburg had received only 650 grams of bread and 750 grams of potatoes per person. One hundred and seventy inhabitants of the town had already died of starvation and seventy had committed suicide.

Soviet 'hunger propaganda' began as soon as the ration cuts were announced in Germany and, in spite of its totally false allegations, was hardly ever refuted by Goebbels because the ration cuts had become the 'hot potato' of German propaganda. According to an SD report, the mood among the public had 'reached a low ebb never previously observed.' The food cuts, contrasting as they did with earlier statements about an assured supply, led to disappointment, embitterment and criticism of the leadership. Goebbels was possibly afraid that major protest demonstrations might in fact be staged.

April 2, 1942
With the progressive improvement in the weather the possibility of a German offensive is clearly moving to the fore of public opinion again. To avoid finding ourselves in the same straits as last year, the Minister directs that reports must be confined to what is actually happening. The task of commentaries is to dampen rather than excite.

Enemy propaganda is using clairvoyance on an increasing scale. The possibility is discussed of inventing two or three well-known clairvoyants with important names and putting in their mouths two or three sentences which must be carefully considered and accurately formulated. There are still a great many people who let themselves be fooled by clairvoyant experiments.

Goebbels more than once, and in subsequent years also, used clairvoyance for propaganda purposes. Thus, at his instigation, a Norwegian paper in early 1944 published the alleged 'revelations of the Swedish clairvoyant Gruenberg', who made a fantastic and crazy prophecy of the war and predicted that, after the greatest of difficulties, Germany would be victorious. After many defeats, 1948 would be Hitler's great year. Finally Germany and the Western Powers would jointly fight against bolshevism and Hitler would be seen as the saviour of Europe. These prophecies were published in excerpts on typed handbills distributed in certain German cities.

April 11, 1942

The Minister discusses the lessons to be learned from his propaganda campaigns over the past few weeks. The articles and other publications brought out by him, designed to convince the German public of the necessity of the imposed restrictions of food supplies and in other spheres of daily life, have produced a response in the form of a vast number of letters, telephone calls, conversations, etc., which prove that the people fully understand these necessities. At the same time, however, there is some doubt in a lot of circles about the matching of theory and practice. The question is asked whether the demands raised by the Minister are not in fact implemented by the broad masses alone, and not by the leading echelons in the Party and the state. The Minister declares that such a discrepancy between theory and practice is intolerable in the minds of the German people. Either the facts are fitted to the theory championed by him, or he must discontinue his propaganda campaign. The Minister points to the attempts made by several Gauleiters and other eminent figures to continue to act in a manner which is unseemly in our present situation and which arouses the sharpest criticism among the public. This applies, among other things, to the big turnout of private cars at receptions, etc. Citing as a typical example of how things should not be done, he criticizes a statement released to the press by the Head of Police in Berlin to the effect that two ladies travelling in a sleeping-car had two suitcases containing jewellery valued at 21,000 RM and 18,000 RM respectively, stolen. It is obvious that the average reader must ask himself what kind of ladies are allowed to make official journeys, or any other absolutely necessary journeys – and, what is more, in a sleeping car – for which they carry with them personal jewellery of that kind of value.

The Minister directs that the Propaganda Department, in conjunction with the OKW, should immediately investigate what kind of help the

German people can give the Eastern Front this summer, after last summer's experience. As an example he mentions the collection of gauze material of all kinds from which NS women's organizations could make protective netting against the intolerable plague of flies and midges which impairs the fighting power of the troops. He points out that the German people will – provided the collections take place in good time – gladly participate, and that this will undoubtedly wipe out the poor impression left among the troops by the belated collection of woollen clothing. The OKW representative is asked to see that the needs are examined by questioning such troops as were fighting on the Eastern Front last summer, and that the OKH should withdraw its earlier refusal of such measures. In this connexion it is pointed out that the Waffen-SS is caring for its troops in an exemplary fashion and has for that purpose repeatedly carried out collections of its own. The objection of the OKW representative that such a procedure is easy for a small formation but seems hardly practicable for the whole army is rejected by the Minister as unconvincing in view of the results shown by the major collections for the Wehrmacht as a whole.

Goebbels announced at the conference of April 9, 1942, that a further textile collection would probably become necessary, even though its result must be expected to be very slight. Towards the end of November 1942 the German press reported that the textile collection of 1942 had made it possible to provide working clothes for an additional four to five million workers.

April 12, 1942
The Minister raises the subject of British threats to make landings on the European mainland and directs that German propaganda should not show the slightest qualms in this respect; instead it should treat this subject entirely in the light of the motto from the Führer's speeches: The more of you come the greater will be your new Dunkirk.

The Minister then raises the subject of the solemn event next Sunday, the 19th, and directs that, in view of the quite exceptionally select audience, measures should be taken in every respect to ensure a dignified and undisturbed procedure.

On April 19, 1942, an NSDAP ceremony was held in the Berlin Philharmonic Hall to mark Hitler's fifty-third birthday. Among the invited guests were armaments workers, soldiers and scientists. The festive oration, simultaneously relayed by radio, was made by Goebbels who drew parallels between Frederick the Great and Hitler. As always on the eve of Hitler's birthday – the last occasion being April 19, 1945 – Goebbels concluded with the words: 'May he remain what to us he always was and is – our Hitler!'

The Minister finally discusses the campaign for the promotion of courtesy, due to start in the Berlin Gau on May 1. He explains that a simple encouragement by press, radio, posters, etc., is not enough, but that, with the public participating, at the end of one month a prize will be awarded to the most courteous conductor, shop-assistant, ticket office employee, waiter, etc. of either sex, and that this must receive great publicity in the press. A proposal by one of the participants of the conference – evidently on the point of being called up for active service – to award a prize also to the most courteous sergeant was turned down.

April 13, 1942

The Minister raises the subject of a DNB report according to which the Japanese General Tatekawa [the Japanese ambassador in the Soviet Union], upon his return to Japan from a stay in Moscow, has made statements about the situation in the Soviet Union which sound exceedingly favourable to the Soviet Russians. The Minister says that these statements are not pleasant for us since they make the Russians appear in an exceedingly rosy light and must bring comfort and encouragement to the public of the other enemy countries. It is, however, conceivable that the Japanese are launching reports of this kind with the definite intention of misleading the world. In that case, needless to say, there is no objection. The Minister requests that it should be ascertained whether the general really made his remarks with the deliberate intention of deception, If not, he requests that the attention of the Japanese government be drawn to the undesirable nature of similar statements.

The German ambassador in Tokyo, General Ott, lodged an objection, with the result that Tatekawa was reprimanded for his remarks by the Japanese Foreign Ministry.

Since the end of February 1942 a letter by a Colonel of the Luftwaffe, Werner Mölders (1913–41), had been circulating in Germany, chiefly in clerical circles. Mölders was killed on November 22, 1941, when his courier aircraft crashed near Breslau. The letter contained fierce criticism of the state leadership and, in particular, of its measures against the Churches. Mölders, a strict catholic and a close follower of Count von Galen, the Bishop of Münster, had been known, even during his lifetime, as a man who never made a secret of his criticism of the Third Reich's Church policy. Hitler nevertheless promised a reward of 100,000 RM. for the capture of the author of the allegedly faked Mölders letter. Investigations showed that the aged Field-Marshal von Mackensen had played a major part in disseminating the letter, but it would have been difficult to take any action against him.

225

The Minister points out that the alleged Mölders letter has been published in a Slovak paper and requests steps with a view to the publication of a denial. Reference may be made to the Reich government's statement of about a fortnight ago that the letter is a forgery. He wishes to be informed about steps taken and points to the particular importance of this letter for the German public as well.

The Mölders letter appeared in two Slovak papers which, however, following intervention by the German legation in Bratislava, dissociated themselves from its contents.

The Minister directs that an American press comment should be taken up in the biggest possible way to the effect that gold is in itself of no value today for the conduct of the war and is useful only as a substitute metal for metals in short supply, e.g. in the manufacture of tins for apple-sauce. The Minister directs that this victory of a fundamental view held for the past two decades by National Socialism about the value of gold as such, in contrast to the value of blood and human labour, should be given particular prominence.

Taken up by the *Völkischer Beobachter* on April 14, 1942, under the heading 'Apple-sauce in gold tins'.

April 15, 1942
The Minister raises the subject of Laval's nomination as Premier and points out that it is not easy to bring this information to the public's notice in the proper manner, seeing that it was forbidden at the time to publish Laval's dismissal in December 1940. As for British and American commentaries on the government reshuffle, he asks that for obvious reasons these should not be taken up just yet. If it should become necessary to deal with the French cabinet reshuffle in some form or other appropriate directives will no doubt be issued.

The German leaders hoped that the return of Laval – to the foreign press the Quisling of France – to head the Vichy cabinet would result in France's closer alignment with Germany. It is typical that in his diaries Goebbels does not by so much as a single word mention the German press's difficulties in handling the Laval report.

April 17, 1942
The Minister states that there is no point in challenging the British to make further raids by putting out malicious or sarcastic German

remarks about the ineffectiveness of British air attacks on Reich territory. If British propaganda now points to the effectiveness of British air raids before the eyes of the world we had best keep quiet about the subject.

The Minister directs that the German press should not attack measures taken by the British government in imitation of Russian government measures. It is, of course, in order and necessary to attack the advance of bolshevik ideological views in Britain and the propaganda being made there in this connexion, such as the singing of the *Internationale,* bolshevik seminars, British-bolshevik celebrations, etc., but it is highly inadvisable to belittle practical measures whose efficacy has been made clear to every critical German observer by the Russian power of resistance. In this context the Minister further points out that the bolshevik system, as far as the mobilization of the whole country's labour force and material resources for the war is concerned, has been so successful as to give many a German food for thought. Only the fact that the German armies in Russia have at every step encountered the most frightful social, sanitary and other conditions among the population has been an effective protection against Germany's infection by bolshevism. This protection, of course, is entirely adequate.

April 18, 1942
The question of the Church in Russia should only be discussed among the German public if entirely unambiguous evidence is available about serious anti-ecclesiastical actions by the Soviets. Even such reports are to be limited to the minimum. Considering the views held by the German public it would be best not to touch on the subject at all.

At the conference of December 1, 1941, Goebbels had already reported an order of the Führer's forbidding German propaganda to touch on the subject of the opening of churches in the occupied territories of the USSR. Edicts about the toleration of the eastern Churches, issued in subsequent months, were similarly prohibited material for the German press since Hitler, and not only Hitler, feared that toleration of the Churches in Russia might be interpreted in the Reich as a fundamental retreat of National Socialism from its anti-ecclesiastical policy.

In connexion with a tendentious report by the Swedish journalist Lindquist, the Minister instructs Herr Brauweiler to have Lindquist most closely watched and to arrange for his instant expulsion in the event of his committing a similar offence again.

227

Nils Eric Lindquist, born 1904, was the Berlin correspondent of the Swedish *Social-Demokrat* from 1940 to 1942.

April 19, 1942

The Minister believes that the British are evidently mounting their air offensive in a big way and will possibly make some propaganda with it during the next few months. The purpose behind their offensive is to demonstrate to the world their aid to Russia.

He requests that the British successes in the air offensive should not be denied. The tactics of keeping silent will, as in the case of the non-stop offensive, prove to be the best method in the long run.

Quite a different matter are the reports which speak of a gigantic accumulation of war material in Britain. This kind of exaggeration must be attacked.

The Times and other British papers have carried observations about the failure of the Russians in their offensive. These assessments are the best confirmation of German news policy which, during the critical months, spoke of fierce fighting but repeatedly pointed out that no vital positions had been lost. Now Britain admits this and our news policy is most brilliantly vindicated.

April 21, 1942

The Minister reports about the increasing British threat of invasion. He directs that there should be no putting one's head in the sand, but the chances of an invasion are to be discussed clearly and unambiguously. After the British experiences so far they can hardly expect to be successful. In addressing the British one can emphasize with assurance that whenever they make the attempt they will meet with a suitable reception on our part. The invasion army may be sure of a cordial and warm reception. Churchill's past record can be used to neutralize the threat. His various failures of landing operations should be made the basis of our polemics. *Pravda* has again lately been publishing atrocities said to have been committed by German troops. As a reply, various reports of cannibalism are being released for the foreign language services.

Ever since June 1941 there were continuous reports, and not only from Soviet sources, about atrocities committed in the occupied eastern territories against civilians and prisoners of war. Almost every month the Soviet Foreign Ministry presented diplomatic protest Notes about German atrocities to all missions accredited to Moscow. As early as January 7, 1942, Fritzsche had said at the Berlin press conference, in connexion with a Note from Molotov, that this must not be discussed before the German public. 'We did not release any details either, in the summer of 1941, about Soviet atrocities in Volhynia, Galicia, the Baltic states, etc. Nor should the issue of the treatment of Soviet prisoners in the Reich be used for our fundamental argument with Molotov. It is quite true that the knout, the stick and the whip play a big part in the treatment of Soviet prisoners of war in German prison camps, since order cannot be maintained with the revolver alone. The Soviet prisoners are used to this kind of treatment and only thus can they be made to work.' All sorts of comments, Fritzsche said, have been made in this country by naïve German witnesses complaining about the use of the knout. But, in point of fact, Molotov is not complaining about this kind of treatment of the prisoners of war; he lists instead the most diabolical atrocities, of a sort as have never been committed by Germans, but only by bolsheviks. (*Cf.* April 28, 1942.)

April 22, 1942
The Minister directs that the British and American propaganda about the imminent setting up of a second front should be countered in German propaganda for abroad with exceedingly sharp and sarcastic references to Dunkirk, Singapore, etc. He explains that this propaganda is evidently intended as a relief offensive for the Russians and designed to make us withdraw troops from the East in order to defend the occupied territories of western Europe.

(*Cf.* May 18, 1942.)

The Minister requests an examination of the possibility of working indirectly on the French public in the following way: dropping of allegedly British but in reality German leaflets over France, which would mention imminent attacks and the inevitable sacrifices in human lives, cities, buildings, property etc.; setting up of a secret transmitter camouflaged as British, which would keep the French public on edge for the same reasons.

The subject of dropping forged British leaflets over France was also considered by Hitler himself. On February 9, 1942, he passed on to General Jodl, the Wehrmacht Chief of Operations, the following suggestion for leaflets which he thought would, 'imperceptibly to the French', be detrimental to the British. Their political line, which would be thought in France to have originated in Britain, was to be: 'Frenchmen! When we left your territory in 1940, unweakened and in full confidence of victory, we did so out of consideration for you, so as to spare your beautiful country further destruction and to save you any further sacrifices for our common cause. Now the whole burden of the struggle is lying on our shoulders alone. You may count on us to

229

see the war through to its victorious conclusion. We count on you to remain standing by our side.'

The Minister directs that the German press and the foreign press should point out that the Americans have again started to steal European patents. He wishes the idea to be clearly expressed that from time to time the Americans intervene in European conflicts in order to gain possession in this way of the achievements of European science and technology.

In connexion with publications by the DAF, the Minister issues most strict instructions to ensure that German propaganda on no account replaces the concept of 'National Socialism' by the concept of 'socialism' or 'nationalism' or 'national-minded socialism'. The term 'National Socialism' has a content which cannot and must not be circumscribed in any other way.

April 27, 1942

It is reported that the fourth raid on Rostock was effected mainly with landmines which caused the extensive collapse of what remnants of the Old City were still standing and also of several previously heavily hit residential areas. Altogether some 40,000 people are now homeless; of these 10,000 are already accommodated in individual quarters in the neighbourhood while the rest still have to be transferred from camps to individual quarters. The Führer has ordered the drawing up of a plan for tough reprisals against appropriate cities. The Minister will propose that in these raids leaflets are also dropped with pictures of Lübeck and Rostock and a reminder that the German raids are reprisal raids.

The RAF bombed the coastal city of Rostock during the nights of April 23–27, 1942. It continued the carpet-bombing of residential areas, first practised at Lübeck, dropping far more incendiary than high-explosive bombs – over 400 tons in two nights alone. By the evening of April 29, 163 killed had been counted in Rostock, including 29 French prisoners of war. There were, moreover, 200 serious and 500 slight casualties. About 100,000 inhabitants of Rostock had been evacuated by April 28. German propaganda recorded the following reaction of the people of Rostock to the air raids: 'The main thing is we are still alive. Whatever we have lost Churchill will have to pay for.'

With his appointment to the rank of Air Marshal, Harris, in March 1942, received the secret order: 'It has been decided that your principal target henceforward will be the morale of the enemy's civilian population, in particular the workers.' The dress rehearsals of the new British bombing strategy at Lübeck and Rostock were eventually followed by the large-scale raid on Cologne. British communiqués about the bombing of Rostock over four consecutive nights, on the other hand, emphasized that the attacks were mainly aimed at the destruction of the Heinkel works and the Neptun shipyard.

The Minister directs that the German press should publish enemy reports about the effect of our raids on Bath and Malta.

Whereas the German air raids on medium-sized British cities were intended as 'reprisal blows' for the British bombing of German cities, the thousand-odd German and Italian air raids on Malta served both the protection of North African convoys and the preparations for the conquest of the British island fortress. In June 1942, however, the landing on Malta was shelved.

The Minister refers to foreign reaction to the Führer's speech and points out that the personal attacks on the Führer must of course be totally ignored on our part. As was to be expected, enemy propaganda is of course trying to read into the Führer's remarks an estrangement between leadership and people and a military weakness. He believes that our propaganda should stress the difference between the situation in Germany and in Britain: In Britain, judging by the press, the public is demanding vigorous government action against all abuses, but without success; by way of contrast, these measures are being taken in Germany by the leadership itself.

The main burden of Hitler's speech to the Berlin Reichstag on April 26, 1942, was its 'legitimation' of the unlimited powers demanded by him as 'supreme law lord' who would 'not be tied to existing legal regulations.' The reasons for this measure were no doubt the effects of the winter crisis of 1941–2, the general slump of morale, and finally Hitler's fear lest the events of November 1918 should repeat themselves. In his table talk at his headquarters on July 28, 1942, Hitler himself explained that the people's 'understanding' was effective only 'so long as the people possess the necessary confidence in their leaders.' Yet the progressive waning of this trust must have been clear to Hitler from the SD reports. For that reason it cannot have been a coincidence that, on April 7, 1942, in his table talk, Hitler likewise developed some very concrete measures to take immediate effect in the event that 'a mutiny should break out anywhere in the Reich today.' The blood bath which he planned for such an event would have outdone all historical parallels.

The suggestion is made that, considering that the British air raids of the past few nights have proved the ineffectiveness of the switching off of the German transmitters, these transmitters should now again be fully placed at the service of propaganda and entertainment in the evening.

231

The Minister rejects this suggestion with the remark that he does not wish to be held responsible at some future date for the success of further British air raids. It must be expected that, if this were to happen, the Luftwaffe would try to saddle him with the responsibility.

April 28, 1942

The Minister raises the subject of the situation in Rostock and emphasizes the brilliant and exemplary organization of Reichsstatthalter and Gauleiter Hildebrand. The necessary relief measures were carried out very quickly and played a major part in avoiding panic among the population. As for handling the Rostock raid for the German public, the Minister points out that we must either tell the whole truth or else pass the whole matter over in silence. The evacuation of a large part of the population enables wise circles of the people to gain a clearer picture of the situation in Rostock and compels us to state quite clearly the number of the victims and the extent of the destruction. The newsreel and the press, therefore, must either tell everything or nothing. A decision is to be solicited from the Führer on whether the full extent of the destruction may be disclosed. As a matter of principle, moreover, an air raid of this nature must be mentioned in the Wehrmacht High Command communiqué.

The Times has published an article which deals with the raid on Lübeck and admits that by far the greater part of the damage has been in residential areas. This article is highly suitable for leaflets placing responsibility for our reprisal raids upon the British leaders who, for the most part, were ordering criminal raids on residential quarters.

By way of reply to the new Molotov Note about atrocities committed by the German troops, individual instances of bolshevik cannibalism and other atrocities are now to be put out on the greatest possible scale. The report about cannibalism by the bolsheviks represents our best reply to the shameless Note of the Russians, who have the impertinence to play-act before the world. These cannibals, priest-murderers and man-eaters are the last people to present the world with stories of atrocities by German troops.

Molotov's Note, broadcast by Moscow radio on April 27–28, 1942, spoke of 'captured documents', etc., concerning the annihilation of Soviet nationality groups, allegedly mentioned in Order No. 431 of Captain Eberhard, the senior garrison officer of Feodosiya.

Goebbels did not stop to ask whether this document was possibly a forgery – as in fact it was – since he was only too well informed about the inhumanities committed by the Germans in the East. Goebbels's reaction to the Soviet atrocity stories betrayed his fear that the world might believe them in the long run.

232

Stories of cannibalism in the Red Army were subsequently collected, or else invented, by the OKW, the Propaganda Ministry and the Ministry of Foreign Affairs. On June 9, 1942, for example, the press in Oslo was shown two captured Soviet spies who were alleged to have murdered and 'eaten up' a third Soviet soldier and two Norwegian companions when their food supplies were exhausted.

Goebbels, on the other hand, banned for the domestic media a report intended solely for the foreign public that a Red Army soldier had bitten through the throat of a German officer.

Referring to an article which has appeared in a German paper, the Minister asks that our restrictions should not be carried to excess. The disappearance of certain comforts, due to wartime conditions, must not lead to a general iconoclasm and thus bring ridicule on an otherwise sound campaign for the avoidance of everything unnecessary.

The occasion for these remarks was an article in the SS paper *Das Schwarze Korps,* directed against hairdressers. 'When all is said and done, we can't run around with hair like the apostles,' was Goebbels's indignant reaction to this symptom of emergent 'primitivism'.

Referring to a conversation with Hitler, Goebbels on May 10, 1943, noted in his diary: 'Most important, total war must not be a war against women. Such a war has never yet been won by any government. Women, after all, represent an enormous power, and the moment one raises a hand against their beauty culture one will make enemies of them.'

April 30, 1942

The Minister desires that polemics against false enemy reports about alleged Italian hopes of a separate peace should point out that Britain and the United States have always spread these stories just when things have been going particularly badly for them. For that reason these false reports are now again a bad sign for their authors.

On December 1, 1942, the government spokesman (Fischer) told the Berlin press conference: 'There is an increasing number of reports coming in about anti-fascist demonstrations in Italy. I need not point out that these have all been fabricated by the paws of Jewish scribes.'

Referring to an article in the German press that the German Luftwaffe will attack in particular those targets in Britain which are marked with three stars in the Baedeker, the Minister points out that it is totally wrong to boast of the destruction of cultural values. Any such destruction remains, as such, an extremely regrettable act. But if one is compelled to carry it out, then this compulsion must be explained logically and convincingly. One must never allow oneself to be carried away into glorifying such actions.

The concept of the 'Baedeker raids' was evolved by Baron Braun von Stumm, the Deputy Director of the Press Department of the Foreign Ministry. The guides published by the Karl Baedeker firm in Leipzig, founded in 1827, were the most widely used guides before the war; all places of particular historic or artistic interest were specially marked in them. Starting with the air raid on Bath, the German raids in the early summer of 1942 were almost exclusively directed at frequently undefended, medium-sized British cities with venerable cultural monuments. In June 1942 Canterbury Cathedral was hit and badly damaged in a German raid.

The Minister directs that arrangements should be made to ensure that supplies are regulated more fairly on the outskirts of those German cities which have a million inhabitants. There are entire sections of the population living a long way outside but having their place of work in the metropolis who, nevertheless, without good reason, are excluded from the special allocations made to the big cities.

In connexion with complaints that the German radio carried no German church music at all, the Minister makes some fundamental observations. He explains that at the beginning of December he did not permit the performance of a Mozart Requiem because its very sombre and world-negating text would have had a bad effect on morale in the exceptionally serious situation then prevailing. He believes, however, that this was intended as a quite exceptional, unique case. German cultural treasures from the past, which include in particular music pervaded with an ecclesiastical content, must not be excluded out of wrongly understood ideological considerations. If every period were to destroy or regard as non-existent the earlier cultural achievements of a people, just because the content of these cultural achievements runs counter to a new ideology which happens to be arising, the people would be deleting their own past and turning themselves into parvenus. The Minister explains that a distinction must be made between a historical approach and enjoyment of the cultural achievements of earlier periods on the one side and the development of one's own new ideology on the other.

May 5, 1942

It is reported that the Reich Marshal [Göring] has decided that no leaflets are to be dropped over Britain. The decision has been justified by Luftwaffe-military considerations.

There was a shortage of aircraft which could have been made available for the dropping of leaflets over Britain.

May 10-11, 1942
Staatssekretär Gutterer deputizes for the Minister in chairing the conferences. It is stated: As for British threats of intensified air raids we must continue to maintain the view, and in very strong language, that such threats do not impress us in the least and that every single attempt will cost the British heavy losses.

On May 28, 1942, Goebbels demanded that, on the subject of British threats of intensified aerial bombardment, it should be stated that 'each bombing of a German city will be answered by the smashing of a British city.'

On May 29 he believed that the threatened British air offensive was a big bluff, designed to convince Britain's Russian allies of her readiness for action.

On the following day, when Goebbels visited Hitler at the Reich Chancellery, Hitler confirmed in him the belief that the German 'reprisal blows' against medium-sized British cities had been of colossally destructive effect and would continue to be so.

The press was given the following additional directive: 'The intensification of British air raids against German residential and cultural centres is due not only to bolshevik pressure but primarily also to Roosevelt's influence. At their talks in London a few weeks ago, Harry Hopkins and General Marshall, acting on Roosevelt's instructions, urged the British to use their air force on an increasing scale for terror raids against the German civilian population. The Americans, just like the bolsheviks, do not care if ancient cities in France, Belgium, Holland, Denmark, Italy and Germany are damaged or if century-old seats of culture are destroyed. They have no understanding for such ancient values since they only appreciate engines, refrigerators and radios.'

As for Churchill's allegations in his speech that Germany intends to use gas, there is a divergence of opinion between the Ministry for Propaganda and the OKW. While the former opposes any mention of gas warfare to the German public, even in this direct context, the OKW would like to see a brief, clear and factual official comment which would refute enemy allegations about German intentions not only to foreign audiences but also to the German public. In this way the OKW wants to make it impossible for enemy propaganda to point to a different treatment of the subject for foreign and for German audiences, or to argue that German propaganda is keeping quiet about the subject at home because workers and servicemen in Germany are accurately informed about the manufacture of poison gas missiles.

Our response to Churchill's speech, generally speaking, should be marked by the sharpest possible pillorying of his falsifications of history and by the sharpest possible attacks on him personally.

In his broadcast speech of May 10, 1942, Churchill dealt extensively with the war in the air and with the very evident British superiority. A long list of German cities to be bombed had been prepared. 'The civil population of Germany have, however, an easy way to escape from these severities. All they have to do is to leave the cities where munition work is being carried on, abandon their work and go out into the fields and watch the home fires burning from a distance. In this way they may find time for meditation and repentance. There they may remember the millions of Russian women and children they have driven out to perish in the snows, and the mass executions of peasantry and prisoners of war which in varying scales they are inflicting upon so many of the ancient and famous peoples of Europe.' On the subject of gas warfare Churchill said: 'The Soviet Government has conveyed to us their view that, in the event of the failure of their attack, the Germans would use poison gas against the armies and the people of Russia. We ourselves are firmly resolved not to use this odious weapon unless it is used first by the Germans. Knowing our Hun, however, we have not neglected to make preparations on a formidable scale.'

May 13, 1942

Churchill's threats of a possible use of gas are to be challenged most sharply in German home propaganda as well. Under the slogan: 'We shan't start it, but heaven help him who does' it should be made clear, among other things, that the secret weapon which has been hinted at in various Führer speeches is certainly not poison gas.

On May 14, 1942, came the instruction that the so-called 'nerve gas' was not to be mentioned in Germany's foreign propaganda either. A few days later Hitler prohibited any publicity for the use of poison gas. Meanwhile there had been much discussion of the use of gas, mainly in the neutral press. A Swiss correspondent expelled from Germany reported about a so-called nerve gas which was said to be non-toxic, but stunned and paralysed the troops. A UP report from Stockholm also claimed that the new German secret weapon was a gas which 'attacks the nerves of the enemy but does not kill people.' New weapons, such as shells with compressed air, had already been used in the Kerch Peninsula, the report stated. The foreign public had in fact been tricked by German propaganda reports. A nerve gas was being produced in Germany but its effect was lethal. German lethal gases were Sarin, Tabun and Soman.

The exaggerated Spanish reports about the opening of the German offensive in the East are not to be published in Germany.

All propaganda media must avoid any geographically defined German military objectives becoming the subject of discussion.

The Führer Directive No. 41 of April 5, 1942, envisaged the penetration of the Russian southern front by three offensive wedges which would converge in the Stalingrad area. The reconquest of the Kerch Peninsula which began on May 8, 1942, after its loss in December 1941, was seen as a secondary operation. On May 12, 1942, however, came the unexpected opening of the Soviet offensive in the Kharkov area which, to begin with, aimed at encircling the German salient including Kharkov by way of a pincer operation.

May 18, 1942

At the request of the Führer's headquarters the question of the 'Second Front' is not to be given any particular prominence in the German press in future.

In a conversation with Goebbels on May 30, 1942, Hitler described the 'talk about a second front' as 'twaddle'. (*Cf.* June 24, 1942.)

May 19, 1942

It is reported that two acts of sabotage have been attempted at the anti-Soviet exhibition, by setting light to phosphorus flares. Whereas in the one instance no one was injured and no material damage was caused, in the other a jet of flame seriously injured two visitors and slightly injured six. The fire damage, however, was so slight that even in this case the damaged area in the exhibition did not even have to be closed.

Gutterer opened the anti-bolshevik exhibition 'The Soviet Paradise' in the Berlin Lustgarten on May 8, 1942. The show, held in marquees covering over a thousand square yards of floorspace and open until June 21, included weapons captured in the eastern campaign, a collective farm building, a Russian factory office, a students' hostel and workers' flats in the Soviet Union. There was also the obligatory 'GPU death cell'. At the exit of the exhibition appeared the 'German infantryman as the defender of Western civilization against bolshevik barbarism.'

Goebbels declared that the exhibition would have to make large-scale propaganda for the justification of the German war against the Soviet Union. For that reason, no exhibit must be included which might 'in any way make good publicity for bolshevism.' (*Cf.* May 26 and 27, 1942.)

May 22, 1942

Vansittart's speech in the House of Lords has led to a discussion among the British public about the treatment of the German people after the war. The Minister once again emphatically points out that the British differentiation between the German people and the National Socialist leadership must be kept out of our reports under all circumstances. We must avoid at all costs ever publishing an enemy comment which attributes responsibility for the war to the National Socialists alone and proposes a differentiated treatment for Nazis and the rest of the people.

In the British discussion about the treatment of the Germans after the war, Lord Vansittart, no doubt in order to justify his 'strategy of annihilation', declared that Germany intended to exterminate twenty million British after the war or to send them to Africa as slaves. Other quarters wanted a distinction to be made between the Nazis and the German people. Goebbels stated on May 23, 1942: 'If they made a distinction between the people and us they would undoubtedly achieve more that way than they have achieved so far.' In late 1942 Goebbels declared that in his propaganda he pursued the principle of acquainting the German people with all 'outbursts of hatred' from the other side, such as the article by the American Kaufmann who had demanded that German men should be sterilized after the war, or suggestions for the deportation of German children. These statements, he pointed out, had resulted in a marked stiffening among the people of their will to resist, simply because measures of that kind go beyond what is humanly bearable. On the other hand, it would be risky to publish detailed political plans, such as about the partitioning of Germany, because these do not touch the individual and merely have an overall depressing effect.

The slogan '1942 – The Year of Decision' which is now appearing in the enemy press must not be taken up. The Minister points out most emphatically that we must keep a free hand for the coming winter. He has no wish, after a summer full of great victories and exuberant optimism, to find himself once more in such a disastrous situation as in October of last year.

The Norwegian telegraph agency carries a report according to which sixty Norwegians have been made to forfeit their civic rights. The Minister most sharply criticizes the fact of this declaration and also of its publication. There is nothing more stupid than to declare patriots, who are fighting for their country, to have forfeited their civic rights. One only need imagine what a wonderful lever for propaganda it would have been for the NSDAP if leading National Socialists had been declared to have forfeited their civic rights during the System* period.

* Derogatory term for the Weimar Republic, *Tr.*

May 26, 1942

According to a report by the Chief of Staff of the Reich Directorate for Propaganda, the perpetrators of the two sabotage actions at the anti-Soviet exhibition have been identified. They are altogether twelve persons, seven of them Jews and five Aryans. The Jews entered the exhibition without the Jewish star and together with the five Aryans placed the phosphorus incendiaries. The manufacturer of the incendiaries is an engineer employed by AEG* in a secret laboratory. The terrorist group was discovered by chance.

May 27, 1942

The Minister directs that enemy reports about the battle of Kharkov should be given maximum publicity right from the start and should be compared with the present situation.

The battle of Kharkov, which resulted in the encirclement of two Soviet armies in the Izyum bridgehead, ended on May 29, 1942. According to a German special announcement of May 30, the number of prisoners taken at Kharkov totalled 240,000.

On May 29, 1942, Goebbels asked that 'the fiasco of the Anglo-American information policy in the case of Kharkov should be dismissed with sovereign superiority.' The neutral journalists' reports about Kerch, he said, were a brilliant testimony to the truthfulness of German reporting and to the mendacity of enemy reporting and of the Soviet communiqués. (According to German reports 149,000 prisoners were taken in the siege of the Kerch Peninsula.)

About mid-May the British and American press had represented the battle of Kharkov as 'the great key position behind whose gates vital decisions will be taken.' Kharkov was labelled as the curtain-raiser for the decisive battle of that decisive year.

At the request of the High Command of the Wehrmacht no comparisons are being made between U-boat sinkings in World War One and in the present war.

The Minister believes that a lot of useful hints about the situation inside Germany are finding their way to Britain through the Swedish correspondents in Germany. The optimism so conspicuously displayed by the enemy powers during the past few weeks is clearly based on hopes of a difficult internal situation in Germany. The foundations for these hopes, the Minister believes, are most probably provided by the Swedish press, which is being increasingly quoted in Britain.

(*Cf.* July 10. 1942.)

* Allgemeine Elektrizitäts-Gesellschaft (General Electric Company). *Tr.*

The Minister says he has submitted to the Führer a proposal for removing the Jews from Berlin. This has been opposed by economic authorities on the grounds that the Jews employed in the armaments industry are very much concerned with precision work and would be difficult to replace. It is now planned to hold five hundred leading Jews as hostages, to stand surety for the decent behaviour of the Jews in Berlin.

In connexion with the incident at the anti-Soviet Exhibition in the Berlin Lustgarten, Goebbels decided to hold five hundred Berlin Jews as hostages. He personally concerned himself with the compilation of their list. In this connexion he was heard to say: 'I'd rather have ten Jews in a concentration camp or below ground than one at liberty.' *The New York Times* reported that, according to information available in Stockholm, 258 Jews had been shot in Berlin-Lichterfelde on May 28.

On the occasion of a visit to the Reich Chancellery on May 30, 1942, Goebbels again urged Hitler to evacuate the forty thousand Jews left in Berlin. Speer was instructed to replace the Jews employed in the armaments industry by foreign workers. Goebbels here again displayed his resolution 'to liquidate the Jewish danger, cost what may.'

The speech by the Japanese Premier Tojo, the Minister believes, is a classic example of brilliant propaganda. The sovereign manner in which Premier Tojo dismissed the British and Americans must be an example to us. Without invectives and without getting involved in the small-scale day-to-day war, Premier Tojo in a superior manner dismissed the enemies and their whole information policy.

In his speech to the newly-elected Japanese diet, Premier Tojo said among other things: 'Burma having been cleared of the enemy, all the British empire's advanced outposts for the defence of India are now in the hands of the imperial troops, and the Indian people therefore now have a golden opportunity to rise and achieve independence. . . .

Following our victorious battle in the Coral Sea, Australia is now facing unaided the attack of the Imperial Army. I would like, therefore, once more to convey to the Australian leaders my sincere wish that they may reflect on my words, that they may have a clear picture of the international situation, and then boldly decide on the most important step for Australia . . . The United States has been compelled to accept defeat after defeat. I can only feel sorry for the people of the United States and Great Britain who have to fight under such leaders. . . .'

May 31, 1942
The Minister refers to the brazen manner in which British and Russian information policies dispute the battle of Kharkov. We must use every

means at our disposal to deal with this biggest-ever fabrication which will simply not recognize this gigantic battle as having taken place. The Minister says he is used to a lot, and he has a thick skin – but this takes his breath away. It is now up to us to produce, on the largest possible scale, documentary evidence of this huge battle of annihilation. The newsreel and the German press are instructed to take the necessary measures.

Tass announced on May 30, 1942, that the German Wehrmacht had lost 90,000 killed and prisoners at Kharkov; Russian losses, on the other hand, amounted to 5,000 killed and 70,000 missing.

June 1, 1942

The Minister regards the bombing of Cologne as a British contribution to the Russian war effort. Churchill's telegram to the Commander-in-Chief of Air Operations about the employment of the bombers proves that the reported figure of 1,250 machines is not correct. However, we should not indulge in any illusions about the number and we should tell the public clearly and accurately how large the number of attacking aircraft was. The reprisal raid on Canterbury is to be given much prominence.

After the RAF's 1,000-bomber raid on Cologne during the night of May 30–31, 1942, the casualties reported were 469 killed and 5,027 injured. Roughly 3,000 tons of incendiary and high-explosive bombs were dropped. *The New York Times* on June 2 claimed to know that the attack on Cologne had cost 20,000 killed and 54,000 wounded. The German Luftwaffe made a 90-bomber reprisal raid on Canterbury.

During the night of May 31–June 1, 1942, the RAF attacked industrial enterprises and cities in the Ruhr with 1,036 bombers and dropped 400 high-explosive and over 31,000 incendiary bombs. Essen, Duisburg and Oberhausen were badly hit; at the last-named place about 100 persons were killed and 300 injured.

The American report about the stockpiling of foodstuffs for the starving people of Europe for peacetime is to be disregarded *under all circumstances*.

June 4, 1942

On May 27, 1942, the Deputy Reichsprotektor and Chief of Security Police, Reinhard Heydrich, was gravely wounded when an attempt was made on his life as he was driving in an open car through a Prague suburb. The perpetrators were Czech exiles, trained in Britain and dropped by parachute from British aircraft. Hitler appointed SS Obergruppenführer and General of Police Daluege (1897–1946) to deputize for Heydrich. On June 4 Heydrich died of his wounds.

The Minister declares that the German side must at once seize the initiative in the question of the assassination of the Deputy Reichsprotektor Heydrich. According to a report from Obergruppenführer Daluege it may be safely assumed that the attempt was mounted by British agents. This fact must be brought out in the German propaganda, at first only at home, but as soon as possible also in our foreign broadcasts, in order to counter any British efforts at falsifying the attempt by representing it as a spontaneous action by the Czech people.

June 9, 1942
The Minister believes that a massive attack on plutocracy would again be in order in the German press.

American speeches about the world they intend to establish should be countered by us by the kind of world which the Americans have established so far and the kind of world we are trying to build. It should be pointed out in this connexion that it is a piece of impertinence for American and bigoted British statesmen to vilify the Führer who has been simple and modest all his life, whereas those social reformers in America and Britain have been unable, in spite of their wealth, to give their people bread and work.

At the conference on June 15, 1942, Goebbels issued the instruction that 'domestic propaganda should express the view that Roosevelt is evidently just as mentally sick as Wilson was.' Goebbels, moreover, aired the plan of using a similar argument for foreign audiences but this was objected to by the Ministry of Foreign Affairs, which pointed to the different mentality of the Americans. Goebbels allowed himself to be convinced. Goebbels's criticism of Roosevelt's speeches which concluded with familiar prayers was not to be used for the American public 'as it was only apt to help Roosevelt in the eyes of his fellow countrymen.'

June 10, 1942
The Minister directs that the American cheating about their great naval victories should be made the target of attack now that the Japanese reports are available. Roosevelt's position on this issue is very weak, for a man who has not yet found the strength to admit the losses of Pearl Harbour must go on scoring paper victories in order to appease the people. He believes that a certain disquiet is beginning to be noticeable

in America and that press comment in Britain, again calling for publication of shipping losses, reflects the uncertainty and disquiet about the situation there.

In the air and naval battles of the Midway Islands from June 3 to 6, 1942, the Japanese lost 4 carriers, 1 heavy cruiser, 253 aircraft and 3,500 men. The battle cost the United States 1 carrier, 1 destroyer, 150 aircraft and 300 men. The battle represented a turning point in the Pacific war in favour of the United States.

As for the fighting at Sevastopol and in North Africa, only comment within the framework of the OKW communiqué should be put out. There can be no harm in pointing to the strength of Sevastopol – probably one of the most powerful fortresses in the world and, moreover, further strengthened by the Russians in recent months – so as not to encourage optimistic comment.

Von Manstein's army launched its offensive against the fortress of Sevastopol on June 7, 1942.

June 12, 1942
The Minister directs that the Anglo-Soviet agreement and the Washington consultations should only be reported briefly at home; moreover, as in the case of the Potomac Declaration,* new expressions are to be used all the time, to prevent the growth of the idea among the German public of an important event associated with a definite concept.

On May 26, 1942, Molotov signed a twenty-year Anglo-Soviet Treaty of Alliance in London. At the same time he received assurances about the establishment of a Second Front in Europe. From May 29 until June 4, 1942, Molotov had negotiations in Washington and there too received assurances about the establishment of a Second Front, as well as of US economic aid. A revised version of the existing lease-lend agreement was signed.

To prevent the Atlantic meeting between Roosevelt and Churchill on August 11, 1941, and the Atlantic Charter proclaimed on this occasion from becoming a crystallized concept in the German public mind, German propaganda was in the habit of referring derogatorily to the so-called 'Potomac Declaration', so named after Roosevelt's yacht. Roosevelt and Churchill met on board the ships *Augusta* and *Prince of Wales*.

* Roosevelt and Churchill met at sea in August 1941 to issue a joint declaration of principles and war aims. A few days prior to the meeting, for reasons of security, the President was reported to be cruising off the Maine coast on his yacht *Potomac*. The joint declaration has therefore sometimes been called the Potomac Declaration. *Tr.*

The Washington consultations about the establishment of a Second Front in Europe are to be commented on by the German side along the lines that such an agreement is totally worthless and meaningless without the decisive partner, i.e. the German Wehrmacht. Enemy forces – and here we should use the Führer's formulations – are still welcome to come to Europe.

June 14, 1942

The Minister explains that the enemy thesis that Germany's offensive strength is exhausted should be countered by the following arguments:

(1) The Anglo-Saxon theatre of war has become very costly owing to the brilliant successes of our U-boats.

(2) On the Eastern Front victories have already been won which, had they been won by our enemies, would undoubtedly have led to British assertions that after such losses there was no hope of our winning the war now.

(3) After these successes we are still a whole fortnight ahead of last year and are already 1,200 kilometres deep in enemy country.

(4) The situation in the Pacific and North Africa is anything but favourable for the Anglo-Saxon powers.

The British large-scale raid on Cologne, in the Minister's view, is the British visiting card for Molotov. At the decisive moment of his negotiations with Russia, Churchill mounted this attack and mobilized for it all available forces. The fact that the most varied types were shot down in the Cologne raid, ranging from single-engined to four-engined bombers, is evidence that all available forces were scraped together for this propaganda raid.

Although loss of life is no absolute yardstick for the success of a bombing raid, it nevertheless provides a certain clue. According to official British statements the loss of life due to German air raids in April and May totalled 1,337 while the number of persons killed by British air raids on Germany during the same period was 1,132.

On June 2, 1942, Goebbels observed about the British air raids 'that in our announcements on the reprisal raids we must on no account use the word terror raids. The British have so far carefully avoided speaking of terror raids on Germany.' The following day he believed that British aircraft losses had resulted in an increasing scepticism in the British assessment of air raids. The number of persons questioning the effectiveness of this method would continue to grow, but this point should not be taken up; on the other hand, the hard reprisal blows against British cities must continue to be strongly emphasized.

June 17, 1942

The Minister issues renewed instructions that, in dealing with the operations in Africa, no alleged German objective must be named, such as Tobruk or Suez – not even in a negative sense.

The German-Italian offensive in North Africa began on May 26, 1942. The British-held fortress of Tobruk surrendered unexpectedly on June 21. The following day Hitler demanded a further advance aimed at the conquest of Egypt, and on June 26 Rommel laid down the next objectives of the attack – El Alamein, the Nile, Alexandria and Cairo, which he wanted to reach by June 30. The press, needless to say, had to keep silent about this.

The Minister issues directives that enquiries should be made at headquarters about the state of investigations in the Heydrich case and points out that British reports, accepting some degree of responsibility by Britain, are evidently designed to exculpate the Czechs. Referring to reports which show that the Czech public is very largely indignant about the assassination, which has cost the Czech people such heavy sacrifices, the Minister believes that it will soon be time for the German side to adopt an unequivocal attitude in propaganda.

June 19, 1942

The Minister declares that, in contrast to the Molotov visit which had been treated with great reserve, German propaganda can use Churchill's present visit to Washington as the occasion for an aggressive sally of propaganda. It might be pointed out, for instance, that whenever he is faced with awkward questions because of a particularly bad military situation, Churchill invariably escapes his questioners in some way or other; that his trip to Washington to receive his orders is a clear indication of Britain's catastrophic situation, especially in North Africa and in the U-boat war; that the Washington meeting is a meeting of two men responsible for the war who now believe they can gloss over the real damage by big publicity, etc. The Minister points out that it is paradoxical to need to make a point of discussing the allegedly good situation at the front since there is not much more one can say about that – one should rather talk about existing difficulties and their removal. As for the Second Front, the present Washington programme makes it clear that this has not by any means been finally fixed with Molotov. From the German side one might point out, under the slogan: 'Why dream of distant shores ...', that North Africa provides an adequate field of activity.

The main purpose of Churchill's talks with Roosevelt in the United States from June 18 to 25 was to achieve the necessary agreement about operational plans for 1942 and 1943. In a secret memorandum drafted on June 20 the landing in French North Africa was considered.

The Minister also deals with the communiqué now issued, about the discovery of the assassins of the Deputy Reichsprotektor [Heydrich]. It is pointed out that this communiqué was directly agreed between the authorities in Prague and headquarters. Supplementary information is that thirteen men were discovered in the Greek Orthodox church in Prague; when an attempt was made to arrest them they immediately put up most fierce opposition and, insofar as they were not killed in the resulting fighting, they took their own lives. They were equipped with plentiful and excellent weapons, ammunition, etc. of British origin. Two weeks before the attempt parachutists had been dropped over Bohemia. The Minister describes it as most regrettable that the communiqué was issued in its present form since, in view of its paucity of precise data, it might easily be questioned. He will try to get a supplementary communiqué issued with precise data.

Heydrich's assassins, as well as twelve members of the Czech resistance organization, found refuge in the Carlo Borromeo church in Prague. The church was besieged by the SS, who eventually killed them to the last man. According to a Gestapo report altogether 1,331 Czechs, including 201 women, were executed in the campaign of revenge for Heydrich's assassination. On June 9, 1942, the massacre of Lidice took place as an act of 'atonement' and deterrence. The village was razed to the ground. About two hundred men and a few women were executed by firing squad. One hundred and ninety-five women from the village were taken to Ravensbrück concentration camp.

June 22, 1942
After his meeting with the Führer, the Minister declares that in our foreign propaganda to Britain the whole responsibility for the loss of Tobruk should be laid at Churchill's door. Generally, it might be pointed out that Churchill always goes off on journeys at times of crisis: thus, during his last trip to America Singapore fell. The fact that 25,000 prisoners were taken in the fortress should not, at the request of military quarters, be interpreted as a sign of a lack of British power of resistance. At home, Egypt is not to be referred to in any way, not even by quotations from the foreign press. The Minister issues the slogan 'Our revenge for Cologne is Tobruk' and directs that attention should be drawn to the fact that the dilettante at the head of the British

government employs his aircraft against militarily worthless targets in Germany while militarily decisive battles are lost for Britain because of a lack of those very aircraft.

The Rumanian Army Command has issued casualty lists. The Minister directs that the Führer be asked to authorize the publication of a German casualty report and until then puts an embargo on the Rumanian figures.

The German losses for the period from June 22, 1941, to June 21, 1942, were announced in the OKW communiqué of July 2, 1942. According to this, the number killed was 271,612 and missing 65,730. These figures, though entirely correct, nevertheless conveyed an incomplete picture and one which was misleading as to the seriousness of German casualties in that it made no mention of the number of wounded. In June July 1942 the number of wounded in the eastern campaign totalled roughly one million. By May 10, 1942, the total had been 851,053 wounded.

Hitler decided to release the German losses only after Tass, on June 23, 1942, had published a comparative table of German and Soviet losses in the Russian campaign, quoting 'fantastic figures'. Total German losses – killed, wounded and prisoners – were estimated at roughly 10,000,000 of which 3,500,000 alone were killed in action. Soviet total losses were quoted at 4,500,000 dead, wounded and missing. Tass simultaneously announced German and Soviet losses of equipment, but these were not taken up by the German side 'for understandable military reasons'.

In order to offset the increasingly noticeable German casualties, General Walter von Unruh (1877–1956) had, as early as April 26, 1942, been appointed by Hitler 'Special Commissioner for the Supervision of a Purposeful War Effort' and charged with the task of pinpointing all men suitable for frontline service and transferring them there. As a result of General von Unruh's work, which has gone down in German military history under the name of 'hero snatching', the OKW in late June 1942 announced that the personnel situation made it necessary 'for all wounded soldiers still suitable for military use to be employed in the Training Army so that men fit for active service may be released for the army in the field.' A decree from Hitler, dated July 29, 1942, moreover, ruled that girls employed by the Reich Labour Service were to be transferred to Wehrmacht and state administration offices.

The same day the Minister received Brigadeführer* Oberg, as well as Colonel Kossmann, the Chief of Staff of the Commander-in-Chief in France, and Colonel von Wedel, Colonel Kratzer, and a number of officers accompanying these gentlemen; present also were the Secretary of State and most of the departmental heads in the Ministry for Propaganda. At the audience, in a talk lasting about three-quarters of an hour, the Minister explained his point of view on the subject of the

---

* SS rank equivalent to major-general. *Tr.*

treatment of the population in the occupied territories. Both at the beginning and again at the end of his exposition he expressly pointed out that he did not wish to interfere in the affairs of other departments or authorities, but that he, as an active champion of freedom, had, after World War One, suffered the enemy occupation of the Rhineland, and, possessing some expertise and experience in the handling of the public, he felt it incumbent on him, in view of the German victims of attacks in France and in view of the important German interests at stake, to set out his views on the best methods for preventing unnecessary casualties.

(1) Penalties must first be threatened and then mercilessly carried out in order to achieve a deterrent effect. These penalties must be shrewdly thought-out so that they should isolate the culprits in the eyes of the population and not induce it to support the outrages. The system of hostages, who should as far as possible be taken from the leading circles of the opposition and made public, and whose execution by firing squad should be threatened, had proved effective in many cases since it had led the entire following of these hostages to concentrate all their efforts on preventing incidents which might lead to the carrying out of the execution.

(2) A Wehrmacht commander-in-chief should not, as far as possible, interfere in the administration, and particularly in difficult tasks, but instead leave these to the native authorities; however, by skilful intervention he should demonstrate his understanding of the hardships of the general public and should intervene whenever injustices are committed in that respect.

Since April–May 1942 the number of attacks on German servicemen in France had been increasing. From the end of April to the end of May 1942 alone the total score was 43 killed and 50 wounded; for these 1,221 French hostages were shot. At the Nuremberg war crimes trial the number of hostages shot in France during the war was given as in excess of 29,000.

Goebbels in early May 1942 regarded the counter-measures taken against attacks on German troops as 'rather pointless and purposeless', mainly because the names of the executed hostages were not published. He also made the proposal that 10,000 bicycles should be confiscated for each attack, since this would hurt the French while the Wehrmacht could 'make exceedingly good use' of the bicycles. On May 23, 1942, Hitler praised Goebbels's proposal for the confiscation of bicycles as a punishment for attacks as 'splendid'.

On the French public, the executions of hostages in April–May 1942 had a shocking and bewildering effect. The measures were unanimously rejected as 'unjust' and the underlying principle of 'collective responsibility' was condemned as intolerable and cruel. However, from June 1942 to August 1944 during the term of office of the Senior SS and Police Leader in France, SS Brigadeführer and Major-General of Police Carl Albrecht Oberg, the number of executions of hostages was said to have gone down. (*Cf.* July 14, 1942.)

June 24, 1942

The Minister directs that the feats of arms of the Italians should receive more publicity in our press. If, in connexion with the capture of Tobruk, those enemy reports are quoted which emphasize the military deeds of the German troops, then our commentaries and leading articles should give prominence to the Italians. We can give the Italian troops this publicity with a clear conscience since the world knows anyway who was victorious.

On the strength of press reports and the debates in the House of Commons, the Minister believes that the situation in Britain is critical. At the same time, however, a certain note of optimism can again be discerned, and the German press must show reserve in judging the British situation and altogether avoid discussing the possibility of the fall of the Churchill régime.

The talk about a Second Front can be made the subject of very strong polemics, pointing out in particular the senselessness of these discussions, since the British and Americans themselves admit that they are short of the most urgently needed weapons everywhere.

Questioned about the problem of the British invasion, Hitler at his dinner-table at the Reich Chancellery on June 22, 1942, observed that the British had three options of a landing – in Spain, Holland or Norway. As he himself considered a landing in Norway to be the most probable, he thought that the most careful security measures must be taken there. Goebbels was present at this dinner. (*Cf.* July 15, 1942.)

The Minister directs that the publication of the secret agreement in the *Göteborgs Morgenpost* should be used in our propaganda in the biggest possible way. This secret agreement cannot be dismissed in a few days but must be used continually in our daily propaganda. We must not enter into any discussion about its authenticity, but we must ceaselessly talk about this document and make it into a fact. He requests that in our day-to-day propaganda phrases like 'as is known' and similar ones are used. The secret agreement must become an established fact.

The alleged Anglo-Soviet secret supplementary agreement, which first appeared in the Swedish *Göteborgs Morgenpost* on June 23, was published in *Völkischer Beobachter* on June 24, 1942. Even without the Reuter and Tass denials the alleged agreement was recognizable as a German forgery from the way in which it as a matter of course presumed the continued existence of the military position of the Axis Powers in Central Europe. The Anglo-Soviet Treaty of Alliance was signed in London on May 26, 1942, without any supplementary secret agreement and without any territorial clauses. It is true that the Soviet government – most recently through Molotov in London – had made territorial claims to eastern Poland and Rumania and had demanded their clear definition in a secret supplementary agreement. However, Eden and Churchill refused – as a matter of principle, or at least for the duration of the war – to conclude any such agreement which would have violated the Atlantic Charter.

June 25, 1942

The Minister points out that Churchill will undoubtedly return [from the United States] with many promises and figures about American aid in order to pacify disturbed British public opinion. It is up to us to begin unmasking these tactics of Churchill's now and to anticipate his probable explanations. In doing so we must point out that these continuous attempts at mitigating defeats and vague promises of American aid are the surest way of losing an empire.

The fall of Tobruk, Goebbels declared at the conference of June 23, 1942, must not produce the impression among the German public that Britain is already finished. 'He pointed out that official British news policy on this subject was evidently working on the principle of first deliberately exaggerating the seriousness of the defeat in order presently to create among the British public the impression that this gloom had been excessive and that the situation was not so desperate after all. This trick had often been used by British propaganda before.'

At the conference of June 26, 1942, Goebbels thought it unlikely that the British defeat in North Africa would trigger off a cabinet crisis. Churchill, he said, was tolerating public criticism to enable the public to 'work its anger out of its system' before his return from America.

According to a DNB report another village in the Protectorate has been razed to the ground because of its support for parachutists. Although the announcement this time has only been in the press and not on the radio, the Minister nevertheless directs that announcements of this kind should as a matter of principle first be submitted to him for comment.

An official report from Prague stated that the village of Ležáky in the Chrudím district had been burnt to the ground on June 24, 1942, and all adult inhabitants put to death. The children were said to have been accommodated in an educational home.

'Don't be too fair'

July-September 1942

July 1, 1942

The Minister points out that the time has now come to activate German propaganda to the Arab world. No purpose is served by attacking the Egyptian government. Nor must any kind of mention be made of the King of Egypt. On the other hand, he considers it appropriate to remind the Egyptians that Britain also intends to apply the 'scorched earth' principle in Egypt. The Minister asks the OKW representative how the military departments judge the suitability of a German propaganda which would carry unrest into the British-occupied Arab countries. The OKW representative replies that such propaganda would seem exceedingly desirable militarily. In particular it would be suitable, for instance, to draw the Palestinian Arabs' attention to the Jewish problem, so as to induce the British to leave their troops where they are, with a view to possible unrest, and not switch them to the Egyptian front.

On June 30, 1942, the German and Italian troops reached El Alamein but because of their exhaustion were unable to continue their advance even though the German command still held great hopes. Goebbels believed that he must give some propaganda support to 'Egypt's power of resistance against British attempts to apply the scorched earth principle.' On July 3, 1942, he coined the slogan: 'Churchill scores victories in parliament, Germany scores them in the war.' It was considered premature to call for a rising of the Arab population in Palestine. On July 2, 1942, the press was informed as follows: 'The struggle of the Axis Powers will also bring Egypt her liberation from British rule and hence the restoration of Egyptian sovereignty; this statement meets the political aspect of this problem.'

The Minister refers to the fact that numerous men from the world of science have travelled about the eastern territories occupied by us and observes that they, just like other travellers of this kind, are now spreading the view in Germany that conditions in the Soviet Union had been good and that the German accounts, although these have been entirely in line with the facts and with the impression of the fighting forces, had been incorrect. The Minister states that the Führer has learnt about this matter and has now issued orders that at all costs such journeys are to be immediately discontinued. He was thinking in particular of journeys by archaeologists, etc. from Reichsleiter Rosenberg's department.

The Minister instructs Herr Staatssekretär Gutterer to get in touch with all authorities concerned with a view to preventing any such journeys which are not absolutely necessary or justified for reasons of the war economy.

July 6, 1942

The Minister issues the directive that the situation in Egypt should be treated with reserve, also in the foreign services. On the other hand he agrees with the OKW that a polemic with Russian denials of our successes on the Don, with Russia's exaggerated German casualty figures and with the alleged rescue of large parts of the Sevastopol garrison, is necessary.

The fall of Sevastopol was announced in the Wehrmacht communiqué of July 1, 1942. On July 3 a Moscow communiqué announced that Soviet troops had evacuated Sevastopol after 250 days' heroic resistance.

As for the work of the secret transmitters, the Minister requests an accurate exposition of existing transmitters with indication of their purpose and method of work. He declares that, generally speaking, the secret transmitters are now no longer topical, just as in 1932, for instance, the leaflet had become outdated in the internal German struggle. The work of the secret transmitters should therefore be continued only in those cases where there are special reasons.

The result of the investigation of the secret transmitters demanded by Goebbels was submitted to him with a letter on July 8, 1942. On the basis of this he authorized on July 9 the suspension of four secret transmitters while seven were to remain in operation. These included four Concordia transmitters: Concordia N = 'New British Broadcasting Station', putting out subversive nationalist propaganda with pacifist overtones; Concordia S = 'Workers' Challenge', responsible for revolutionary working-class propaganda; Concordia H = 'The Voice of Free India' under the overall direction of Subhas Chandra Bose; and Concordia A = 'The Voice of the Free Arabs'. Of the secret transmitters to the east, only East Transmitter V = 'Radio of Lenin's Old Guard' remained in operation; this conducted subversive Leninist propaganda, aimed against Stalin, and was directed by Karl Albrecht. The 'Free American Radio' was camouflaged as the organ of a group of independent Americans living in Europe who opposed

'Roosevelt's catastrophic policy'. Finally there was a special camouflaged agents' transmitter (Secret Transmitter Z) which put out coded instructions for agents.

As for propaganda directed at Egypt, this should now, in so far as it is conducted openly, be handled somewhat more calmly. The German-Italian government declaration should be emphasized. Calls for acts of sabotage and disturbances in Egypt may, however, continue to be made through suitable channels.

On July 3, 1942, Germany and Italy issued a joint government statement which said, among other things: 'At the moment when their armed forces are penetrating into Egyptian territory, the Axis Powers solemnly restate their firm determination to respect and safeguard Egypt's independence and Egypt's sovereignty.' The possibilities which would follow the Africa Korps's penetration into Egypt were already discussed by Hitler in his table-talk on June 28, 1942. He believed that King Farouk might possibly have to be induced to flee the country in order to prevent the British from abducting him. After the occupation of Egypt, however, he would be prepared solemnly to re-enthrone the king in Egypt. 'In such a case I have nothing against the monarchy.' On July 9 he opposed the suggestion that the Ministry of Foreign Affairs should send a Resident to Cairo or Alexandria after the occupation of Egypt. He wanted to assign Egypt to the Italians who could, if they wished, install a Resident in Egypt as Rommel's deputy.

The Minister points out that it is now no longer advisable to deal in our German propaganda with the difficulties of the fighting during the past winter. If this subject were now to be discussed, the public would no longer feel that sense of relief as at the end of the winter, when it was all over and done with, but would feel anxious about what the coming winter might bring in terms of sacrifices, hardships and demands. The Minister therefore issues a binding directive for internal German propaganda not to touch upon this subject again.

In a discussion on the Russians' power of resistance, the OKW representative points out that, according to the unanimous evidence of prisoners, the Russians are fighting so stubbornly only because they cannot associate any kind of hope for themselves with the idea of a German victory. The morale of the Russian troops as such is exceedingly low. Even so the Russians still consider it better 'to die on their feet than to live on their knees.' The participants in the ministerial conference express the view that a propaganda which would make a German victory appear advantageous to the Russians would contribute decisively to the paralysis of the Russian power of resistance.

July 7–9, 1942

A number of broadcast talks during the past few days about the fighting for Sevastopol, as well as reports about the operations by foreign journalists sent to Sevastopol, as described to them by German officers, are seized on by the Minister as an occasion for some fundamental observations on the question of how the manner of fighting of the Soviets should be depicted and assessed:

During the past few days we have heard some moving and stirring war reports. However, there is the danger that sections of the German public may draw false conclusions from them. Several reports were psychologically exceedingly dangerous. There was a suggestion in them that the Soviets, too, had ideals which inspired them to fanaticism and heroic resistance so that they would not shrink from any privations or efforts in the war. Indeed this went so far that thousands of soldiers and civilians, including women and children, preferred to blow themselves up or let themselves be buried in bunkers rather than capitulate, and that, during an attack on a factory held by 'true bolsheviks, members of the Young Communist League and fanatical commissars,' these resisted to their last breath.

The reports of foreign correspondents similarly contained statements by German officers along these lines. One officer remarked that the Russians had fought 'truly heroically', or it is said: 'The commissars see to the propaganda; they practise iron discipline; anyone yielding is shot. . . .' Another report actually says: 'Whatever is the secret of the Russian power of resistance, German military authorities see it in the political commissars. . . .' In this way the political commissar, an institution we reject for the German Wehrmacht, is suddenly made into the hero and the secret of bolshevik resistance, of toughness and perseverance.

This kind of reporting, unless it is opposed, is bound to shake the German people's attitude to bolshevism and very shortly produce a kind of pro-bolshevik enthusiasm. National Socialism teaches that bolshevism must not be seen as an idea but as the excrescence of sub-humanity and criminal Jewish instincts.

It must further be borne in mind that although National Socialism has freed the German people from the *disease* of bolshevism, a certain proneness to it continues to be present and that this may increase as the war continues and sacrifices are multiplied. It is exactly the same thing as a tubercular patient who has been cured by treatment. The cured person will still remain vulnerable to his former disease. The bacilli are still present, encapsuled, and it would be the peak of folly and could well produce a spiritual catastrophe in Germany if we ourselves were to soften these capsule walls and thus allow the whole poison of the bacilli to penetrate once more into the German national body. It must not be forgotten that there are still five million people alive in our nation who, at some time in the past voted communist. Moreover the kind of reporting that we have now experienced lacks all ability of historical understanding and appreciation of the principles by which great ideological movements have successfully struggled to victory and have established themselves for hundreds and thousands of years.

By way of comparison, surely it is not even conceivable that in the Thirty Years' War the catholic Church, in an account of the war, would have pointed out that the struggle was so hard because on the enemy side the original protestants (the young protestants spiritually educated by Luther) led by their priests, were inspired to fierce tenacity and obsession, or to the most furious resistance; or that, in the conflict of the ancient Roman Empire with young Christianity, a Roman senator should have referred to the heroic attitude of the Christians who, obsessed by their idea, would rather die than surrender. Nor have the bolsheviks for their part ever uttered a word about, say, the heroic and eventually victorious German resistance in the fortress of Demyansk.

Besides, this resistance by the bolsheviks is not a case of heroism or gallantry at all. What we are encountering here in the Russian soul is nothing other than the primitive animal instincts of Slavdom organized into resistance by ferocious terror. It is a mistake to see in it the secret of the Russian soul as represented by Dostoevsky's philosophy. They are creatures which are capable of resistance because they are so inferior. A street mongrel is also more resistant than a pure-bred sheepdog. But that does not mean that the street mongrel is more valuable. A rat, similarly, is more resistant than a domestic animal because it lives in such poor environmental and economic conditions that it simply has to acquire a healthy power of resistance in order to survive at all. The bolsheviks, too, are resistant. The secret behind it is that the Slav mentality has allied itself with an infernal Jewish 'education' which has kept everything else from the Russian people. For twenty years the Russians were not allowed to know anything about Europe, and now they are being told that the German barbarians would shoot everyone, mutilate everyone, torture everyone, etc. The result of this Jewish 'education' which is so subtly exploiting these primitive animal traits is bolshevism. This has nothing in common with heroic resistance.

History shows that in earlier wars (the Seven Years' War, the Crimean War, the defence of the fortress of Port Arthur) the Russians were just the same as we experience them today. The attitude of the Russians is in marked contrast to the conscious heroism of the man who possesses the strength of standing up for a great cause and dying for it.

This is a decisive, fundamental question. For that reason a definite scale of concepts must be created for our reporting, one which clearly differentiates the bravery and heroism of the German soldier from the primitive animal attitude of the bolshevik. In reporting about the bolsheviks we must avoid:

(1) any expression or indication of what we would regard as soldierly behaviour or any alleged ideal of bolshevism,

(2) any concept which must remain reserved for the description of the feats of our own soldiers.

The German language has sufficient forms of expression to distinguish between these fundamental differences, while nevertheless fully reflecting the gravity and ferocity of the fighting.

A few days after the fall of Sevastopol, Colonel von Choltitz, the commander of the Sixteenth Infantry Regiment which particularly distinguished itself in the capture of the fiercely defended forts of Sevastopol, described the fighting for the fortress at the Berlin press conferences and over the radio. His broadcast was immediately used by the BBC's transmissions to France, chiefly in order to emphasize the heroism of the Russians. This was one more reason for Goebbels to criticize the broadcast from the political point of view at the conferences of July 7 and 9, 1942. He went on to say:

Of course, the description of his experiences was entirely correct in every respect. What was wrong – and the political censorship authorities will have to answer for this – was the fact that bolshevism was shown to be the motivation of the enemy's resistance. Referring to his experience, the Minister points out that the German people are free from bolshevism at the moment but nevertheless continue to have a heightened susceptibility to some idealized form of it. The longer the war goes on, the more the German public will ask itself whether the heavy sacrifices and privations are necessary; if German propaganda were then to contain suggestions that the bolsheviks too are fighting for an exalted idea which lends them such great power of resistance, then the German offensive spirit, which is so decisive in this battle of life and death, will be shaken. Nothing is further from him – the Minister – than to belittle the motives which guide, say, de Gaulle. But in the present struggle it is a matter of either you or me – and no elements of weakness must therefore be conveyed to the people. The German people are a people without nuances. They know only black or white, and nothing in between. For this reason too, for instance, the Führer hesitates to give the nations of Russia autonomy under German overlordship – because he is afraid that the German tendency for recognizing the claims of foreign nations is limitless and would very shortly lead to very serious difficulties.

As for the situation in the East, this is favourable enough to be given more publicity. At the same time care must be taken not to exploit too readily the strikingly pessimistic assessment of the situation in the East in enemy propaganda, since our experience teaches us that we may be dealing here with deliberate pessimism laid on by enemy propaganda.

July 10, 1942

The bolsheviks are again reporting statements by prisoners who claim to have been ill-treated by the German Wehrmacht. These reports are clearly designed to prevent desertion and counteract a possible demoralization because of the offensive. Statements by prisoners about the good treatment they have received are to be published more extensively in the press as a counter blow.

The Minister again raises the subject of the expulsion of the Danish correspondent and requests that a clear answer should be obtained from the competent quarters on whether censorship may now be introduced. In any case, no one in the world believes that we have no censorship and everybody is convinced that censorship has long been in existence in Germany. Besides, everybody throughout the world today knows where he stands and everybody believes that the press is no longer free anyway. For that reason any report which slips through will gain particular weight because world opinion believes that if such information has passed through the German censorship then surely there must be something behind it. He believes this question to be so important that, if necessary, he would like to discuss it with the Führer. Non-censorship will not help us any longer, whereas introduction of censorship cannot do us any harm.

Reports in the Swedish press about German peace feelers were the occasion on July 8 for Goebbels to raise again the subject of 'introducing complete censorship of foreign journalists'. To begin with, this was to be merely threatened to the foreign journalists. On July 9, 1942, Goebbels directed that the fact of the expulsion of the Danish journalist should be published in the domestic press without mentioning 'that he spread peace rumours'. Only to the foreign public was the full justification for his expulsion to be given, since this would simultaneously represent a denial of his allegations about German peace feelers.

The *Völkischer Beobachter* of July 10, 1942, carried the following note: 'The Danish correspondent Hjelm Hansen [1878–1957] has been expelled from Germany at short notice for sending untruthful and tendentious reports to the Swedish *Socialdemokraten* and other papers.'

July 13, 1942

The Minister raises the subject of introducing censorship of the reports of all foreign correspondents working in Germany and requests the speediest possible final clarification. He points out that, in the present situation, not only political disturbances but far more extensive and serious damage might accrue to the Reich, for which he cannot bear the responsibility. As a result of the reporting by foreign correspondents, Berlin has lately developed into a kind of news sewer; this state of affairs must be reversed.

As for day-to-day propaganda, the Minister directs that it should be borne in mind that the exceptionally pessimistic Russian reports about the situation on the Eastern Front may well be a trap; for that reason we should in every respect keep within the framework of the OKW communiqué. In particular, the naming of the Caucasus and its connexion with Russia continues to be undesirable.

Mention of the Caucasus as a strategic objective was repeatedly forbidden to the German press in July 1942. The Führer Directive No. 43 of July 11, 1942, set the Eleventh Army the task of making all preparations for a crossing of the Kerch Strait not later than mid-August, with a view to thrusting into the Caucasus and taking possession principally of the oil region around Maykop. The Führer Directive No. 45 of July 23, 1942, envisaged a thrust forward as far as the Caspian and the conquest of the area around Baku.

July 14, 1942

The Minister points out that German propaganda must of course continue to keep within the framework of the OKW communiqués, but that the exceptionally pessimistic enemy reports about the situation in the East nevertheless suggest that one might now, under the overall slogan 'Demolished illusions', demonstrate how wrong enemy propaganda has been and how much it has lied. Under this heading come, e.g. references to the fact that those German soldiers who were reported by enemy propaganda to have been killed are now making their appearance in the East, that alleged German losses of equipment are refuted by the fact that a Second Front has not been established, and that the hopes placed in the African campaign have been dashed by the Germans. The Minister points out that propaganda of this sort is particularly useful now for abroad. Special emphasis should be given to the fact of how much the enemy nations have been cheated and fed on lies.

The Minister finally touches upon the decree of the Supreme SS Führer in France, Oberg, concerning the seizure of hostages and executions, etc.

Oberg's decree was posted up in Paris on July 13, 1942. It stated that all male relations of assassins would be executed within ten days, their wives sentenced to compulsory labour and their children placed in orphanages.

He points out emphatically that he has nothing to do with the decree in the form it has now been published and that he considers it totally wrong psychologically in almost every respect. First of all, it is wrong to issue such a decree without very special justification, e.g. the assassination of a German officer known for his francophile and helpful attitude, and who leaves a large family. Secondly, it is totally wrong to threaten measures against women, let alone against children. Enemy propaganda will eagerly exploit this German mistake. Thirdly, it is wrong to take hostages from among the blood relations of those men who are suspected of being the culprits. The yardsticks to be applied must not be those of blood but political, i.e. men detained as hostages should be politically close to the accused, and these are the men whose execution should be threatened if necessary. In that case the relations and acquaintances of the men arrested as hostages and threatened with death will co-operate in the discovery of the real perpetrators. The Minister requests that his view about the new decree should be conveyed to the competent quarters in the Ministry of Foreign Affairs too.

July 15, 1942

The new argument lately appearing in enemy news services that we shall not survive the winter will be ignored by us. A British paper mentions that the campaign in Russia is developing in accordance with Allied expectations. This should be countered by quoting the grandiloquent and extravagant reports of the winter campaign about the annihilation of the German army.

On July 26, 1942, a ban on the phrase 'General Winter', as used in enemy propaganda, was issued.

An English transmission reported that a survey among ordinary British people had shown that the Second Front was not urgent. We should make a good note of this dishonest excuse of the British, the Minister points out, as it will probably herald a general retreat from the idea of a Second Front.

The following day Goebbels declared that an Allied attempt to establish a Second Front in Europe or Africa was quite conceivable, and that care must therefore be taken to avoid creating the impression among the public that any such attempt would come as a surprise. Nevertheless, no mention should be made of the Second Front at home, and it should only be mentioned for foreign audiences if the enemy himself has referred to it to any extent.

'The best arguments against the talk of a Second Front,' Goebbels remarked at the conference of July 21, were weekly newsreel reports about military preparations in the West and about the fortifications there.

Reports from inside Germany reveal that a change has occurred in public reaction to the attitude of the Russians. Our thesis that the Russian army is being kept together by commissars wielding the knout is no longer believed; instead, the conviction is gaining more ground every day that the Russian soldier is a convinced believer in bolshevism and fights for it.

As the OKW communiqué continued to report persistent heavy defensive fighting on the northern and central sectors of the Eastern Front it was becoming more or less obvious that the initiative was now with the Soviet armies, and extensive sections of the population were beginning to ask themselves 'whether bolshevism can ever be crushingly defeated'.

July 16, 1942

The Minister again raises the subject of introducing pre-publication censorship for the reports of foreign correspondents and points out that although in the past he thought it right to dispense with the introduction of such preliminary censorship, circumstances have now developed in such a way, and the considerations now calling for a change in the present practice are so weighty, that he can in no circumstances agree with a continuation of this state of affairs. He would otherwise have to decline personal responsibility, even towards the Führer himself.

In the further course of the conversation the Minister explains his way of thinking and says that what he has in mind is not the sudden introduction of complete censorship. Instead, he considers it advisable to proceed step by step; he sees it on the lines of first naming a few subjects on which the submission of reports would be obligatory for foreign correspondents.

He lists, for example, military events and the situation at the front, matters connected with the Church, the situation in countries allied with Germany, the peace question. If it turns out that the introduction of obligatory submission within this limited scope – which of course must

be adjusted to conditions prevailing at any given moment – is successful, then matters could be allowed to stop at this point; otherwise the
practice could be extended, if necessary to the point of complete
pre-censorship.

At the foreign press conference of September 7, 1942, Brauweiler informed
the correspondents that the Reichspressechef had decreed new directives for
foreign journalists in Berlin. These directives would come into force on
September 15. As a general principle, 'free reporting' was to be preserved, but
existing regulations were to be supplemented. In future, all reports for the
foreign public would have to agree with the authentic source. Correspondents'
own reports would first have to be submitted to the control authority for
checking, and would have to conform in content and trend with the regulations
of the Ministry for Propaganda and the Ministry of Foreign Affairs. Anyone
contravening the directives would be liable to expulsion or to the penalties for
treason.

July 19, 1942

The Minister requests that a brake should be put on reports from the
Eastern Front in the German press and radio. He refers in particular to
an article in *DAZ* of the 18th of this month which speaks about the
far-reaching consequence of the Russian defeat. The Minister points out
that once before, during the previous autumn, there was talk of the
collapse of the Russian armies without such a collapse coming about.
When the heavy defensive fighting began in the winter, the very circles
which during the autumn had wallowed in optimism were suddenly
predicting the collapse of the Eastern Front in the winter. These people
are not now entitled to talk about the seriousness of the operations in the
East. Altogether this struggle cannot be comprehended by the military
experts since it is essentially an ideological conflict, and no one can
know whether the Russians will not once again very soon face us with a
few more million men.

Goebbels here referred to his observations at the conference of June 17,
1942, when he had warned against optimistic expectations concerning the
speed of the operations. He pointed out that 'in order to avoid the difficulties
encountered during the past winter, supply routes would have to be put in
order, including the resetting of the rail tracks, which, in view of the 350 to
400 km covered by the advance, must inevitably lead to a temporary halt in
the advance.'

The report about Timoshenko's dismissal, which has been put out by
a Turkish news agency, must not be taken up since we have already

dismissed Timoshenko repeatedly during the past year. An official Russian announcement should be awaited.

Marshal Semen Konstantinovich Timoshenko (b. 1895) was Commander-in-Chief of the Soviet Southern Front from October 1941 to December 1942. On July 23, 1942, Lieutenant-General Gorodov replaced Timoshenko as Commander-in-Chief of the newly-established Soviet Army Group Stalingrad. When Timoshenko and Budennyy did not appear on the list of candidates of the Soviet Youth Congress in mid-October 1942 Goebbels cautiously directed: 'Last year we came adrift so often with reports of this nature that it would be a dangerous mistake to publish this kind of unverifiable rumour' about their dismissal.

July 20, 1942

The enemy powers are again using disruptive propaganda in a big way by claiming that Göring, Himmler and others have been relieved of their posts. This requires a few denials which should dismiss these ludicrous reports rather condescendingly.

July 22, 1942

Enemy news policy during the past few days has been divided into an optimistic and a pessimistic note. The Minister directs that the optimistic and the pessimistic reports should be well mixed, and that care should be taken in any event not to allow the impression to arise among the German people that the Russian army on the Southern Front is heading for catastrophe. He asks that the city of Rostov should not be named in German reports until the OKW communiqué announces its fall or encirclement.

The city of Rostov-on-Don, which had been in German hands for a few days in November–December 1941, was captured for the second time on July 25, 1942. From July 23 to 25 there was bitter street fighting in the city.

At the conference of July 21, 1942, Goebbels demanded that foreign press comment on the disastrous situation of the Russian Southern Front should not be taken up. On the other hand, he directed that Soviet reports of victories were to be challenged. In case it was alleged that the Russian retreat was taking place in complete order, attention was to be drawn to the coming newsreel.

On the discussion about the Second Front the Minister observes that reports in certain papers to the effect that it had been put off are no evidence that it is in fact no longer topical. The talk about the Second

Front might be countered, by way of argument, by the supposition that Beaverbrook will probably enter Churchill's cabinet as a kind of Minister for the Second Front. This plan might be presented on the lines that Churchill is now taking Beaverbrook into the government so that, when the Second Front fails, he can always later kick him out as a scapegoat.

Subhas Chandra Bose (1897–1945), the Indian nationalist leader, was the chief of the 'Free India Centre' set up and maintained in Berlin. He served the Germans as a propaganda figure and was earmarked, in case of need, to head an Indian 'counter-government'. In the meantime, his task was to co-operate with German propaganda to India and, as far as it was possible from Berlin, promote an anti-British underground movement in India. Bose, until the outbreak of the war president of the Indian Freedom Movement, had been Mayor of Calcutta until his escape to Germany in 1942. In 1943 he was taken to Japan by German U-boat.

Goebbels received Bose in Berlin on July 21, 1942. After his conversation he remarked that here 'the right man is being used in the right way'. During his conversation with Bose, Goebbels talked about the liberation of India and about propaganda to India.

The slogan, in his opinion, should be: 'We want to make India free and independent of the British.' Bose compared the situation in India with that of the Nazi movement in 1931; he compared Gandhi with Hindenburg and pointed out that his movement required the elimination of out-dated nationalist concepts and a 'revolution of action'.

In connexion with his conversation with S.C. Bose, the minister requests that careful attention should continue to be paid to the Indian question. At the same time he directs that no mention should be made of actions in India until these are in fact imminent.

July 26, 1942

In connexion with a letter from Ministerialdirektor Berndt, at present serving on Field-Marshal Rommel's staff as an orderly officer, in which Berndt describes the bitterness of the German troops over the publicity given in the German press to Italian troops, the Minister points out that the Italians must nevertheless be given prominent treatment in the German press, etc., on every suitable occasion. Besides, this is also in line with directives from the Führer's headquarters. The question is then raised whether it might not be possible to draw Field-Marshal Rommel's attention to this political necessity. In agreement with the OKW representative the Minister proposes to despatch a suitable member of his Ministry to Field-Marshal Rommel in order to convince him that prominent treatment of the Italians is essential in German domestic propaganda.

On July 27, 1942, Goebbels again gave instructions that, in spite of irritation over the performance of the Italian troops, their 'merits' must continue to be emphasized in German propaganda.

July 28, 1942

The Minister points out: There is no German interest in the successful establishment of a Second Front. It would therefore be a mistake for German propaganda to provoke the enemy into establishing one and to ridicule, say, the reasons he gives for not doing so. Rather, our interests demand that we should help the British to get an alibi [sic] that would suit Russia, such as the air raids on German cities. For that reason it would be a mistake for German propaganda to belittle these raids. In this connexion the Minister points out that Germany by no means intends to continue fighting Stalin under all circumstances; should Stalin, who is already highly incensed over the failure to establish a Second Front, be prepared one day to come to an arrangement which would offer us a strategically good frontier and security against Russian rearmament, then such a possibility will certainly not be rejected out of hand on the German side.

At the conference of July 27 Goebbels announced that his editorial article in *Das Reich* about the Second Front would deal with the subject in the most authoritative manner.

The article was published on August 2, 1942, under the significant headline 'Even the Attempt is Punishable' and ended with the words: 'We therefore assure the British of a cordial welcome. We hope they will also bring along a few Americans. The MacArthurs would then make their first acquaintance with German troops who may not carry tennis-rackets or golf balls in their luggage, but who are equipped with first-rate weapons and with superlative combat experience gathered in all the theatres of war in Europe. They would be happy to have the opportunity to make it clear to the Yankees that admission to Europe is forbidden to them too.'

August 2, 1942

The Minister raises the subject of the Second Front and believes that the large-scale British employment of aircraft for the bombing of German cities is proof that a landing is not to be made. The British air force cannot afford to shed as much blood as it does in its raids on Germany if it is really to set up a Second Front. As for the exaggerated British reports of successes, we should quietly accept these and not deny them. If the British believe that their air raids are an adequate contribution to the Second Front then they should be allowed to do so. On the other hand, needless to say, we must not allow a suspicious silence to arise in Germany about the air raids since this again would not meet the desired end.

Goebbels on July 29, 1942, prohibited notice to be taken of Swedish press reports suggesting that 'the idea of a Second Front has been dropped for the moment' in Britain.

August 3, 1942
The Minister directs that the reports on air raids on German cities must be formulated with particular caution. In particular, all remarks and hints that the air raids are not decisive for the war must be avoided.

The Moscow press is now dealing with the Second Front. This circumstance makes it a political issue of prime importance. The Minister requests that there should be no reaction to the Russian comment so that this 'tender little plant' is not destroyed by applause from us. Our most effective response will be to hold back, because in this way we shall probably best foment the quarrel between the others.

August 7, 1942
The journeys to Moscow of the American and British ambassadors are to be described as a symptom of the crisis within the Allied camp. Rumours about a trip by Churchill to Moscow are to be passed over by us in silence as before. The Minister similarly requests that the rumours from Lisbon about a German-Russian separate peace should not be taken up.

In August 1942 various reports appeared in the world press about peace-feelers between Germany and the Soviet Union. It was said in the Ministry for Propaganda that these reports had been launched by Britain and the United States in order to induce the Soviet Union to issue a denial. On the other hand, it is not impossible that the reports, which cropped up first in Tokyo and Lisbon, had been inspired by the German side in order to sound out the attitude of the Soviet Union. Yet more rumours were being spread about peace-feelers submitted to the British by Germany. Thus the Gaullist Free French news agency reported from London on April 29, 1942, that Germany had addressed peace proposals to Britain via three channels during the past six

K

weeks – namely Turkey, Switzerland and Sweden. In all these peace proposals Germany was said to have demanded control of Europe. In Moscow, a conference of Allied ambassadors was held on August 7, 1942, attended among others by the US ambassador in Moscow, Admiral William H. Standley, and the British ambassador, Sir Archibald Clark Kerr. The purpose of the conference was to prepare visits to Moscow by Churchill and by Roosevelt's special envoy. It was officially denied that the subject of the Second Front was on the agenda.

The subject of 'peace rumours' was discussed at meetings of officials of the Ministry for Propaganda's Foreign Affairs Department on August 31 and September 2, 1942. The upshot of the talks was as follows: 'Rumours about an early conclusion of peace are again widespread among the German population at this moment; the rumours are being spread not only by whispered propaganda, as in the past, but now also by way of chain letters. In the whispered propaganda the date named for the conclusion of peace is "the autumn", whereas the chain letter propaganda, allegedly "Christian", mentions "Christmas". This whispered and chain letter propaganda (an official of the Foreign Department of the RMVP succeeded in gaining possession of a copy of one such chain letter) can only have been started by the enemy. Apart from placing an additional load on the postal services, it pursues the aim of arousing unfulfilled or at any rate excessive hopes among the German people in order, when these unfounded hopes are dashed, to make them susceptible to the influences of defeatist propaganda. This propaganda must be countered emphatically. Measures against it, however, are meeting with particular difficulties because these peace slogans are for once readily and gladly believed.'

The Minister requests that the Indian problem should continue to be given great prominence. We may confidently do this in expectation of the clashes which will probably occur between the British and the Indians. We must, however, take care not to emphasize internal differences between the various Indian factions. It is our task to show up the precarious position of the British and to exploit it for our purposes.

On the subject of India it was said at the conference of August 6, 1942: 'We might well point out in our press that India's hour will soon strike. . . .' In order to pacify the Indian sub-continent, Britain in March 1942 offered India dominion status as well as the right to leave the British commonwealth; but these regulations were not to come into effect until after the war. The Indian leaders rejected the proposal. At the beginning of August 1942 unrest in India threatened to grow into a rebellion. The leaders of the Indian Congress Party, including Gandhi and Nehru, were thereupon arrested and interned. However, fear of a Japanese invasion very quickly caused the Indian public to calm down and made it possible for India to continue as the main arsenal of the Allied forces in the East.

266

August 10, 1942

The Minister requests that the situation in India should be presented in a strongly polemic form. The bamboo truncheon, by which the British are now trying to keep the Indians down, must be made into the symbol of British rule, just as the police truncheon had been the symbol during the System Period.

In our reporting on India we should above all point to the low standard of living and stress the sanctimonious regret of the British about their repressive measures against the Indians. He requests that all details should also be published about the arrest of the leading men of the Congress Party.

August 11, 1942

After his return from a lecture tour in western Germany the Minister talks at length about the situation in the bombed areas. The Rhineland-Westphalian cities are undoubtedly going through a difficult time, the extent of which the authorities in Berlin cannot, unfortunately, picture correctly. Besides, we are not handling the subject of the air raids in the right manner; indeed he found that we made some considerable psychological blunders. We might very well learn here from the British who, at the time of the heavy raids on London, glorified the attitude of the British population and made London into a myth. This myth undoubtedly was a considerable factor in stiffening the resistance of the population and in keeping public morale high. The Minister says he believes that, for one thing, the raids must be described much more impressively in the OKW communiqués and, for another, the population must receive greater recognition. He proposes among other things that men and women who particularly distinguish themselves during air raids should be awarded the Iron Cross, or even, when they have quite outstandingly distinguished themselves, the Knight's Cross, and that individual heroic feats should be given far more prominence in the German press.

The Minister sharply attacks the German administration in the Netherlands which is displaying an incredible attitude to the Rhineland-Westphalian population. The people there require large quantities of fruit and vegetables, but the German civilian administration in Holland is only allowing exceedingly small quantities to go to Germany. In Holland anybody can buy fruit and vegetables on an unlimited scale, while in the hard-working Rhineland-Westphalian industrial area there are none to be had. One frequently gets the impression that it is not Holland that is the defeated country which was at war with us. Among other things he relates the case of the Düsseldorf Regierungspräsident*

* The head of the civilian administration of an urban or rural district. *Tr.*

whose Dutch maidservant told him, the Regierungspräsident, that she could no longer watch this shortage of vegetables and fruit in his family and would therefore write to her parents and ask them to send them some fruit and vegetables. The Minister says that, on the strength of the full powers given him by the Führer, he will tackle this problem very firmly and see that a sensible and fair solution is found at all costs.

The Minister requests that the Indian question should continue to be given the greatest prominence; we should follow the example of British propaganda which makes every trivial incident in the Protectorate or in other occupied territories into something big. The Reuter reports should serve us only as the material basis on which we can then build up our stories. The bamboo truncheons should again and again be emphasized by us as the symbol of British rule. He requests that the book by the American journalist Miller, *I Found No Peace,* should be exploited for our propaganda and that those parts should be emphasized in particular where Miller pillories British police procedure against the Indians. The Minister requests that in our propaganda about India the detailed differences between Gandhi and the rest of the Congress representatives or indeed with other Indian parties should not be highlighted, but that the common aim of the Indian parties should be emphasized. We must not at present differentiate between the views of the Indian parties, but only stress their common struggle against Britain.

August 13, 1942
Major evacuations of Jews are again being carried out in Berlin these days. The Minister requests that, especially in the bourgeois papers, a few reports should be carried during the next few days about Jewish agitation in the enemy countries.

According to figures submitted to Goebbels there were 72,327 Jews living in Berlin at the end of August 1940; by the end of August 1941 the figure was roughly 76,000 and at the end of October 1942 roughly 40,000. At the so-called Wannsee Conference of January 1942 it had been decided to solve the Jewish question systematically by 'resettlement' in the East and by 'other measures'. (*Cf.* November 3, 1942.)

August 15, 1942
The Minister raises the subject of the powerful mood of optimism in the Reich and in particular refers to various reports by the SD and the

Gauleiters which all agree in pointing out that the German people are full of hope of an early end to the war. Even the smallest news items in the press or on the radio serve to strengthen that belief and to make it into a certainty for many people. The Minister says that he has done nothing to nourish such optimism and that he regards it as extremely dangerous. For this reason, German propaganda should tread very warily in the immediate future and in particular display caution in taking up pessimistic comment from the enemy countries.

August 17, 1942

The Minister warns against the wave of optimism. No member of the staff of the Ministry for Propaganda must arouse illusions among the public which cannot be fulfilled.

August 18, 1942

In connexion with Churchill's visit to Moscow the Minister remarks that we should represent it as a desperate step by the British Prime Minister, ridiculing in particular the whole hullabaloo of taking salutes, inspecting guards of honour and such like. We must highlight the humiliating aspects of the whole journey and in particular point out that, according to the official reports, Stalin did not even appear at the airport but was said to have been busy at the Kremlin. We might add the remark that Winston Churchill has brought the British Empire to a pretty pass if the British Prime Minister on his arrival in Moscow is not even welcomed by the bolshevik chieftain. Stalin's attitude, moreover, is a special sign of the 'sincerity' of the Russians. The many ridiculous features with which the visit has been embroidered merely prove that not much has come out of it. In connexion with Churchill's visit to Moscow one might now also again recall the whole of Churchill's many remarks about the Russians.

August 22, 1942

In some of the commentaries on Churchill's trip to Moscow the thesis has appeared that Churchill demanded from Stalin that Maisky should keep out of British domestic politics. These reports have been more or less strongly supported by British propaganda. The British papers have meanwhile also reported communist demands in the sphere of domestic politics. This proves that Churchill did not appear in Moscow as a man putting forward demands but as a humble petitioner – exactly as we have repeatedly pointed out.

Churchill was in Moscow from August 12 to 16, 1942, for consultations with the Soviet government. At Moscow airport he was welcomed by Molotov. That same evening, August 12, at the Kremlin he had his 'first meeting with the great revolutionary chief'. In what was at first a very tense conversation, Stalin suggested that the British, by their bombing raids on Germany, were evidently 'trying to avoid getting involved'. Churchill thereupon explained the planned Allied landing in North Africa. But Stalin demanded a landing near Cherbourg. The final communiqué about the conversations between Churchill and Stalin naturally made no reference to the serious differences of opinion; it merely confirmed that the two governments were resolved to continue the 'just war of liberation' until the total annihilation of Hitlerism and of 'any similar tyranny.'

August 21, 1942
The Minister has returned from his trip to the Führer's headquarters and reports about his talks with him. The Führer believes, like the Minister, that the illusionist atmosphere in the Reich must be damped down a little. On the subject of air raid alarms the Führer has ordered a change in the present practice, to the effect that the warning will now be given in two stages. Moreover, the bomb-damaged areas will receive special allocations on a major scale.

The air-raid warning system was reorganized at the beginning of September 1942. From then onwards the alarm was given in two stages – the first on the appearance of up to three enemy aircraft and the second in the event of more than three aircraft. At night the second alarm stage was given as a matter of normal routine.

The Führer is determined at all costs to increase the bread and potato rations in the Reich in the autumn. For this purpose the occupied territories will be drawn upon in an even greater measure and their standard of living, if necessary, reduced in favour of that of the German people.

About mid-September 1942 came the announcement of an increase in food rations, effective from October 19, 1942. Göring reserved the right to make the announcement in person. He intended to point out, above all, that the ration increase in the fourth year of the war 'is due principally to the magnificent achievements of the German army'. About mid-September 1942 it was announced in the press that at Göring's order the meat and bread rations would be increased with effect from October 19, 1942. A normal consumer now received 350 grams instead of 300 grams of meat, and 2,250 grams instead of 2,000 grams of bread per week.

With unusual sharpness the Minister criticizes the interview given by Reich Commissioner Koch to the German press, in which he said, among other things, that German people would be amazed if they knew to what extent the Ukraine is already contributing to the feeding of the German people. The Minister regards this kind of propaganda as irresponsible and instructs that his directives must be followed more strictly. It is irresponsible to make this kind of statement at the present moment and to create among the German people illusions which will not perhaps subsequently come true.

The *Völkischer Beobachter* of August 20, 1942, carried a lengthy article by the Reich Commissioner for the Ukraine, Erich Koch, headed 'One Year of German Ukraine'. This stated: 'The first task was to support and safeguard the German war economy and the German war effort with the country's extraordinary food and raw material resources, so that Germany and Europe might survive a war of no matter what duration . . . The German people therefore – and even optimists would not have thought this possible last year – may in future expect additional yields for the Reich which will make their food supply situation more favourable.' The DNB on August 19 put out a summary of a Koch interview with the representative of the *Deutsche Ukraine-Zeitung*.

August 24, 1942
In view of the favourable development of the military situation at Stalingrad, the Minister points out, there is no reason why this subject should be discussed before the OKW communiqué deals with the operations.

August 26, 1942
The Russians are evidently indulging in deliberate pessimism [over Stalingrad]. The situation at the moment is not such that we should emphasize this Russian pessimism in the German press. British comment on the importance of Stalingrad is being collected so that, if Stalingrad falls, it can be used in our propaganda. It is to be expected that the British will apply their old method and, once Stalingrad has fallen, will claim that the city was only of slight value to the Russians. In connexion with this manoeuvre their earlier comments on the importance of Stalingrad will prove of considerable value to us.

On August 19, 1942, Hitler issued orders to the Commander-in-Chief of the Sixth Army (Paulus) to attack the city of Stalingrad. The Fourth Panzer Army (Hoth) advanced close to the city by August 23, but at the end of August and the beginning of September 1942 the two armies were still outside the outer belt of fortifications surrounding Stalingrad. Nevertheless, the OKW communiqué mentioned Stalingrad almost every day for a month, even before any German troops had reached the city's outskirts. Not until mid-September was heavy street fighting reported on the outskirts of the city.

The failure of the British landing at Dieppe should continue to be featured in the German press. This failure is so extensive that we should deal with it continually. Likewise, the question should now be raised in the German press of whether a British statement about the Mediterranean convoy has meanwhile become possible. At the time they announced that they could not comment on the Axis Powers' 'allegations' about the catastrophe so long as the military operation was not concluded. Since then some considerable time has elapsed without the British Admiralty having said anything about the convoy. We should now ask what the British have in fact lost.

The Anglo-Canadian landing near Dieppe on the Channel coast on August 19, 1942, was a complete failure. The town and harbour, which served the German convoys as an intermediate port, was to have been seized in a surprise coup by 6,000 men, mostly Canadians. The port installations and any craft in port were to have been destroyed. In view of the strong German defences the weak remnants of the landing troops were forced to re-embark by mid-day. They lost 3,600 men, 28 tanks and numerous landing craft. A report from Ottawa about mid-September stated that Canadian losses at Dieppe totalled 3,350 killed, wounded and prisoners.

When the fighting was over, the people of Dieppe and of the countryside around it were publicly praised by the German fortress commandant for their bearing during the operation. At Hitler's request about 1,000 French prisoners of war whose homes were in that area, were released. Goebbels protested at the Führer's headquarters against the publication of this report in the German press since it would merely increase 'the widespread francophile complex in our nation'.

At the conference of August 26 it was announced that Hitler had endorsed Goebbels's view and had given instructions that only an inconspicuous and brief report was to be put out about the release of prisoners from the villages around Dieppe.

On September 6, 1942, *Das Reich* published Goebbels's leading article 'Don't Be Too Fair!'. Millions of copies of the article, which Goebbels viewed as an urgent popular-educational task, were dropped by aeroplane and distributed at home and on the front. In this article Goebbels criticized what he regarded as the weaknesses or disadvantages of the German national character, which caused the German people to be 'still vulnerable to attacks from many sides'. To the detriment of 'their own interests', he pointed out, the Germans had an inadequately developed national consciousness and suffered from an over-developed sense of justice and a 'kind of super-objectivity'. Only

National Socialism had tried to bring about a change – but all that was still 'young and fragile'.

He cited this example: 'One cannot even visualize what our people would do with a government which would cheat it in the way that, say, Mr Churchill's cheats the British. And yet there are people amongst us who try to discern a kind of political style even in that ... We are so much afraid of doing an injustice to someone else that, in case of doubt, we prefer to be unjust to ourselves ... We Germans still have to learn how to hate. We are not well suited to chauvinism, and if anyone really wants to bring our national soul to the boil he has to set about it very cleverly ... Are these the qualities which make us particularly loved in the world? By no means! This German shortcoming is a matter of contempt rather than of admiration ... We Germans have a lot to learn before we can finally make our mark spiritually and socially. . . .' Instead of, more properly, using the first person singular, Goebbels continued: 'We do not want to make an objective judgement when our existence is at stake or when questions of our national life are in the balance; then we are all Party, all prejudice, all blind and stubborn bias. Let no one object that this is not German. Maybe the opposite is German – but if so, it is a bad and a dangerous side of our national character, and one which we must fight.'

In conclusion Goebbels said that objectivity, a mania for justice and sentimentality would prevent the Germans from discharging their mission in the world, a mission which consisted not of carrying culture and education into the world but of 'taking grain and oil out of it'. The age of false and lying concepts of humanity was gone.

On September 12, 1942, Goebbels reported at the conference that his article had been well received among the German public and had met with much agreement.

September 9, 1942

On the subject of Churchill's speech, the Minister remarks that American press comment about the lack of interest shown by British MPs during the speech should be particularly featured. These reports in the American papers should be published on the lines that they confirm the accuracy of our belief that no one is any longer interested in the tales Churchill is telling the British people. It should be added that British press comment, which again refers to a magnificent speech by the British Premier, means nothing since this is ordered from above. The sentences where Churchill says that Smuts had talked to him 'massively' and Stalin 'brusquely' should be particularly noted.

In his speech in the Commons on September 8, 1942, Churchill, reporting on the war situation, emphasized British superiority in the air and at sea, and suggested that military developments were heralding a turn in favour of the Allies.

273

The question of an effective propaganda slogan for the winter has been put to the Minister by the Reich Propaganda Directorate. In this connexion the Minister points out that we should not yet start talking about the winter. This is only early autumn, and we had better first wait and see how military operations develop. He has always urged that no excessive optimism should be aroused in Germany, and we have therefore enough time to tackle these problems at the end of September, when the situation will be clearer.

On the subject of Stalingrad the Minister points out that we must not arouse any illusions about a rapid course of the operation, and that it is quite all right to reproduce comment such as that by Exchange Telegraph referring to the ferocity and gigantic scale of the fighting. Our people should be told plainly how difficult, tough and costly the fighting for Stalingrad is.

By the end of August it was stated in Moscow that Stalingrad would turn out to be 'another Sevastopol'. In early September Moscow radio put out commentaries of this kind: 'Rejoice at the sight of rivers of the enemy's red blood.' The heavy German losses on the Eastern Front were sufficient justification for the British Exchange Telegraph agency to cable to London front reports reflecting restrained optimism.

Criticism of Roosevelt's speech did not deal sufficiently with his dictatorial appetites. His speech, with its demand for full powers, is a clear admission by Roosevelt that he wants dictatorship – and this we can make good use of in our propaganda. The Minister objects to the term 'world governess' which we must not apply to him on any account. The concept of a 'governess' suggests something relatively harmless, something that may be ridiculous but is basically decent. Roosevelt is a war criminal, an enemy of the world, a hireling of Jewry – and this is how he must be represented to the German people. The term 'world governess' will not be used again in future.

On September 7, 1942, President Roosevelt addressed a message to Congress in which he requested approval for a draft bill which would authorize the President to set up an administration to control the cost of living and the prices of all agricultural products. The purpose of this measure was the stabilization of prices and wages by way of appropriate taxation, introduction of maximum wholesale prices and suspension of hire purchase transactions.

Roosevelt's letter about Christian questions is likewise not to be taken up, even though it represents an attractive issue for a polemic. There are many minds in Germany which allow themselves to be ensnared by his phrases.

A Turkish paper has raised the question of the humanity of the war. The Minister says that this is an exceedingly dangerous question. It would be particularly dangerous in the fourth year of the war, and we cannot nowadays indulge in any philosophy of war. There are many Germans and also many people in the world who ask themselves, whenever they see a war picture, what sense is there in all this destruction. If we were now to allow any philosophizing about the humanity of the war, the German people's sense of security would be undermined.

September 11, 1942

The Minister points out that during the past few days the German press has depicted the situation at Stalingrad in much too rosy a light. Accounts of the fighting there will from now on emphasize mainly the toughness and complexity and stop talking about nothing but penetrations, widening, and such like. The reason why Stalingrad is being defended so stubbornly by the Russians is in itself a convincing argument for the stubbornness of the fighting. Here one can no longer speak of a fortress or of fortified terrain; here one bunker is next to another. The city is a focal point of Russian defensive strength and is therefore being fiercely defended by them.

September 12, 1942

The Minister again warns against quoting pessimistic enemy comment on the situation at Stalingrad. On the other hand, any comment on the consequences of a loss of the city may be published, since for the most part these show how important Stalingrad is for the Russian defence and how much the Russian leadership is therefore trying to stem the assault of the German troops. All naming of fixed dates, for instance that Stalingrad is bound to fall within forty-eight hours, or any similar prediction, must of course be kept out.

At the conference of September 13, 1942, Goebbels most sharply criticized a Berlin paper 'which talks of the Russians' heroic struggle at Stalingrad and quotes the nationalist slogans of the bolshevik leaders. The Minister regards this as a clear case of sabotage by the papers. This article can only arouse sympathy for the bolsheviks. The Minister does not propose to take any action against the paper for the moment, but requests the representative of the German Press Department to use this article at the press conference as an occasion for issuing a sharp and serious reminder to the press.'

The Minister believes that the time has come to adopt a fundamental attitude to the war in the air. It is not possible to leave the discussion of this exceedingly important subject to the German people themselves. Millions of people are concerned each day with the increasingly serious air situation in the West and are asking themselves how it will all end. We must issue a statement or at least raise the hope that things will be different one day. It may even be in order to tell the people the full seriousness of the situation and draw their attention to the fact that the German Luftwaffe cannot be equally strong everywhere. So far we have not yet struck the right note on the subject of the air war.

September 15, 1942

In connexion with the increase in the food rations the Minister points out that an official comment will be issued at the beginning of October. Meanwhile, on his own initiative, he is setting down the following points of view which must be brought out at all costs:

(1) The British, and also the Americans, have placed their entire hopes of victory on starving the German population. From the outset they never believed in military victory, but as in 1918 placed their hopes in the gradual demoralization of the people through food shortages. Now that we are increasing our food rations, British hopes in this field are collapsing and they cannot even talk their way out of it by saying that we are only pretending to increase our rations without in fact giving the people any more. Any food rations we have granted the people have invariably been distributed.

(2) The great slogan of the British has always been that, as the war wears on, the food supply situation will progressively worsen. But now we have a situation when in the fourth year of the war our rations have not been reduced as much as they had in the last war, but have, in fact, increased.

(3) These increased rations are the first modest interest paid back to us on our conduct of the war. They are the first fruits of the gallant efforts of our soldiers. We are proving, moreover, that we are not just chasing after bloodless ideals but are waging the war in the East for very real reasons.

(4) The raising of the rations, of course, is only a beginning but it clearly refutes the slogan that the British lose all battles except the last, since the raising of the food ration proves that battles won in the course of the war also lead to a heightening of the war potential and to the winning of that last battle. We can most emphatically point out how much our war potential has been strengthened if we are now in a position to raise food rations.

The Minister believes the British slogan that we started the civilian air war might become dangerous. He therefore directs that a few leading articles and reports should point out – without, however, making this too obvious – that the civilian air war was started by the British side. Our raid on Warsaw in 1939 was aimed at a fortress crowded with troops and military objectives and was not aimed at the civilian population.

September 16, 1942

Reports from the Reich Propaganda Offices show that the talk about the conclusion of some pact between the Reich government and the British government concerning a truce over the [bombing of the] two capitals is widespread in many parts of the country. The Minister fears that this may give rise to hostility towards Berlin, especially as in times of war the capital city of a country is always very unpopular. In military quarters it is believed that there is no need to act against this rumour since we shall probably have to expect raids on Berlin in the late autumn and this speculation will thus collapse of its own accord.

According to reports from various parts of the Ruhr, workers from Soviet Russia and our own miners have been talking to each other at work about working conditions. The Russians, on some occasions, have referred to better working conditions in their country and are also talking about the better food which they used to have. The Minister regards such discussions as exceedingly dangerous and asks for suggestions on how this danger can be best countered.

In a few German papers the practice has sprung up of factually discussing British propaganda speeches. The Minister directs the German Press Department to put an end to this malpractice and to see to it at all costs that there are no factual discussions with the enemy. In a war one must make sure that the fronts are quite clearly drawn and no bridges across them are permissible. He himself was repeatedly attacked during 1931–2 whenever he deliberately launched an attack on or gave publicity to certain representatives of the System. Only afterwards was it realized how important this had been, and we must now do exactly the same thing, and on no account deal factually with the propaganda theories of the others.

On September 10 Goebbels had issued directives that nothing was to be published about speeches by enemy statesmen unless they were to be polemically dismissed. 'After all, the speeches of enemy statesmen are made not to conduct any factual argument but solely to make propaganda for their policies.'

The Minister very sharply attacks the talk about the 'New Europe'. He believes it is not right for such a hullabaloo to be made about this subject on our side at present. No one in the world will believe that we are fighting for a new Europe without pursuing material interests. They might just about credit the Germans in general with fighting for an idea alone, but where the Nazis are concerned it is known that they are waging a struggle for oil and grain and the material improvement of our people and that they are not just chasing a mirage.

September 18, 1942

Now that the fall of Stalingrad may be expected for certain, the enemy is again beginning to use his old methods of playing down the importance of that city. However, extensive collections of press comment are available from the past few weeks, unequivocally stressing Stalingrad's importance to the enemy side. These will be taken up at a suitable moment.

The Reichspressechef's Slogan of the Day of September 15, 1942, had said: 'The struggle for Stalingrad is nearing its successful conclusion. Important announcements by the OKW about the successes achieved so far are to be expected in the course of today or tomorrow. The German press will have to make preparations for featuring in the most effective way the victorious outcome of this vast struggle for Stalin's city – if necessary by the publication of special editions.'

Although the foreshadowed special announcement about Stalingrad failed to materialize on September 15 and on the subsequent days, special editions were published on September 15 and 16, 1942, about Stalingrad, with banner headlines (as in the Stuttgart *NS-Kurier*) 'Final Stage of the Battle for Stalingrad'. On closer inspection one discovered that this was the view expressed in certain foreign reports. The OKW communiqués merely referred to the penetration of German forces into the city area. On September 18 the press reported stubborn 'fighting for every pile of rubble'.

A 'European Youth Congress', staged by von Schirach, was held in Vienna from September 14 to 18, 1942; youth delegations from Germany's thirteen satellites took part. A 'European Youth League' was founded. Ribbentrop had tried to prevent the Congress, and Goebbels banned all reporting of it. Nevertheless, there were some fairly elaborate events, demonstrations with oath-taking, receptions, parades and gala occasions. The Viennese made fun of the 'important-looking youths' and called it 'Baldur's children's party'. Viennese humour linked the expensive festivities with the increasingly obvious failure in the East: 'You know why the tanks on the Volga have stopped advancing?' 'No – why?' 'Because they've had to give up their fuel for Baldur's children's party.'

278

In connexion with reports on the European Youth Congress in Vienna, the Minister again touches on various remarks concerning the New Order in Europe and clearly defines his position. It is necessary in the present situation that we should express our idealism, but we should not do so in a form which no one will believe. There are two possible forms of a New Order in Europe – the pan-European, which of course is rejected by us, and the establishment of a central power which would attract all other countries with magnetic force. European history, and history generally, shows that in any conflict one rival always ends up victorious, and it is towards him that the others orientate their political concepts, more or less subordinating themselves to his leadership. We must emphasize quite clearly at this juncture that we are the rival who will be victorious one day and that the other European nations will sooner or later align themselves with us. In this connexion it must be emphasized that we are not facing the other European countries as beggars but that we are the givers, the ones giving Europe its New Order. It is a fact that Germany will one day be the richest country in Europe and it is now up to each nation to decide whether it wishes to live in friendship with this richest country of all. The European Youth Congress in Vienna, however, is the most unsuitable occasion conceivable for making the European countries realize this situation. Vienna seems to him [the Minister] like a repetition of the Congress of Frankfurt – only then it was a meeting of men with beards whereas this time it is a lot of kids indulging in pointless chatter.

September 21, 1942
The Minister points out that we must switch over to new headlines and not always highlight Stalingrad. For weeks we have been keeping the people in a state of high excitement but this will soon no longer be possible. The question about the fall of Stalingrad has been asked among the people for some considerable time now, but military progress is not such that a final capture of the city can be expected just yet. For this reason other subjects will now be brought to the fore.

September 22, 1942
The Minister directs that the business of the 'internationalization' of German children which, much to his satisfaction, has now been taken up by the British side and has been made known by Britain to the whole world, should be treated on the lines that the official British Reuter agency has put out this proposal to South America; German propaganda should not in any way take up any other British information

about the origin of the report. The Minister declares that this plan, which can now be proved to have been spread by Britain, should be so persistently rammed down the public's throats that it will become as familiar as Clemenceau's dictum about the twenty million Germans. A suggestion by the Reich Propaganda Directorate that women's rallies should be held in Germany in protest against the British proposal is rejected by the Minister on the grounds that such events would seem forced and would merely create the impression among the German public that the leadership intends to exploit this public improperly.

The German press reported that *Vrij Nederland,* the Dutch paper published in London, had announced that after an Allied victory all German children aged from two to six would be seized from their mothers and sent abroad for a period of twenty-five years. The way in which this report in fact originated is clearly reflected in Goebbels's words. It was launched by Germany for foreign consumption.

The OKW representative reports: The fighting is exceptionally stubborn as the city [Stalingrad] is ideally suited to defence because of the natural ravines throughout the terrain and the way it is laid out. The German troops are making only very slow progress. The fate of the fighting may well be decided, and in a negative sense, by the weather. If, for instance, prolonged rain should set in before the conclusion of the operations, the German supplies, which have to be brought up over seven hundred kilometres by road, will be more or less cut off, whereas supplies for the Russian troops can be brought across the Volga right up to the fighting units on any scale desired. But even if the weather were to continue favourable the duration of the fighting in the city cannot yet be judged.

Along the entire front the Russians are still in a position to appear with large quantities of material and with an unexpected number of men. Admittedly, the quality has noticeably deteriorated lately. In the course of the past month, for instance, over 3,000 Russians have deserted – a figure not even remotely approached ever before.

September 27, 1942

The Minister makes some fundamental observations about the inadequacies of German propaganda methods. On the basis of a number of reports submitted to him, he remarks that the public at home, but also abroad, no longer accepts German propaganda for the reason that its expressions and style have become so worn and shabby that they produce a sense of distaste in the listener or reader. The choice of expressions, for instance, used in reproducing military events is in line with 1939 and 1940 but certainly not with the present moment. Phrases like 'readiness for sacrifice', 'the German soldier is fulfilling his duty', etc., have become so hackneyed that they no longer make the slightest impression. The Minister issues a mandatory instruction to all propaganda bodies such as the press, the radio, the weekly newsreels, the speakers' pool, to move away from this method of cliché-ridden and unthinking repetition of propaganda terms and to make an effort from now on to prevent any further decline of public interest in information, announcements, articles, lectures, etc.

The Minister declares once again that such mistakes as occurred by the preparation of a special edition about Stalingrad a few weeks ago will in future be mercilessly punished because they jeopardize his own credibility and hence also the credibility of German news generally at home and abroad. It is not the task of propaganda to make predictions but to report facts. The Minister draws a parallel with the menu in a restaurant which lists not what is intended to be served in a few days' time but what the guest may find ready to eat.

Goebbels also made made some lengthy observations on the subject at the conference of September 26. They were clearly aimed at Reichspressechef Dietrich. Goebbels once again made him the scapegoat for all propaganda failures, although he must have known that Dietrich was wholly under Hitler's influence and that it would be unreasonable therefore to expect Dietrich to raise objections or misgivings about Hitler's instructions. Dietrich, moreover, records that 'the fully edited special announcement about the fall of Stalingrad being expected at any moment' had been lying 'on Hitler's desk' ever since the middle of August 1942.

'We are digesting the conquered territories'

October-December 1942

October 1, 1942

The Minister directs that in the propaganda treatment of the Führer's speech, both at home and for abroad, the main emphasis should be placed on the argument that this war is now no longer concerned with theories but with realities. The most essential mineral wealth and territorial gains are in our hands. All that is needed now is a certain degree of patience and time to exploit them. Time is on our side. In our propaganda for abroad we should on no account take up the small and trivial 'trouble-making' by foreign propaganda. Instead, German propaganda should deal calmly and confidently with such arguments on the Führer's speech as have any substance.

At home, emphasis is to be put mainly on the short shrift to be made of rumour-mongers and the hankerers after the past – as he [Goebbels] has already said at the beginning of his own speech.

The Berlin Sportspalast rally of September 30, 1942, which marked the inauguration of the Winter Relief Drive 1942–3, was opened with a speech by Goebbels. On the subject of rumour-mongering he declared: 'Those dubious political characters who then [1932], during the final phase of the struggle for power in the Reich, were ranged against us, are now once more ranged abroad against the National-Socialist state in order to try to snatch victory from it at the very last moment, in the decisive phase of the struggle for German freedom. Now, as then, they are hoping, by the dissemination of stupid and foolish rumours, to carry unrest into the German people's community and to weaken and undermine our people's faith in final victory.'

Hitler's speech, following Goebbels's, was in effect a volley of superficial insults hurled at his opponents abroad. Goebbels himself deplored the low standard of the speech. Hitler assured his audience that he would 'batter Stalingrad and also take it' and that no human being would 'dislodge him from this spot'. In connexion with future British invasion attempts he prophesied that Churchill could 'count himself lucky if he stayed ashore for nine hours!'

October 2, 1942

The Minister directs that enemy assertions that the Führer's speech proves Germany to be turning from the offensive to the defensive should be opposed. In doing so the emphasis should be put on the Führer's observations that we are now developing what we have taken possession of.

The Minister requests, in connexion with British reports of more than 43,000 civilians killed by bombing, that our foreign propaganda should point out that German casualty figures are considerably lower than the British claims. The number of civilians killed by the air war in Germany has been given as 10,900.

The Minister directs that enemy attacks on his article about the New Europe – which has been submitted to the Foreign Minister by way of Herr Gesandter* Schmidt – should not be taken up.

Das Reich in its issue of October 4, 1942, carried a leader, 'The New Europe', in which Goebbels dealt, above all, with the fate of the German-occupied and also the neutral small countries of Europe – criticizing the latter for their neutrality. He went as far as to say: 'The fact that more meat and fat is being eaten today in the capitals of the neutral states is no proof whatever that this will still be the case in ten years' time. In order to become rich one must have the courage to suffer poverty and want for a time – but this pays off later.'

October 4–5, 1942

The Minister directs that the most important feature to be stressed, especially for the foreign audiences, from the various speeches of the past week is the statement that we can now withstand a war of unlimited duration. He instructs the officials responsible to buttress this thesis by compiling and publishing real figures, especially about former Russian production of foodstuffs and raw materials. These figures must be explained on the lines that (1) Russia now lacks them and (2) they are now beginning to be useful to us. The main theme must always be: 'The fact is you can't win the war any longer.' This theme should also be underlined by pictorial propaganda. The Minister explains that this propaganda must be conducted on similar lines as, years ago, after the seizure of power, the propaganda about the elimination of unemployment in Germany.

The Minister further directs that the passage in the Reich Marshal's speech, where he refers to the occupation forces being fed exclusively by the occupied territories, should not be given too much prominence for abroad.

* Envoy Extraordinary – rank in the diplomatic service below that of ambassador. *Tr.*

In his 'Harvest Thanksgiving' address at the Berlin Sportspalast on October 4, 1942, Göring announced that the meat ration in the air-raid danger areas was being increased by a further 50 grams and that a special issue could be expected for Christmas. However – as so often – he was rather too boastful when he said: 'From now onwards things will be getting better all the time – because we now possess the territories with the most fertile soil ... eggs, butter, flour exist there [in the eastern territories] in quantities which you cannot even imagine.' In view of this abundance of foodstuffs he expressed the hope that he would be able to raise food rations again in the coming year.

Since the British especially took up those passages in Göring's speech which dealt with Germany's food supplies at the expense of the occupied European countries, Goebbels, on October 6, 1942, announced that he intended 'by means of a fundamentally positive propaganda shortly to divert foreign attention from this subject. If this does not come off then he reserves the right to launch a direct refutation of the relevant enemy propaganda next week.'

As for the Stockholm and Ankara reports that Stalin has given up supreme command of the Soviet armies, these are not to be published for the time being. He explains that he cannot without further evidence believe that these rumours are true. If, however, they are accurate then they should not be prematurely assessed as a sign of weakness. It has been found, for instance, that years ago the execution of the generals, which we regarded as a sign of the incipient decline of Stalin's power, in effect meant an extraordinary strengthening of his position and his régime by the liquidation of weak generals and their replacement by 'real fellows'.

These rumours, which were devoid of foundation, were to the effect that Marshal Shaposhnikov, the Chief of the Soviet General Staff, was replacing Stalin as 'People's Commissar for Defence'.

October 7–8, 1942
As for President Roosevelt's threat that so-called war criminals will be held responsible after the war, the Minister desires comment to take the line that such threats leave us entirely cold and that Herr Roosevelt would be well advised to be careful in case his idea turns against him.

A few months later all foreign references to the punishment of Nazi war criminals after the war had to be passed over in silence by German propaganda. Goebbels on October 16, 1942, had this to say on the subject of war criminals: 'Our situation is not such that we can readily make the same point in our propaganda that the British are now doing.'

October 10, 1942
The Minister observes that the time has now come to work out generally valid principles for the publicity and propaganda treatment of the war in the air. Anything that two years ago, or even one year ago, may have had a repulsive, offensive, convincing or any other effect on the public will have a different effect today. People everywhere have become less sentimental and harder. In his opinion, therefore, it is not advisable to give too much publicity in our propaganda to the destruction of cultural values – for one thing, because the average reader or viewer will turn not so much against the enemy as against the war as such, and secondly because cultural values have been destroyed on both sides. German propaganda should instead put its main emphasis on individual feats in the fighting of fires, the saving of human lives, etc.

The Minister further makes some fundamental observations about the news, which he describes as highly significant, that the institution of political commissars has been abolished in the Soviet army. The Minister says that he is not yet quite clear about what is behind this measure. But if one views it in conjunction with the rumours about Shaposhnikov, with the Stalin interview and with other reports from and about Russia, it is certainly not impossible that we are dealing here with symptoms of a fundamental transformation which may possibly mean a shifting of the centre of gravity away from the Party towards the Red Army. But no-one should have any illusions about Stalin's popularity.

On October 9, 1942, Stalin decreed for the Red Army the abolition of the separation of military from political command. This meant a strengthening of military authority by the abolition of the political commissar, the political supervising officer of the Party. Although this post had originally been abolished on August 13, 1940, it was reintroduced on July 16, 1941. On October 16 the Soviet army daily *Krasnaya Zvezda* announced that so-called regimental agitators were now to be employed in the army with the task of stiffening the morale of the troops and replacing the political commissars.

October 14, 1942
The Minister bans the subject of winter equipment for the German Wehrmacht both for the German press and for the radio. In this way the blunders are to be avoided which occurred last year when the weekly newsreel and the press referred to the good winter clothing of the Wehrmacht whereas in fact hardly anything had been provided.

On October 6, 1942, Goebbels ordered that particular emphasis should be given to the fact 'that "Generals Winter, Cold, Time, Hunger, etc." are no longer doing Germany any harm but are in fact working for Germany.'

At the conference of October 20 it was announced: 'At the Eastern Front winter has already set in in a few places. For the time being, no mention is to be made of the subject of winter until the OKW communiqué issues an official announcement.' (*Cf.* November 25–26, 1942.)

October 16, 1942

The Minister requests that in replying to enemy commentaries which speak of Germany having gone over to the defensive, the word 'defensive' is avoided as a matter of principle. The word 'defensive' has a defeatist ring. He suggests the use of such formulations as 'we are digesting the conquered territories', 'we are fighting against a continent and organizing it', and suchlike.

The Minister will publish an article in *Das Reich* next week under the heading 'For whom is time working?'. In this all the objections made by the enemy to our conduct of the war will be taken into account and refuted. The burden of his article will be that not time but space is the decisive factor and that whoever utilizes space also has time on his side.

Goebbels's article 'For whom is time working?' appeared in *Das Reich* on October 25, 1942. In it Goebbels tried to disprove the numerous arguments of foreign journalists to the effect that Hitler had now definitely lost his 'race against time'. In connexion with the armaments industry the American press, ever since the beginning of the year, had been using the slogan: 'We want to beat Germany at production.' And in view of the late start of the German summer offensive of 1942 it was said: 'Hitler has lost his race against the calendar.' Goebbels arrived at a different conclusion and made such optimistic forecasts that in the following year he was careful not to include this article in his collection of articles published in 1943 under the title 'The Steep Climb'.

The article was followed by a domestic propaganda campaign. Broadcasts to foreign audiences attacked foreign comment.

On the subject of the manacling of the prisoners of war, the Minister says that restraint should continue to be practised. The manacling of prisoners is an unpopular business, as shown by British press comment and also by reports from the Reich.

On October 12 Goebbels issued a ban on the disclosure that three times as many prisoners had been handcuffed in Germany as in Britain. He stated: 'Our propaganda must instead emphasize that Britain has been compelled to admit everything we claimed. We should not allow ourselves to be drawn into legalistic disputations but state clearly that an order that prisoners were to be handcuffed had existed and had been applied. When informed that the OKW

286

today or tomorrow will release a final overall report, the Minister remarks that this is rather late in the day but that at least no time was lost in the propaganda handling of the affair.'

On October 13, 1942, Churchill made a statement in the House of Commons on the manacling of prisoners of war. He conceded that manacling was 'sometimes necessary under the pressure of circumstances' in order to protect the prisoners from danger. This applied only for the duration of the fighting but not to prisoners who 'are in secure captivity' and whose treatment is governed by the rules of the Geneva Convention which are binding also upon Germany. Germany, on the other hand, had violated these rules by having 1,376 British prisoners put in chains. The British government had lodged with the protecting power a 'solemn protest' to the German government against this breach of the Geneva Convention.

On October 16, 1942, the OKW issued an extensive statement on the British Prime Minister's remarks 'concerning the maltreatment of German prisoners.' This was the first detailed information the German public had about the whole affair.

The subject was thereafter very largely dropped, since its discussion before the world public was embarrassing to both sides.

The German prisoners in Canada had their manacles removed at the beginning of December 1942. The British prisoners in Germany were due to have theirs removed on December 15 and Goebbels assumed that he would now at long last 'get out of this tiresome business'. He was wrong. The prisoners remained handcuffed. Not until after the surrender of the German army in Tunisia, at the end of May 1943, did Hitler decide to approach the question of ordering the unshackling of the British prisoners of war. This was to be done unobtrusively. On May 17, 1943, Goebbels remarked: 'We can now no longer engage in any prestige competition with the British on this point since the British now hold many more German prisoners than we do British.'

October 17, 1942

The Minister again warns against the term 'defensive' and believes that we must definitely abandon this concept in our propaganda. It is dangerous for any state to create the impression that it is sated. This fact of saturation leads to a defensive concept and is exceedingly dangerous for any revolutionary régime. Moreover, the word 'defensive' is reminiscent of 1914 and gives rise to dangerous parallels.

On October 18, 1942, at a mass rally outside the Feldherrnhalle in Munich, Goebbels declared: 'Whoever has wheat, oil, iron and coal, and moreover the strongest armed forces, will win the war . . . If, up to a point, we are now busy digesting what we have swallowed then this digestive process will also come to an end.' What Goebbels intended to suggest was that after this 'digestion' the German offensive would be resumed.

287

October 19, 1942

The Minister points out that the fall of Stalingrad may take a few days yet so that all commentaries today should again keep within the framework of the OKW communiqué.

At the conference of the following day Goebbels again called for restraint in the handling of the Stalingrad topic. On October 18 the OKW communiqué had reported the 'penetration' into the furiously defended Red Barricade Ordnance Works in Stalingrad: on October 20 the bombing of the Red October Ironworks was reported, and its partial capture was announced in the OKW communiqué of October 24. The fall of Stalingrad, on which the German command had again counted in mid-October 1942, remained an elusive mirage.

On October 17 the OKW had made propaganda preparations for the fall of Stalingrad which was expected 'within the next few days'. It was intended to publish the number of men killed in Stalingrad, to point to the decisive intervention of Soviet artillery positioned on the eastern bank of the Volga, to bring back all bearers of the Knight's Cross from Stalingrad to Berlin in order to interview them in the press, on the radio and on the screen, to publish an article, preferably by General Schmundt, Hitler's ADC, about the difficulties of street fighting in great cities, and finally to launch 'horror articles' in the foreign press (also 'by way of our contact inside United Press') about the new German close combat weapons employed in Stalingrad. The document continues: 'In our foreign propaganda it should be hinted that, whereas last autumn Germany had underestimated her Russian opponent and as a result of this underestimation got stuck outside Moscow, the military leaders of the Reich have this year correctly judged the difficulties of the offensive against Stalingrad... One day after the capture of Stalingrad a short note should be published to the effect that for once the Germans have come to an excellent arrangement with the weather god since, right up to the fall of Stalingrad, the weather and temperature had favoured the attack; only now when the city is in German hands and the weather can no longer influence the outcome of the operations have the rains begun which will result in a rising of the water level in the Volga which will as good as rule out any attacks across it by the enemy. This was precisely what the Germans had intended since they would now use the period of the floods to settle in among the ruins of Stalingrad so that, once the Volga has frozen over, bolshevik attacks will find us prepared.'

The suggestion is made that signposts should be put up in a few German cities showing the distance to the principal towns and operational sectors of the front. The Minister welcomes the suggestion and believes that this will have a good psychological effect and will take the wind out of the sails of critics who refer to the slowness of our war in Russia compared with the other campaigns of this war.

The erection of signposts giving distances – the suggestion came from Berndt – was intended to demonstrate the extent of German power and Germany's absolute security. The OKW, on the other hand, objected that if gigantic distances of several thousand kilometres were kept in front of the eyes of the troops and of their relations day after day this would hardly produce much enthusiasm.

October 22, 1942
The Minister points out that the use of the names 'Red Barricade' or 'Red October' for the big factories in Stalingrad and a reference to these factories being defended by their workers is undesirable in German propaganda; these names might appeal to those communist-infected circles which still exist here and there. For the same reason the Führer issued orders, at the time, that the term 'Red Army' was not to be used in internal German propaganda.

On the strength of his experiences during his last few journeys in Germany, the Minister points out that the illusionism which persists about the war in the East among certain German circles is intolerable and exceedingly dangerous. For months he has warned again and again that the situation must not be depicted as easier than it is. The German people are entitled to be informed about the situation in such a way that no false illusions are created. Since his own concept of confidence without illusions has not been put across everywhere he must now decline to be held responsible for the public mood. These remarks by the Minister are clearly aimed at the Wehrmacht communiqués.

On October 29 the press was instructed to publish again, 'as a deterrent', a number of sentences for illicit listening-in to foreign radios.

The Minister sharply criticizes the German press for publishing Japanese reports of reprisals against American airmen. He points out that in the event of further air raids the German population might take their revenge on crash-landed enemy airmen in the belief that, as suggested by the Japanese reports, they had committed deliberate murder of children and women. Such a practice would lead to reprisals, and one would drift into a stage of complete lawlessness in which the German prisoners in British hands would be at the mercy of the British. The Japanese, as a matter of fundamental attitude, have no consideration for prisoners since they are regarded as cowards and are written off. Europe holds different views in this respect, and it is dangerous, therefore, to allow a confusion of Asiatic and European concepts. In this connexion the Minister recalls that the manacling of prisoners of war, for instance, with its mutual escalation, was wholly unpopular among the German people since it runs counter to western attitudes.

A report from Tokyo on October 21 stated that American pilots who dropped bombs on the civilian population and were hence guilty of atrocities against it would be severely punished in Japan. This was reported in the *Völkischer Beobachter* of October 22, 1942.

The Minister also sharply criticizes the opening words of the leading article in today's *Völkischer Beobachter* in which it is said that the Russian resistance is 'inexplicable' to us. Such a remark from the pen of a National Socialist in the leading paper of the NSDAP is intolerable.

The *Völkischer Beobachter* of October 22, 1942, had a leading article by J. Schieferdecker, the editor-in-chief of the paper's Berlin edition, under the heading 'Incomprehensible'. It began with the words: 'We cannot understand the bolsheviks. They are offering a stubborn resistance which we cannot explain in terms of our concepts.' Nevertheless, the author of the article was merely expressing something which was incomprehensible also to the leadership and to large sections of the German people. Stalingrad was confidently expected to surrender but did not do so.

Current rumours about alleged armistice negotiations with Russia are treated as a particularly serious matter. The OKW representative reports that papers have been found on servicemen on leave which linked their leave with such negotiations. An investigation is under way to establish whether this is a case of enemy propaganda, sabotage or stupidity. The Minister directs that enquiries should be made at the Führer's headquarters on this point and the suggestion put forward there that these reports should now be most vigorously contradicted. He declares that any misgivings about such a denial will presumably now be satisfied in view of the serious risk of a reverse in German morale. Generally speaking, he repeated several times that he must have lost his power of judgement if there is a single world of truth in these rumours. He is firmly convinced of the contrary.

At the conference of October 26, 1942, Goebbels believed that he did not need to contradict the rumours about armistice negotiations with Russia since these would soon peter out anyway. (*Cf.* October 28, 1942.)

October 24, 1942
The Minister again directs that the fighting for Stalingrad must be treated only within the framework of the OKW communiqué and that

the incredibly exaggerated Russian reports of German losses must be vigorously contradicted.

Enemy reports about German losses could not, however, be effectively contradicted by the disclosure of the heavy losses actually suffered by the Germans. As early as October 10, 1942, Goebbels had unsuccessfully requested the OKW 'to see to it that the astronomical figures of German losses put out by the Russians in the fighting near Lake Ilmen are continually and most energetically repudiated. It is impossible to let enemy lies have the final word in this matter. If the OKW will not issue any announcement of its own then he must instruct his agencies to keep on branding the Russian reports as lies.'

As for Mrs Roosevelt's visit [to London], the Minister directs that care should be taken that the visit is not, in a sense, publicized for us by, say, a chronological record of the events of her journey. He requests Herr Fritzsche to ensure that any comment on this journey in the German press is written only by journalists possessing special journalistic ability. Experience shows that an exceptional amount of persuasive wit is required to attack a woman in such a way that the attack will not look tasteless to the broad German public, but convincing. In this connexion the Minister sharply criticizes a few flat glosses which appeared in this morning's papers.

Eleanor Roosevelt arrived in London on October 23, 1942, on a visit lasting nearly four weeks. She received, among others, exiled European politicians as well as European monarchs living in exile in London. On November 2, 1942, Goebbels issued this directive: 'The hullabaloo about Eleanor Roosevelt should be left to die down gradually and should not result in Mrs Roosevelt's journey being popularized or invested with a certain importance.'

The Minister prohibits the German press to draw attention to the fact that the 20,000 million lire made available by the [Italian] fascist régime for social purposes over the past twenty years cannot even equal the result of one single German Winter Relief Campaign, or to the fact that more than forty Italian generals are in enemy captivity.

The Minister finally deals at length with the fact that in the field of armaments propaganda we have now completely got on to the defensive towards the United States. At the beginning of the war German expressions like Stuka, encirclement, Panzer, etc., had the world over become concepts of the invincibility of German armaments and of the German method; but today the world is spellbound by the American bluff with figures. The Minister directs that State Secretary Gutterer, acting together with the Munitions Ministry, should set up a special working party which would, within a week, supply him with a vast body of figures and other data for use in a large-scale propaganda campaign in the armaments field. The Minister points out that he has time and again found that the Führer, in spite of his sense of security for military secrecy on such questions, is much more liberal than the military censors. He has also reason to believe that Minister Speer will show a good deal of understanding. Moreover, it might well be useful to drop hints, by way of whispered propaganda or in some other form, about the existence of new and unbelievably effective weapons – naturally without giving any further details. A similar propaganda drive last winter was most effective and was subsequently reinforced by the emphasis given to the giant gun employed at Sevastopol.

The new armaments propaganda drive, under the slogan 'The best weapons ensure victory', made an embarrassingly false start at the end of November. At the conference on November 27, 1942, Goebbels criticized the disclosures about new weapons as having been 'made at the worst possible moment'. He ordered an investigation into who launched the report and demanded: 'The factory which manufactures the machine-guns is to be visited by the foreign press, so that the Soviet statement that these machine-guns do not even exist can be refuted.'

About November 24, 1942, the news was being spread both in Germany and abroad that a new flame-throwing tank had been employed at Stalingrad; this was said to be capable of hurling its jets of flame over buildings five and more storeys high. It was further claimed that heavy losses had been inflicted on the Soviets by a new type of machine-gun which could fire 3,000 rounds per minute. The Soviets, it was said, were calling the new machine-gun, instantly identifiable by its sound of firing, the 'electric' machine-gun. Both reports were instances of wishful thinking by German armaments propaganda. As recently as September 1942 Hitler at his meetings with Speer had suggested that heavy tanks should be constructed for house-to-house fighting in big cities. As for the so-called 'electric' machine-gun, its inspiration no doubt was the MG 45 which was then under construction. Although it was not manufactured in time to be used before the end of the war, it did in fact achieve a rate of fire of 40 rounds per second, although in continuous fire its performance was definitely below 1,000 rounds per minute. The figures for the MG 42, on the other hand, were about 25 rounds per second, and up to 400 rounds per minute continuous.

October 28, 1942
Mention is made of a British report to the effect that the OKW has requested a four-day armistice at Stalingrad. It is stated that, to the best knowledge of the most varied authorities, the report does not accord

with the facts. The Minister proposes that an entirely unambiguous denial should be issued and that it should be emphasized that the report is a downright fake, invented by the enemy solely in order to nourish an artificial optimism.

The assertion, put out by London radio on October 27, that the German side, through the good offices of the Red Cross, had proposed an armistice for the Stalingrad sector was refuted in the OKW communiqué of October 28, 1942.

October 30, 1942
The Minister takes the opportunity to make a few fundamental observations on our propaganda: from the very start, National-Socialist propaganda has always addressed itself to the common people and has never attempted to convert the intellectual. The popular language of National-Socialist propaganda appealed to the man in the street and brought him closer to the National-Socialist ideas. It is thus a mistake to conduct propaganda in such a way that it will stand up to the critical examination of the intellectual. The intellectual will never have the strength to make the man in the street conversant with his ideas; on the contrary, it is the intellectual who will take his cue from what the ordinary person thinks and wants. The Minister emphasizes that, in connexion with his most recent speeches, he has again noticed that the most primitive arguments are the most effective and meet with the greatest agreement among the masses. Intellectuals always yield to the stronger, and this will be the ordinary man in the street.

November 3, 1942
The punishment of managers in Russia for tolerating sabotage in their factories is to be reproduced without comment, in order to show certain people in the Reich how the Soviet Union is dealing with layabouts.

In connexion with an article published in a British paper under the heading 'How is a target chosen for the RAF?', the Minister deals with careless press reports and the thoughtless repeating of information which could be useful to the enemy. This British article explains that a raid was mounted on a German city because it had emerged from a newspaper report that a factory in that city had been doing particularly good business. The Minister points out that we cannot be too careful with reports of this kind: we have had repeated irrefutable evidence of how well the intelligence services of the enemy powers are working. The most trivial and seemingly unimportant pieces of news may provide the enemy with valuable hints. The Minister believes in particular that the Jews still remaining in the Reich represent an important basis for British intelligence. He wishes the 40,000 Jews still in Berlin to be evacuated from the Reich capital as soon as possible, and this evacuation to be carried out as quickly as possible. It is hoped that all Jews will have been removed from Berlin by March.

On March 2, 1943, Goebbels said: 'The Führer is happy to hear from me that most of the Jews have now been evacuated from Berlin. The Jews will certainly be the losers in this war – one way or another.'

November 4, 1942

As for the elections in the United States, we shall not comment on them until we have a clear picture of the outcome. In the event of a Republican victory we must be careful not to display any optimism which might arouse hopes in the German public which, in the Minister's opinion, cannot be fulfilled. The alignment of the fronts in America is a purely domestic one and must be seen as such. Generally speaking, he is convinced that an overthrow of the government is not possible in any of the belligerent countries in the near future. The authoritarian form of government makes it exceedingly difficult to do anything against the government, and it would be a mistaken speculation to hope for an overthrow of the government, say, in Britain or America, just as such an overthrow is impossible in Italy or Japan or Russia. It is our task merely to weaken by our work the enthusiasm for the war and the morale of the people on the other side. Looking at the situation in Britain, for instance, he [the Minister] does not believe that any rift can be discerned between the government and the people. So long as a belligerent country is not occupied one cannot hope for the war to end as if by a miracle. We Germans, unfortunately, often indulge in vain hopes since we ourselves came to grief once, in 1918, because of our ideologists and because of our own lack of political education. We now believe the others could one day do the same, simply because we did so once. We must keep this attitude out of our reflections and calculations because it is dangerous.

The elections in the United States resulted in a victory for the Democrats, who won 218 seats in the House of Representatives as against 208 for the Republicans. In the Senate the Democrats had 66 seats and the Republicans 28.

November 5, 1942

The Minister uses very sharp words in directing the press and the radio to observe the utmost reserve in dealing with the fighting in North Africa. British special announcements and reports of victories are to be ignored. We can afford to let the British speak uncontradicted for twenty-four hours, as we have repeatedly done before; later, when the situation is clarified, we shall reply in the appropriate manner. For the next few days the Minister prohibits the publication of pictures about supplies to North Africa. These measures, however, should not induce us to create abroad an impression of pessimism or internal disquiet. The point has not yet been reached where an all-out effort must be made, since Rommel no doubt will make the best of the present situation. For the time being, North Africa is to be handled only in terms of news until a different trend emerges from the OKW communiqué.

November 6, 1942

The Minister discusses the events in North Africa and charges all his collaborators not to display any pessimism to outsiders during these critical days. He explains the military situation in broad outline and expresses the hope that Field Marshal Rommel, as so often before, will master the situation. We cannot tell yet how the fighting is going to end, but one thing is certain – that the gallantry of our soldiers and the genius of the Field Marshal will do the very best that is possible for the Reich. For the time being we had better tread warily in our propaganda and deal with events in terms of news only. At the moment we do not know what we can say, and therefore we had best say nothing.

In spite of Hitler's order of November 3, 1942: 'Hold on at all costs', the German-Italian Panzer Army in North Africa had been in retreat since November 2. On November 4 it was clear to the British that they had won the battle. Rommel succeeded, however, in evading pursuit and the threat of encirclement. On November 6 General Alexander reported to his Prime Minister that an estimated 20,000 prisoners had been taken. The British lost over 10,000 men killed, wounded or missing. In Britain the church bells were rung for the victory of El Alamein.

The OKW communiqué did not mention the North African theatre of war for a few days; only on November 10 did it report 'disengagement' in a westerly direction.

November 8, 1942

The landing in North Africa is to be branded as an infamous breach of law by the gangster President. An American statement emphasizes that the initiative and the plan for this operation came from the Americans and that Britain merely gave her agreement to this seizure of European colonial possessions. The Minister observes that Britain has readily given her consent to this seizure of European property by America, since America is gradually taking over Britain's colonial possessions anyway. Roosevelt's justification that he wanted to forestall an Axis attack must be sharply repudiated and it must be pointed out that throughout three years we have done nothing to appropriate possessions in Africa, although we had the chance to do so.

Operation 'Torch', the Anglo-American landing of roughly 110,000 men in Morocco and Algeria, began on November 7–8, 1942. On November 8 a report from Vichy stated that American and British forces had landed on the coasts of French North Africa the previous day. Attempts to land at Algiers and Oran were repulsed with heavy losses. Further landings were being attempted.

At the conference of November 10, 1942, Goebbels voiced the suspicion that French resistance in North Africa was being made out to be stronger than in fact it was. A 'certain distrust' was therefore in order. On November 11 Admiral Darlan, who had meanwhile moved from Vichy to Algiers, ordered the French forces in North Africa to cease fire against the Allies. The order was obeyed.

November 10, 1942

Following his return from Munich the Minister makes a few observations on the political situation, evidently designed to urge the departmental heads of the RMVP* not to transmit any disquiet to the public by any change whatever in their own outward attitude. The Minister compares the present general situation with that of a football team which makes an all-out effort during the first half of a match and achieves a lead of four goals to nil. After half-time the other side then succeeds in shooting a surprise goal and this has somewhat unnerved our own team. The task now is to overcome this temporary crisis and not to make any psychological mistakes in doing so. The present situation gives no cause for pessimism, let alone for doubts of our victory. Only by comparing the present days with the grave crises of 1932 and 1934 does he [the Minister] fully realize how much more difficult and critical things were then. Nor can the situation be compared in any way with our retreat during the winter of last year, when the fate of the nation was really frequently in the balance. What matters in the present phase of the war is to parry a blow dealt by the other side and go over to the counter-attack.

* Reichsministerium für Volksaufklärung und Propaganda (Reich Ministry for People's Enlightenment and Propaganda). *Tr.*

He [the Minister] does not know what will come of the negotiations in Munich, but he hopes that we may get some guidelines for our propaganda on which we can then enlarge. Admittedly we have said a great deal about Europe in the past, but we have also threshed a lot of Europeans with flails– which is no overture to collaboration. He now hopes that the negotiations in Munich will lead to a different policy.

The Minister outlines the difficulties of Italy's situation and draws attention to the contrast between France and Italy. The difficulties of the negotiations must not be underrated, and particular understanding must be shown for Italy's position. To date we alone have profited from the war, whereas the Italians have not so far received anything. If the war were to end suddenly today we should be left holding a lot of pawns while the Italians would have nothing to show except their lost empire.

If we are now sitting down at the negotiating table with the French we must not overlook the fact that their position has become totally different as a result of the American attack. The French know very well that we must have Tunis, and so no doubt we shall not come off scot-free ourselves in these negotiations.

Hitler made a speech in the Munich Löwenbräukeller at a ceremony to commemorate November 8. He denied that a German peace proposal was being submitted, he belittled the defeat in North Africa, and he gave prominence to the successes of the U-boats. The events of the past winter, he assured his audience, would not be repeated. He did not want Stalingrad to become another Verdun, and for that reason he would 'prefer to attack with quite small assault parties.' There was not a word about a rapid, overwhelming victory. Instead he said: 'The old Germany [in 1918] laid down its arms at a quarter to twelve – I never, as a matter of principle, stop until five minutes past twelve!'

On November 10, 1942, Hitler arrived in Munich for conversations with Laval and Ciano. From Laval he expected that the French army would, on Germany's side, defend the French frontiers and North Africa, but he was not prepared to make any compromise with Vichy France. The following day Laval was informed of the occupation of the remaining part of France – already prepared by the Führer Directive No. 42 of May 29, 1942 – as well as of Corsica and Tunisia.

If Goebbels really believed that a genuine arrangement would be reached in Munich between Vichy France and Germany then he overlooked not only Hitler's uncompromising attitude but also misjudged the military situation in the Mediterranean area which demanded rapid military counter-measures and left no time for the 'wooing of an ally'. On November 11, 1942, Goebbels issued the instruction: 'We must express the most friendly feelings towards France and Spain. It is important to influence the French in the sense that they will keep calm, and to shape German broadcasts for abroad in such a way that they reflect the assurance and confidence of the German leadership.'

I.

The Secret Conferences of Dr. Goebbels

November 12, 1942
The Minister points out that the situation is gradually clarifying itself. For the time being at least, it may be assumed that Marshal Pétain will ensure correct and calm behaviour by the French population in Europe, whereas North Africa will, generally speaking, have to be written off. Darlan has gone over to the enemy; the question of how Tunisia will act is still open.

Although Marshal Pétain gave orders on November 8 for resistance in North Africa, Algiers was occupied by the Allies on November 8, Oran on November 10 and Casablanca on November 11, 1942. On November 9 German airborne landings began in Tunisia, and German troops, in spite of Pétain's protest, marched into unoccupied France.

The Minister continues to point out that things are not easy for German propaganda in the present circumstances. Its most important principle must be to act with firmness and assurance, not to betray any weakness, not to allow the possibility of a crack in the European front, and, just as Churchill did after Dunkirk, to whip up every ounce of energy. For that reason this is not the moment to explain or even mention defeats. Just as the gravity of the situation in the winter of 1941 was allowed to be seen only at a moment when the danger was banished, so the same practice must again be adopted now.

November 14, 1942
Stalin's interview is not to be touched on in any way whatever by the German media.

On November 13 Stalin answered three questions on the war situation submitted to him in writing by Henry Cassidy, the Moscow correspondent of Associated Press. Stalin emphasized that the campaign in Africa, insofar as the initiative has been seized by the Allies, 'fundamentally alters the military-political situation in Europe in favour of the Anglo-Soviet-American coalition.' The campaign in Africa, Stalin declared, created 'the prerequisites for a Second Front being organized in Europe in closest proximity to the vital centres of Germany, which will be of decisive importance for the organization of victory over the Hitlerite tyranny.'

The Minister makes some fundamental observations about the Wehrmacht communiqué. He bitterly and sharply criticizes the circumstance that, for instance, the fall of Tobruk has not so far been announced by the German side although any German, without offending against the listening ban, can listen to the German news in

298

English on the Deutschlandsender and thus discover that Tobruk has in fact fallen. This mistaken news policy has led the German public to find out about the real situation by roundabout methods and to show interest in the official German announcement only in order to discover to what extent the German people are being informed by their own government about the real state of affairs. The danger of a very serious crisis of confidence has now arisen, at least in the field of information policy. He [the Minister] must most emphatically draw the OKW's attention to this point because ultimately the responsibility will be put on him as the Propaganda Minister. The OKW representative explains that the German Wehrmacht communiqué about North Africa is now always made consistent with the Italian communiqué or at any rate is not drafted until the Italian communiqué has been received.

The Minister proposes to make his own representations to the Führer on this issue. He points out in conclusion that the morale of the German public is low enough as it is and that the leadership must not further depress this morale by abusing the people's confidence. He compares the present situation with that of a sick person; not to tell the public about the inescapable facts of the military situation is like not telling a patient that he is sick, merely in order not to excite him. But by not doing so one is depriving oneself of the chance of fighting the illness with medicines and by the patient's own powers of resistance, and one thus gets into an absurd situation.

British troops captured the fortress of Tobruk on November 12–13, 1942. The OKW communiqué of November 14 had this to say: 'German and Italian troops have evacuated Tobruk according to plan, following the destruction of all military installations.'

November 20, 1942

The Minister makes a few observations about his trip to the west and to Holland. In his opinion the available reports on morale in the Reich do not accurately reflect the real morale among the people. The circles reached by the Security Service, by the propaganda offices of the Party and by the other official agencies are nearly always the same. The people covered by them are, as a rule, so interested in day-to-day political events that their morale is extensively affected by favourable or unfavourable happenings of the moment. Among the people at large, on the other hand, a firmly rooted conservatism can be discerned which looks beyond the events of the day and faithfully discharges the tasks set to it. These people are difficult to shift from their attitude, and they do not become hysterical if things do not go according to plan. They perform a tremendous service for our Reich in their everyday work. All over the West and in Holland the chimney stacks have been smoking and it is an impressive picture to see so many million people working for our armaments industry today.

The Minister opposes certain enemy concepts which have crept into the German vocabulary in a dangerous way. We should carefully avoid using concepts like 'the United Nations', or 'the Allies', because these have propagandist connotations and remind us of World War One and hence terrify many people. We should therefore always speak merely of 'our enemies', 'the enemy side' and such like.

On February 8, 1943, Goebbels wanted the 'United Nations' to be described as 'satellites' of the Soviet Union.

November 22, 1942

As for the alleged conspiracy of German officers against National Socialism, the Minister issues instructions that this ridiculous report should not be dealt with in talks or long speeches but that these excrescences of the British and Americans should be ridiculed in brief, effective glosses. At the end of these brief reports it should always be emphasized that here is a case of the wish being father to the thought and that the British are pretending to possess strength and power where there is none.

November 23, 1942

The Minister discusses the present situation on the Eastern Front and points out that the situation today cannot remotely be compared with that of last winter. It somehow seems to be a fact that November always brings serious reverses for us. The Russians have undoubtedly been able to force certain advantages, although no clear picture can yet be formed of their offensive thrusts. So far they have not achieved any offensive success and the counter-measures launched by us will soon bear fruit. It is obvious that at this moment the entire enemy propaganda will pounce on this subject and make a big noise. We should allow the situation to clarify itself first and for the time being keep within the framework of the OKW communiqué. At the same time, it is now particularly important to conduct an offensive news policy. Now is the time to counter enemy propaganda with impertinent, overbearing and sovereign unconcern. Our press must not be dominated by news at this moment – now it will be revealed whether the press really is an instrument of leadership. In this context he again reprimands a Berlin paper.

The Soviet counter-offensive at Stalingrad began on November 19, 1942. About 300,000 men – Paulus's Sixth Army and parts of the Fourth Panzer Army – were encircled. In the evening of November 22 Hitler ordered: 'Sixth Army to form hedgehog and await relief from outside.' Throughout the next two months, or very nearly, the Wehrmacht communiqué edited by Hitler was an illustration of the 'art of non-information'. In so far as the Wehrmacht communiqué mentioned the Stalingrad front at all, it was not until January 16, 1942, that it was evident from it that a German army was encircled there and awaiting annihilation.

November 25–26, 1942

The Minister points out that the press must now turn even more from being a vehicle of news policy into becoming an instrument of propaganda guidance. In view of the present situation it is in order to overcome our reverses by a skilful compilation of available material. On the lines of the military method of clearing up any enemy penetrations, we must now also iron out the propaganda penetrations of the past few days. In doing so we must not of course be over-optimistic, but on no account should we lend support to enemy propaganda information by displaying pessimism. He [the Minister] had been a realist in the summer too and had warned against the great optimism which was trying in many places to gain ground among the people; now that pessimism seemed to be gaining the upper hand he can act against it and diminish its scope too. He himself feels entitled to do so, for if one has acted against an excessive optimism one can also act against pessimism. He requests that enemy news in our favour should be published. The German people should not be kept in the dark about the seriousness of the situation, but on the other hand the impression must not arise that this has been a decisive blow of the war.

On the operations at Stalingrad the Minister remarks that the ferocity and difficulty of the fighting should be given prominence. Nothing should be said for the moment about winter clothing since not all units have received their full quota.

On November 27, 1942, there followed the directive: 'We should again counteract and most resolutely deny the astronomical figures published by the bolsheviks about our losses in the fighting at Stalingrad.'

Since the beginning of the Soviet offensive at Stalingrad almost daily communiqués were issued in Moscow, including casualty figures for the German Wehrmacht and its allies at Stalingrad. On November 26, 1942, for instance, Moscow gave the total number of men killed in the fighting for Stalingrad on the German side since November 19 as 51,000 and the number of prisoners as 63,000. (*Cf.* December 1, 1942.)

On December 4, 1942, came the instruction: 'By far the greatest part of the winter clothing has now arrived at the Eastern Front. The Minister nevertheless recommends that the topic of winter clothing should not be taken up in German propaganda since silence on this point is the best propaganda for us. Word will go round by itself that this winter the Eastern Front is well supplied with winter clothing.'

The Minister is going to publish an article about political passions; this will, above all, castigate the objectivity of the Germans. The time has come to make it clear to the people once again that we must be fanatics in our struggle to safeguard the future of the Reich. Just as the British cared nothing for justice or injustice when the survival and furtherance of their nation were at stake, so we must do likewise.

On November 29, 1942, Goebbels's leading article 'On Political Passion' appeared in *Das Reich*. In it he accused the Germans of certain 'national vices': they were 'fanatics for objectivity', they were guided by sentimentality and they paid homage to a philistine sense of justice. All that, he said, was dangerous and troublesome, especially in a war which was ultimately decided by success alone. Goebbels again complained that an atrophied national instinct was preventing the people from 'coming to the boil'. What was needed now was 'the most radical fanaticism and the most ardent passion for our great cause . . . For the enemy we must have only hatred and the will to destroy him. If anyone talks to us in this war about the right of the enemy then we shall square up to him bravely and manfully because he diminishes the right of his own people.'

November 27, 1942

German troops occupied the French naval base of Toulon in the south of France on November 27, 1942. The French warships at anchor there neither left port nor allowed themselves to be seized by the Germans; they were put out of action by their crews. The fleet at Toulon included 3 battleships, 7 cruisers, 25 destroyers and 26 submarines.

The scuttling of the French fleet at Toulon should be reported only within the framework of the OKW communiqué. In our propaganda we may now point out that the word of honour of a French general or admiral has no validity for us – as was proved by what has happened with Darlan, Giraud and Nogues. Besides, the German Reich cannot build its future on the word of honour of French military men. To do this would be unpardonable recklessness after the experience we have had of the French so far.

The latent conflict between Giraud, Darlan and de Gaulle is worth exploiting by us. We could, moreover, point out to the French that in

North Africa all French mine owners have been removed and replaced by Americans on the grounds that they are followers of Pétain. We might point out in this connexion that, needless to say, the Americans will now never quit North Africa, and this is the result of France not making a clear decision at the crucial moment.

At the conferences of November 28 and 29, 1942, Goebbels repeated his directive that the quarrel between de Gaulle and Darlan should be 'lovingly' fanned. As a matter of principle, de Gaulle for the German press was the 'hireling' of Churchill and Darlan that of Roosevelt. After Darlan's death Giraud was chosen for this part. At the beginning of December 1942 Goebbels said: 'The Darlan–de Gaulle conflict continues to deserve attentive handling. The quarrel, however, must not be made into a clash between these two men but into a political conflict behind which stand Britain on the one side and America on the other.'

November 28, 1942

The Minister thinks it advisable to get off the Toulon subject as soon as possible so as to avoid the danger that this scuttling of the French fleet might become a legend and be compared with the scuttling of the German fleet at Scapa Flow. Instead, the breach of the word of honour, as emphasized by the Führer in his letter to Marshal Pétain, should be given greater prominence. The fact that the fleet broke its word of honour to the Marshal who has always represented a nationalist France, should be highlighted. In countering enemy propaganda we must point out that we never wanted the French fleet at Toulon, but that France has now lost her last trump card. This is the result of *attentism* and of the belief that at the moment of the greatest historic decision one can just sit on the fence, rub one's hands and act as a spectator.

November 29, 1942

Before marching into unoccupied France Hitler on November 11, 1942, addressed a letter to Marshal Pétain and a proclamation to the French people. On November 26 he wrote another letter to Pétain in which he attempted above all, to justify the occupation of the French naval base of Toulon. He wrote: 'Having learnt of new breaches of the word of honour of French officers, generals and admirals, and of their now proved intention to open France, just like North Africa, to the Anglo-Jewish war criminals, I have now given orders for Toulon to be occupied at once, for the ships to be prevented from leaving port or to be destroyed, and for all resistance to be broken, if necessary with extreme force.' Hitler then voiced the hope that it must be possible to give the French state once more its armed forces and added the assurance that Germany would help France in every way possible in regaining her colonial empire.

On the subject of the Führer's letter to Pétain, the Minister observes that it has unravelled the political situation in a truly classic manner. He points out in this connexion that there is a danger, amidst the continuous changes of day-to-day politics, that the great guidelines of the war may be lost to our view. He considers it necessary at this moment to launch a systematic campaign in press, radio and the other media to reshape public opinion, and to remind the people of the fact that this war was neither desired nor started by us. The fact that the war was triggered off over Danzig must not be lost in the clash of day-to-day argument and must be continually recalled to the world. For a certain period all Party spokesmen, all slogans of the week and all leading articles are to open with the sentence 'We did not want this war!'

November 30, 1942

In his broadcast speech of November 29, 1942, Churchill first referred to the successful Allied landing in North Africa. At the same time he warned against hopes that the war – which he predicted would be concluded in Europe rather than in Asia – would not last a great deal longer. It must be remembered, he said, that Hitler was holding nearly the whole of Europe under his domination, that the U-boat war might get worse still, and that the German leaders, 'those scoundrels, know that their lives are at stake.'

In connexion with Churchill's speech the Minister remarks that we should introduce our criticism with the sentence that it was Churchill who made this war and that his guilty conscience about being responsible for the war is reflected in his speech. Churchill was one of the principal warmongers in World War One, and according to a British report he burst into roars of laughter when the first world war actually began. In just the same way as he was responsible for World War One he is responsible for this one. We should pick out from his speech the passages where he draws attention to the difficulties of fighting this war. The fact that the Americans are in control of operations in North Africa should be emphasized to the British. Churchill's boasts about German U-boats sunk are best answered by reminding the British that in World War One, according to their own information, they claimed to have sunk more U-boats than we actually possessed. Churchill's hope that we would meet the fate of Napoleon no longer holds. This parallel lost its edge in the past winter. If Churchill attacks Adolf Hitler's generalship then it should be pointed out to him, by way of reply, that it was the corporal Adolf Hitler who smashed the mightiest land power in Europe, i.e. France.

December 1, 1942
Our successes in the U-boat war and pessimistic comment from the other side should be featured more prominently in order to give a slight fillip to morale in the Reich. The people are worrying more about the situation in the East than is appropriate at the moment, and for that reason the U-boat successes can be given greater prominence.

On December 2, 1942, the sinking of 166 ships with a total of 1,035,200 gross registered tonnage during the month of November – the highest monthly total so far – made banner headlines in the German press.

The Russians have again made exaggerated claims about our losses. It is now proposed to add up all the losses reported hitherto by the Russians, plus the losses which we are alleged to have suffered in operations against the British and French. Added together, according to enemy statements, we would by now have lost over 12,000,000 dead. These lying reports are to be brought to the world's notice quite soon, in order to demonstrate that, if the Russian figures were correct, about one sixth of our population would by now be dead. This arithmetic would undoubtedly be embarrassing to the British, just as their calculation was to us when they showed that the aircraft carriers which we reported we had sunk exceeded the number of aircraft carriers which they possessed at the outbreak of the war. The Minister believes that he can in this way put a slight damper on the faking of figures by the other side.

December 2, 1942

William Henry Beveridge, the British economist and statistician, in 1942 produced a *Report on Social Insurance and Allied Services* which became generally known as the Beveridge Plan and which to this day remains the basis of Britain's welfare policy. Under a directive of December 5, 1942, all post-war plans of the enemy countries, including the Beveridge Plan, were to be 'unequivocally unmasked as Utopian or designed to trick simpletons.'

On the subject of the Beveridge Plan the Minister remarks that our criticism should highlight the salient features of this social welfare plan and disregard its inessential aspects, Our criticism should confine itself to a few major points. Among these the Minister lists the following:

(1) The Beveridge Plan is roughly on the level of Bismarck's social legislation and thus proves Britain's social backwardness.

(2) The Plan means good business for the private insurance companies, since insurance is not to be nationalized but to remain privately owned. The social insurance envisaged is therefore just like a fire insurance.

(3) Even this primitive social welfare plan is described as unacceptable by the British capitalists, as shown by *The Times* and the *Daily Telegraph*.

(4) The Beveridge Plan, moreover, lays down the figure of 1,500,000 unemployed as the norm. Thus the British empire believes that even after a victory it will be unable to solve its unemployment problem.

December 4, 1942
The Minister believes that in spite of the increasing stabilization of the Eastern Front the German people should nevertheless be told about the fierceness of the fighting. Nothing, on the other hand, should be said about the extent of the operations. The foreign audience could now be presented with an overall picture of the situation, with reference to what our enemies intended and what they have in fact achieved. The following objectives might be listed for this purpose:

(1) The enemy tried to eject the Axis Powers from North Africa. In this he has failed.

(2) From North Africa he wanted to cross over to Italy in order to make the Axis edifice collapse by striking at it from the south. In this too he has failed.

(3) He then tried to undermine Italy by an intensive propaganda drive. This attempt was unmasked by Mussolini and the propaganda drive was made to collapse.

Further on this subject on December 3, 1942: 'The good Italian comment on Mussolini's speech should be highlighted. In our foreign propaganda we must in particular attack the British thesis about a 'war-weary Italy' and emphasize the fact that Britain is faced with a new European consciousness which cannot be defeated by old, worn-out propaganda methods. Morrison's figures about destruction caused by air raids should not be published.'

After a period of eighteen months, during which time he had made no public speeches, Mussolini addressed the Legislative Committee of the Fascist Chamber on December 2, 1942. He surveyed the war situation, called the war a 'holy war' and described as its fundamental feature the fact that the Germans had defeated the Russians. From his fellow countrymen he demanded that they should bring him captured enemy flags.

Mussolini in his speech of December 2, 1942, gave Italy's total losses during the first thirty months of the war as 230,738 prisoners, 37,713 missing, 40,219 killed in action and 85,968 wounded. Goebbels remarked that by this frank announcement of Italian losses the Duce had 'earned himself unprecedented credit.'

(4) The enemy had hopes of a collapse in the East and already saw his forces in Rostov.

Rostov had to be evacuated by the Wehrmacht in mid-February 1943.

These objectives, which the enemy undoubtedly had, are to be supported by press reports and radio commentaries. *The Times* and other British and American papers have on more than one occasion made these objectives the subject of their discussions. We may therefore point out that, just as all enemy offensives have so far failed to produce any results, so they will invariably fail to do so in future. Considering the extent of the fronts, they may of course succeed here or there in achieving a penetration, but this will always be sealed off again.

Goebbels was now using the method of which he had been accusing the British for a number of years. He attributed to the enemy far-reaching strategic objectives and then proved that these had not been reached; from this he concluded that Germany had scored a magnificent defensive victory and brilliantly survived a difficult situation. In reality, of course, matters were different.

December 5, 1942

Men on home leave from the East will be informed by OKW authorities in Germany during the next few days that their leave has been extended until further notice. In reply to questions the OKW representative explains that the real reason lies in the need temporarily to employ all available east-bound transport for other purposes. The announcement of this measure is expected to produce considerable excitement – in part a resurgence of rumours about an imminent armistice in the East and in part rumours about serious collapses or other unfavourable developments there. Since a public announcement of the measure, accompanied by the real reasons, is not desirable, and since false reasons cannot be adduced, the Minister will inform the Gauleiters about the true state of affairs and instruct them by way of the Party organizations to repudiate most emphatically all rumours from the very start by way of personal propaganda and implying the real reason for the extension of leave.

December 7, 1942

The term 'fortress of Europe' must not be used. It is defensive and contains only negative elements. A fortress can be besieged and it is only a question of time before it will fall.

The concept of the 'fortress of Europe' was first introduced into the German media by propaganda experts of the Foreign Ministry. By the end of November 1943, however, the foreign press reported that the greatest siege in history was beginning, the 'attack on the fortress of Europe'.

December 12, 1942

British propaganda is taken up so much with the alleged anti-Jewish atrocities in the East that the Minister believes the time has now come to do something about this propaganda campaign. The subject, of course, is rather delicate, and we had best not engage in polemics but instead give particular prominence to British atrocities in India, in Iran and in Egypt. Our best weapon against this propaganda campaign is an offensive, and for that the British are providing us with enough material. The atrocity stories, however, must be presented by us on a stronger note and must be vigorously supported by the German press so that they really make an impact in the world.

In the winter of 1942–3 not only the American but in particular also the British press carried a mass of articles about German executions of Jews and became, more than ever before, accusers against those inhuman practices.

The 'maltreatment of the Jews in Poland', Goebbels had said on December 8, 1942, was 'a delicate question' which had better not be touched on at all.

December 14, 1942

The Minister refers to the world-wide Jewish propaganda campaign against Germany and declares that this action, which has been noticeable for a few weeks, must at all costs be opposed by a German counter-action. There can be no question of a complete or partial refutation of the allegations of anti-Jewish atrocities, but merely a German campaign concerned with British and American atrocities throughout the world. There must be reports therefore about India, Iran, North Africa, and about acts of violence by

Britain and America generally, and these extensive reports must be put out again and again with the greatest emphasis. This news policy must be carried out at home too, even though the German public does not wish to hear about it any longer, in order to avoid any discrepancy between our domestic and foreign propaganda which might be exploited against us.

The Minister requests that steps should be taken to ensure that the Foreign Ministry also takes appropriate measures where it can. He is thinking, among other things, of appeals or proclamations by the two Boses, the Grand Mufti of Jerusalem, etc.

On December 18, 1942, the Grand Mufti of Jerusalem, addressing a rally in Berlin, declared that the United States and Great Britain would support Jewish aims in every respect and, in conjunction with the Jews, would crush all protests by Arabs and Islam with terror, blood and fire.

On December 22, 1942, Subhas Chandra Bose, in a broadcast appeal to India, referred to the Allied 'atrocity propaganda' and countered it with an account of the barbaric nature of British rule in India.

December 16, 1942

In our offensive against British atrocity stories we must not confine ourselves only to British atrocities but must also refer to various acts of violence and extortion by the Americans and to Russian atrocities. The Minister regards a general hullabaloo about atrocities as our best chance of getting away from the embarrassing subject of the Jews. Things must be so arranged that each party accuses every other of committing atrocities. This general hullabaloo will then eventually result in this subject disappearing from the agenda.

In his Sportspalast speech of February 18, 1943, Goebbels was to describe Jewry 'as the incarnation of evil, as the embodiment of the demon of decay' and as an 'infectious phenomenon'. Foreign protests against Germany's anti-Jewish policy, 'the shedding of hypocritical crocodile's tears', could not stop Germany from countering the Jewish threat by the 'exter ...' – then Goebbels corrected himself and said – the 'elimination of Jewry'.

A total of six hundred postcards from German prisoners of war in Russia have reached the Reich via the Red Cross. As the mail censorship was closed for some time these postcards were passed on to the men's families without examination. The question of whether this matter should be made public is still under discussion. Further letters and postcards are being collected and will probably be passed on to the men's families at a suitable opportunity. But no general ruling has yet been made.

Goebbels in his diaries, on December 17, 1942, refers to 'about four to six hundred postcards' from German prisoners of war in Russia. The cards had been passed on to the men's families but with an 'explanatory covering letter'. In future, however, these cards were no longer to be delivered to the families because they would open 'a gate for bolshevik propaganda to pour into Germany'.

December 18, 1942

In a lengthy statement the Minister complains in the sharpest possible tone that every attempt to counter the wave of American armament propaganda, which is holding the whole world spellbound, by way of German reconstruction and armament propaganda, has been frustrated by lack of understanding from the censorship authorities. He used the sharpest possible terms to describe this grotesque attitude of theirs, quoting as an example the case when the military censorship banned the publication of a picture of an enemy aircraft shot down over Reich territory on the grounds that this aircraft has not yet been reproduced in the appropriate military calendar. The Minister very sharply instructs his collaborators to submit to him proposals at once, which he will go over with the Reichspressechef and sum up in a memorandum to the Führer.

German armament propaganda had been set back by publications about two weapons which were not even in use yet. For the moment all those concerned 'had cold feet and did not feel like venturing out on to this slippery ground again.' At the beginning of January 1943 German journalists were given a demonstration of new weapons at the army training ground of Döberitz near Berlin.

December 22, 1942

The Minister points out that we must not allow ourselves to be rattled or irritated in our propaganda by the inflated reports from the enemy side. On the contrary, it is necessary to make a big noise ourselves and to create an impression of confidence towards foreign audiences. Phrases such as 'serious' or 'critical situation' must not be used, since if we say 'serious' in our propaganda then the others will make this out to mean 'catastrophical'. This is quite natural, since the side affected will of course always try to make things out to be less than they are.

On the situation in Stalingrad Goebbels in his diary merely noted on December 20, 1942, that it was giving 'cause for some concern. Because of the bad weather, air supplies are not functioning in the way one would wish. Our troops no longer have enough to eat.'

The order for the evacuation of the Sixth Army from Stalingrad, planned for December 22–23, 1942, was not given because Hitler had refused to authorize it. The troops were then waiting in vain for the arrival of the relief army which was to have thrust forward into the neighbourhood of the Stalingrad pocket.

December 31, 1942

All favourable foreign comment about the situation in the East should be published. The exaggerated Soviet reports should be countered by pointing out that last year the Russians also presented the world with great successes which subsequently turned out to be of no great importance. Last year they had intended to reach the Polish frontier, whereas this year they are contenting themselves with Rostov. Generally speaking, it is necessary to show a steely firmness and resolution in all annual balance-sheets and not yield to the temptation of examining how many kilometres we have retreated but rather how many we have reached in the past year. The twenty kilometres which we have had to move back are unimportant compared with the thousands which we have advanced.

In his New Year's Eve address Goebbels thought it advisable to deceive his audience about the real seriousness of the situation. He said, among other things: 'We have deprived the enemy of his most important raw material, armament and grain centres. He has thus suffered a blow from which, for the purpose of continuing the war, he cannot any more recover . . . We are now sitting on the longer arm of the lever . . . The Reich is being defended by a front which is equal to any stress . . . Today we already see a distant light – the light of a new morning which awaits us, which we are fighting and working for, and which we are striving for with all the strength in our hearts.'

'Do you want total war?'

January - March 1943

Goebbels's 'New Year Message' for 1943 was addressed to the troops at the front. In it he said that 'a historic year of the first order' had come to a close and 'a historic year of the first order' was beginning. Without making definite forecasts he declared: 'Just as the war began suddenly so one day it will end suddenly. The totalization of the war effort merely leads to an acceleration of the war itself ... This war is our great but also our last historical opportunity ... This war therefore must end with such a total victory that it need never be repeated again ... The year ahead will not spare us any trials or stresses. It will be a lively year and we shall have to hold on fast when its storms roar around us ...' Nevertheless, Goebbels believed that the new year would bring nearer Germany's 'final victory', the 'ultimate victory'.

January 4, 1943

The Minister makes a few fundamental observations on the war situation and emphasizes the seriousness of the position and the need to make every effort to mobilize the very last forces for the war effort. At the beginning of the new year it is necessary to review the work done so far and to draw conclusions from it for the future. He is happy to see that his demand for a more total war effort is now gradually asserting itself. He has always emphasized at the ministerial conferences that only a more radical civilian war effort can achieve military success for us. Every day furnishes further proof that in the East we are facing a brutal enemy who can only be forced to his knees by the most brutal means, and for that purpose we must achieve total mobilization of all our forces and reserves. In consequence, German propaganda is coming into its own again, and the discrepancy between theory and practice is being eliminated. Once the people feel that what is happening is not just propaganda for total war but that the necessary conclusions are also being drawn, propaganda will have gained its proper substance and effect. The time has now come for action, and it would be quite wrong to be fobbed off with hopes of spring. If we do not mobilize all our reserves now it should not be thought that we will catch up in the spring or the summer when optimism usually gains a lot of ground anyway. Now, when our difficulties are so great, we must make the most of our time and go over to a total war effort.

As for war propaganda itself, the Minister points out that we must reduce it to a few basic axioms. With the prolonged duration of the war it was unavoidable for our propaganda to become fragmented by day-to-day events and for the basic principles of this war to be progressively lost sight of. The history of National Socialist propaganda, however, proves that principles are always decisive, and a true propagandist will seize every opportunity to show up these fundamental aspects of the war in the individual, day-to-day events. It is necessary to emphasize a few solid principles continually and ceaselessly at every opportunity, and to hammer them into the consciousness of the people. Among these he [the Minister] listed the following:

(1) The war was forced upon the German people;

(2) This war is a matter of life or death;

(3) We now need a total war effort.

The Minister likens these principles to the *leitmotifs* in Wagner's operas and believes that these phrases must again and again appear in variations. There is daily some occasion for recalling these fundamental tenets to the people's mind. . . . The Minister believes that these fundamental ideas will, among other things, also dismiss the rubbish that is talked about who it was who started the bombing of cities.

As for the post-war plans of our enemies, currently being featured in enemy propaganda, the Minister believes that it is better not to take any notice of them. It cannot be denied that they might have some effect in many circles. The massive publication of these plans is instilling fear into many people who have little idea of the real situation. These post-war plans, of course, are pure propaganda and ultimately pursue the aim of feigning assurance to their own people. For that reason we had better not deal with them at all in future.

The Minister discusses the slogan that 'We cannot lose the war.' He regards this phrase as absolutely wrong since Providence has not decreed in advance who shall win the war and who shall lose it. Of course we could lose the war if we did not mobilize all our strength for the war effort. If on the other hand we mobilize all the forces of our people and apply them correctly, then it may well be that Russia will be smashed this summer. He is pleased that the right kind of language is now being used; this can only work to our advantage in our war effort.

According to Semler, Goebbels declared: 'It is my conviction – and not even the greatest national catastrophe will shake it – that we shall win the war easily if we now mobilize all our strength. We hold all the trump cards. What we need is to devote our entire moral effort to it, and to employ every reserve we have. We must mobilize all our reserves – that is what has to be done on the greatest scale.

I believe we can now force the Soviet Union to her knees next summer provided we now use to the full the strength which is still present, untapped, among the German people. We should have done so last winter.'

January 5, 1943

Further to his fundamental observations yesterday, the Minister, emphasizing the particular duty of all present to keep this secret, announces that a working party consisting of Reichsleiter Bormann, Reich Minister Lammers and Reich Minister Goebbels is expected to work out a plan of action for the realization of total war and that this will be submitted to the Führer in the very near future. It is necessary to make one million men available for the front. He intends to propose the closure of numerous shops and department stores which are not selling anything anyway and are merely tying down unemployed staff, and likewise the closure of all luxury restaurants, in particular night clubs and similar establishments. Needless to say, theatres, cinemas and other places of genuine recreation will be kept for the people who work hard throughout the day. For men a labour conscription is envisaged from the age of 15 to 65 and for women from 17 to 50. At the same time, all departments will be combed through again, and he intends, of his own accord, to set an example in his Ministry. The Minister expresses the conviction that, once the first shock has passed which this announcement will trigger off among the public, a sense of greater security will arise – once the measures show that total war is not only being talked about but that appropriate action is in fact being taken. The public must be made to understand that the most radical war is also the shortest. What must be produced is a realism free from illusions which will serve as a foundation for an optimistically inspired, unlimited effort by all available forces.

January 6, 1943

Supplementing his observations of yesterday about the measures for the realization of total war, the Minister points out that our propaganda must of course avoid producing a basically defensive attitude among the German people. On no account must publicity be given to slogans such as 'Life or Death' or 'The Fortress of Europe', which give rise to undesirable ideas. Since the beginning of the war our propaganda has taken the following mistaken line of development:

First year of the war: We have won.
Second year of the war: We shall win.
Third year of the war: We must win.
Fourth year of the war: We cannot be defeated.

Such a development is disastrous and must on no account be continued. Instead, the German public must be made to realize that we not only want to win and must win, but more particularly that we are also *able* to win because the prerequisites exist as soon as work and effort in the country are fully placed at the service of the war.

January 8, 1943

The discussion in Britain about the failure of the announced air raids on German cities to materialize must not be treated by us as a cause for gloating criticism. This might only provoke the British, and if they then really came the people would blame us for having brought it about by our propaganda.

The Minister once more points out that there is no cause for panic-mongering, even though we should not view the situation with too many illusions. He is making this point more particularly with a view to the new draft laws about the totalization of the war which are to be published very shortly. We should view the situation seriously, but we should also always remember that if we intensify our war efforts the situation will change.

January 13–14, 1943

The Minister announces that the Führer has signed a decree ordering the total mobilization of the homeland for the war effort.

The Minister believes that all comment dealing with the totalization of the war in the other belligerent countries may now be published. Thus, further totalization efforts in Russia may be mentioned, as may similar moves in Britain. The Minister is convinced that the enemy countries will not be able to say much about our totalization efforts, and even if they do in fact scream for a couple of days our measures will soon cease to be a subject of polemic on anybody's part.

The Minister points out that the present practice of special announcements gives cause for criticism. Our special announcements are no longer special announcements at all since they are always released at the same time, between 13.00 and 14.00 hours, and everybody knows that what is coming now is a U-boat announcement about 100,000 GRT. The Minister believes that, first, the timing must be varied and, second, the announcements should not always be only about 100,000 GRT but, if it has been a particularly successful day, they could be below 100,000 GRT or, if the total tonnage sunk covers a longer period, one could occasionally wait until it has reached 160,000 GRT to 180,000 GRT.

January 16, 1943

The Minister discusses the impression produced by a film, obtained from abroad, about the defence of Leningrad during the past winter. He directs that the responsible heads of German propaganda should see this film because it demonstrates the enormous difference between the German and the Russian war efforts and because it shows how slight is the German civilian population's contribution compared with the Russian. The film also shows the Russians' masterly skill at improvization; one of the secrets of the Russian successes is the employment of the most ruthless and the toughest men in leading positions. The Minister points out that if necessary we must oppose these by the same type of men in order to cope with them.

January 19, 1943

The Minister comes back to the subject of the air raids and directs that on no account must we raise a howl of triumph over the figure of aircraft shot down, since one can never predict just how many British airmen will be shot down during the next raid. Altogether, our reporting of the air raids should be purely factual and not coloured by propaganda. Any swaggering or frivolous reporting of the air raids is altogether out of tune with the present situation.

During the night of January 16–17, 1943, some 400 to 500 British bombers attacked Berlin; according to British reports 22 bombers were lost. The OKW communiqué reported that 25 enemy aircraft had been shot down by flak and night fighters during the attack on the capital.

On January 18, 1943, Moscow announced the reconquest of Schlüsselburg.

Similarly, we do not wish to touch on the alleged loss of Schlüsselburg;* we should counter the Russian special announcements with the argument that things were just the same last year and the very opposite then happened during the summer. This is virtually the only argument left to us and therefore we should use it all the time.

The Minister raises the subject of neutral press comment and in particular deals with our attitude to the Swedish, Swiss and Turkish

* A town and island fortress on the Neva forty miles east of Leningrad. *Tr.*

316

papers. He points out that he is often greatly annoyed by the impertinent and uncomprehending reporting of the neutral press and that he is frequently revolted by their attitude. Nevertheless he thinks it advisable not to reply to such instances of rudeness since it cannot be denied that the neutral countries are working for us on a major scale. He refers to Switzerland which, by manufacturing industrial goods, is very considerably contributing to German armament output, and to Swedish ore deliveries without which we should find it very difficult to wage war. The neutral countries are now trying to neutralize their contribution to Germany's armament effort by adopting a different attitude in their press. Even though the attitude expressed in the papers frequently reflects conviction, it is still not advisable to argue with it in the long run. It is best to ignore neutral press comment as far as possible and, if necessary, to refute it in a dignified manner. It does not behove a great power continually to raise its finger without following up its warning by action. As a great power one can threaten only once; the second time one must strike. Since at the moment we are in no position to do so, and since it would conflict with our own war effort, he believes that the correct thing is as far as possible to ignore all press sallies from the neutral countries. After all, their work for our German armament effort is worth more to us than the screaming of their press.

January 20, 1943
On the subject of the situation in the East, the Minister observes that events this winter are presenting the same picture as last year. We should not, therefore, be drawn into discussing details since everything at the moment is in a state of flux and there is some uncertainty about the situation. We should view the situation in a generous way and not be drawn into squabbles about the names of places and towns. Like last winter we are again undergoing great trials but this year we have the advantage that the necessary conclusions are now also being drawn at home. This is the positive feature about the military crisis, and he [the Minister] is firmly convinced that, once the total potential of the German people is enlisted, we shall finish the business in the East before the end of this year. We must not be shaken in our conviction and must continue fighting indefatigably.

A careful reading of the OKW communiqué of January 16, 1943, revealed for the first time that the German troops in Stalingrad had been surrounded for several weeks. The OKW communiqué ran: 'In the Stalingrad area our troops, which have for some weeks been engaged in heroic defensive fighting against an enemy attacking from all sides, continued yesterday to repulse powerful attacks by enemy infantry and armoured formations with heavy losses for the bolsheviks. Commanders and troops thus again set a brilliant example of heroic German soldierly spirit.'

January 21, 1943

The Minister deals extensively with the totalization measures and makes the following observations: The labour service very shortly to be introduced for women and men will cover all women between 17 and 50 and all men between 16 and 65. Exempt are women who have a child under 6 or two children under 14, or have a household to look after. Applications for exemption on health grounds can be considered only if accompanied by a certificate from a medical officer of health. The Minister will see to it that the daughters of the plutocrats do not dodge this duty. The aim of the new measure, the Minister states, is to scrap one million reserved jobs so that the present age group (1925) will be able to supply one-and-a-half million soldiers by the spring. It is necessary to start recruiting for the Wehrmacht at once and not to allow any great delays, to make sure the totalization measures produce an immediate effect. Once the soldiers have been recruited and a vacuum created, we will be forced to enlist the women too. He even considers it necessary to create a shortage of labour in order to lend real force to the law.

In quoting these figures Goebbels must have deliberately indulged in enormous exaggeration. It was planned to make 800,000 men available for the Wehrmacht in the spring of 1943; on March 9, 1943, Goebbels voiced his concern to Hitler that this plan was not feasible, and that his own recommendation of 500,000 men would be closer to the mark.

The Minister issues the following directives for the propaganda campaign to implement this law:

The intensification of the war situation and the persistence of heavy fighting compel us to draw on all our human reserves. We expected too much from the front without, at the same time, making everybody participate in the war back home. However, he issues the express instruction not to enlist people for work by browbeating them but to use persuasion and kind words alone. They should be informed of the realities of the situation in a clear and authoritative manner, and be told how much manpower is still needed. Most of our fellow Germans will understand that they are needed at this critical hour and will gladly comply with the law. Besides, the law expressly provides that not everybody has to go into an armament works, but may first look around to see where he can find a suitable job. For the initial period, at any rate, preferences may be expressed. Moreover, those enlisted should be employed according to their abilities. The Minister considers it particularly important that those enlisted are employed rationally. There is no intention of merely plaguing anybody, and we can say quite plainly in our commentaries that we do not begrudge anybody a comfortable life, but that their employment on war work is necessary at this moment. Formulations such as 'we hope everyone will understand these measures' or 'we cannot see any possible objection to these measures' are most suitable for commentaries. People are not to be bludgeoned but should be persuaded to do their work with conviction. Any opposition to the law can be attacked by us later. No doubt, this will be confined to groups of weaklings, since the others will follow the call of duty. The appeal to national solidarity will not remain unheard and will undoubtedly contribute to a rise in morale.

Referring to an issue of the Moscow *Pravda* the Minister illustrates the propaganda methods of the Russians. The success of Russian propaganda is due to continuous repetition. The Russians have set up few principles of propaganda, but these principles run through all their newspapers. These are that the Russians will have their throats cut or be led into slavery. A leading article in *Pravda* is entirely filled with quotations from the *Deutsche Ukrainische Zeitung* [*Deutsche Ukraine-Zeitung*] which unambiguously expresses our intentions to exploit Russia. The result of this Russian propaganda is that Stalin today has behind him a united Russian people, and one cannot avoid admitting that the Russians have accomplished a masterpiece of propaganda. They have succeeded in getting their nation, sceptical as it is with regard to bolshevism, mobilized for a total effort. We can only learn from them, and we too should reiterate our principles again and again. One of these principles is that, no matter what an individual German's attitude is to National Socialism, everybody will have his throat cut if we are defeated. This propaganda slogan will be effective. Besides, repetition is what the people want. The Church has been living on nothing but continuous repetition and yet the churches are not empty. National Socialism, at the time of its struggle for power, similarly attracted people and turned them into fighters by repeating slogans to them.

The Minister sharply criticizes the practice of talking to the Russians about our plans of conquest in the East. He refers to the parallel of the National Socialist struggle for power and says that if we had then, before our seizure of power, talked about belief in Wotan or the dissolution of the German National Party or the prohibition of the Social Democrats or the locking up of the communists, or about fighting the Churches, surely no one would have voted for us. Similarly it is lunacy today to talk to the Russians about our intentions in the East.

There is only one slogan which must be proclaimed again and again, and that is our fight against bolshevism. Today Russia is waging her war under the slogan of nationalism and can therefore find support among all sections of the nation. Our propaganda slogan for the East must therefore be that we are not fighting against the Russian nation but only against bolshevism.

January 23, 1943
Available U-boat comment may continue to be used although certain misgivings are being voiced. This topic is of importance to us at the present moment as it offsets the situation in the East.

The U-boat war, which Goebbels had called 'our big ace', was engaged in a race against time, trying to sink Allied ships faster than they were being produced. In 1943 Allied tonnage of new ships amounted to over 12,000,000 GRT. For Germany to retain the lead, at least 1,000,000 GRT had to be sunk each month – a figure which was not attainable, if only because of Allied technical innovations in anti-U-boat operations. The U-boat war finally collapsed in the North Atlantic at the end of May 1943.

A pastoral letter from the Bishop of Berlin about human rights was read out in the United States Senate. This fact will be added to the existing record on the Church's attitude in this war.

January 24, 1943
Following his trip to the Führer's headquarters the Minister discusses the present situation at length and points out that Ministerialdirektor Naumann transmitted the directive to his Department on Saturday. Ministerialdirektor Naumann on Saturday evening gave a brief account of the talks with the Führer to the most important departmental heads and pointed out that the Führer is now determined to carry out the total warfare measures proposed by the Minister. The Führer agrees that complete and unreserved frankness should now be practised in our news policy. The Minister points out that, in spite of the seriousness of the situation at the fronts, we may now enjoy a sense of relief since our propaganda is once more based on solid fact. The momentary crisis through which we are passing cannot be remotely compared with the gravity of the British crisis after Dunkirk. At that time Winston Churchill displayed admirable frankness in drawing the necessary conclusions and telling the British people the absolute truth. At the time we did not understand this, but with these tactics Churchill aroused the

conservative forces in his nation. The task today is to arouse the same conservative forces in the German people and to mobilize them. Our people, at this moment, are not desperate but they are serious and deeply moved by the situation. They are demanding a strong hand at the helm and they must feel that the government knows what it wants. Today there can be but one slogan, and that is: Work, work and total war. The many boils which have formed on the German national body must be sliced off. He [the Minister] himself will act mercilessly in this respect and draw the necessary conclusions. However, we should always conclude all our reflections by saying that at the end of our great war effort stands victory. We must not paint things in black colours only and we must not be serious solely for the sake of seriousness.

On January 23, 1943, the Reichspressechef's Slogan of the Day ran as follows: 'The great and stirring heroic sacrifices made for the German nation by the German troops encircled at Stalingrad, in conjunction with the imminent labour duty for women and other far-reaching organizational measures for total war, will become the moral mainspring of a truly heroic attitude of the entire German people and the starting point of a new period of German determination for victory and the upsurge of all forces. The German press at this moment is given the special task of shaking up every single citizen by publishing moving accounts of the unique self-sacrifice of the heroes of Stalingrad, so that every German will take his place in the great front of resistance and will to victory. Editorial offices are asked to prepare themselves to follow this serious line of thought, which will continue right up to January 30, so that, as soon as the expected appeals and announcements are made, they can ensure that their papers will produce the necessary moving effect.'

The Minister states that the Führer has given him the most far-reaching powers and that he will now use them. He mentions in this connexion that the Führer has an open mind on everything, and if some people do not get anywhere with him then this is because they do not know how to speak to him. The Führer has told him [the Minister] that for the next three months he will not receive anyone who comes to him to beef about him, the Minister. The Führer knows that the vast measures which are now being put into effect will involve a great deal of injustice. If one-and-a-half to two million soldiers are recruited and if such radical measures are put into effect, some injustice is bound to be done to some individual or other. The Minister says that in his own Ministry he does not want any rows during the next few months either, because he wants to be able to devote himself fully to his work. He compares his own situation with that in 1932 when he was also [subsequently deleted] the most hated man. At that time some soft-centred groups within the NSDAP were against him because he demanded all or nothing. He will now again take radical measures and carry them through, and he knows that the people will unreservedly approve them. Already the people are welcoming his articles in *Das Reich* with enthusiasm; at headquarters too the men are deeply impressed by them. He is convinced that the people today are crying out for leadership and are happy when they feel a strong hand over them. Now even those forces which have hitherto always kept aloof will, of their own accord, range themselves on his side.

We are today the bulwark of European culture against bolshevism; we are Europe's protective wall against the red hordes. Even when speaking to Britain, we may raise the question of what would happen to her empire if the European continent became bolshevik. British reports, by the way, suggest that many discerning minds there have realized the danger of bolshevism. It is the greatest merit of National Socialism – and this will be generally understood one day – that it annihilated communism in Germany and called a halt to Russian bolshevism.

On the subject of news policy the Minister points out that we should not repudiate the Russian special announcements or their reports on the progress of their offensive. For the time being we should allow the Russian reports to take their course so that the rest of Europe becomes alarmed about the danger they present.

On January 25, 1943, Goebbels supplemented his directive to let reports of Soviet victories pass without denial: 'He is convinced that the British are slowly getting cold feet and beginning to see the danger of a possible victory of the bolsheviks. He recalls his slogan of yesterday, which we should continue repeating to the world, i.e. "What would have happened if National Socialism had not come to power, and what would happen if we lost the war?!" We should ask the European nations what would happen to them if the German Wehrmacht were no longer standing in the East. The time has come to winkle out the anti-bolshevik trends in other countries and gradually to build up an anti-bolshevik front. In Africa we must see the situation totally differently: there we must present the course of operations as being in our favour.'

At the conference of January 26, 1943, it was noted that 'the propaganda tactics of greatly stressing the bolshevik danger' were already paying off.

January 26, 1943

Stalin's order of the day to the bolshevik army should be ignored by us. Moreover, we should not publish the pessimistic Russian comment on the war situation either since it does not fit into our propaganda slogan at the moment. On the other hand, neutral comment should now be featured on a bigger scale since the neutrals are beginning to have the jitters at the thought of bolshevism. Churchill's slogan of 'blood, sweat and tears' must not be taken up; we must think up a slogan of our own.

On January 25, 1943, Stalin issued an order of the day to all troops at the front. As the result of two months of Soviet offensive operations he listed the smashing of 102 divisions and gave the number of enemy prisoners as in excess of 200,000. The Red Army, he said, had advanced by up to 250 miles. The order emphasized the victory of Stalingrad, mentioned the breach of the blockade of Leningrad and named a large number of cities which had been recaptured – including Velikiye Luki, Schlüsselburg and Voronezh.

January 27, 1943

The Casablanca conference between Roosevelt and Churchill, as well as between the two military staffs of the Allies, was held from January 14 to 26, 1943. The envisaged tripartite meeting with Stalin did not come off as Stalin did not wish to leave his country at the moment of the Russian winter offensive. The Casablanca conference had been a well-kept secret until an official press conference on January 24, when Roosevelt announced that the Allies would insist on the 'unconditional surrender' of the Axis Powers. The conference was concerned mainly with planning the war during 1943, including preparations for landings in Sicily and northern France.

In connexion with the meeting of Roosevelt and Churchill at Casablanca the Minister points out that we must be careful in future in reporting details of alleged meetings between Churchill and Roosevelt so as not to commit a bad blunder. Only yesterday the German press referred to a meeting in Washington and today we have to admit that they spent ten days together at Casablanca. He issues the following directive for the treatment of the meeting:

(1) On no account do we take any part in the sensation-mongering;

(2) The German people are to be told frankly that Churchill and Roosevelt have met at Casablanca to discuss the further conduct of the war against the Axis Powers. The German people will be told where they have met and how long they have negotiated.

As for the purpose of their trip, we shall point out that the grave differences between the Americans and British in North Africa urgently necessitated some sort of settlement. Added to this is the U-boat problem which is of considerable importance to the enemy's war effort. Besides, we shall not conceal from the people the fact that the Allies are planning offensive operations. Likewise, the German people must be informed that the enemy laid down as his aim the unconditional surrender of the Axis Powers. Against these aims we hold the following trump cards:

Although at present we are going through a crisis in the East, we shall master the situation somehow. The U-boats are causing the greatest

323

difficulties to the enemy's war effort and furthermore we can now refer to our totalization measures, since these will lead to the full utilization of all the forces of the German people.

Stalin's absence, we should point out, proves how little the Russians are interested in the relationship between Britain and America. Stalin is now hoping to bag Europe without the help of the others. He no longer attaches any importance to the Second Front and therefore has not even sent a representative to this meeting.

On the German side the Casablanca conference was at first assessed as a sign of Allied disunity. It was believed that there had been arguments in Casablanca in favour of an arrangement with Germany. In order to check this trend Roosevelt had coined the slogan of unconditional surrender. This interpretation was lent support by US comment, after March 1943, to the effect: 'German people, dissociate yourself from Adolf Hitler and National Socialism and you will get a moderate peace!'

Reports from Stalingrad indicate that the heroic struggle of our soldiers is nearing its end. This unique event in German military history – for never before have German soldiers been in such a hopeless fight – must be exploited psychologically for the strengthening of our people. He [the Minister] urges the press to remember that every word about this heroic struggle will go down in history. The OKW communiqué, in particular, must be formulated in a way which will stir people's hearts for centuries to come. The OKW communiqué must be so drafted that it will rank equal with Caesar's addresses to his troops, Frederick the Great's appeal to his generals before the Battle of Leuthen, and Napoleon's appeals to his guards. The few sentences about the heroic epic of Stalingrad must be simple, direct and modest, as if engraved in bronze.

January 28, 1943

The Minister directs that caution must be practised in handling the meeting between Churchill and Roosevelt. He, personally, is convinced that the two have cooked up something. Last time, when they met in Washington, the plan for the landing in North Africa was hatched, and if they now had a ten-day meeting then this must mean something. At this moment, when the war has reached a dramatic point, some new plans have undoubtedly been discussed. We should not be fooled by the well-acted show of disappointment put up by the British in connexion with the final communiqué.

The Minister again emphasizes that we must intensify our anti-bolshevik propaganda and he coins the slogan that ideas need no convoys. Once bolshevism has reached the Channel coast – and Britain had better realize this – it will leap across the narrow Channel and encompass Britain also.

January 29, 1943

The Minister describes the comment on the Labour Duty Law in today's press as good and issues instructions to continue along these lines. The closure of luxury restaurants, luxury shops and other superfluous institutions will follow next week. In handling this subject, the Minister declares, the press and radio must point out that these are shops which in fact no longer serve any useful purpose because they have no merchandise to sell and are at most the scene of a barter trade which is offensive to the public. The Minister directs that it must again and again be pointed out that all vitally necessary places of production or business will of course be kept going to their full capacity.

January 30, 1943

As for the treatment of today's rally, he [the Minister] issues instructions that particular prominence is to be given to portraying the positive mood of the German people at the rally. In factual terms, particular publicity should be given to the report, now released by him, about the Soviet government's intention to deport the German people for forced labour in Russia after the war.

Goebbels made a speech at the Berlin Sportspalast on the tenth anniversary of the 'National-Socialist seizure of power'. His speech referred to the 'unimaginable ferocity' of the fighting in the East and hinted at the disastrous situation at the front. 'If the enemy believed,' Goebbels said, 'that he could dishearten us by a few blows then he is very much mistaken. These blows were and are for us merely a warning signal to embark on total war as we are now firmly determined to do ... For us it has always been a firm and unshakable principle that the word capitulation does not exist in our vocabulary. We still hold to this view and shall always hold to it!' Goebbels further stated: 'We have faith in victory! We have faith in it because we have the Führer ... Faith moves mountains. This faith must pervade us all.' The new elements in this speech were, on the one hand, Goebbels's express mention of the idea of capitulation and, on the other, his emphasis on faith in victory.

January 31–February 1, 1943

The Minister points out that the Führer's proclamation will naturally provide the basis for our propaganda in the immediate future. Particular emphasis is to be given to the point that Germany is fighting for Europe. As for the East, a further directive from the Führer will be issued in due course. He [the Minister] has been instructed by the Führer to draft the text of a proclamation to the Russian people. Meanwhile the Führer's remarks about the East are to be used in the occupied eastern territories.

The 'Eastern Proclamation' proposed by Goebbels did not at first meet with Hitler's approval. In a conversation with Goebbels on March 9, 1943, Hitler expressed the view 'that bolshevism is hated and feared so much among the eastern peoples that the anti-bolshevik trend of our propaganda is fully adequate.' Hitler feared that a proclamation might be interpreted as a sign of weakness and yielding. Goebbels therefore confined himself for the time being to spreading his ideas in general directives issued to all German authorities subordinate to him. (*Cf.* February 15, 1943.)

The drive for the closure of luxury restaurants in Berlin started at the beginning of February 1943. Until then these places had served Lucullan dinners for the 'top thousand', without coupons but at prices from 50 Marks to 100 Marks. The best-known gourmets' restaurant was Horcher's in the Lutherstrasse, whose chef, incidentally, enjoyed the particular favour of Göring. The restaurant's windows were smashed by a few SA men on Goebbels's instructions.

The Minister points out that the German people are now expecting practical measures for the totalization of the war and that he himself will on no account be a party to disappointing the public. Just because twice during the past few days Horcher's have had their windows broken he certainly cannot therefore demand police protection for this gourmets' restaurant, since the public is instinctively right in demanding its closure in view of events in the East and the totalization measures announced.

Hitler's proclamation, read out at the Berlin Sportspalast by Goebbels on January 30, 1943, declared that 'victory is not a gift from Providence' and that 'in this war there will be neither victors nor vanquished, but only survivors and annihilated.' As a war aim Hitler named 'the Germanic State of the German nation, as the eternal and equal home of all men and women of our nation – the National Socialist Greater German Reich.'

The Minister points out that the British press has not reported the Führer's proclamation at all. This method, which he has in the past recommended to the German press when the situation was reversed, should be seen as an instructive example since it shows that even in a democratic Britain awkward announcements by the enemy are passed over in complete silence by the press.

The German press, moreover, should not take up enemy comment on the establishment of a Second Front. Likewise, the Russian report about the alleged capture of the commander-in-chief at Stalingrad is not to be published.

Paulus, the Commander-in-Chief of the Sixth Army, promoted Field Marshal by Hitler as recently as January 31, 1943, went into Soviet captivity a few hours after receiving notification of his promotion. The capture of the 'Field Marshal' was announced in a Moscow communiqué of January 31, 1943. The capture of further generals was reported on February 2. The German media kept silent on the subject.

Finally, General Giraud's statement* is also prohibited for the German press because its publication would lend new support to criticism among the German public of the inadequate way in which he was guarded while in German captivity.

A reconciliation between Giraud and de Gaulle took place at the Casablanca meeting. The French General Henri-Honoré Giraud (1879–1949), who escaped from German captivity during World War One, had again been in German captivity since May 1940. On April 17, 1942, however, Giraud – having persistently refused to give his word of honour that he would not escape – succeeded in escaping from the fortress of Königstein. Not until ten days after news of his escape became known did Hitler – although he had offered a reward of 100,000 Marks for Giraud's capture – allow the press to join in the search for him. But this did not produce the desired result either. Giraud made good his escape to North Africa and there, from 1942 to 1944, was Commander-in-Chief of the French forces. The German leadership at first feared that Giraud might become the head of the French exile government in London, replacing de Gaulle. Goebbels said: 'That would be most awkward . . .' since de Gaulle was 'of slight intellectual and moral calibre.'

February 3, 1943

The Minister announces that immediately upon the issuing of the report on the conclusion of the fighting in Stalingrad a national remembrance of three times 24 hours will be held. During that period all places of entertainment, including theatres and cinemas, will be closed. It is intended, on the first and last days, to have a minute's standstill of all traffic.

For the publicity treatment he issues the following directive: there can be no question of mourning or sentimentality, let alone swagger. The three days of remembrance must serve reflection, contemplation and the

* Broadcast on January 28, 1943. *Tr.*

concentration of strength. Within this general framework, therefore, no flags will be flown and papers will be forbidden to appear with black margins. German propaganda in its entirety must cause a legend to be created around the heroism of Stalingrad, a legend which will be a most precious possession of German history. It is necessary, to compel every individual to ask himself whether and how he can make an even greater contribution to the war.

On February 2, 1943, a Moscow communiqué announced the end of the battle of Stalingrad which had begun on August 22, 1942 and in which the Axis troops, according to unofficial estimates, had lost 503,650 men.

On February 1, the OKW communiqué reported the capitulation of 'the southern group in Stalingrad under the leadership of Field Marshal Paulus'; on February 3 it stated that 'the battle of Stalingrad is over'. The Reich-pressechef's Slogan of the Day of February 3 ran:

'The heroic fighting for Stalingrad has come to an end. In several days of mourning the German people will remember its gallant sons who did their duty to their last breath and to their last round, and thereby broke the main force of the bolshevik onslaught against the Eastern Front. The heroic struggle for Stalingrad will now become the greatest heroic epic of German history. This faces the German press with one of its greatest tasks. In line with and in the spirit of the OKW special announcement expected today, the German press must pay tribute to the moving event which outshines the greatest feats of military heroism in world history; it must hold up this exalted example of supreme heroic bearing and ultimate self-sacrifice for the sake of victory as a sacred torch before the eyes of the German people. From the immortal heroism of the men of Stalingrad there will unfold within the German nation, more strongly than ever before, the spirit and the forces which will ensure the victory which it is now more than ever fanatically determined to achieve.'

Not a word was said about German losses at Stalingrad, and the press was not even allowed to 'intone words of mourning.' A few days later, on the other hand, came a report that 47,000 wounded had been saved from the battlefield.

February 8, 1943

The Minister, who has today returned from the Gauleiter conference and a personal reception at the Führer's, reports that the Führer has in every respect approved the policy of extreme totalization of the war which he, the Minister, has been demanding for the past eighteen months, and has indeed made several demands which go beyond what the Minister had in mind. This applies not only to the home country, where the Führer desires that the people's exceptional readiness for sacrifice and work should be fully utilized and various unpleasant features eliminated, which in the present circumstances seem incomprehensible to the public, but also to the occupied countries. It is intended to summon the Reich Commissioners, etc., to Germany shortly and to issue to them very strict instructions in this respect.

On February 5 and 6, 1943, a conference of Reichsleiters and Gauleiters was held at Posen. The conference was addressed by, among others, Bormann, Goebbels, Speer, Sauckel, Backe and General von Unruh. The Reichsleiters and Gauleiters were subsequently summoned to the Führer's headquarters. Only a brief communiqué was published in the press about the speech made to them by Hitler on February 7. The exact text of his speech is still not known to researchers.

The Minister points out in this connexion that, according to preliminary and still quite incomplete reports, the result of yesterday's collection in Berlin was 92 per cent more than the corresponding figure last year, even though no badges were distributed. As the Defence Commissioner and Gauleiter of Berlin he has among other things issued instructions that the racecourse of Ruhleben is to be closed at once and released for the erection of hutments and for the storage of vital materials, and that the issue of collection badges is to be stopped altogether until further notice. The slogan should be put about that the next badge will be the victory rune.* The public has for some time been at a loss to understand why material urgently needed for other purposes should be used for such badges.

The Minister points out that the Führer has expressed his quite particular satisfaction with German propaganda, especially with the treatment of the Stalingrad topic.

The Minister charges his collaborators not to betray under any circumstances the fact that they know that the rupture of the front over a width of about 450 km began with the failure of certain of our allies.†
These things cannot be discussed at all until after the war.

February 11, 1943

The Minister requests that the German press should keep off cartoons which belittle our opponents. We have no reason at the present moment to portray our opponents as being smaller than in fact they are, especially as the people would not go along with us in this respect.

When Stalin was appointed Marshal of the Soviet Union on March 7, 1943, Goebbels expressly prohibited any 'poking of fun' at the appointment.

---

* The revival and use of some of the ancient Germanic runes (the early Nordic alphabet in which certain letters also stood for concepts) formed part of the Nazi mystique. *Tr.*
† The Rumanian Third Army cracked at a vital point on the Stalingrad Front. *Tr.*

The Minister believes that the reference in the German press today to the mobilization of our last reserves could not have been more unfortunate. This is an expression which not only does not do justice to the actual situation but also gives rise to pessimism. In consultation with the appropriate authorities it has been agreed that professional sport is to be suspended altogether for the duration of the war. Football championships, friendly matches and inter-city fixtures, as well as all kinds of races are not to be held any longer. The Minister has, moreover, issued a ban on riding in the Grunewald and the Tiergarten. Golf, tennis and such sports are to be ignored by the German press.

February 12, 1943

The Minister points out that we have now a great and unique chance of issuing a striking propaganda slogan. The struggle against bolshevism and the danger of the bolshevization of Europe are at present occupying our friends and enemies in an equal measure. Our struggle against bolshevism must now dominate all propaganda media as the great and all-pervading propaganda theme. From this point of view the lesser day-to-day questions are to recede into the background and occupy only a subordinate position. As the bolshevik danger draws nearer the fear of the neutrals is growing and so is the sense of allegiance of the countries which are our friends and allies. The topic of bolshevism concerns them all. Even in Britain there are bound to be circles which are aware of its danger. The Minister says he cannot imagine that bolshevik-baiter Churchill suddenly turning pro-bolshevik overnight; British policy on Russia, therefore, is only an alliance of convenience. The British are hoping that the bolsheviks and National Socialists will kill each other off so that Britain can then assert her policy and her hegemony at the decisive moment. In connexion with our anti-bolshevik propaganda the Minister refers to the NSDAP Party congresses, some of which were entirely dominated by the slogan of the struggle against bolshevism. From their opening down to the final proclamation everything used to be dominated by the one over-riding formula of the struggle against bolshevism. Many people were then fed up to the teeth with this, but it did in the end produce results. Even the most stupid began to prick up their ears and the world received a clear picture of bolshevism. In propaganda the decisive element is keeping to a systematic pattern; he [the Minister] will see to it therefore that anti-bolshevism dominates our propaganda for the coming weeks and months. He is having some pamphlets drafted at the moment which are to be disseminated by the million.

330

Great care must be taken in this propaganda campaign that there is no mention of a struggle against the Slavs or against the Russian people.

It is important that in our propaganda we should also let bishops and other princes of the Church, scientists, famous scholars, etc., express their views. Likewise we might use in our propaganda Churchill's remarks about bolshevism and other observations by statesmen from the enemy camp.

The Minister instructs the head of the Press Department to keep on referring to bolshevism when discussing the Slogan of the Day at his press conference. The Minister points out that we must always say bolshevism and not communism, since the word communism has a different ring and is possibly apt to strike a reminiscent chord here or there.

The Minister issues instructions for the setting up of a propaganda committee headed by the Reich Propaganda Directorate to direct and guide this propaganda. Right up to the end of the war the theme of bolshevism will now be continually bandied about and the struggle against bolshevism must be the alpha and the omega at every rally.

February 15, 1943

On February 15, 1943, Goebbels, in his capacity as Reichspropagandaleiter, issued a decree addressed to all Reichsleiters and Gauleiters and also to all army headquarters. In this decree Goebbels outlined the universally binding directives from Hitler's proclamation of January 30, 1943, concerning the treatment of the European nations insofar as these were living within the German sphere of power. It contained the following directives:

(1) We must mobilize for victory not only all still available and usable forces of the German people but also those of the peoples inhabiting the countries occupied or conquered by us in the course of the war so far. All forces on the European continent, and in particular also those of the eastern peoples, must be employed in the struggle against Jewish bolshevism.

(2) The entire propaganda effort of the NSDAP and the National-Socialist state must therefore be aimed at convincing not only the German people but also all the other peoples of Europe, including the peoples in the occupied eastern territory and in the countries still under bolshevik rule, that the victory of Adolf Hitler and of German arms is in their own best interest.

(3) It is therefore incompatible with the aforegoing to belittle these nations, in particular the members of the eastern nations, either directly

M *

or indirectly, and especially in public speeches or articles, or to affront their self-esteem.

(4) Equally out of place is any description of the future New Order in Europe from which the members of foreign nations might gain the impression that the German leadership intends to keep them in a state of permanent subjection.

(5) It is equally mistaken to speak of new German settlements or even large-scale settlements and land expropriation, or to work out theoretical articles on the question of whether the nations or the soil must be Germanized. Even less must there be any discussion of any deportation of the indigenous population.

(6) On the other hand, prominence must be given on every suitable occasion to the will to be free, to the determination to fight against the bolshevik terror régime which inspires the nations subjugated by the Soviets, to their soldierly prowess and to their willingness to work. Proof for this is to be provided by the employment of eastern nations in their own autonomous troop contingents, as has already been emphasized in the Wehrmacht communiqué, the employment of eastern workers on Reich territory, and the work with which the eastern nations, in the industrial or agricultural enterprises of their homeland, are, under German leadership, contributing their share to victory, to the German armament effort and to getting the harvest safely home.

(7) After their systematic destruction by bolshevism (in accordance with Stalin's scorched-earth order), the occupied eastern territories will be built up anew under German leadership. This, together with their mineral wealth, will ensure for Germany, for the whole of Europe, and hence also for the nations living in the East, independence in respect of foodstuffs and raw materials and social progress for all time.

February 16, 1943
On the subject of our anti-bolshevik campaign the Minister points out that one can already clearly observe the nervousness on the other side. The growing danger is having a profound effect on the European nations and the argument that help might come from Britain has no effect.

The Minister, moreover, in his Sportspalast speech next Thursday [February 18], in addition to his observations on the total war measures, intends to speak in particular about the bolshevik danger. His references to the totalization measures are to be reported only in a small way whereas his treatment of the bolshevik danger must be given a very big show.

Further directives for his Sportspalast speech were issued by Goebbels on February 18, 1943: 'The arguments about bolshevism concern not only the German people but the whole world, whereas the remarks in the speech about the totalization of the war effort are a matter predominantly for the home public. The Minister further points out that reasonable comment from the neutral countries on the bolshevik danger should not be taken up by the German side, while, on the other hand, German propaganda should take up the spate of reports arriving daily from the enemy countries with evidence of how the British and the Americans are betraying the cause of Europe.'

February 17, 1943
In view of repeated transgressions against the present guidelines of our eastern policy in speeches by prominent personages, the Minister directs that care should be taken that at least all those speeches which may be expected to be noticed abroad should first be subjected to an examination as to their compatibility with the present principles of German policy in the East.

On the strength of reports from inside Germany the Minister points out that the following four slogans on the subject of bolshevism are at present circulating in Germany; these must be opposed:

(1) 'Bolshevism has lost its teeth.' This mistaken view must be countered by quoting practical examples, from recent rather than early years of bolshevik rule, showing the treatment of nations falling under the bolshevik rule of terror (countries on the periphery of the Soviet Union [the Baltic States], Bessarabia, etc.);

(2) 'The British and Americans will surely prevent bolshevization.' This view, which is particularly widespread in intellectual circles at home, should be countered by the continuous reproduction of such British and American comment as tends to show that Britain and America are prepared to surrender Europe to the bolsheviks;

(3) 'A man can't do more than work whatever happens.' This view, which is particularly widespread among the German workers, should be refuted by vivid descriptions of labour camps in the Russian Arctic, etc.;

(4) 'The Bolsheviks will only hang the Nazis.' This slogan should be countered by the publication of figures about the murder and deportation of workers and other members of the broad masses in the territories overrun by the bolsheviks.

The Minister emphasizes most particularly that German propaganda must give undiminished prominence to Britain's and America's betrayal of Europe. As for the general line of domestic propaganda, he further issues the directive that lesser events of subordinate importance, as for example personal attacks by Mrs Roosevelt or differences between Giraud and de Gaulle, should not be given particular prominence; the German people are in a serious mood and want to be informed about the great issues and their development; they do not wish to concern themselves with trivial matters.

On February 18, 1943, Goebbels made his speech at the Berlin Sportspalast about 'total war'. (For details see the Introduction to this book.)

February 19, 1943

The Minister issues instructions that domestic propaganda should allow yesterday's speech to produce its full effect, first of all, on the domestic political front before going over on a major scale to its repercussions abroad. He emphasizes the disciplined and politically mature behaviour of the Berlin population which turned up at the Sportspalast, as reflected in particular in the applause for Italy. In German propaganda, the main themes to be emphasized again and again are the struggle against bolshevism, total war, and the people's reply to the questions put at the end of the speech. From tomorrow onwards foreign comment should then be utilized, especially such comment as would also show that hopes of an internal German collapse are totally illusory.

February 20, 1943

The Minister points out that the success of the anti-bolshevik campaign has been greater than could have reasonably been expected. Foreign comment shows that the danger of bolshevism has been placed in the forefront of discussions and that everybody has taken notice of our slogan. In various countries existing complexes are rising to the top and are certainly receiving further buoyancy by our propaganda.

The Minister points out that regrettably we have left the great theme of bolshevism and have thus exposed ourselves to many attacks. For that reason we should now no longer speak of our conquests in the East, but of the crusade against bolshevism. In this connexion he mentions that he has received various telegrams from the front approving his Sportspalast speech. He particularly commends the Berlin population which has proved itself a political public of the first order.

Our day-to-day routine work must further develop the three themes of his Sportspalast speech – that of bolshevism, total war, and the Sportspalast plebiscite for the continuation of total war. The readiness in our people must be given direction; he now intends to issue an announcement at the end of each week, about the measures taken during that week to step up the war effort. This is necessary in order to keep the people's readiness alive and to apply pressure on the authorities to follow up the measures suggested by him. The weekly communiqué will contain a moral principle whose practical application the people will be able to watch at all times.

The Minister once more points out that we must dispute all selfish aims in the East and speak of the twentieth century's sacred crusade against bolshevism. The concepts of order, discipline and humanity must stand in the forefront of our propaganda.

February 22, 1943
The Minister requests that the favourable reports about the military situation on the Eastern Front should on no account be reflected in our propaganda. It would be the worst possible mistake to be triumphant at the present moment or to regard the danger as averted. There has been no fundamental change on the Eastern Front as a result of the stabilization of the line; there has merely been a drop in the fever chart. The reasons for the stabilization of the front are first of all, in the Minister's opinion, the early onset of the muddy period, secondly, the supply difficulties encountered by the Soviets due to the lengthening of their routes. We must not be induced by the improved situation on the Eastern Front and the momentarily favourable weather to repeat the old cardinal mistake of the past years.

We have always indulged in illusions about the East and he absolutely refuses to make this mistake again. We got through the first winter crisis relatively well, through the second one not nearly so well, and in the event of a third winter crisis he would have no wish to be Propaganda Minister any longer. The people will lose confidence if every spring and summer we sound our fanfares and in the winter we then find ourselves in a crisis. We must not delude ourselves about the fact that this winter has made an inroad into our reserves of confidence. Besides, an illusionist note at the present moment would undermine all our measures for the totalization of the war.

The Minister sharply criticizes the German press treatment of the twenty-fifth anniversary of the Red Army. The treatment of this subject went wrong. Our press, he says, made propaganda for the socialist trends and failed to observe the directives he had issued. The principal *VB* [*Völkischer Beobachter*] article on the subject was so formulated that the reverse of what was intended was in fact done. The article refers to the Russian people, the Russian army, the Russian Church, the Russian personality. He issued strict instructions that the words 'Russian' and 'Slav' were to be kept out of all articles and speeches, and

335

'bolshevik' used instead at all times. The use of the term 'bolshevik' enables us to make propaganda use of the British propaganda hullabaloo on the twenty-fifth anniversary of the Red Army. The Minister very sharply demands that his directives are followed in all circumstances.

The article '25th Anniversary of the Soviet Army – a British National Holiday' provided the main feature of the *Völkischer Beobachter* of February 22, 1943.

February 26, 1943

The Minister again refers to his Sportspalast speech and points out that he has received an unprecedented flood of letters. Ninety per cent demand the most radical measures for the war effort, while only a few insulting letters have come in – evidently written by Jews. All these letters reflect concern about whether we shall really carry out those measures. The Minister explains that in order to keep up morale we must continue to emphasize the toughness of the fighting and repeat this to the people every day. The slogan now dominating our propaganda must be: 'No more crises!' This time we must start preparing for the winter in spring, because after the two crises we have suffered one cannot expect the people to continue to have confidence in us if a third one occurs.

The SD report of February 22, 1943, shows that Goebbels's speech with its description of the gravity of the situation had a cathartic effect, and again strengthened confidence in the leadership. Some sections of the public suggested that Goebbels had painted things so black in order to lend emphasis to the totalization measures. The announcement of the most radical measures, however, had 'triggered off the greatest approval everywhere', even though the ten questions in the final part of the speech had met with 'a varied reception'.

March 3, 1943

A Moscow communiqué of March 3, 1943, reported that the Red Army had recaptured Rzhev 'today'. The OKW communiqué of March 3 announced that Rzhev had been evacuated unobserved by the enemy, 'as part of our systematic design to shorten the front'. On March 14, 1943, *Das Reich* carried Goebbels's article 'The Winter Crisis and Total War'.

The Minister requests that, in announcing the evacuation of the Rzhev salient, the planned nature of the move is strongly emphasized. According to a report from the competent military authorities the evacuation took place without any enemy interference or obstruction so that, by emphasizing the planned nature of the move, we are depriving the Russians of the chance of trumpeting a great victory to the world. The Minister will arrange for an article on the Eastern Front to appear in the next issue of *Das Reich,* which will have as its main theme the slogan coined by him: 'No more crises!'

In connexion with the bombing raid on Berlin he [the Minister] points out that the papers have attached too much importance to descriptions of the effects and not given enough publicity to the efforts of the people. The public has behaved pretty well, and it is now up to the leadership to set them a good example during the next few days by particular restraint on the one side and an effort on the other. It is the special task of the Party to look after the population since the problem of getting over this period of emergency is principally psychological. The Minister paid a visit to the Church of St Hedwig in Berlin and was received by the provost there who petitioned him to have a small emergency chapel made available for divine service. In his capacity as Reich Defence Commissioner of Berlin the Minister issues instructions to comply with this request.

In the British air raid during the night of March 2–3, 1943, some 900 tons of bombs were dropped on Berlin. The catholic Church of St Hedwig, in the immediate vicinity of the state opera house, and four other churches were burnt out. The priests of St Hedwig's Church were assigned a hall in the Academy of Singing as an emergency chapel.

March 5, 1943
The Minister directs that no great denials should be issued of the alleged major Russian victory at Rzhev. We should let them sound their victory fanfares since this Russian 'victory' does not cost us anything militarily and in fact supports our anti-bolshevik campaign. The situation on the Eastern Front is otherwise to be handled within the framework of the OKW communiqué alone. Favourable comment on the situation on the front is to be disregarded.

In connexion with the Russian victory at Rzhev it was stated at the conference of March 4, 1943: 'We shall ignore the Russian shouting about Rzhev. We shall also disregard their reports about the large amount of captured material. The OKW representative in this connexion points out that the Russians found nothing but wreckage and destroyed railway installations in Rzhev and that their reports about large quantities of loot are complete fabrications.'

337

In his diary of March 5, Goebbels scoffed at the 'idiotic denials' of the OKW. On March 14, 1943, came the directive that 'most rigorous action' was to be taken against Russian atrocity stories concerning Rzhev, etc.

A German industrialist has approached the Minister and drawn his attention to the bad treatment men and women workers from the East were receiving in the Reich. The Minister points out that he has spoken to a great variety of people, including the Reich Marshal, all of whom oppose bad treatment of foreign labour. It is widely agreed that we cannot keep the eastern nations committed to our cause if we continue with our past methods. The Minister says that he has never yet come across a person or an authority issuing a decree declaring that the eastern nations are to be treated badly – but in actual fact they are being harshly handled all the time. He sharply objects to the method of shoving these auxiliary workers, who are so important to us, behind barbed wire or beating them up. He directs State Secretary Gutterer to convene an early meeting of all authorities concerned, in order to bring about a final clarification on this point. The Minister will then issue a decree which will regulate the whole issue down to the last detail. He will then most resolutely and mercilessly punish all infringements against his decree. Once the decree is issued no one will any longer be able to hide behind the argument that it is a particular National-Socialist virtue to insult and maltreat the eastern nations. The regulation of this problem is not a matter of principle but of tactics. He also objects sharply to badges for the eastern workers and believes that it is impossible to win these people over to our side with such methods.

Since the end of 1941 workers from the occupied territories of Soviet Russia had been compelled to wear a conspicuous square on their clothes with the lettering *Ost*. Goebbels's attempts to abolish this were just as unsuccessful as his attempts to achieve a change of direction in Germany's policy towards the East.

March 10, 1943
The question of the air war is a serious worry at the moment. The Minister is afraid that the German people might fall into a certain mood of resignation. Such resignation is very easily possible since no one knows when this unnerving air war will end. We must make an all-out effort to eliminate this danger and plan all our measures with this in mind. He does not wish the word 'mood' to be used in future since one cannot speak about mood when people's homes have been burnt down and cities devastated.

338

In future he wants mention to be made only of a high morale. One cannot expect the people to burst into cheers after air raids. The British propaganda conducted in the autumn of 1940 to cope with their own domestic air raid problems is unsuitable for us. In Germany any propagandist who, like the British in the autumn of 1940, were to ask why the next bombs weren't coming yet would simply be given the boot. The Minister believes that the air war can be eliminated only when a counter-attack is made on Britain on a major scale. Our defensive measures are not able to deter the British from further attacks. In the raid on Munich, in which two hundred machines took part, only nine were shot down; one can therefore work out on the fingers of one's hands that the British can keep up this kind of attack for a long time yet, especially if one considers that their production will continue to rise owing to the American armament industry. The Minister therefore requests that caution should be practised in the propaganda treatment of this subject. It would be totally wrong for our propaganda today to make great promises of retaliation. The only reply that can be given is a counter-attack. The sole task of propaganda therefore is to stiffen the spirit of resistance – but here, too it must on no account cause annoyance among the public.

The Minister points out that it would be a mistake, after our outspoken reporting, if we now went to the other extreme and described matters as graver than in fact they are. We do not know yet how many people were killed as a result of our last raid on London, whereas we have currently and truthfully reported the casualties in Berlin. We had better not now over-indulge in love of truth when not so long ago we outbid each other in hushing things up. All information releases must be judged on their suitability alone. Figures, as for instance those of air raid casualties, should be published only if necessary. He [the Minister] also directs that publication of sentences for looting should now cease so as not to create the impression that there has been a lot of looting in Berlin.

The Minister announces that the Führer is full of praise for the anti-bolshevik propaganda and has in particular described the Minister's Sportspalast speech as a psychological masterpiece. We should continue with this propaganda and steadily strike at the same spot. After all, a 150-year-old oak will crash down only when the same spot is hit time and again and not if only an occasional blow is struck at it. At the same time, we must on no account register the successes scored with our anti-bolshevik propaganda. It would be equally wrong to rub our hands and gloat because enemy propaganda has now got itself into a certain dilemma thanks to our anti-bolshevik campaign.

The successes on the Eastern Front make it difficult for us to continue dealing in pessimism. But so long as the Russians continue to make a big show of success at our voluntary evacuation of a few territories in the north we had better pretend to be displeased about what suits us very well. At the same time we should begin to prepare to substantiate our anti-bolshevik propaganda on matters of principle in the way this was done principally at the Party congresses in 1936–7.

March 12, 1943

The Minister points out that it is desirable to continue to publicize to foreign audiences the fact that we are evacuating certain territories in Russia. In handling this favourable development on the Eastern Front we should on no account, when speaking to our foreign audience, go beyond the OKW communiqués, and when addressing the German public we must avoid creating illusions. In this connexion the Minister requests the OKW to dispense with a special announcement concerning the recapture of Kharkov.

The city of Kharkov, abandoned during the Soviet winter offensive in mid-February, was the objective of a German offensive in March 1943. By March 12 German forces had penetrated into the city. On March 15, in spite of Goebbels's efforts, a special announcement was issued to the effect that Kharkov had been recaptured by an enveloping attack.

The Minister deals with reports of insulting behaviour to which well-dressed ladies have been exposed on the part of certain people who appear to have completely misunderstood the requirements of total war. We must deal most rigorously with any attempt by the mob to throw its weight about now. The German press will receive appropriate instructions.

The SD report of March 1, 1943, pointed out, among other things, that the public was taking objection to 'trousered women painted like Red Indians'. There had been complaints in Berlin, for instance, that certain ladies were showing themselves in the streets wearing trousers made of gentlemen's best suiting and making it clear that they were wearing these trousers not for occupational reasons. On March 16 the press received the directive 'that the measures for total war must not arouse instincts of mutual snooping, in particular in such outward things as behaviour, clothes, etc. It would be appropriate to take up this subject positively once more in the readers' columns and point out that it is no infringement of war discipline if, for instance, a woman dresses herself attractively in the things she possesses or otherwise makes herself pretty. We are interested not in outward appearance but solely in attitude and achievement.'

The ban on permanent waves, imposed by decree of the Reich Economics Minister, was rescinded at the end of March 1943. On March 29, 1943, a DNB report announced that 'the production of permanent waves has been authorized uniformly throughout the Reich.'

March 13, 1943

The Minister reports that, according to the OKW, the main theme running through all letters received from the front is approval of the total war measures. The troops are unanimous in referring enthusiastically to the measures which are to be carried out in the home country.

On the subject of the struggle against bolshevism, the Minister points out that it has been propagated by us in a form which has made it impossible for the world not to take notice. We must now find a peg for this subject without, however, getting hooked on it. What the Minister means is that we must on no account record reaction to our propaganda. The Minister criticizes certain papers which desperately comment on every speech made by foreign statesmen. The Minister considers this a very dangerous practice; he believes that our polemics and lengthy quotations would only induce our critical Germans to switch on the British radio and hear what the man really said. In future we should confine ourselves to picking out only those things which can be utilized within the framework of our propaganda. He also warns against cartoons which for the most part produce a totally different reaction from that intended. Even the seemingly most hostile cartoons frequently lead the viewer to tell himself: This man must be a great personality after all if our propaganda is so obsessed with him. Cartoons result in popularity and we should therefore show more restraint about them than in the past.

On the subject of the air war the Minister points out that the British are always accurately informed about what has been destroyed, whereas we do not receive any accurate factual reports about our air raids. We are far too open and honest in our reporting and we launch news items into the world when in fact we should be making propaganda.

In this connexion the Minister rejects the idea of releasing details about the destruction of churches, since we have invariably deduced the measure of our own success from British reports of churches destroyed. From the percentage of churches hit we have assessed the destruction at railway stations and industrial objectives. We must not therefore give the British these useful pieces of information in the future. On the other hand, needless to say, reports about the destruction of individual world-renowned cultural monuments will be released.

The situation in the East continues to stabilize itself and thus, in a sense, deprives the total war propaganda of its force. The Minister therefore issues directives to make it clear to the people that total war is a thing in itself and must be implemented regardless of sunshine or other positive features. Total war has nothing to do with the crisis in the East but is designed to avoid future crises. Our slogan must be: 'No more crises!'

In his diary Goebbels noted: 'The advancing bolshevik steam-roller has been halted and the Germans have once again performed a miracle. They have overcome the danger in the East, and all those who last winter, while praising the bolshevik successes, were secretly experiencing the greatest anxiety and alarm, are now like men reborn.'

Appendix

List of Participants

(Titles and designations of the regular participants in the conference, as given below, apply to the period October 1939 to June 1941)

Goebbels, Dr Paul Joseph; Reich Minister for Popular Enlightenment and Propaganda, Reichspropagandaleiter of the NSDAP and President of the Reich Chamber of Culture.

Berndt, Alfred-Ingemar; Ministerialdirigent, head of Radio Dept in RMVP. (February–August 1940, then called up).

Böker, Erich; head of RPA Berlin (from April 1941).

Bömer, Prof. Dr Karl; Ministerialrat/Ministerialdirigent, head of Foreign Press Dept in RMVP. (Suspended end of May 1941).

Braeckow, Ernst; Oberregierungsrat, deputy head of German Press Dept (until June 1940) deputy head of Propaganda Dept (June–August 1940), head of Propaganda Dept in RMVP (from August 1940).

Brauweiler, Ernst; Oberregierungsrat/Ministerialrat, deputy head of Foreign Press Dept in RMVP, in addition head of Foreign Dept of RMVP (December 1939–September 1940).

Cohrs, Wilhelm Heinrich; Major, liaison officer of OKW Wehrmacht Propaganda Dept (to mid-January 1940).

Diewerge, Wolfgang; Oberregierungsrat, deputy head of Radio Dept in RMVP.

Dittmar, Walter Wilhelm; Direktor/Intendant, head of News Service of the German Radio (Reichsrundfunkgesellschaft).

Drewitz, Carl Albert; Regierungsrat, official in Press Dept of RMVP.

Fangauf, Eberhard; Regierungsrat, in charge of film newsreels in Film Dept of RMVP; OKW censor for film reporting.

Fischer, Erich; Regierungsrat/Oberregierungsrat, deputy head of German Press Dept in RMVP (from June 1940).

Fischer, Hugo; official in NSDAP Reichspropagandaleitung (Reich Propaganda Directorate of the Party).

343

Fritzsche, Hans; Ministerialrat/Ministerialdirigent, head of German Press Dept in RMVP.

Froelich, Hans; senoir NSDAP official in Berlin Gau (to March 1941).

Frowein, Kurt; Regierungsrat, Goebbels's personal assistant (from April 1940).

Glasmeier, Dr Heinrich; Reichsintendant (Controller) of Greater German Radio.

Greiner, Dr Erich; Ministerialdirektor, Director (I) of the three administrative departments of RMVP.

Greiner, Hansjörg; Regierungsrat, official in the Minister's office at RMVP.

Gutterer, Leopold; Ministerialdirektor/Staatssekretär, head of Propaganda Dept in RMVP (to August 1940).

Hadamovsky, Eugen; Reichssendeleiter, head of Radio Dept in RMVP (February–August 1940).

Hahn, Klaus-Friedrich; Lieutenant/Lieutenant-Commander, head of information office of OKW Wehrmacht Propaganda Dept, Wehrmacht liaison o:ficer with German Press Dept in RMVP and liaison officer of the Navy (from March to July 1940 on active service).

Hinkel, Hans; Ministerialrat/Minsterialdirigent, head of Dept for Special Cultural Tasks in RMVP.

Hippler, Dr Fritz; Oberregierungsrat/Ministerialrat, head of Film Dept in RMVP.

Heiduschke, Herbert; Regierungsrat, Goebbels's personal aide (from January 1940).

Hunke, Prof. Dr Heinrich; Ministerialdirigent, head of Foreign Dept of RMVP (from December 1940).

Jetter, Heinz; Inspector of NSDAP Berlin Gauleitung (Gau Directorate) (to November 1939).

Köhn, Willi; Consul-General, head of Foreign Dept of RMVP (to December 1939).

Kurzbein, Heiner; Regierungsrat/Oberregierungsrat, in charge of illustrated papers in German Press Dept in RMVP.

Mahlo, Dr Friedrich; Ministerialrat, head of Tourist Traffic Dept in RMVP.

Martin, Hans; Major/Lieutenant-Colonel, senior official in OKW Wehrmacht Propaganda Dept, Wehrmacht liaison officer with Goebbels (from February 1940).

Müller, Dr Erich; Ministerialdirigent, head of Personnel Dept of RMVP.

Müller, Georg Wilhelm; Ministerialrat, personal assistant to Goebbels (to April 1940).

Naumann, Dr Werner; Ministerialrat, head of the Minister's office in RMVP (some of the time on active service).

Neumann, Karl; Oberregierungsrat, in charge of technical production of propaganda material in Propaganda Dept in RMVP (to April 1940).

Ott, Dr Karl; Ministerialdirigent, head of Budget Dept of RMVP.

Otte, Richard; Regierungsrat, Goebbels's personal secretary.

Raskin, Dr Adolf; Director of External Broadcasting in German Radio (Reichsrundfunkgesellschaft) (to November 1940).

Rechenberg, Hans; Oberregierungsrat, official in German Press Dept in RMVP; government spokesman at the economic press conference (May–June 1940).

Schaudinn, Hans; Oberregierungsrat, head of central radio office in Radio Dept in RMVP.

Schaumburg-Lippe, Friedrich Christian, Prince of; Oberregierungsrat, Goebbels's personal assistant (from November 1940).

Schippert, Wilhelm; Oberregierungsrat, official in Foreign Press Dept in RMVP.

Schirmeister, Moritz Augustus von; Regierungsrat/Oberregierungsrat, Goebbels's personal press officer.

Schmidt, Dr Erich; Chief Secretary of Reich Chamber of Culture, presiding over the economic press conference (to May 1940).

Schmidt, Fritz; NSDAP official, liaison officer with the 'Staff of the Führer's Deputy' (to May 1940).

Schmidt-Decker, Felix; NSDAP Gau propaganda chief, head of RPA for Abroad (from September 1940).

Schmidt-Leonhardt, Prof. Dr Hans; Ministerialdirigent, head of Legal Dept of RMVP.

Schmidtke, Heinz; Major, senior official in OKW Wehrmacht Propaganda Dept, head of its information office and Wehrmacht liaison officer with German Press Dept in RMVP (March–July 1940).

Schwarz van Berk, Hans; chief editor, head of a news bureau subordinate to Foreign Press Dept in RMVP.

Semler, Dr Rudolf; Regierungsrat, Goebbels's personal press officer (from January 1941).

Sommerfeldt, Martin H.; Captain, OKW liaison officer with Foreign Press Dept in RMVP.

Spieler, Christian; Chief Prosecutor/Ministerialrat, Goebbels's personal assistant (from November 1940).

Splettstösser, Jürgen; radio commentator.

Stephan, Werner; Ministerialrat and Lieutenant (Reserve), personal assistant to the Reich Press Chief and OKW censor for spoken reports by Wehrmacht propaganda companies.

Theill, Dr Karl; radio commentator.

Tiessler, Walter; head of the Reich Circle for National Socialist Propaganda and Public Enlightenment within the NSDAP Reichspropagandaleitung (Reich Propaganda Directorate), liaison officer with the 'Staff of the Führer's Deputy' and with the head of the Party Chancellery (from mid-1940).

Titel, Walter; Major of Police, head of Operations Staff in RMVP and of the Defence of the Reich section (from February 1940).

Wächter, Werner; head of RPA Berlin (to March 1941).

Wentscher, Bruno; Lieutenant-Colonel, Wehrmacht liaison officer and head of the Defence of the Reich section in RMVP (to January 1940).

Wildoner, Franz; head of Foreign Language Service of German Radio (Reichsrundfunkgesellschaft).

Winkelnkemper, Dr Toni; Director of External Broadcasting of German Radio (Reichsrundfunkgesellschaft) (from January 1941).

Wodarg, Rudolf; Major on the Luftwaffe Operations Staff, Luftwaffe liaison officer with RMVP (from March 1940).

Some Ranks under the Third Reich:

The German Army and the Waffen-SS

Army	*Waffen-SS*	*Conventional translation (not always strictly equivalent to British or US ranks)*
	(Corresponding Ranks)	
Leutnant	SS-Untersturmführer	2nd Lieutenant
Oberleutnant	SS-Obersturmführer	Lieutenant
Hauptmann	SS-Hauptsturmführer	Captain
Major	SS-Sturmbannführer	Major
Oberstleutnant	SS-Obersturmbannführer	Lieutenant-Colonel
Oberst	SS-Standartenführer	Colonel
Generalmajor	SS-Brigadeführer	Major-General
Generalleutnant	SS-Gruppenführer	Lieutenant-General
General	SS-Obergruppenführer*	General
Generaloberst		Colonel-General
Generalfeldmarschall		Field Marshal

The Senior Ranks of the German Civil Service

Minister
Staatssekretär
Ministerialdirektor
Ministerialdirigent
Ministerialrat
Oberregierungsrat
Regierungsrat

---

* The SS-Obergruppenführer in command of a division had the additional title of General der Waffen-SS.

The Nazi Party Hierarchy

Reichsleitung der NSDAP	(Several *Reichsleiter* with specific 'portfolios', the Führer's Deputy in charge of Party matters, the Party Treasurer, etc.)
Landesinspekteur	Originally nine, each for four or five *Gaue*. (This level gradually faded out as Gauleiters were directly appointed and dismissed by Hitler and later by Himmler.)
Gauleiter	Thirty-six in the 'Old Reich', their number increased with the German annexation of Austria, the Sudetenland, Danzig, Western Poland (the 'Warthegau'), etc. A *Gau* (plural *Gaue*) was a 'province' (e.g. Saxony, Silesia) and often corresponded to the traditional administrative territorial division of Germany.
Kreisleiter	A *Kreis* (plural *Kreise*) was, and still is, an administrative unit in Germany, comparable to a rural district council in Britain.
Ortsgruppenleiter	The *Ortsgruppe* ('local group') was the local primary organization of the Nazi Party.
Zellenleiter	The Party 'cell' could be based either on a neighbourhood unit or on an employment unit (a workshop in a factory, an office, etc.)
Blockwart	The 'Block Warden' was the lowest official in the Nazi Party above the ordinary rank-and-file member.
PG = Parteigenosse	'Party Comrade'; the ordinary member.

List of Abbreviations

AEG	Allgemeine Elektrizitäts-Gesellschaft (General Electric Company)
AP	Associated Press
BBZ	*Berliner Börsen-Zeitung*
BDM	Bund Deutscher Mädel (German Girls' League)
DAF	Deutsche Arbeitsfront (German Labour Front)
DAZ	*Deutsche Allgemeine Zeitung*
DNB	Deutsches Nachrichtenbüro (German News Agency)
HJ	Hitler-Jugend (Hitler youth)
KdF	'Kraft durch Freude' ('Strength through Joy' organization)
NSDAP	Nationalsozialistische Deutsche Arbeiterpartei (National Socialist German Workers' Party)
NSV	Nationalsozialistische Volkswohlfahrt (National Socialist People's Welfare Organization)
OKH	Oberkommando des Heeres (High Command of Land Forces)
OKL	Oberkommando der Luftwaffe (High Command of the Air Force)
OKM	Oberkommando der Marine (High Command of the Navy)
OKW	Oberkommando der Wehrmacht (High Command of the German Armed Forces)
Pg	Parteigenosse (Party Comrade)
PK	Propagandakompanie (Propaganda Company)
RMVP	Reichsministerium für Volksaufklärung und Propaganda (Reich Ministry for Popular Enlightenment and Propaganda)
RPA	Reichspropagandaamt (Reich Propaganda Office)
SA	Schutz-Abteilung (the 'Brown-shirts')
SD	Sicherheitsdienst (Security Service)
SPD	Sozialdemokratische Partei Deutschlands (Social Democratic Party of Germany)
SS	Schutz-Staffel (the 'Black-shirts')
TASS	Soviet Telegraph Agency
TO	Transocean (German news agency)
UP	United Press
VB	*Völkischer Beobachter*
WHW	Winterhilfswerk (Winter Relief Scheme)

349

Sources

The minutes and other records of the ministerial conferences at the Reich Ministry for Propaganda, as published in the present volume, are scattered among several archives. A few amplifications have been taken from published memoirs as well as from Goebbels's published and unpublished war diaries. The source material is as follows:

Pages 1-173: Reichsministerium für Volksaufklärung und Propaganda, Ministerbüro, No. la/lg, Deutsches Zentralarchiv Potsdam [German Central Archives, Potsdam, East Germany].

Pages 108-109: (Molotov's visit) ZSg 109/16, Vertrauliche Informationen (Oberheitmann collection), Bundesarchiv Koblenz [Federal German Archives, Koblenz].

Pages 174-180: R. Semmler [should be: Semler], *Goebbels, The Man Next to Hitler,* London, 1947, p.39.

Pages 175-176: ZSg 109/22, Vertrauliche Informationen (Oberheitmann collection), Bundesarchiv Koblenz, and W. Stephan, *Joseph Goebbels, Dämon einer Diktatur,* Stuttgart, 1949, p. 226.

Pages 176-178: ZSg 109/22 and 23, Vertrauliche Informationen (Oberheitmann collection), Bundesarchiv Koblenz.

Pages 178-183: ZSg 101/40 (Brammer collection), Bundesarchiv Koblenz.

Pages 183-184: ZSg 109/25 and 26, Vertrauliche Informationen (Oberheitmann collection), Bundesarchiv Koblenz.

Pages 185-187: ZSg 101/41 (Brammer collection), Bundesarchiv Koblenz.

Page 188: ZSg 109/26, Vertrauliche Informationen (Oberheitmann collection), Bundesarchiv Koblenz.

Pages 190-192: ZSg 109/27, Vertrauliche Informationen (Oberheitmann collection), Bundesarchiv Koblenz.

Pages 192-253: Auswärtiges Amt, Krümmer, Aufzeichnungen über Teilnahme an der Ministerkonferenz im Promi, etc., Vol. 1, Politisches Archiv des Auswärtigen Amts Bonn [Political Archives of the Bonn Foreign Office].

Pages 254-257: OKW No. 638, Militärgeschichtliches Forschungsamt Freiburg [Research Centre for Military History, Freiburg].

Pages 257–331: Auswärtiges Amt, Krümmer, Aufzeichnungen über Teilnahme an der Ministerkonferenz im Promi, etc., Vols. 1 and 2, Politisches Archiv des Auswärtigen Amts Bonn.

Page 293: (October 30, 1942) Auswärtiges Amt (V-Stelle B.f.l.), Auslandspropaganda-Leitstelle, Politisches Archiv des Auswärtigen Amts Bonn.

Pages 331–332: Panzer AOK 2, Militärgeschichtliches Forschungsamt Freiburg. (The author is indebted for this Goebbels decree to a suggestion made to him by Dr E. Klink of the Militärgeschichtliches Forschungsamt Freiburg.)

Pages 332–342: Auswärtiges Amt, Krümmer, Aufzeichnungen über Teilnahme an der Ministerkonferenz im Promi, etc., Vol. 2, Politisches Archiv des Auswärtigen Amts Bonn.

Editorial interpolations in the text of the sources are indicated by square brackets. In the Introduction, as well as in the amplifications in the explanatory passages, use has been made not only of extant sound recordings of Goebbels's speeches but also of countless documents from a variety of archives, of a mass of scholarly publications, and above all of contemporary reports in the German and foreign press. To list all these publications would exceed the framework of the present volume. A large number of the publications drawn upon are listed in the extensive documentary volume *Kriegspropaganda 1939-1941, Geheime Ministerkonferenzen im Reichspropagandaministerium,* ed. Willi A. Boelcke, Stuttgart, 1966. The following, however, deserve special mention:

G. Moltmann, *Goebbels' Rede zum totalen Krieg am 18. Febr. 1943,* in *Vierteljahreshefte für Zeitgeschichte,* Vol. 12, 1964, pp. 13–43.

A. Hillgruber (Ed.), *Staatsmänner und Diplomaten bei Hitler. Vertrauliche Aufzeichnungen über Unterredungen mit Vertretern des Auslandes 1939-1941,* Frankfurt am Main, 1967.

A. Philippi and F. Heim, *Der Feldzug gegen Sowjetrussland 1941-1945. Ein operativer Überblick,* Stuttgart, 1962.

To all those who have helped me, by word and deed, in the compilation of this book I express my warmest thanks. To them, as to all thoughtful readers, this book is dedicated.

Willi A. Boelcke

Stuttgart, September 20, 1967

Index